Good and • Evil

THE ETERNAL CONFLICT WITHIN

An Agenda for Helping the Good Within,
Without Destroying the Evil

BHIMESWARA CHALLA

GOOD AND EVIL—
THE ETERNAL CONFLICT WITHIN

iUniverse books may be ordered through booksellers or by contacting:

iUniverse
1663 Liberty Drive
Bloomington, IN 47403
www.iuniverse.com
844-349-9409

ISBN: 978-1-6632-2626-6 (sc)
ISBN: 978-1-6632-2627-3 (hc)
ISBN: 978-1-6632-2628-0 (e)

Library of Congress Control Number: 2021908523

Print information available on the last page.

iUniverse rev. date: 09/01/2021

Dedication to a Daughter

In fond remembrance of my daughter Padma Priya Challa, who died, solitary through her life, at the age of 54, on 22nd March 2020. She was innately loving and giving, exceptionally endowed—a rare blend of beauty, brilliance, and above all, as a friend described her, an 'enormous heart'—much admired but much misunderstood. She was a bundle of pure joy while growing up, scaled high academic and professional heights, but a slew of fateful setbacks, professional and personal, set in, and a life of uncommon promise went woefully wrong. She was carefree about her future, and whenever I worried, she used to heartrendingly reassure me: "Don't worry, Dad; I will die before you'. Doubtless, she is now in a far, far better and more caring place, surely to join the many she loved down here who are already up there.

By the way she led her life, she helped me to settle my karmic dues of this life at her own expense, and, as per this book, by her very inability to sufficiently 'feed' the 'good wolf' in its fight with the 'bad wolf' in her 'war within', she aided me in waging my own war. What more can any daughter do? After saying thanks to her, even if posthumously—for thanks must be said wherever they are due, as my mother once said—I will now meander in the remains of my time, bearing, in the words of the Greek philosopher Aeschylus (*Agamemnon*, 1602), "even in my sleep pain that cannot forget falls drop by drop upon my heart".

So long, my love! Rest in paradisiacal peace. And please take my hand when I come there. God! I implore on bended knees: give her your merciful forgiveness she longed and prayed for. Free her from all sin and future pain; and shelter her at your lotus feet.

Contents

What This Book Is About... Why *Now*

The year 2020 in the human calendar was like no other, for at least the last hundred years. It is too early to tell how the current year will look like a year from now, much less, how history will mark this year a hundred years from now. Whichever way, blissful or baneful hindsight can only unravel, but it is most certainly a consequential time "in that dawn to be alive", to paraphrase Wordsworth.[1] Right or wrong, we are making history. What makes us so meaningful is, of all things an awful thing, a pandemic that we have named *Covid-19*. Nothing else in living memory has so transformatively left its mark on the way we live, work, socialize, play, mate, and amuse ourselves. And never before has death seemed such a high possibility, and sadness, grief, and suffering, so universal. It has shattered the illusion of safety that despite the belief that 'something destructive will happen to *us*', we are convinced that 'nothing will happen to *me*'. While the world indeed has survived many other scourges incomparably more lethal, this pandemic has come to showcase the shadow that stalks all of us, the dread of the unknown, the baddy under the bed, the ghost in the hallway.

---

[1] William Wordsworth. 1850. *The Prelude*. Book 10.

It has rudely reminded us that, despite delusions to the contrary, we will never be immortal or impregnable and that, contrary to what technology promises us, we will remain indispensable to each other. Yet we know deep down that we have no one to blame but ourselves, we are our own worst enemy, that we, by our own comfort-seeking behavior, have chosen this disaster—and the impending climate catastrophe.

Most of us, albeit grudgingly, will willy-nilly go along with this line of thought. Where we go wrong is to believe that behavior—how we relate with one another and with the world—is conditioned by faith, taste, class, upbringing, education, or the company we keep, and when we believe that it can be qualitatively altered externally by commandments or codes of conduct, custom or culture, laws, or regulations. It is such a facile 'belief' that has betrayed all our efforts and aborted all expectations. Fact is that the basic cause is embedded in the essence of what anthropologists call the human condition—more precisely the lack of any authentic attribute that is solely, squarely, and irreplaceably 'human'. In 1857, Charles Darwin scribbled in a notebook the phrase, "One species does not change into another". That may be biologically true of all other species except the human. The human can effectively be any other without becoming. The human animal is really a kind of a conglomerate, a hotchpotch of all the rest and, as a result, it can, and does, show many of their trademark characteristics—like the aggression of a tiger or the docility of a lamb, the cunning of a jackal or the focus of a hedgehog, the sneakiness of a snake or the nobility of a peacock—at some time or the other. That is a mixed blessing, and it is due to the fact that we harbor, unlike other fellow-animals, such a wide mélange of instincts, emotions, traits, attributes, drives, and urges. The only extra we have is the one that makes such a menace to one another: malice. In consequence, we often behave in a way we feel deeply embarrassed. It is because of malice that our natural and normal desires and how we desire each other are so detrimental to our common good. We all know that the next pandemic is near-inevitable, perhaps far more virulent and vicious, unless we desist from 'earth abuse', but still we persist. Most often, most of us don't "mean to be unkind—but the other goes away weeping." The answer to the obvious 'why' is within.

The 'world within' is, in its reach, farther than the farthest star in the sky and more alien than any extraterrestrial out there. And yet it is ensconced in our inner space. Our external behavior is a mirror image of our internal behavior. What we experience outside is actually *ex post facto*; the real experience is what constantly churns in the world within. It is a two-way street; life outside affects the 'life inside' and vice versa. But our phenomenal world—the world as it appears to human beings as a result of being conditioned by human understanding—is so tainted and putrid that it has coarsened, corroded, and corrupted our inner world. We now live with both our 'worlds' locked in a toxic embrace, like two scorpions in a bottle.

Even as much of mankind is exhausted fighting for its breath of life and drowned in the drudgery and dread of day-to-day living, there are still many who feel in their bones that something truly big is in the offing, that, in the words of Benjamin Franklin, 'the chaos of noise and nonsense' we hear all around is the crack of doom, the beginning of the end of the world as we know it. A recent report[2] on the human impact on earth says that "we are at the dawn of what must be a transformative decade", possibly on the edge of the abyss of a comprehensive civilizational collapse. Some shrink the timeline to just five years. Modern man may think it is catastrophic, but history might record it as a 'lucky break for humanity as a whole', provided we muster the will and wisdom to seize the chance. During this short stretch, we have the daunting challenge of transforming human society from an *imperial* civilization, which organizes around hierarchies of domination and exploitation, into an *ecological* civilization—"restoring

---

[2] Report prepared by the Potsdam Institute for Climate Impact Research for the Nobel Prize Summit 2021, '*Our Planet, Our Future*', 26–28 April 2021.

the health of the living earth's regenerative systems while securing material sufficiency and spiritual abundance for all people".[3]

With stakes so scary, so much being up in the air and our vision so blurry and fuzzy, we are yet compelled to plan for the world of the future, not merely post-pandemic, certainly post-climate, but possibly *post-human*. Man must either be thrown into an inferno to be winnowed, alchemized, and reborn, or get abolished, wiped clean off the face of the earth. Who will step in to fill the void, we do not know. We cannot even imagine what nature might assuredly do, but we have made known our studied preference: to mediate a technological 'marriage' between man and machine. To the crossbreed resulting from this 'mating', which we expect will be super-intelligent and superhuman, we fully intend to pass on our terrestrial mandate. What we are prepared to offer at the altar is our essential identity and humanity, our reason for being, our niche in nature. What really the trade-off could be, no one can tell. Instead, the odds are that the resultant 'being' will be even more self-righteous and self-destructive, narcissistic and nihilistic. That is because, despite science-fiction-come-true innovations, the hybrid-human will carry the same errant mindset that brought us to this perilous pass. It is hard to believe that any other so-called 'lower animal' will so cheerfully and assiduously choose its own execution or emasculation, ironically in pursuit of permanence and perfection. That is perhaps why human stupidity, Einstein once sardonically said, is the only infinite in the cosmos.

It is against this bleak backdrop and in this despairing setting that this book makes its daring debut—daring because what it says is what we rather *not* hear. To keep the record straight, I am not the one who 'wrote' the book... *the book got written by me*; I was the chosen one. The real author is not known; at least not to me. What is utterly astounding is why no book on such a topical and timeless subject has never been written, or at least been published so far. The book sets a somber tone and says that

---

[3] David Korten. *Ecological Civilization: The Vision*. Living Economics Forum.

there is a fair chance that, as William Yeats wrote over a hundred years ago, "Things fall apart; the centre cannot hold; mere anarchy is loosened upon the world" (*The Second Coming*, 1919). The book reminds us that this all, in one sense, is *déjà vu*; that we have known for centuries what needs to be done and yet, time and again, we have stumbled despite scriptures, sages, philosophers, and scientists, all well-meaning and wise.

That is because we have not found, and not even likely to find, an answer to what Saint Paul lamented: "I do not understand what I do. For what I want to do I do not do, but what I hate I do". That epitomizes the agony of the human condition. This book rephrases that angst as the two questions that occupy our lives—*Why can't I be good? Why do I do bad?*—and makes them its central theme and centerpiece. In so doing, it makes a crucial point, namely, it is not that all of us are bad or do evil all the time. There is plenty of goodness in us, what Abraham Lincoln called 'better angels' of our nature, and most of us, maybe much to our surprise, actually do more good more often. The problem is that most of the time it requires strenuous, almost extra-human effort. The challenge is to make doing good easy, even reflexive. How to make that happen has always been a huge part of the human quest but to no avail. This book says that the way we have ignored, the *only* way, is to wage and win this war the right way.

This war is another name and form of the epic clash between two sides of our own Self, what we usually characterize as 'good' and 'evil' in their broadest meaning, what Hindu scriptures call *dharma* (righteousness) and *adharma* (wickedness), and in psychic terms what Carl Jung called *persona* and *shadow*. Actually, our consciousness is nothing but a bundle of binaries, *dwandas* in Sanskrit, like good and evil, love and hate, compassion and callousness, kindness and cruelty, indifference and altruism, and so on. And their concurrent coexistence and conflict inside each of us is the war within. This line of thought is in accordance with what the British poet Samuel Coleridge expressed as follows: "Every power in nature and in spirit must evolve an opposite as the sole means and condition of its manifestation: and all opposition is a tendency to re-union. This is the universal law of polarity or essential dualism" (*The Friend*, 1812). What we call 'daily life' is nothing but a facsimile, if you will, of the state of this war on a particular day in a person's life. It is the centerpiece of all major religions and all great literature. Many great saints, like Saint Augustine, Saint Theresa de Lisieux, Saint Mary of Egypt, and, in our own times, Mother Teresa (later anointed as Saint Teresa of Calcutta), to name a few, all fought their own war within.

This book's signal contribution is to connect our two worlds (the 'inner' and the 'outer') and this inner struggle, to the nuts and bolts and odds and ends of our daily doings. The book argues that to win this war we don't need to become saints or heroes or martyrs. What needs to be done is for a critical mass of ordinary people to do ordinary things ordinarily, but with a new mindset, a mindset that is free from malice and is not mind-dominated but heart-centric. But first, we must acknowledge that the intellectual and existential paradigm we have relied upon lies shattered. Only then will it be possible to cathartically cleanse, or detoxify our consciousness and trigger a radical *contextual-change*. And such a change entails and requires a radical shift in the way we view, think through, and deal with the critical dimensions of morality, money, and mortality. The book suggests specific steps in that direction.

In life, for anything meaningful to be useful, it has to be done at an opportune time. That is why the Bible tells us, "To everything there is a season, and a time for every purpose under heaven". As a weary and wounded world strives and stumbles to get back on its feet, to confront its past to prepare for the future, the 'season' for this book is now, and its purpose is to *help win this war and save the world.*

What I Owe to Whom

We all know that no man is an island, and that nothing in life can be done in anyone's life without the involvement of many others in some way or the other. We cannot live through a single day, even physically, without being obligated to a host of others. We seldom notice it, but in whatever we do, we constantly make each other, and merge the 'I' with the 'We'.

If the purpose of life, as George Eliot once said, was to make life less difficult to those around us, be it one's spouse or a servant or stranger, or even a murderer, then writing too serves a purpose. It is a way to encapsulate countless hours of one person's sustained suffering, introspective reflection, and inspired imagination into a few fleeting hours of laid-back reading by the rest of humanity.

What I wrote in the preface to my previous book, I cannot do any better: "If 'no one is a stranger' on the voyage of life, any potential reader would be my soul-mate, those who yearn, as Richard Bach (*Jonathan Livingston Seagull*) said, 'to make life come to life'… we know that a book does not just happen". In that preface, I also said, "Apart from the actual author and publisher, there are always unseen forces and invisible actors who facilitate the process and the product. Being invisible should not deny the right to be remembered; death should not annihilate deserved gratitude". In that context, I expressed my gratitude to my beloved parents and siblings, "who gave me boundless love, without which any urge for creativity would have long been smothered". To that list I must now add another, the closest and dearest to me—my own daughter *Padmalu*, as I used to lovingly call her. No other calamity can befall a parent than the unhappy life of a child meeting an untimely end. But then, my daughter's life had a purpose, the noblest; to save a father from his *karmic* debt and to liberate him from all worries and fears...

But, among those who are 'down here', I must mention my family— my wife Nirmala, my son Ram, my daughter-in-law Margie, my grandson Varun, and my daughter's (and now our) 'divine' dog *Whiskey*, truly the best of us. In particular, my wife's silent and steadfast cooperation greatly helped me to keep writing for so long, through thick and thin, when many other more mundane things got neglected.

Like my earlier book, this tome is also entirely the fruit of my own lonely travail, and the offspring of the promptings of the unseen author. But among the things that made this practically possible, I must mention the dedicated contribution of my editorial support, more appropriately my collaborator, Vijay Ramchander. He was a thorough professional as well as a person of the highest integrity, a rare blend these days. Without his painstaking effort, this book, indeed like the previous one, would not have seen the light of the day. There are several other individuals who anonymously assisted me in subtler, but nevertheless instrumental ways, much like the janitor at NASA's space facility in 1962: when the visiting President John F Kennedy asked him about the nature of his work, the janitor solemnly said, "*I am helping put a man on the Moon*".

However, even the most ordinary of our accomplishments would have involved innumerable and 'invisible' people—many of whom we might have hurt at some point in time, and to whom we owe an apology. This brings to mind the grace that Buddhists offer as a prayer before a meal:

"Innumerable beings brought us this food. We should know how it comes to us." This book is no exception.

Last and most importantly, I would be committing one of the *panchamaha-patakams* (most heinous sins) characterized in Hinduism—ingratitude—if I do not place on record my profound gratitude to the divine 'Author' who hand-picked me to be his human scribe in the writing of this book, and made sure my life does not end before it reaches the eye of a reader.

The Setting

The Twin Questions and Twin Inabilities

Why can't I be good when I want to be? Why do I do bad when I don't want to? These simple angst-full questions, which are really twin inabilities, have been at the epicenter of everything that has marred much of human history and troubled the best of us. And these questions—or inabilities, if you will—are the crux of what went so horribly astray with what has come to be known as the 'human way of being'. It is these inabilities that have held us back from fulfilling our full potential, our capability and capacity. These are at the very nub of every crisis and exigency, of every hue and headwind that the human world has had to deal with. It is our being unable to do what we want to, and desist from doing what we shouldn't, that has caused both of the current two crises: the coronavirus pandemic and the climate crisis. And our overcoming these inabilities is the only solution; as well as the only way to preempt future crises. Without addressing these elemental and elephantine issues, we cannot make much sense of the most baffling enigma, the most impenetrable riddle: why human history is so stained and sullied, and why, despite uncommon God-given endowments and entitlements—and the advent and appearance of great religions, prophets, philosophers, messiahs and mahatmas, path-breaking altruists and high-minded anarchists, humanists and transhumanists—none could arrest, much less reverse, the temporal and spiritual decline and deterioration of human character and persona. And why, notwithstanding all our well-earned glory and grandeur, a species avowedly poised at the zenith of creation, and after over a million years of evolution and millenniums of 'progress', we 'talk our extinction to death', to paraphrase Robert Lowell (*Fall 1961*). One of our wisest, Socrates, once said that "no one goes willingly towards the bad". It depends what 'willingly' is, or, more to the point, is not. We are all conscious, at some depth or dimension, of what needs to be done, but the real problem is our poor skill in navigating the seas of selfishness, short-sightedness, and self-indulgence. There is hardly anything bad or evil in human history that we did not know was an imminent possibility and yet didn't do anything in particular to avert or abort it. Making matters even worse, we often act against our better judgment and wonder why. We take risks that are too risky, never know how soon is too late, and often choose an OBT (Obviously Bad Thing), a condition of cognition that the ancient Greeks called *akrasia*. Every day, we are offered a fresh chance to make a difference to make life on earth, at the very least one single life, better or a bit less difficult, but we don't know why we don't. The bottom line is that we don't even know what we don't know, and yet are obliged to act on what we think we know.

For anything that is abhorrent and revolting, distasteful and depressing, we have played the victim card, blaming it all on the State, the system, on evolution, or on hard-wired human nature. To top it all, we have come to convince ourselves that man's manifest destiny is, to borrow Peter Lawler's words, "to free ourselves from Nature and God"; and through that, to do the unfinished business of what we might characterize as human wholeness. What we have not realized is that the opposite of 'perfection' is affection, and being 'unfinished' or incomplete is our natural and permanent state of existence. As a result, we have been indulging in all sorts of things to get the better of this road bump to our wholeness. If there is one crucial takeaway from the current wacky times when we are tossed between 'gloomy laughter' and 'comic despair' (Margaret Atwood; *The Edible Woman*, 1969), it is that nothing is stand-alone, that the most mundane human activity is at once casual and galactic, and that it sets off a "butterfly-effect". And that we cannot any more shirk becoming, the 'change we want to see', as Gandhi once said. Jalal ad-Din Rumi said that a clever man wants to change the world, and a wise man will change himself.

Each of us must become an agency of change inside. If we want to change the narrative of our future, *we* are the ones to stimulate the 'alienation effect', a jolt that should be strong enough to force us to come awake. There is no particular archetype. Everyone has to find their own Road to Damascus, their own path to inner transformation. Everyone is for change, except when it comes to the extant social order and power equation and one's posture and position in that. It is a charade, as Anand Giridharadas (*Winners Take All: The Elite Charade of Changing the World*, 2018) characterizes it. As citizens, we have always been ambivalent about our nexus with society. By and large, we expect much and give little. The change we are all for is, to paraphrase Tolstoy, like a man who sits on another's back and chokes him, and professes to do everything to help except to get off his back.[4] The fact is that we live in society, not the other way around, and at the same time we should not get lost in it. The appropriate analogy we can emulate is what the Buddhist text *Muni Sutta* says about the life of a sage in society: live like the 'wind not caught in a net', or like the lotus flower that blooms most from the thickest mud.

Almost every calamity or cataclysm, or trouble or tribulation that man has faced, including the present coronavirus pathogen is caused by these inabilities. If we can do good when we want to, and refrain from doing bad when we don't want to, there wouldn't be a climate or a corona crisis. The two are in fact linked. There is growing evidence that "climate

---

[4] Tolstoy, L. 1899. What Then Must We Do?

change could have played a role in the Covid-19 outbreak".[5] Now there is evidence that addressing the climate crisis can save millions of lives, the one reason why we didn't exhibit half the zeal for the climate as we did for corona. And the coronavirus outbreak was eerily foreseen by many. Before his final passage, astrophysicist Stephen Hawking said that one of his haunting fears was that mankind could be wiped out one day by a pathogen which jumps from animals to humans. We have not been wiped out, at least not yet, but the global outbreak has thrown into disarray the normal temporal rhythms of almost every human alive, while smoking out our mortally uneven relationship to those rhythms. Indeed, the sweep and scope of the expected aftermath of the present pandemic is such that some are already calling the year 2020 a liminal moment, that we have become a sort of non-person. Some others see a lot of similarities with the likes of civilizational collapses or *in situ* implosions, dating as far back as to the Bronze Age. Comparisons apart, what the current crisis has done is to force us to rethink and revisit our response from the perspective that nothing is 'as-is' and that everything is 'as we are'. And that, in turn, revolves around what happens at the deepest depths of our being, at the level of our soul.

We somehow fail to notice that the real voyage of discovery consists not in seeking new landscapes, but in discovering those hidden inside. While we have plenty of help to journey to the far corners of the world, we have none for this inner journey, or *yatra*. What we do not appreciate is that there's always something deeper, and life is grander, because there's so much underneath all of what appears to be. While being paralyzed in the face of imminent danger, we humans also yearn for something that uplifts and arouses us, that we can all share and rally around, one grand battle cry like Alexandre Dumas' "All for one and one for all, united we stand, divided we fall".[6] But sadly, the only idea currently in our grasp is

[5] Bressan, D. 2021. Climate Change Could Have Played A Role In The Covid-19 Outbreak. *Forbes Magazine*, 8 February 2021.

[6] Dumas, A. 1844. The Three Musketeers.

the cold, raw fear for life, of one another, of our own power, of loneliness, of loss of livelihood, of starvation, of a faceless danger lurking in the shadows somewhere. A new study shows that ninety-seven percent of young people are concerned about bringing a baby into a world as damaged as ours.[7] Peter Berger once noted, "Every society is, in the last resort, [human beings] banded together in the face of death" (*The Sacred Canopy*, 1967).

Death, rather *dodging* death, is what is keeping everyone alive. But once the present pandemic loses its potency and virulence and mutations run their course, 'the dead cold light of tomorrow' dawns, to borrow the words of Katherine Anne Porter (*Pale Horse, Pale Rider*, 1939). That is when *Tikkun olam*, or 'world repair', will begin.[8] As frail, feeble, and flawed men and women of this make-or-break century, we are subjected and susceptible to greater enticements and allurements than anyone else, has faced before. Faced with a significant chance of becoming extinct, we humans are being summoned to make a kind of determination few, if any, have been asked before: to consider who we irrefutably are, shorn of sophistry and sugar-coating, and who we deserve to be, and what kind of world we will build for our grandchildren and great-grandchildren. While the searchlight is directed at the medical pandemic, little is left to the other, even more pernicious, psychological pandemic of disempowerment, deprivation, and depressive restlessness. While a huge chunk of intellectual and influential pondering is being devoted to resetting, rebooting, and redesigning aspects of our outer life like economy and our relationship with nature, barely a word is heard about aspects of our inner life, or, in the words of the Benedictine monk Bede Griffiths, about our 'interior experience', the experience that counts most and is the most consequential. In the words of Andrew Jackson Davis, "The interior of all things is the

---

[7] Cited in: McKibben, B. 2020. Can Wall Street's Heaviest Hitter Step Up to the Plate on Climate Change? The Climate Crisis, *The New Yorker Magazine*. 24 December 2020.

[8] *Tikkun olam* is the idea, in Orthodox Judaism, that [humans] bear responsibility not only for their own moral, spiritual, and material welfare, but also for the welfare of society at large. Source: Wikipedia: The Free Encyclopedia. Wikimedia Foundation.

only 'real Reality'—the external is the mere transient expression…. all their external communications with each other are inflowings of interior affection" (*The Principles of Nature, Her Divine Revelations, and a Voice to Mankind*, 1847). Some of our greatest thinkers like Samuel Beckett, for example, drew inspiration from 'the innermost place of human frailty and lowliness'.[9]

Perhaps the worst that the current virus has done is to further deepen our alienation, not only from one another, and even more from our inner life. One of the fundamental truths we overlook is that, at the most elemental level, none of us are aware how much any of us mean and owe to another person, and how important physical contact and tactile sensation are for our mental health. That is one reason why the present trauma and upheaval has pushed so many to go into or through what Christian mysticism calls the 'dark night of the soul', what in Russian is called *toska*, 'a constraint of the soul, a yearning of the spirit, an agonizing gnawing', and a sense of impending 'unrecoverable dystopia' (Toby Ord, *The Precipice*). Yet, amid such gloom, some still see a silver lining, signs of the advent of a messiah or an avatar, who will rescue the righteous and take humanity to a higher realm of spiritual awareness. What we must now accept as a fact of life or price of our parasitical *persona*, is that we have entered an era of 'constant emergency'. But precisely moments like this can be times of high calling, for truly great game-changing things to incubate.

Everything in life is situational and it is in this somber, if not scary, setting that we have to delve deep into these timeless topics. Especially since this is a long haul, it is important that we take the first step right. That step here is to recognize that this is a *crisis of consciousness*. That is because the problem comes from consciousness, and that is where we must seek a resolution. This could be one of the those long-awaited, or dreaded,

---

[9] Cited in: Wimbush, A. 2021. The Wisdom of Surrender. *Aeon Magazine*. 18 January 2021. Retrieved from <https://aeon.co/essays/how-samuel-beckett-sought-salvation-in-the-midst-of-suffering>.

moments when everything we deem entirely 'unique' to human—society, culture, cognition, civilization, way of life—gets thrown open and all bets are off. Will we pole-vault from what the virus has forced us to be—masked, distanced, de-individuated humans—to transhumans or post-humans? Could what the United Nations calls 'shadow pandemic' (domestic, gender-based violence) become permanent? One of the paradoxes this pandemic, which seemed stranger than science fiction in so many ways, has brought to light is the 'effect of human proximate presence': those who lived alone suffered from single angst, and those who were coupled-up couldn't cope with the demands of 'constant and complete presence' of another person. Will this ordeal do a great favor and incentivize us to seek and discover our essential elemental essence? Or will it end with a whimper... and a few years from now we will learn to live with it like other infectious diseases, and life comes back on course with some redacts and revisions?

What we will at first see, if we can step up and look down, is that we lead a life on autopilot, following the same routines and doing the same activities every week or every day. Our brains have developed an unconscious decision-making system so we can take care of routine tasks necessary for life. We must move to 'conscious living'—being conscious of what we consume with our senses, and of the effect it has on us and on others. If we do that, then we can do what we want to do, and desist from doing what we don't, and go a long way to overcome the twin inabilities. Some of our greatest saints and *rishis*, epic heroes, prophets, philosophers, and poets, but even evil geniuses and plain folks like any of us, have spoken or written about their struggle with these inabilities. Notable among them were Saint Paul, acclaimed as one of the authors of the New Testament,[10]

---

[10] "I do not understand my own actions because I do not do what I want to. But I do the very thing that I hate. ... I can will what is right but I cannot do it. For I do not do the good that I want, but the evil I do not want is what I do." [Romans 7:15]. "Why is a person impelled to commit sinful acts, even unwillingly, as if by force, O descendent of Vrishni?" [Chapter 3, verse 36].

Saint Augustine, the author of *The City of God*,[11] and Sage Veda Vyasa, the author of the great Indian epic *Mahabharata*.[12] The *Pandava* prince Arjuna, a central character in the same epic, asked Lord Krishna, "Why is a person impelled to commit sinful acts, even unwillingly, as if by force?"[13] What is interesting is that the epic's arch enemy and villain, Duryodhana, also strikes a similar rueful refrain and confesses, "I know what is *dharma* (righteousness),[14] but am not able to practice it. I know what is *not* dharma, but I am not able to keep away from it".[15] In our own times, Gandhi, the ardent advocate of ahimsa or nonviolence, lamented, "What evil resides in me?" But it takes a Gandhi or a Saint Teresa of Calcutta (Mother Teresa) to be aware of the evil within, the sinister underbelly of being human, or what René Dubos[16] calls "the paleolithic bull". Such remarkable people still managed to lead the lives they led because they were consciously cognizant that despite the deluge of evidence to the contrary there is abundance of goodness within. As Eckhart Tolle tells us, "Acknowledging the good already in your life is the foundation for all abundance"—and to aid the forces of good within. Just as we cannot value presence without knowing absence, and we cannot value light without knowing darkness, we cannot experience good without suffering evil. And it is not only evil that we must

---

[11] "It is not we who sin, but some other nature that sins within us... My sin was all the more incurable because I did not think myself a sinner." Confessions, Book V, Section 10.

[12] "Mahabharata XVIII.5.49: With uplifted arms I am crying aloud but nobody hears me. From Righteousness comes Wealth, also Pleasure; Why should not Righteousness, therefore, be courted?

[13] Bhagavad Gita, 3.36.

[14] *Dharma* is the foundation of Hinduism. This Sanskrit word has multiple meanings, and there is no single-word translation for it in Western languages. It is somewhat similar to the ancient Chinese concept of Tao. In practical terms, it is, as defined in the Mahabharata (XVIII.113.8), "One should never do to another what one regards as injurious to oneself. This, in brief, is the law of dharma". Some say that the Egyptian word *maat* comes closest—truth, balance, order, harmony, law, morality, and justice.

[15] Source: Pandava Gita, 57:58.

[16] René Dubos, author of *So Human an Animal*, 1968.

learn to suffer, but suffering itself. As Thomas à Kempis says, "He that can well suffer shall find the most peace".[17]

From Arjuna to Saint Paul to Gandhi, no one has been able to come to terms with who they seemed to be from the outside, and who they felt they really were deep within their own selves. Could it really be that, as Ralph Barton[18] said, "the human soul would be a hideous object if it were possible to lay it bare"? But the mixed message of human nature is that each of us is equally capable of reaching Himalayan heights of cascading altruism, as well as descending to pornographic depths of lascivious living. Fact is that man has repeatedly shown his ability to empathize, to identify himself with a suffering person or able to shed, in Virgil's words, "there are tears for things and mortal things touch the mind" (*sunt lacrimae rerum et mentem mortalia tangunt*).[19] We have long wondered, when mutual support is so obviously self-advantageous, why do we waste our lives in mutual struggle?[20] We are befuddled why man is so money-minded, mean-spirited, and malice-filled, and if he even comes close to the depiction "magnificent miracle and a wondrous creation".[21] We wonder why, as Robert Wright (*Moral Animal*, 1994) says, "Nature has gone to great lengths to hide our subconscious from ourselves", particularly if, as biologist Rupert Sheldrake says, there is memory within nature. Some other biologists say that it is because "our moral brains evolved to help us spread our genes, not to maximize our collective happiness".[22]

Happy or horrified we may be, but the point of departure is to contrast ourselves as, on the one hand, one of tens of millions of species on the cosmic canvas, and, on the other hand, what import we carry as by far the

---

[17] Thomas à Kempis. *The Imitation of Christ*, 1427.

[18] Ralph Barton, 20th-century American cartoonist and caricaturist.

[19] Book I of the ancient Roman poet Virgil's masterpiece, the *Aeneid*, c.29–19 BCE.

[20] Peter Kropotkin. 1902. Mutual Aid: A Factor of Evolution.

[21] Depiction of man by the Italian Renaissance philosopher Giovanni Pico della Mirandola, in his *Oration on the Dignity of Man*, 1486.

[22] Greene, J. 2013. Moral Tribes: Emotion, Reason and the Gap Between Us and Them.

most menacing form of life on this planetary outpost. Nothing about what we do is any longer innocent or irrelevant. Every time we act badly despite not wanting to, could trigger a domino effect. This makes the overcoming of the twin inabilities a matter of ecumenical prominence. We have to bring about a drastic directional course correction, from the outward to inward, external to internal. The distance we cover is often less important than the *direction* we take. For, as Tolstoy used to say, "Just because he walks the road like a drunk, doesn't mean it's the wrong road". We have consistently disregarded our inner potential and inner blossoming, and failed to develop what spiritualists call 'spiritual infrastructure', similar to physical, economic, social, and technological infrastructures. For that, we need to do what is being described in esoteric circles as 'inner work' or 'self-audit', to dive deep into our inner self for the purposes of self-exploration and changing the controls and coordinates of our consciousness. It is here that we fail to live up to our billing. Wisdom is what man has long lusted for, and it is for this that, in Norse mythology, the god Odin sacrificed an eye. In Buddhism, good versus evil is not the central issue; it is ignorance, called *avidya*, versus wisdom, called *panna* in Pali. Socrates too laid down his life persuading Athenians to pursue wisdom. While wisdom-deficit has always been a huge handicap to human blooming, what we confront now is more nuanced and menacing: a growing imbalance and disequilibrium between our fantastic nuclear, industrial, technological, and mechanical powers, and our underdeveloped wisdom.

It is this deficit that drags and distorts how we behave. It is our own behavior that triggers a blend of bewilderment and breakdown, of being rooted and being rootless. It is through behavior that we make the choices that define life. It is the sum of salad-bowl choices we have made personally that has brought us to where we are today. The power to make choices is a great gift of God; in the words of Giovanni Pico della Mirandola. Although it may be a gift of God, the reality is that we live on autopilot, and very little of what we do every day is the ineluctable result of a considered choice-making. The real 'choice' is made actually elsewhere: in the maelstrom of our consciousness. As the philosophy of *panpsychism* postulates, consciousness is a fundamental feature of all physical matter, the intricate web of all existence should be regarded as a state and level of consciousness, all the way from the mineral to the post-human. And, as mystic and spiritual master George Gurdjieff says, "Evolution of man is the evolution of his consciousness, and 'consciousness' cannot evolve unconsciously". That is not merely a mystical vision. Even scientists like Jonas Salk, the inventor of the polio vaccine, say the same: "The evolutionary need is to increase our breadth of consciousness as human beings, to expand our range of choice for the wisest alternatives. The human capacity to anticipate and select will be the means whereby the future of human evolution will be determined" (*The Anatomy of Reality*, 1983).

Our incapacity to anticipate and to be prepared for anything that radically upsets our regular, predictable, routine patterns of everyday living has been the story of our history. The latest that demonstrated it is the coronavirus pandemic. That incapacity, time and again, we see, is innately constrained, as so vividly and visually unmasked by the current coronavirus crisis. While we are, like never before, united as a world, fighting a common enemy, what the world is also experiencing is a perilous pause in the 'normal' that held life together for so long. The cliché 'everyone dies' has acquired an all-new menacing meaning and immediate relevance. Unlike most disasters, the pandemic is restricted neither to a specific geography nor to one particular population. For better or worse, remote work, distance learning, and outdoor living is catching on. We have absolutely no idea of what kind of imprint all these and others are going to leave on human character and conduct, once the dust settles down, and how human life will look like.

Views vary on whether and, if so, which of the so-called Green Swans— climate change or Covid-19—qualifies as a greater 'existential risk'; the

Australian philosopher Toby Ord defines this as a "risk that threatens the destruction of humanity's long-term potential" (*The Precipice: Existential Risk and the Future of Humanity*, 2020). Both are expansive global negative externalities, and both are related to changes in our natural ecosystems. Of the two, climate change is the more severe, if only because "there is no vaccine against climate change".[23] And our chaotic and dysfunctional response to Covid-19 is a grim preview of what might ensue if something far more deadly like full-fledged nuclear or biological conflict were to happen. Some nuclear arms control experts even suggest, "A pandemic [natural or engineered] is just a kind of nuclear war in slow motion. Preventing nuclear war and managing a pandemic require the same conceptual approach".[24] There could be other Toby-Ord-type of existential threats, some we cannot now foretell, and some still incipient and carry immensity required to qualify. One such could be embedded in the most basic of it all: human fecundity. While the population bomb (Paul Ehrlich, 1968) was viewed until recently as a potential threat to human continuity on earth, it now seems more likely that the predicted doom—"nothing can prevent a substantial increase in the world death rate"—could happen from the other end: mass-scale birth-abnegation. If that attains 'critical mass', then mankind itself can become involuntarily infertile and result in human extinction. That is, unless, in the meantime, medicine makes a 'vaccine for mortality'.

But that is still way down the line. How the world will look like even after a couple of years we cannot even envision, but clearly, we are at a climacteric moment of a cathartic transition, and we need to lean into this opening, rather than brush past it. We have to consciously, carefully, and collectively reimagine a volte-face in human deportment and demeanor, a new routine that supports our long-term durability, and the robustness of the earth that supports us. And it will be a waste if we do not hammer

---

[23] Cox, R. 2020. There is No Vaccine for Climate Change. Resilience by Design Lab.

[24] Lewis, J. and Krzyzaniak, J. 2020. How the coronavirus outbreak is like a nuclear attack: an interview with Jeffrey Lewis. *Bulletin of the Atomic Scientists*. 20 March 2020.

out what cultural anthropologist Angeles Arrien describes as 'honorable closure'—a process through which we avoid that kind of waste, and awake to fresh pastures of promise (John O'Donohue). Without the hope of such a process, the terrible toll and mass death, agony and mourning, and the loss of precious 'freedoms', will have gone to that very waste. To be fair, it is not all that bad or our full fault. It is what we have made ourselves to be; our full range of powers of understanding and analysis, comprehension and cognition are still limited, confined and captive to our mind. As the Buddhist *Dhammapada* tells us, "There's a mess inside you: You clean the outside". The 'mess inside' is caused by our own consciousness bastardized by our own mind. Often, we go wrong not because the 'dark side' in our consciousness is deep, but because it is "easier, more seductive", as Yoda, the mystic Jedi Master told Luke Skywalker, in the *Star Wars* universe. It is easier because it better suits what our senses—which, as Stanislaw Lem (*Fiasco*, 1986) reminds us, are "no different from those of a baboon"— crave for: power, pleasure, and comfort. Our senses are fine-tuned for subjective utility, not objective reality. We have now gone a huge step ahead: we have developed what Scott Galloway calls 'refusal',[25] refusal to bear minor inconvenience. While in the case of the baboon such craving is fairly anodyne, when it incubates in the human mind, man's free choice "only lead him to sin", as St. Augustine lamented.

It is such gloom that prompts authors like Roy Scranton to ask: "Not one of us is innocent, not one of us is safe. We are doomed: Now what?"[26] That sense and query are now more palpable and pertinent. To reverse the slide down the slippery slope, we must return to the root and recognize two basics: one, that the world is but a conglomerate of all of us; two, that all of us have a world within. Our intent and intensity, passion and prejudice,

[25] Galloway, S. 2020. Post Corona: From Crisis to Opportunity. New York, USA: Portfolio/ Penguin.

[26] Scranton, R. 2018. We're Doomed. Now What? Essays on War and Climate Change. Soho Press.

compassion and malice, freedom and fire, all come this world. We don't realize, but, as Nietzsche said, "The 'apparent inner world' is governed by just the same forms and procedures as the 'outer' world" (*Will to Power*, 1910). He also suggests that "sense impressions naively supposed to be conditioned by the outer world [which he describes as the perspective world, this world for the eye, tongue, and ear] are, on the contrary, conditioned by the inner world". We should also be mindful that even though the question *Why be moral?* (or phrased otherwise, 'What *moral* reasons are there to be moral?') has always been high on human thought, it never got satisfactorily addressed, because we did not sufficiently take note that the very "meaning and morality of one's life comes from within oneself".[27] In fact, as Joseph Campbell, author of *The Hero with a Thousand Faces*, (1949) summarizes the Upanishadic vision, "All the gods, all the heavens, all the worlds, are within us". In his work *The Power of Myth* (1988), Campbell makes it more practical: "The inner world is the world of your requirements, your energies and your structure and possibilities that meets the outer world".[28]

The mystic master Gurdjieff resonates the same refrain when he says, "There are two struggles: an Inner-world struggle and an Outer-world struggle… you must make an intentional contact between these two worlds". The Greek philosopher Plutarch wrote, "What you achieve inwardly will change the outer reality" (*Plutarch's Lives*, 1470). We have always, at some depth or the other, known that the real action is within, but what we have failed to realize is that the nature of such action is that of a war, an '(un)civil war' between two siblings of our own integral self. And Jacob Needleman sums it up well: "Life is not so much defined by the external situation as it is by the internal one" (*I Am Not I*, 2016).

It is our all-consuming gaze on the outer world that gives rise to the predicament which is succinctly expressed by scientist Francis Collins: "We

---

[27] Hergenhahn, R. and Henley, T.B. 2013. An Introduction to the History of Psychology. UK: Wadsworth.

[28] Osho. 1989. The Rebel.

may understand a lot about biology, we may understand a lot about how to prevent illness, and we may understand the life span. But I don't think we will figure out how to stop humans from doing bad things to each other" (*The Language of God*, 2006). Much of the bad that many do, some say, is out of nescience. Lincoln simplified and simply said, "I don't like that man. I must get to know him better". It is also equally true that many of our shortcomings do not spring from not 'knowing', but not acting on what we do 'know'. What we must also acknowledge is that we harbor inside us not just little weaknesses, innocuous *hamartia,* and innocent foibles, but a demon—in Shirley Jackson's[29] words, "The demon in men's minds which prompts hatred, anger and fear, an irrational demon which shows a different face to every generation but never gives up its fight to win over the world".[30] To that we might add, 'and to win the war within,' between good and evil. It is a terrible thing: our soul is in immutable flux imprisoned by our fantasies and fallacies. We live in terror of what terrible things *we* might ourselves do *any* moment, which temptation might turn out to be too tempting, and what provocation or seduction might make honorable people do utterly dishonorable things. Some of our greatest heroes have been deeply flawed persons who used their public eminence to hurt and humiliate others, particularly those closest to them and dependent on them. Some of our holy men and women were not always holy; they were "cutthroats, crooks, trollops, con men, and devil-worshippers".[31] What gives us some cheer is that they were just like us. They too sinned during their lifetime, and often led lives of decadence and depravity before their lives were converted. Doors were not closed to any sin, even murder or prostitution. Even the Bible tells us, "Just so, I tell you, there will be more joy in heaven over one sinner who repents than over ninety-nine

---

[29] Shirley Jackson, author of *The Witchcraft of Salem Village*, 1987.

[30] From the book *The Letters of Shirley Jackson*, by Shirley Jackson (Hyman, L. and Murphy, B.M., eds.), to be published July 2021.

[31] Craughwell, T.J. 2006. Saints Behaving Badly: The Cutthroats, Crooks, Trollops, Con Men, and Devil-Worshippers Who Became Saints. Penguin Random House.

righteous persons who need no repentance".[32] And yet we must be fully cognizant that our capacity for destruction has far outpaced our ability to act responsibly. We are at risk, now more than ever, to acting irresponsibly that it prompts a nettling question: what are we capable of being induced or tempted or compelled to do? At the crux of all the stubborn issues that vex us is our instinctive inability to measure up to the ideal expressed by Jean-Jacques Rousseau: "Identify myself with my fellow, and I feel that I am, so to speak, in him, it is in order not to suffer that I do not want him to suffer. I am more interested in him for love of myself".

What is true enough is that all humans are responsible for any single human action, bringing to mind the famous saying of the Roman playwright Publius Terentius Afer: "*Homo sum, humani nihil a me alienum puto*", or "I am human, and I think nothing human is alien to me" (*Heauton Timorumenos*). With that kind of consciousness, we will realize that everyone is guilty for everyone else, and we will learn to treat others as subjects and not objects, and acquire a sense of responsibility—the moral culpability which we accept and ascribe to our actions and to those of others. Each of us carry our own brand of 'moral ulcers and scars', to borrow the words of Thomas de Quincey,[33] which we like to conceal from public gaze. Whether we like it or not, everyone we come in contact with leaves a residue on us. The imprint stays with us forever, becomes a part of us, and modifies us. As the Elder Zossima in Dostoevsky's *The Brothers Karamazov* (1880) says, "There is only one way to salvation and that is to make yourself responsible for all men's sins".

In the warp and woof of everyday life, we usually adopt one of two courses: the Pollyanna-ish way of ignoring an evil, or the pessimistic acquiescence of evil as an immutable characteristic of our finite, and futile, existence. What we must learn to accept is that evil is not some sort of alien value system, and instead see it as a malfunctioning of our own

---

[32] Luke 15.7.

[33] Thomas de Quincey. 1821. Confessions of an English Opium-Eater.

mind. So commanding is evil in our consciousness that we have failed to give due weight to the reservoir of our 'secret goodness' (Jack Kornfield; *The Wise Heart*, 2008). Iris Murdoch, in her book *The Sovereignty of Good* (1970), says, "Goodness appears to be both rare and hard to picture. It is perhaps most convincingly met with in simple people". It is also sadly true that goodness and good conduct do not compel our interest the way evil and grief do. But the 'gales of grief', a Beckettian phrase, like grace, is also a gift of God. It is up to us how we internalize it. What is disheartening is that even when we do good, we rarely feel that good, as much as we don't feel bad when we do bad. Yet paradoxically, feeling bad isn't actually that *bad*; it pushes you to do good; it's what helped us survive. And, we must never forget that, as Daniel Deronda (in George Eliot's 1876 novel by the same name) says, "No evil dooms us hopelessly except the evil we love… and make no effort to escape from". What we do not realize is that evil can be infectious; if we are constantly or repeatedly in its presence, like the coronavirus, we can catch it. The evil we denounce in our shambolic world is nothing but our refusal to see it as an engaged expression of our own self in others. In its stead, we picture ourselves as 'victims' ventriloquized by others. And evil is always 'absolutely' relative to good; but also, paradoxically, if we refuse to perceive and resist it as evil, then it becomes evil absolute and utterly sabotages the very way man likes to live with it. What is missing is that we inexplicably ignore our own reflexive goodness; we fail to see that magnanimity is as natural to us as monstrosity. That is because we make everything personal and selectively reciprocal. 'Tit for tat' is bad, but putting oneself in another's shoes is good. St. Francis says, "Kindness is the overflowing of self upon others. We put others in the place of self" (*My Prayer Book*, 1912). The *Taittiriya* Upanishad says, "Those acts that you consider good when done to you, do those to others, none else". This is similar to what Jesus says in the Sermon on the Mount: "All things whatsoever ye would that men should do to you, do ye even so to them". To imbibe that spirit in our life has long been our ambition but it has usually eluded us because we view it as a problem of behavior, of external environment, out of joint with, not an inadequacy or malfunctioning of, our consciousness. We have forever engaged in discourses and debates about issues such as if man is an agent of free will, or if we should, as the Latin phrase goes, *amor fati*, "love our fate". Or if we should rebel and die fighting. The foundational fact is that everything begins, occurs, and ends inside; everything else is a reflection, refraction, and extension. Evil is no exception.

Evil exercises its influence anonymously in our corrosive contemporary culture not only as injustice, indifference, and intolerance, but even as obscene affluence in the interpersonal realm, as well as in our tendency to see another person or another people or race as 'inferior'. It is so smooth and seamless that nobody can be held directly liable or responsible. And that anonymity and ambiguity allows us to do evil while still feeling good about ourselves. Indeed, more than not 'being bad' it is the escapist 'feel good' that we feel so good about. And it is *feelings* that are our deepest, most authentic essence, even existence. And if they lead us astray, we are truly star-crossed. Anyone can be a wolf in a sheep's clothing; even more unnerving is how everybody knows that it is a wolf but *pretends* not to know. Because we fear what we might actually see. One could always become the other; one is forever hounded and haunted. Interpersonal and invisible evil[34] has never been so pervasive and penetrative as it has been over the past century. It is 'evil, on evil, piled on evil',[35] so unremitting that we are sliding into a state of Stockholm syndrome. But, this, we must understand, is a reflection of the state of our consciousness.

Two gravest global abominations in human history are unravelling in our lifetimes. One is how we treat the 'people of the abyss'[36] those who, for

---

[34] Source: Lerner, M. (ed.). 2007. Tikkun Reader: Twentieth Anniversary. New York, USA: Rowman and Littlefield. p.282.

[35] Miller, W.M. 1960. A Canticle for Leibowitz. USA: Lippincott.

[36] London, J. 1907. The Iron Heel.

no fault of theirs, get the short end of the stick, the insulted and injured, in every society. The other is how we treat our young people who, to borrow the words of Louise Glück[37], are "born and then forced to exist", and then, adding insult to injury, are left to die in the wasteland that we are turning the earth into. A notable feature is the ever-growing imperative to often choose the lesser evil and the greater good, although we also say in the same breath that good and evil, like true and false, beautiful and ugly, or white and black, are simply another mind-made label, and that our real aim ought to be to go beyond both. As Jalal ad-Din Rumi (*A Great Wagon*) says, we should go "out beyond ideas of wrongdoing and right-doing... Ideas, language, even the phrase *each other* doesn't make any sense". The reality is that the same deep chemistry that fosters goodness, in a heartbeat, pivots to evil, and the pluralities between right and wrong are usually opaque and blurred. Indeed, there have always been those like the Sophists of classical Greece who thought that notions such as *right* and *wrong* were considered to be not only arbitrary creations of a weak-willed society, but also of 'natural justice'. Since it is too taxing to distinguish the two in the daily context, many feel that to live in accordance with what is averred by others to be right or wrong will amount to erring on the 'safer' side.

The basic reality is that anything, or anyone, can be both good or evil, depending on the context and purpose. A saint is not always saintly, and a sinner need not always sin. Even anger, envy, and violence can be 'good' if they are well-oriented; and 'good' things like tolerance, tranquility, gentleness can be 'bad' if directed at the wrong person or purpose. Human evil now is technified, impersonal, invisible, and integrated into daily life. It is channeled through plutocracies, oligarchies, technocracies, meritocracies, bureaucracies, and corporations. Institutional, increasingly incendiary, evil far outweighs the classical evil perpetrated by wicked or wacky individuals. And, as German playwright Bertolt Brecht said, "When evil-doing comes like falling rain, nobody calls out 'stop!'" Like a virus, this

---

[37] Louise Glück, winner of the 2020 Nobel Prize in Literature.

evil is getting better at being evil and is jumping from person to person. The present pandemic has offered a perfect platform. We should constantly remember that all is not well that ends well, and that good does not always come out in the wash. Evil is so detached from the doer and so deeply impregnated in how we do anything that, as Andrew Kimbrell points out, "The very idea of our society being characterized by masses of evil people seems somewhat comical".[38] In a world shattered by and saturated with everyday evil, none is in the clear, and silence is complicity. There are three reasons why there is more evil in contemporary society: one, we leave public life 'morally quarantined'; two, we think that anything done as 'duty' indemnifies us against any judgment; three, our willingness to give absolute ethical *carte blanche* to those who wield political and economic power over our lives. Machiavelli says, "Hence a prince who wants to keep his authority must learn how not to be good, and use that knowledge, or refrain from using it, as necessity requires" (*The Prince*). It is a message that our present day master-class have taken to authority like a duck to water. The State frowns upon—rightly so—citizens having weapons, but the State itself has become the deadliest weapon. What can one do if the fence, meant to protect the crop, itself starts eating the crop?! As a moral society, we are aimlessly inching to the place to which Satan's choice inexorably led, in Milton's *Paradise Lost*: "All Good to me is lost... Evil be thou my Good". In his play *Antigone*[39], Sophocles says, "Evil sometimes seems good to a man whose mind a god leads to destruction". Have we slipped into such a quagmire? Is it because evil is our 'good' that even when we do evil, we think we are being good? Evil "has become the grey eminence infiltrating all areas of human existence".[40] In Hindu scriptures, it is said that God incarnates on earth to slay evil demons, and that in our present

[38] Kimbrell, A. 2000. Cold Evil: Technology and Modern Ethics. Annual E.F. Schumacher Lecture. Schumacher Center for a New Economics. Lecture delivered on 28 Oct 2000.

[39] Antigone. Verses 620–623.

[40] Kimbrell, A. 2000. Cold Evil: Technology and Modern Ethics. Annual E.F. Schumacher Lecture. Schumacher Center for a New Economics. Lecture delivered on 28 Oct 2000.

age, the *Kali Yuga,* evil manifests not as individual demons but makes the mind of man itself 'demonic'.

Man is bent on now is bent on bettering the brain and mending the mind, as ways to bend others to our will and whim. The underlying premise is that you and I and every human being is reducible to the processes and content of our brain; brain equals mind and mind consciousness. There are many scientists who doubt the validity of these premises and attendant assumptions. In fact, some like philosopher Dan Dennett make a compelling argument that not only do we not understand like our own consciousness, but that, half the time, our brains are actively fooling us. What is not in such serious doubt is that we all harbor in the world within in our mind a hydra of Lerna[41]—the habits, tendencies, and behavior patterns or reactions that seem like a beast within us that we don't want to even acknowledge. Every time we try to quash them, new heads seem to spring up. This much most of us at some level of consciousness we are aware of, but not that we all have within a Hercules too—our own innate goodness—to slay such monsters. It is interesting that one of the heads that Hercules chopped off was immortal. What we are trying to do is the opposite: while Hercules had to cut off this head to kill the hydra, we want to 'grow' it to acquire such a 'head'. At the most basic level, the dialectic between good and evil has baffled human thought, and our inability to get a grip on their interplay has shaped history. Biblically, it was man's inability to measure up to and submit to God's vision, and man's desire to 'know' good and evil, that led to his Edenic banishment. And, truth be told, it was of no avail; we still do not know good and evil—or how to choose good over evil. We have long blinded our own minds through absolutist notions of good and evil, and by asking how can there can be evil in a world made by a 'good' God. But, on the same token, one should ask, as the Roman philosopher Boethius asks: "How can there be good if

---

[41] The Hydra of Lerna is a multi-headed, serpentine water monster in Greek and Roman mythology. Hercules is sent to overpower and slay the monster.

He exists not?" (*The Consolation of Philosophy*, 524). The German mystic Jakob Bohme amplifies and says, "There is nothing in nature wherein there is not good and evil; everything moveth and liveth in this double impulse, working or operation, be it what it will". Some draw the analogy of the chimera, a mythic beast having the body of a goat and the head of a lion.[42]

The discipline of determining what is good and what is bad, what is, in fact, virtuous, or what virtue consists of and how we might best attain it, is generally viewed as the judicial branch of philosophy. It has preoccupied the abiding interest of philosophers from Aristotle onwards. The nexus between good and evil is subtle, and it is almost superhuman to neatly summarize. It can be any of the following: polar opposites, Siamese twins, sniping siblings, two sides of the same coin, or, what in German is called *doppelganger*. Maybe a more accurate approximation is that man is not truly one, but truly two, or may be many more. As RL Stevenson's famous character Dr. Henry Jekyll says, "Man will be ultimately known for a mere polity of multifarious, incongruous, and independent denizens".[43] He also refers to a 'perennial war among [his] members'. Intrinsically, good and evil are intertwined and have the same face; not opposite or complementary. They house the same psychic space, but there is no love lost between them; they fight tooth and nail for suzerainty of the same space. But we want to exorcize one, evil, and, at the same time, overcome the fragility of human goodness. The inconvenient truth is that we will never cathartically purge ourselves of the impulses that threaten to wreak havoc with our lives. The way out is not to weed out bad people or worship good people. For each of us has the capacity for appalling atrocities and appealing altruism, for rousing joy and sinking despair, and we have long wondered about who is the culprit: disposition or situation. To use, or rather misuse, the analogy

---

[42] Wrangham, R. 2019. The Goodness Paradox: The Strange Relationship Between Virtue and Violence in Human Evolution. Pantheon.

[43] Stevenson, R.L. 1886. The Strange Case of Dr. Jekyll and Mr. Hyde. Chapter 10: Henry Jekyll's Full Statement of the Case.

of Philip Zimbardo (*The Lucifer Effect*, 2007), what is rotten is neither the apple nor the basket; it is the *worm* within.

Everyone longs to be known as a good person, good spouse, good citizen, and everyone covets leading a good life. Even if one must die, one longs to have a good death. And in every case, what good entails is subjective and situational. That doesn't deter many among us to act with the illusory attitude that 'good is commendable but evil is dependable!', to quote Lucy Harris from the musical *Jekyll & Hyde*.[44] It brings to mind Susan Wolf's essay *Moral Saints* (1982), in which she asks: "What makes a moral saint? Is it what we do? Or what motivates us?" That equally applies to a good person or a bad person. The best way to answer is to say 'none-of-the-above'. There is no moral saint or good or bad *person* per se; there are good and bad actions depending on the motive and its fallout and ripple effect. Sometimes, in the words of Guy De Maupassant, "an action reprehensible in itself often derives merit from the thought which inspires it", or the end justifies the means. Good or evil is not what separates us and our enemies. What separates us is our failure on two fronts: the inability not to do the right thing not because it makes us happy but because it is our duty to others; and, the inability to factor in the truth that we are each other's destiny, or that anyone can find himself in anyone else's shoes. It is good to bear in mind what is attributed to the 20th-century Austrian philosopher Ludwig Wittgenstein: "I don't know why we are here, but I'm pretty sure that it is not in order to enjoy ourselves". It is also good to remember that everything we say or do, by default, hurts or helps another person. And, as Lewis Carroll (*Alice in Wonderland*) says, "One of the deep secrets of life is that all that is really worth doing is what we do for others". And then, the human intellect has not found its way to prevent plurality from descending into depersonalization, and differentiation into discrimination. While it is

---

[44] *Jekyll & Hyde* is a 1997 musical loosely based on the 1886 novella *Strange Case of Dr. Jekyll and Mr. Hyde* by R.L. Stevenson. This quote is from the song *Good 'N' Evil*, sung by the character Lucy Harris.

almost impossible to lead any human life without causing harm or hurting any other sentient being, at the very least the human beast, by conscious and purposeful practice, it is possible to meliorate, minimize, and mitigate the intensity of repercussions. Learning not to cause harm to others or ourselves is a basic Buddhist teaching on the healing power of nonaggression. It is our different standpoints, our perspectives, our fears, our prejudices that set us apart, and different people interpret them differently from different vantage points. We must also reckon with the realism that being prejudiced is a part of the package of being human. That is the bitter by-product of the ability, unique to humans, to like and dislike, to differentiate one from another. For, if it is not race or color or caste or class, we will invent something else. The dare we face is to see that prejudice or bigotry does not obfuscate considerateness, justness, and fairness. This becomes all the more pointed and poignant when we realize that most of us enjoy the luxuries of life that are extracted from the tears and toils, sweat and servitude of many others who are often underfed and overworked. Even our beliefs are prejudiced, our mercy is tainted with might. To such an extent that we can 'believe' things or persons that we don't believe in. To muddy the matters even more, to do good or bad is not a matter of pure choice; neither can be stopped once it happens within. Nothing is neutral; not even science or silence or sin. And nothing goes in vain, good or bad. It is interesting to note that in *Paradise Lost*, Milton establishes good and evil as constantly shifting forces that both God and Satan seem to mobilize in opposition to each other. Some scholars even speculate that "the conflicting discourse between the two forces redefines Heaven's God as a being capable of evil, and Hell's Satan as a creature seemingly capable of good".[45]

The moral quandary endemic in the twin questions has gained emergent resonance and greater rigor than ever before when so many feel that they

---

[45] Hensell, K. 2009. The Shifting Concept of Good and Evil in Paradise Lost." Edifice Project. The University of Alabama, USA. Retrieved from <http://edificeproject.ua.edu/wp-content/uploads/2009/05/shifting-concept-of-good-and-evil.pdf>.

are complicit with evil but feel too helpless to either hack it or break free. A great number even think that there is little merit in worrying why we cannot do good when we want to, when being good is no good for any good; and being bad is not bad, by far better than being dead. Some ask: If by being nasty I can get all nice things, why be nice at all? And unlike in earlier times, everything man does deeply affects the natural world—our world, the only one we have. We have made that very world both unviable and increasingly unlivable. The plunder and predation of the planet are the bedrock of our 'civilized' civilization to such an extent that many feel that nothing short of an organized, orchestrated rollback, if you will—of what Roman Krznaric[46] describes as the 'tyranny of the now' and 'pathological short-termism'—can reprieve our planet. And how can we do that if we cannot even desist or resist from doing bad against our will, when we are unwilling to accept the short-term cost for longer and larger good? The climate crisis, dubbed as the klaxon-kind of emergency of our time, is a direct consequence of these two inabilities: inability to live how we want to live, frugally, virtuously and ethically; and inability to refrain from doing what we know is self-destructive (pollute and poison our planet). Our ongoing assault on outer space will only make matters worse, by increasing emissions of carbon dioxide, particulates, and other noxious substances.[47] Experts warn that the climate crisis, which, it is said, is changing the geography of the planet, might also trigger the onset of a pandemic era, caused by "shaking up the natural world and rewriting disease algorithms on the planet". And 'the fire next time' (James Baldwin) and the coming 'fire storm of change' (Alvin Toffler) might be all-consuming and vaccine-proof. Even in the wake of the present, some say that the world will experience a 'psychological pandemic'.[48] The odds

---

[46] Krznaric, R. 2020. The Good Ancestor: How to Think Long Term in a Short-Term World. New York: WH Allen.

[47] Ross, M.N. and David, L. 2020. An Underappreciated Danger of the New Space Age: Global Air Pollution. *Scientific American*. 6 November 2020.

[48] Cocozza, P. 2020. Has a Year of Living With Covid-19 Rewired Our Brains? *The Guardian*. 13 December 2020.

are that we will read such reports and pass on to the next, less ominous and more boisterous story. But all is not down the drain; whatever we experience, something sticks on and becomes part of us. Our paralysis in the face of clear and transparent threats to our very existence, our inexhaustible aptitude to evade seeing what stares us in the face in the mirror, are symptomatic of the fact that "something seismic, something utterly mysterious has happened in the human spirit and psyche at the deepest level, and equally mystifying is that we do not have the foggiest idea what it could possibly be".[49]

Not having the foggiest idea of any answers to the twin questions, and perceiving a threat to its own dominance, the human mind has mounted a twin strategy: *self-righteousness*, and *self-destruction*. Each reinforces the other in a vicious whirl. It is self-righteousness that consumes us with a bottomless compulsion to dominate others, that doesn't let us concede even in thought that others can arrive at different beliefs in their honest search for truth. It was perhaps necessary for self-preservation, but the risk is that we can be so self-righteous about self-righteousness, that we may fall into the trap of thinking it is righteousness. That leads to self-destruction. That is what makes every human being a risk factor that can go awry anytime. The two risk factors of the Covid-19 pandemic and suicidality, or so-called deaths of despair, converge to create what is flagged as 'GG vulnerability'. Covid-19 has been doubly-deadly: one, as a major cause of death; two, as a trigger for suicides.

It is from this somber standpoint that we should try to place in perspective the trauma and toll that the coronavirus has wreaked on humankind. Like in any life-threatening crisis, it has stripped human hubris of its veneer, cover, and camouflage, and exposed the toxic, acquisitive, profit-motivated society. It has laid bare to the bone the twin dangers of endemic poverty not only in the developing world, but also in rich countries like USA, and the grotesque disparities in wealth and

---

[49] Bhimeswara Challa. 2011. Man's Fate and God's Choice—An Agenda for Human Transformation. New Delhi, India: Kalpaz. p.3.

well-being. According to the World Bank, while the Covid-19 pandemic pushed an additional 88 million to 115 million into extreme poverty in 2020, the combined wealth of the world's ten richest rose by $540 billion. The rich, come hell or highwater, always seem to find a way to maneuver around any medical calamity or economic depression or natural disaster, and get richer. But when the bottom half of the globe by income realizes they can double their wealth by taking the wealth of the richest eight families—who have more money than 3.6 billion people—it is hard to tell what they wouldn't do. Recent research suggests that being rich or poor has a significant bearing on longevity too.[50] A study indicates that "wealth appears to be more strongly associated with mortality than other socioeconomic position measures".[51] Big-money-muscled 'immortality' research will further widen this disparity. From all this, it does appear that, to bring about some semblance of transformative justice, there may be no other way than to anoint, as suggested by Sam Pizzigati (*The Case for a Maximum Wage*, 2018), "a world without a super-rich" as a global goal. It is poverty that forces tens of millions to be ineligible for healthcare and makes them economically so fragile that a single paycheck is what stands between a heated home and living on the street.

The Covid-19 pandemic has reinforced the long-evident reality that global problems require global imagination, coherent cooperation, and holistic solutions. In the shadow of the pandemic, we did things which we never imagined we will do. We invented a new way of life: life in *cordon sanitaire*, a time when human presence even in silence risks playing a game of Russian roulette. Security gave way to safety. Unpleasant it may be, but once more it has become apparent that, even in the face of mass death and

---

[50] Johnson, B.W. and Raub, B. 2018. How Much Longevity Can Money Buy? Estimating Mortality Rates for Wealthy Individuals. *Statistical Journal of the IAOS*: 34(1)91–98. IOS Press.

[51] Demakakos, P., Biddulph, J.P., Bobak, M., and Marmot, M.G. 2016. Aging; Wealth and Mortality at Older Ages: a Prospective Cohort Study. Journal of Epidemiology and Community Health. BMJ Journals. 70(4):346–353.

a mountain of misery, some lives matter more than others, based on factors like color and class, and that none of us can throw the first stone; that we are all partners in the crime. The positive part is that we are learning 'how to be at home' externally; what we need to learn is how to be at home *internally*. The time is now, for, as Austrian author Marc Elsberg warned us, "tomorrow will be too late".[52] We have reached a stage when it will do us a world of good to remember the moral message contained in ancient Sanskrit animal fables (*Panchatantra: The Two-headed Weaver*), and in a 1902 horror story by WW Jacob (*The Monkey's Paw*): "Beware of what you wish, lest you might just get it". More than our wishes, it is our *wants* that can be harmful. Every want of anyone is no longer 'his' alone; because its fetishistic pursuit has implications, more than intended by the intent, that impact not only 'his life', but also life in general. The model of our wants has moved from necessity to contentment, from what Adam Smith called 'ease of body and of mind' to luxury—which Karl Marx dubbed as the opposite of naturally necessary—and from luxury to the redundant. For anything to go right in today's world, we must get a hold on the ways of our wants. We must draw, as the philosopher Harry Frankfurt suggested, a sharp distinction between the things that we simply want and the ones that, after consideration, we intend or *want to want* (*Freedom of the Will and the Concept of a Person*, 1971). Sometimes, even the effort to know what we 'want to want' can be effective if it is affective. As Albert Camus said about Sisyphus, "the struggle itself toward the heights is enough to fill a man's heart".

The conundrum is that even though man is basically a desiring being who strives to extract things from the world, morally he lacks the capability to veto what he 'wants to want' and be able to calibrate the desirability of his desires; in short, he becomes the kind of creature that his unhinged individualism and algorithm-fuelled acceleration of consumer culture has

---

[52] Marc Elsberg, author of the disaster thriller, *Blackout: Tomorrow Will Be Too Late*. Penguin. 2017.

turned him into. And the wages of unbridled desire result in the agony of unfulfillment. God's honest truth is that there is enough for all of us on this very planet if only we give up on greed and grifters. As Kim Stanley Robinson tells us, "Enough should be a human right, a floor below which no one can fall; also a ceiling above which no one can rise" (*The Ministry for the Future*, 2020). In monetary terms, it means that we need both a 'minimum wage' and a 'maximum wage'. It is revolting that hundreds of millions of global elites wallow in licentious luxury when billions struggle to meet their basic needs. Equally offensive it should be to divert so much of collective sweat and skill towards achieving what Ernst Bloch calls "the final medical wishful dream…. the abolition of death" (*The Principle of Hope*, 1995), when a child under 15 dies every five seconds around the world, and 2.5 million newborns die in their first month, due to preventable causes, according to a study of the World Bank. Our growing appetite for self-damnation and self-sabotage, individually and as a species, could be death's way of paying us back. That is why even as we try to 'abolish' death, the more death is becoming too irresistible to so many as a kind of a corrective to life.

Equally important to ponder over, particularly in the current coronavirus context, is, all said and done, what we owe to one another. That is all there is. As Immanuel Kant elaborated, each human being is "not merely as a means to ends… but as an end in itself". Whenever we are in doubt about what to do, we should ask ourselves a simple but colossal question: would we be content to live the lives that the least fortunate, the left-behinds, in our society actually live? The time is now for us as a weedy but responsible species to reevaluate how to ensure that every human being will live what philosopher Nicole Hassoun calls a 'minimally good life' (*Globalization and Global Justice*, 2014). It is a life that aims to rid ourselves of life's excess in favor of what is basic. In our ever-growing life as a ravenous consumer, we should train ourselves to reflect on questions such as: Who made this thing? Where did they make this? What is their life like? Who profits from this transaction? In earlier times, 'good life' philosophers like Aristotle associated with *eudaimonia* or human flourishing. They also linked it with the well-being and the spiritual growth of society. In fact, Indian philosopher Radhakrishnan's depiction of 'what it is for a human life to go well' is universal salvation or *sarvamukti*. As every man is considered potentially divine, good life had to be a means to realize that divine potential. Modern man has brought it down to the purely humdrum level, to a life of hassle-free ease and conveniences—incubated license, leisure, and luxury.

While only barely a year ago everyone was busy chasing time and dreaming of free time, suddenly all of them became too abundant to be of any use. A life of 'doing nothing' is no longer our idea of unicorn or utopia. It also underlined the question: how does one wriggle out of the grip of creature comforts and material attachments? Fact is that we are so inured to the sumptuous life in the shade that we are sore afraid of sunshine. Since primordial times, man has struggled to make sense of the absurdity of the human condition, strived to do what the Delphic Oracle termed as 'Know thyself', and what the Upanishads called *Atma-vichara* or self-inquiry. An essential step towards that knowing, that inquiry is to 'know' that there is a 'world within', and that, in that world, an epic, eternal war is raging, and that it is in our own power to intervene and influence its course in the desirable direction. The way to influence is as direct and simple as how we use time in our life every day. It is the warped way we live, and our barely concealed contempt of the laws of nature, that has brought us to the brink of the abyss. But it is ironic to recall that the earliest man conceived gods as personifications of the forces of nature; even today, the Hindu religion worships the five basic elements of nature, the *panchamahabhutas* as they are termed—*prithvi* (earth), water *jala* (water), *tejas* (fire), *vayu* (wind), and *akasha* (space). It also postulates that all of creation, including the human body, is made up of these five essential elements, and that, upon death, the human body dissolves into these five elements of nature.

And it is nature that we must get back to in order to go to the root of the ongoing pandemic. It has taken the world's foremost expert on chimpanzees, Jane Goodall to tell us where the root is: "Disrespect of nature... forcing animals into closer contact with each other and some of them with humans".[53] A major manifestation of that disrespect is modern man's attempt to make himself a *Homo Immortalis Omnipotent*, an immortal and impregnable superman with super intelligence. Actually, in practical terms, man today is a virtual superman compared to a man even a half century ago. But what man truly wants is more than all of the above: he wants to survive death and stay in his own skin, and as Woody Allen said, he wants 'to live on in [his] apartment'. Man has always labored to come to terms with death. The Stoic philosopher Epicurus wondered, "Why should I fear death? If I am, death is not. If death is, I am not. Why should I fear that which cannot exist when I do?" But the best is how the Greek hero Achilles turns 180 degrees his assessment after his death. When alive he said, "The gods envy us. They envy us because we are mortal, because any moment may be our last. Everything is more beautiful because we are doomed",[54] but after being dead, he told the visiting Odysseus, "Say not a word in death's favor; I would rather be a paid servant in a poor man's house and be above ground than a king of kings among the dead".[55] Fact is that despite prophecies of 'impending immortality' and transiting into a space-faring species, almost the foremost thought in the mind of every human alive now is how to stay alive here and now. We must also have a global conversation on the ethics of bodily enhancement. There is no question that enhancement of a specific body part can make that part 'superhuman' in its efficiency and help medically. But if we use it non-medically as a way to make man himself a 'superman' that raises a different

---

[53] Cited in: Mirsky, S. 2020. Jane Goodall: We Can Learn From This Pandemic. Scientific American podcast. Conservation, 60-Second Science. *Scientific American*. 21 April 2020.

[54] Homer. *The Iliad*.

[55] Homer. *The Odyssey*. Book XI.

and more complex issue. For superman may be a super-man but not man. And does it—should it—make any difference? Should speed, strength, efficiency and all that matter?

Although we think that life and death are polar opposites, many religions do not view mortality and immortality as incompatibles *per se*. In the cosmic perspective, as the Egyptian mystic and philosopher Hermes Trismegistus puts it, "Birth is not the beginning of life—only of an individual awareness. Change into another state is not death—only the ending of this awareness" (*Corpus Hermeticum*). Immortality was viewed as symbolic and spiritual, not physical. Pema Chodron says, "To live is to be willing to die over and over again (*When Things Fall Apart*, 1996). St. Francis says, "It is in dying that one is raised to eternal life" (*My Prayer Book*, 1912). The Upanashadic *shanti* (peace) mantra says, *mrtyor ma amritam gamaya*, translated as "lead me from death to immortality". The Katha Upanishad tells how to become immortal: "When all desires lurking in the heart are removed, then a mortal person becomes immortal, and attains *Brahman* in this world. When the knots in the heart that bind one to this world are all cut, then a mortal becomes an immortal". Human civilization has always been driven by our utterly unique ability to create and innovate. We now have added another dimension, the full import of which we are too close to and too soon to tell: the ability to create an 'autopoietic'—self-maintaining and self-regulating—machine, which, some apprehend, will compel us to 'abolish our own future', and others suggest will give us a huge leg up to overcome the biological limits of being human, and take us to the next, and ultimate, level of evolution. Although we have long fiddled with automata, we have now concluded that there is no other way to further the power and capacity of 'species *Man*' other than making the machine more intelligent, more reliable, and more amicable, and to piggy back on that. Perhaps the most pressing matter that we should calmly and coherently consider is this: should we go wherever or do whatever to cross all limits, limb by limb and enhance in every way we can, regardless of how the human might end up as?

A crucial issue is: what, anyway, is 'intelligence', and what has that to do with who we are? At a more basic level, according to cognitive scientist Andy Clark, one obstacle why artificial intelligence—building machines that have the same capabilities that human beings have—hasn't really taken off is that "we simply misconstrued the nature of intelligence itself".[56] After all, computing is not the same as intelligence. We should fear as much about what our intelligence might push us into doing, as about our tools misbehaving. But our tools and toolkit are the creations of our inherited intelligence. Even in pre-*sapiens* times, as professor of philosophy Robert Doede points out, "using tools to modify their environment, early hominids were themselves modified by their tool use". These days, we prefer a variant of 'modified' or 'optimized' to describe what we are doing with our body and with every organ in it—with our brain, even our souls—to turn us into a cyborg (Elon Musk says we already are one such being). We are tapping technologies to optimize our corporeal limitations, treating our bodies more like software with which we can experiment.

The blaring irony is that with such a possibility, we could not come up with anything better than a drab and dull machine as our role model and gold standard and, some fear, as the agent of our own absolute obsolescence. What we are trying to give is nothing less than a mind of its own to the machine. We have pretty much concluded that our salvation lies through 'surrender', what in Hinduism is called *prapatti* (unconditional surrender to the Almighty), and what in Sufism is called *tawakkul* (offering complete trust to a person who knows the way out of a vast desert). By the time we are done with the machine, what it will do is anybody's guess. What we tend to forget is that what we create cannot be very different from those who create it. Will it become self-destructive or sadistic? We have,

---

[56] Quoted in: MacFarquhar, L. 2018. The Mind-Expanding Ideas of Andy Clark. *The New Yorker*. 26 March 2018.

as a species, a quirky liaison with our bodies—a kind of love-and-hate ambivalence, venerated and vilified, all the way from a 'temple of God' to a 'doorway to the devil', microcosm of the macrocosm and a numinous vehicle to a purely carnal frame—"all are of the dust, and all turn to dust again" (Ecclesiastes 3). We have also long been both fascinated as well as frightened by the human–animal hybrid, by the likes of centaur in Greek mythology, and the Lord Narasimha *avatar* (lion's head and human body) in Hindu mythology—and we are now stretching that to the making of this man–machine 'hybrid'.

The exact nexus between God and man has long been debated, theologically, theoretically, and temporally. In the view of Rudolf Steiner, "Man is at the same time a fallen god and a god in their becoming" (*An Outline of Occult Science—Sleep and Death*, 1914). Man's highest spiritual ethos is echoed by the Bible ('Being like Him'); and Jesus was believed to be, at the same time, 'fully divine' and 'fully human'. God as Jesus, a man, suffered on the Cross, and Lord Vishnu as Rama, a man, suffered the pangs of separation from his wife. Man always, envious of 'gods', wanted to be one of them. Jakob Bohme, expressed the same sense this way: "For God is himself the Being of all Beings, and we are as gods in him, through whom he revealeth himself". Man has long railed against 'gods' for the injustice done by monopolizing immortality, and now he feels that he needs to pay them in their coin and be a 'god' himself.

The Covid pandemic has brought home, if nothing else, the fragility and frailty of life more than ever before in recent memory, and has impelled us to grudgingly concede that, at least in the near term, we cannot dodge death. The way each of us reconciled with this planetary-scale peril brought to the frontline who we are, or not, a 'moral animal' (Robert Wright). For, as Charles Darwin wrote, "Of all the differences between man and the lower animals, the moral sense or conscience is by far the most important". Without such a 'sense', we find it very difficult to understand one's relations to wrongs wrought or wrongs we might do to others. Unwilling to do what it takes, and in line with our penchant for the easier way, the human mind has come up with a fail-proof formula: enlist the machine to 'moralize' us while we pursue our ageless and insatiable search for warmth and comfort. To fortify this line of thought and to quell any qualms in our comatose conscience, we contrast with what machines wouldn't do: "Robot soldiers would not commit rape, burn down a village in anger…". And then, after all, who are we but, as Thomas Hobbes said, 'automata' (*The Leviathan*, 1651). In a world brimming with burnout beyond all bounds, man is finding in the machine the balm he needs. It all brings to mind what EM Forster envisioned way back in 1909, when he wrote: "It is we that are dying, and down here the only thing that really lives is the Machine. We created the Machine, to do our will, but we cannot make it do our will now. It has robbed us of the sense of space and of the sense of touch, it has blurred every human relation" (*The Machine Stops*, 1909).

The Lure of the Forbidden and the Streak of Cruelty

Our obstinate quest for the grail of immortality also stems from another spur. Right down from Adam, the Biblical first man, to the present man, we have always done what we should not have. As Mark Twain wryly quipped, "It was not that Adam ate the apple for the apple's sake, but because it was forbidden. It would have been better for us—oh infinitely better for us—if the serpent had been forbidden". While the world cries for a fresh, fair-hearted internal calculus by which we calculate and choose, and reflect, interpret, react, and respond to situations, what science is doing is 'humanizing' machines and 'de-humanizing' humans. This could well be one of "our most radical scientific experiments" that might turn out to be what Toby Ord calls "other anthropogenic risks" to our existence (*The Precipice*, 2020). Yet until less than a year back, it all seemed to be on track and target. Our dreams or delusions of giving 'death to death' have received a near death-blow. What is more important is that whichever way this pandemic passes or pauses, or peters out into an epidemic and stays put, we will still be propelled by the same mentality, and will continue, as the Buddha warned over 2,500 years ago, to be 'lured to evil ways'.[57] If we want to end or drastically diminish the ingrained trio of oppression, exploitation, and cruelty in the world, we must lift our sight to this power-struggle between good and evil in our consciousness, and in the direction of what stands *before* us, not what stands *between* us. Those at the receiving end are not inferior; the perpetrators are the ones who are inhuman. Every stomach-turning abomination—mass murder, school shooting, sadistic violence, perverted rape—that hangs in the world and causes us so much anguish and tumult is a signal that our mind has come to occupy the commanding heights of consciousness of a critical mass of mankind. As Pedro Okoro puts it, "There is a furious, fierce, and ferocious battle raging in the realm of the spirit between the forces of God and the forces of evil" (*Crushing the Devil*, 2012). Warfare happens every day, all the time, everywhere, even in the womb. It is the cause of—as well as the resolution to—every riddle and ordeal we face. If we want to 'tame the savageness of man' and 'make gentle the life of this world', we have to get a grip on the flow and fluctuations of this war. Our tireless talk of human transmutation across millenniums has remained just that and no more because we have not realized that it calls for a radical realignment and reengineering of something we are not even conscious of—our consciousness. It is human beings that have to beget any amelioration in the human behavior, and that cannot happen if the doer remains unchanged from within. For, we are powerless about what we do because we are helpless over what happens inside in the war within. This the war we must fight to surmount the two inabilities that are so central to whatever we yearn to achieve. This is the war that holds out an explanation as to why, when all of us are made of the same mud, blood, and bones, with the same package of impulses, emotions, drives, and cravings, why we lead such dissimilar and diverse lives, why

---

[57] Warrior wisdom quote of the Buddha. The full quote reads as: 'It is a man's own mind, not his enemy or foe, that lures him to evil ways'.

some act like Mother Teresa, and others like moral monsters. This war is the response to what biologists call 'our behavioral randomness', and, we might add, brazenness. The simplest and the safest way to lead our lives is to ask ourselves, whenever we are about to do anything: 'Which of the two forces at war—good or evil—is our action likely to help or hurt?' That will enable us to consciously make the choice that aids the good far more than the evil.

This war is the answer to the baffling actuality that the same inputs often do not yield the same output. The war is universal—it rages within everyone—but it is not replicable and recursive in anyone else. That explains why one person becomes a killer and another a sucker in a copybook situation. It also explains what is called the *Pareto principle*, that a small number of events or people are responsible for the majority of consequences. We also have to reckon with another law—the law of unintended consequences—that when we do anything, there is always, more often than not, an embedded possibility that something unexpected might result. And then another law could pop up to complete the picture, a wittier Murphy's Fourteenth Law—It is impossible to make anything foolproof because fools are so ingenious. It all comes down to this. We live in two parallel universes, one within and the other without. Only through a radical reengineering within can we revolutionize life outside. If we allow a *status quo* in the world within to continue, then we should not expect any alteration in the state of the world at large. According to one of the seven principles of the universe propounded by Hermes Trismegistus, "As above, so below; as below, so above; as within, so without; as without, so within, as the universe, so the soul". It means that the events in our world are actually a reflection of our inner state, and that whatever takes place in the outer world is but an extension of our inner experience. If we view it as a malfunctioning of life in the world, it is 'wishful innocence'. What is ironic is that we, as it were, declare a war at the drop of a hat to tackle every societal crisis, be it terrorism or egotism, vice or virus, poverty or pandemic, but pay no heed to the 'mother of all wars', the only war that truly counts, the one we are powerless not to wage but are utterly oblivious of it. In fact, we use the metaphor of war so reflexively because it is such a huge part of what goes on continuously in our own, as it were, backyard. It is almost as if man is so made that he cannot summon his best effort unless his brain manages to convince itself it is a *war*. This war is difficult to fight partly because it is not easy to grasp or clasp: it has no *casus belli*; it is unprovoked; it is a perpetual war and an immediate war, a sibling war and a spiritual war. This war has to be fought in silence and solitude, and no one can help us, save, perhaps, in the words of the Aeschylus, the "awful grace of God" (*Agamemnon*, 1602). Unlike any other war, this one was not started by anyone, nor can it be ended by anyone. It is a strange war because in this war one of the opponents, *good*, must win and yet, the other, *evil*, must not be allowed to lose.

The thorny challenge is that we have to shape—and win the right way—a war whose occurrence we are even oblivious of. Some of the greatest events and cathartic conversions in human history were the products, direct or indirect, of this war within. This war is central to everything that happens every day in our lives as well as whatever happened to the human race in its star-crossed history. John Stuart Mill (1867) once said, "Bad men need nothing more to compass their ends, than that good men should look on and do nothing". Tales of battles between good and evil, and of power encounters between good gods and evil demons are replete in all religions. The Bhagavad Gita says that all of us harbor two traits, what it calls *Daiva sampad* and *Asura sampad*—divine qualities and demonic qualities.[58] Considered as the oldest scripture in the world, the Hindu *Rig Veda* includes many references to warfare of its time. The two great Hindu epics *Ramayana* and *Mahabharata* both have war as their centerpiece. More than wars between worldly foes, it is the inhouse struggle of individuals who, to borrow a Homeric phrase, do 'deeds of daring', which has hewed

---

[58] Bhagavad Gita. Chapter 16, verses 4–8.

human history. What Prince Siddhartha faced and fought and won that fateful night under the *Bodhi* tree was his own war within, which gave us a great religion, Buddhism. When Prince Arjuna refused to fight and kill those whom he revered, what Lord Krishna realized was that unless he helped Arjuna to win his war within, He [Krishna] would not be able to make him fight the outer war, the war of Kurukshetra. It gave us the much-revered Bhagavad Gita. In another great religion, Christianity, some suggest that the events of what was called the 'Temptation of Christ' in the desert, where he was sought to be tempted by Satan, were not literal events; in their view "the whole transaction with him [Satan] passed from beginning to end within the recesses of the soul of Jesus", a consciousness in conflict with itself, struggling for harmony and peace.[59] In other words, the spiritual struggle that Jesus battled in the Judean desert for forty days was his own war within.

This war is the central event of our lives. It defines our personality, and what we do and how we live, but we are utterly oblivious to its very occurrence. Arthur Conan Doyle's famous sleuth Sherlock Holmes puts it this way to Watson: "The world is full of obvious things which nobody by any chance ever observes" (*The Hound of the Baskervilles*, 1902). It is not a squabble, skirmish, schism, scuffle or a brawl or clash; it is a full-blown, fierce war, and unless we recognize it in that way, we cannot fight it. Recognition of the war's very reality has eluded us for so long that one wonders why. It has not only complicated everyday life but has also impeded progress towards realizing what Buddhists call "a state of spiritual wholeness that underlies and supports one's everyday consciousness". We have tried all sorts and stripes of utopian models to embody spirituality into everyday 'lived experience': egalitarian communes, communitarian living, arcadias, ashrams, *gurukulas*, spiritual settlements, and so on. We have tried all 'isms'—feudalism, communism, socialism, capitalism—and

---

[59] Strauss, D.F. [Eliot, G., trans.; Hudson, P.C., ed.]. 1972. Das Leben Jesu (1ˢᵗ edition 1835). *The Life of Jesus Critically Examined*. Philadelphia, USA: Fortress Press. pp. 255–256.

experimented with all sorts of models of governance: empires, kingdoms, city-states, nation-states, democracies, dictatorships. They all fell far short because human beings grievously failed to live together in mutual respect. The nation-state, in particular, has become the main stumbling block to resolving almost every problem the world faces, including the current coronavirus and climate crises; to such a degree that we now have, as Jonathan Schell said, to choose between species survival or national sovereignty (*The Fate of the Earth*, 1982).

A long-held belief has been, across all customs and cultures, that there is another invisible world up somewhere, populated by angels, demons, and a beneficent God. Because we know almost nothing of the goings-on in our own 'inner home', our effort has always been to make and remake ourselves from the outside, through haphazard improvisations and trial and error. What we need is a breakthrough moment of revelation or revolution from *within*, something akin to what Aristotle called *peripeteia* (literally, 'turning around'). What Arjuna, the Buddha, and Christ— indeed all prophets, saints, rishis, and mystics—did not have to face (and which *we* do) is the toxic temptation of technology, or, as psychiatrists like to call 'addiction to technology', and what Andrew Kimbrell called the 'technification of evil'. Technology, which physicist Freeman Dyson called 'the gift of God' is now threatening to do Satan's bidding, ensnaring and enslaving us with the promise to give us a cozier version of what he tempted Eve with in Eden; a life of ease sans death. The sensitive ones now face a stark choice: tending for themselves or caring for the world. In fact, it is a *faux* choice. As Jane Goodall puts it, "Only if we care, we will help. Only if we help, we shall be saved".[60] All told, our behavior is unhinged: now, we find ourselves in a globe longing for panic to feel the prick of the real, *in medias res* of strange and surreal, copy and counterfeit, inconvenient truth

---

[60] Jane Goodall Institute. 2000. Jane Goodall: 40 Years at Gombe. New York, USA: Stewart, Tabori, & Chang. The full quote reads: "Only if we understand, can we care. Only if we care, we will help. Only if we help, we shall be saved".

and post-truth, presumable facts and alternative facts, ideal and ordeal, etc. We are marooned in a world in which shams and imitators reign over 'our way of life', and anything 'real' remains seductively out of reach. There are no more taboos or forbidden zones or safe havens from evil. When the crunch comes, we do not know whom to be wary of the most—spouse, or stranger, relative or recluse, friend or foe, snake-oil salesman or a pseudo-spiritual guru. That is truer now than ever. All of us treat someone or the other—a servant, a subordinate, employee, moneyless and powerless—as, in flesh, if not in spirit, those whom the Nazis called *Untermensch*, inferior or sub-human people. That is the basis of much callousness, enmity, and cruelty in the world.

That is why philosophers like Michel de Montaigne have long argued that cruelty should be considered the supreme evil, and that we should put it first among the vices. Yet, a man revered as a *mahatma*, like Gandhi, confessed to his own cruelty. Marquis de Sade believed that "cruelty, very far from being a vice, is the first sentiment that nature injects in us all". In fact, as Jonathan Glover tells us, "The festival of cruelty is in full swing" (*Humanity: A Moral History of the Twentieth Century*, 1999). And being cruel is not the exclusive trait of sadists and serial-killers or school-shooters. In fact, much as we want to insulate ourselves from such 'evil' people, the actuality is that they are, in Philip Zimbardo's words "terribly and terrifyingly normal". Often, as Michael Fischer rightly reminds us, those who inflict an exceptional amount of violence are, with very few exceptions, subjected to an even greater amount themselves.[61] David Buss strikes the same note and says, "Most killers, in a nutshell, are not crazy. They kill for specific causes, such as lust, greed, envy, fear, revenge, status, and reputation, or to get rid of someone who they perceive is inflicting

---

[61] Fischer, M. 2020. On the Language of Nonviolence and the US Criminal Justice System. *Literary Hub*. 2 November 2020.

costs on them. They are like you. They are like me".[62] It means that one can be both virtuous and violent, greedy and grateful, respectful and revengeful at different times or under different circumstances. Just as the Greek philosopher Heraclitus said that you cannot step into the same river twice, we need not react the same way to the same circumstance.

We have in us both the divine and the devil, and managing the tension between the two is the central challenge of being human. That such a conflict is always extant within us was mentioned in scriptures too. For example, in the Jewish Torah, God tells the matriarch Rebecca that "There are two nations in your belly".[63] The two nations are the 'good' Jacob, and the 'evil' Esau, the twin sons of Isaac and Rebecca. The two were engaged in a power struggle before they were even born. The "spirit of Esau" with which we all grapple is our own material self and its lecherous longings and dizzying desires. This war is the central event of our life; it defines what Martin Luther King Jr. called 'the content of our character'. It is at the same time a civil war and a tug of war, an internal war and an unceasing war. Conversely, how we live and what we do heavily influence how the war wages. What happens inside does not just happen: it depends on what happens outside. What we tend to forget is that the greatest gifts we have with us are one another, the greatest sins we commit are also against each other. As George Eliot said, "what do we live for, if not to make life less difficult to each other?"[64] We must make life less difficult particularly for the less fortunate among us. A famous quote of anthropologist Margaret Meade reads, "Helping someone else through difficulty is where civilization starts". But then, what 'civilization' has come to stand for is quite the opposite: the strong survive; the weak suffer what they must. We do not

---

[62] Buss, D.M. 2005. The Murderer Next Door: Why the Mind is Designed to Kill. New York, USA: The Penguin Press.

[63] Genesis 25:23.

[64] Eliot, G. 1871. Middlemarch: A Study of Provincial Life. London, UK: William Blackwood.

any longer entertain what Lewis Lapham[65] called 'thoughtful regard' for a fellow-citizen. Contrary to how we view ourselves as normally moral and a largely peace-loving species, the fact also is, as a recent study reveals, that "we are the most relentless yet oblivious killers on earth".[66] That is not because we were doomed to be evil in the womb, but because our evil inclinations have gotten much meaner, stronger, and ingenious. Long considered as the handiwork of an aberrant mind or a morbid man, killing is now very much within the realms of a tolerable termination to any overly irksome problem. In fact, that is not that outlandish. As Jennifer Hecht says, "We all sometimes feel a sort of fleeting homicidal thought…" (*Stay: A History of Suicide and the Philosophies Against It*, 2013). Irony is that we want to abolish 'death', but we want to fine-tune killing.[67]

In truth, as a species, we have always been ambiguous, ambivalent, and Janus-faced. On the one hand, we have elevated saving life as the highest moral virtue. On the other hand, unlike other animals which kill primarily for the stomach, we kill for as many reasons as there are to live. We also extol taking life, under particular circumstances, as heroic. Our sacred books say that even an evil man, if he dies in battle, will go to paradise; and the Quran promises a *shahid* (martyr) something more tangible and tempting: the sensual company of virgins. While earlier much of killing was messy and disagreeable, we have now made it, in line with everything else, less messy and more efficient. Whether it is in business or on the battle field or back at home, the watch-word is 'efficiency'. It means doing things economically and cost-effectively, more speedily and smoothly, with less time and labor. It serves us well mostly but there is a

---

[65] Lewis H. Lapham, founder of *Lapham's Quarterly*, and former editor of the American monthly *Harper's Magazine*.

[66] Fields, R.D. 2016. Humans Are Genetically Predisposed to Kill Each Other. Psychology Today. 02 Oct 2016. Retrieved from <https://www.psychologytoday.com/us/blog/the-new-brain/201610/humans-are-genetically-predisposed-kill-each-other>.

[67] Tippett, K. 2020. Jennifer Michael Hecht: We Believe Each Other Into Being. *On Being with Krista Tippett*. 7 December 2020.

downside too. Some say that the unpreparedness of countries like USA to the present pandemic is a fallout from becoming 'too efficient with transactions', and "one lesson, then, is that to be better prepared next time, we need to learn to live less efficiently in the here and now".[68] The most macabre manifest of this approach was what the Nazis, by common consent, called the *Final Solution to the Jewish Question*—the 'efficient' extermination of over six million human beings perhaps in 'record time'. While that solution has come to be the metaphor for organized evil, it seemed to have unknowingly seeped into human consciousness and taken root. So much so, many employ that ghoulish method to resolve even routine problems and garden-variety grievances. The idea is stunningly simple: if there is no 'person' there can be no 'problem'. With the loss of our moral compass, the repugnance associated with snuffing a life has lost its horrific effect on our senses. And, horror is so addictive and afflictive, that some fear that it may be slipping into what is being called 'habituation of horror' and normalization of fatal violence, or what Rob Nixon calls 'slow violence'.[69] As a result, financial crimes that shatter millions of lives are given the cultured 'white collar' tag, and environmental violence attracts little notice. Most do not realize but we have become tacit terminators "by approving the actions and principles that inevitably led to them", to quote the character Jean Tarrou, in Albert Camus' novel *The Plague* (1947).

It is also necessary to remember that while every act of evil is the same, every individual is singular and separate, and so is our reaction to the contingencies of a contingent world. Some, like Polish philosopher Karol Wojtyla, who advocated the school of thought called 'personalism', even say that not recognizing evil *itself* is evil. And, even more, not recognizing that acquiring combat capability to fight evil in the world requires such capability-building in our consciousness. To preempt, penetrate, and

---

[68] Schwartz, B. 2020. Why Efficiency Is Dangerous and Slowing Down Makes Life Better. *Aeon Magazine, Psyche.* 19 August 2020.

[69] Nixon, R. 2013. Slow Violence and the Environmentalism of the Poor.

prevent evil in the world, we need endogenous capacity-building. The Greek philosopher Sophocles said, "With so much evil stored up in that cold dark soul of yours, you breed enemies everywhere you touch". But 'evil within' we must remember, is not all that evil in its effect. As Mr. Spock says about his boss Captain Kirk in *Star Trek*,[70] "We see indications that it's his negative side which makes him strong, that his evil side, controlled and disciplined, is vital to his strength". Kirk himself says about his 'evil side': "I can't survive without him. I don't want to take him back. He's like an animal, a thoughtless, brutal animal. And yet it's Me!" Implicit in all of them is that, as recent research suggests, "the capacity to experience some degree of pleasure from other people's pain is surprisingly common". Modern man finds himself in company with what in Greece was known as *Cyrenaic hedonism*, which holds that the only good in life is that which is pleasurable, and that the best life is one which is most pleasurable. It advocates unbridled indulgence as a way to attain 'best life'. As the father of pragmatism, CS Peirce puts it: "You must abjure this metaphysics of wickedness. In the first place, your neighbors are, in a measure, yourself, and in far greater measure than, without deep studies in psychology, you would believe. Really, the selfhood you like to attribute to yourself is, for the most part, the vulgarest delusion of vanity."[71]

While all life, and everything we do, is a binary choice—between good and evil, why is it so taxing to choose good? Essentially, human behavior is elastic, open equally to both altruism and narcissism, empathy, and barbarism. In Shakespeare's words, "The web of our life is of a mingled yarn, good and ill together" (*All Is Well That Ends Well*). Science says,[72] "Nothing is either good or bad, desirable or undesirable, or anything else except that it is made so by laboratories inside us producing the emotions

---

[70] *Star Trek*. American media franchise originating from the 1960s science fiction television series created by Gene Roddenberry. Fifth Episode, *The Evil Within*. 1967.

[71] Peirce, C.S. 1893. Immortality in the Light of Synechism.

[72] Ligotti, T. 2011. The Conspiracy Against the Human Race: A Contrivance of Horror. New York, USA: Hippocampus Press.

on which we live". There is something beautiful in the worst and hideous among us, as illustrated in the story of Jesus kneeling before a stinking carcass of a dog and exclaiming, "Praise be to God, what beautiful teeth this creature has". A thought leader can be a mean man and a lustful man can love dearly. And there is terror not only in the darkness of the unknown, but even more in the bright lights of the known. Good and evil are seen as extreme opposites, but they cannot do without each other. Gandhi, in his comments on the Mahabharata, said, "Human life is like a fabric woven with black and white threads—threads of good and evil". He also said, "None can be said to be evil personified". For if everything is good, then nothing would be good. The reality is that we all contain within ourselves the capacity for callous cruelty, as much as for *anrsamsya*, which in Sanskrit means embodying empathy, altruism and non-injury to any sentient being. At a loftier level, in the Bhagavad Gita, it is said that a *sthitaprajna* (person of steady disposition) sees the presence of God not merely in the good and noble, but also in the wicked and ignoble.

The notion of a shady 'shadow' inside each of us was famously propounded by the Swiss psychiatrist Carl Jung. He said, "Beneath the social mask we wear every day, we have a hidden shadow side: an impulsive, wounded, sad, or isolated part that we generally try to ignore". According to him, the *Persona* is the lovable face we present to the world, while the *Shadow* is the face we hide. In the war within, the persona fights on the side of the good, and the shadow fights alongside the evil. In Hinduism, such a shadow is represented by the *Arishadvargas*, the six enemies of the mind—*kama* (desire), *krodha* (anger), *lobha* (greed), *moha* (infatuation), *mada* (pride), and *matsarya* (malice). Of these, the Bhagavad Gita[73] points out, anger, lust, and greed are the 'three gates to hell'. What we have to understand is that these are as natural to us as their opposites like love, kindness, and empathy. They cannot be exorcized or eliminated; they can only be kept in check by constantly strengthening the 'better angels' of

---

[73] Bhagavad Gita, Chapter 16, verse 21.

our nature, to borrow a phrase from Abraham Lincoln's first inaugural in 1861.[74] And the best in human nature, do please stand up 'before it is too late'.

The Struggle for Supremacy Over Consciousness

We must constantly and actively ensure that the forces of evil and darkness do not overwhelm the good and light in the war. But once we recognize this dimension of our creaturely existence, many of the things we don't like about ourselves suddenly cease to be so intractable. We would feel liberated. But if we don't make any sustained and studied effort, and continue to deal with our troubles and tribulations as we have been, the evil in the world will get us. It is this war that the Bible alludes to, when it says, "For the sinful nature desires what is contrary to the Spirit, and the Spirit what is contrary to the sinful nature. They are in conflict with each other, so that you do not do what you want".[75] This was the inner battle that the American theologian Thomas Merton alluded to when he said that he "felt in his bones that his own life constituted a battleground between conflicting interests, warring tendencies, mutually exclusive selves". Contrary to what we are often told by spiritual masters, we cannot 'fight' the evil within. How can you fight when you cannot even enter the arena where the 'enemy' is? Actually, it is the good within that battles the bad within. For, the *we* that we refer to includes the two sides, the good and the evil. We are all, in different degrees and ways, like Harry Haller of Hermann Hesse's *Steppenwolf* (1929). Two souls war inside him: "the beast", yearning for savagery and isolation, and "the man" seeking culture, society, and love. Hesse wrote that one might argue the point whether Harry "had been given the soul of a wolf, though born as a human being; or whether, on the other hand, this belief that he was a wolf was no more

---

[74] Abraham Lincoln's first inaugural address, delivered on Monday, 4 March 1861.

[75] Galatians 5:17.

than a fancy or a disease of his". We do not know the beginning but we do know that there can be no end. It is a war in which capitulation of either good or evil will be a disaster. For we need *both* sets of adversaries—good and the bad, light and darkness, head and heart. We need both "instinct and conscious intellect", to borrow Jeremy Griffith's words, for our very survival, if not salvation. The optimal condition of the conflict should be that the forces of good maintain a consistent 'upper hand' over the forces of evil. This war goes on unnoticed because no blood or body bags come out of our body, and we remain trapped in what in Greek is called *ataraxia*, a state of tranquility and liberation from life's vagaries and vicissitudes.

We are incapable of transcending ourselves wholly through whatever we create because, as Jim Holt says, "the world creates us, and we in turn create the world" (*Why Does the World Exist?—An Existential Detective Story*, 2002). And all creation, and decimation, is within. But if we win the war within the right way, it can be doubly beneficial: it will not only make the human a more humane being, but it could also empower him to make truly soft machines. To fight the war within, we must understand how the world within functions. That world within, the very pith of our being, what Keats called 'the abyss of himself,' is the spiritual space at our innermost depth. Many great men drew their inspiration from their own storyline within. Socrates said, "A voice which comes to me and always forbids me to do something which I am planning to do, but never commands me to do anything". Tolstoy and Gandhi spoke about their inner voice, and the Quakers have their own concept of Inner Light. The Indian mystic Osho said, "Enjoy whatever your inner feeling is". Some have spoken about a 'wounded inner child'. Rumi asks us to listen to the 'inspiration within'. Emily Dickinson said a voice inside her—she called it her 'faithful monitor'—had commanded her to write. The traditional Jewish view on this complex subject is well-defined in rabbinic literature. Man's inclinations are therefore poised between good (*Yetzer HaTov*) and evil (*Yetzer HaRa*), and he is not compelled towards either of them. He has the power of choice and is able to choose one or the other knowingly and willingly. The *yetzer hara* is not a demonic force, but rather man's misuse of things the physical body needs to survive. In fact, a Jew's very purpose in this physical world is to ultimately triumph in this epic battle. Islam too echoes this line of thought. After returning from a battle, A companion of Prophet Muhammad was quoted as saying, "We have returned from the lesser jihad to the greater jihad", the fight against the evil within; an individual's effort to master the dark side of his or her character. This intramural spiritual struggle, in Islam, according to some scholars, is the major struggle (*Al-jihad al-Akbar*), higher than the external 'holy war'. In other words, the higher *jihad* is another name for the war within. If the major war against evil in Islam is within our soul, the Christian war[76] is a 'war in heaven' between God and the Devil. It is also between flesh and spirit, which, according to St. Paul are the two antithetical principles of creaturely existence. The Bible says, "Walk by the spirit and do not gratify the desires of the flesh". Alyosha of Dostoyevsky's *Brothers Karamazov* reconfigures the scene of action and says, "God and the devil are fighting there and the battlefield is the heart of man".

The subject of what Lars Svendsen called the 'demonic evil' (*The Philosophy of Evil*, 2010), and the showdown between good and evil, has been a perennial theme in great literature like Mary Shelley's *Frankenstein* (1818), RL Stevenson's *The Strange Case of Dr. Jekyll and Mr. Hyde* (1886), JRR Tolkien's *The Lord of the Rings* (1937–1955), William Golding's *Lord of the Flies* (1954), and John Steinbeck's *East of Eden* (1952). The common theme in all of these is that humanity is continuously immersed in a struggle of good versus evil. Steinbeck sums it up: "I believe that there is one story in the world, and only one… Humans are caught—in their lives, in their thoughts, in their hungers and ambitions, in their avarice and cruelty, and in their kindness and generosity too—in a net of good and evil". Steinbeck calls it, "the way in which this sense of opposed absolutes rises from deep

---

[76] Revelation 12:7–10.

within man, representing something profound and inevitable in human consciousness". Before Steinbeck, we have Shakespeare, in whose entire oeuvre the fight between good and evil is a recurring refrain. In *Hamlet*, he says, "For there is nothing either good or bad, but thinking makes it so". And in *Macbeth*, throughout the play, Macbeth and his wife, after the murder of Duncan, are engaged in a constant combat between the good and evil within. A much-acclaimed work of this genre is Joseph Conrad's classic *Heart of Darkness* (1899), which highlights the struggle that humans go through, with their own morals, and their own battles with their hidden evils. In the Harry Potter books, there is no magic in the world without a fight between good and evil. Not only modern literature but also scriptures underscore this issue. According to Jewish belief, the goal of the battle between good and evil is not mastery over the outside world, but over the soul of the human individual. The contestants are man's conscience against man's cravings, man's spirituality against the physical life force. The Indian scripture *Katha* Upanishad says that all life is a choice between two paths—*sreyas* (goodness) and *preyas* (pleasantness)—and implores us to tread the former. It says that the wise prefer the good to the pleasant; the foolish, driven by sensual desires, prefer the pleasant to the good. Preyas sizzles with sensual pleasure, while sreyas leads to spiritual joy. In the Bhagavad Gita, Krishna compares sense-born pleasures to 'wombs of pain and sorrow'.[77] And it is not an evolutionary accident. As Robert Wright says, "Sensual pleasures are the whip natural selection uses to control us, to keep us in the thrall of its warped values system". And as Jeremy Bentham says,[78] "Nature has placed mankind under the governance of two sovereign masters, pain and pleasure". The Buddha went beyond and advocated "abandoning of pleasure, pain and all former states of joy and dissatisfaction" as a way to awakening.

---

[77] Bhagavad Gita. Chapter 5, Verse 22.
[78] Bentham, J. 1789. An Introduction to the Principles of Morals and Legislation.

Homo sapiens to *Homo Deus*

Scientists say that there were seven *Homo* species close to the present humans, the *Homo sapiens sapiens*. What is referred to as 'techno-humanism' argues that *Homo sapiens* have reached the end of the tether, and need to be upgraded to a new superhuman model: *Homo Deus*. The philosopher Thomas Hobbes (*Leviathan*) fashioned the phrase *Homo homini deus* (For man, man is a god), as a reply to the famous rebuke by the Roman poet Plautus, *Homo homini lupus* (For man, man is a wolf). The difference between a god, man or wolf, or, for that matter, anything from anything, is essentially a state of consciousness and, in scientific terms, a state of energy. In life, everything manifests as a dual, identical in nature but different in degree. According to Gurdjieff, most of us actually live in what he called 'hypnotic waking sleep'. The twin dangers we would encounter by the time the human acquires god-like powers are: exclusion of the mass of mankind from its benefits; and a *status quo* of consciousness. In fact, we have had god-like powers for some time; having gotten a bit stale, man now wants to be a walking 'god' on earth. But that won't be a stroll in the park or a cakewalk. We must realize that if we do become a god, it throws on us an awesome responsibility. As Albert Camus puts it across, "When the throne of God is overturned, the rebel realizes that it is now his own responsibility to create the justice, the order, and the unity that he sought in vain within his own condition, and in this way to justify the fall of God" (*The Rebel*, 1945). Come to think of it, it is how and to what end their power is put to use that separates God and the devil, Superman and Lex Luthor!

And then, it is far easier to strive to be a 'god' than having a role model to that end. The mythic model that we have stumbled upon roughly resembles that of the Homeric Greek gods, or of the *devas* of the Hindus. Like them, we do not want to be tied to fate. In trying to be a god, we take heart, even if vicariously, in what Plato (*Euthyphro*) said of them, "Gods 'sin' and engage in immoral behavior a lot—they murder, steal, cheat, go to war, and act out of spite". We think, they are like us; why can't we become one of them? Fortunately or unfortunately, in nature, changing places with or becoming another species is not possible; if it were not so, God would not have created us disparately; we cannot be another even individually, how can a species be any other? What is truly tragic is that as 'humans' we obsessively seek and search every way to acquire more power and capability and leverage over life, and yet each of us has almost limitless inner power and potential that lies untapped. Sant Kabir said in one of his *dohe*: *'Tera sai tujh mein hai, tu jaag sake to jag'*—divine power is within you, realize this if you can. Shunya, the author of *Immortal Talks* (2017), says that "to get godly powers, you must have godly qualities..." What we are trying to do is exactly the opposite of what Kabir and Shunya have suggested. We want godly powers without godly consciousness. We want to be good at being a 'god' without embarking on any internal *yatra* or pilgrimage to divinity within us. Osho, the Indian mystic said, "The inner journey leads to the end of all conflict and to lasting peace". And, as Marya Mannes puts it, this "long journey in inner space" is of "far greater importance than outer to the future of man" (*My Journey Through Inner Space*, 1965). But there will be no future for man if we continue to "treat it [future] like a distant colonial outpost devoid of people where we can freely dump ecological degradation, technological risk and nuclear waste—as if nobody will be there".[79] Not that we care much about the present; the Covid-19 that has been so disruptive of our daily life is itself a result of the disruption of ecosystems.

For a start, we should aim to be a *humane*-human, not transhuman; more spiritual and less sensual. We may well go down, not as the first species in evolution to create its own successors, providing a cyclic process of rebirth of our universe, but as the first species that, for no one's any good, callously disrupted the order of 'The Great Chain of Being'. And, even if science has its way and *Homo sapiens* does become *Homo Deus*, it

---

[79] Krznaric, R. 2020. Future Generations Deserve Good Ancestors. Will You Be One? *Aeon Magazine, Psyche.* 21 July 2020.

still does not mean that we will all wake up one fine morning as 'gods', or that all births will *ipso facto* become immaculate births. As Albert Camus once said, "Nothing can discourage the appetite for divinity in the heart of man". That is because man thinks that it is the only way he can be what he truly longs for: to be limitless. But in fact, in the Indian tradition, it was believed that some human beings, the great Vedic rishis, transcendent beings who lived better than gods, and that the latter when in trouble, came seeking their advice and help. And that the ancient rishis even 'made' gods, whom the Indian sage Sadguru Vasudeva calls 'energy robots', for a particular purpose.

In the Melting Pot of Life and Death

Our new-found longing to be *Homo Deus* undermines the basic dynamics of life and death and highlights our basic inability to live well with death. We have long brooded over the question that Immanuel Kant brought out clearly: what are our powers of disposal over our life? We are not still not sure which is more 'desirable', birth or death. The only reason we keep living despite the horrors that life brings us is because of the fear of the unknown, but when the fear of the *known* becomes stronger, then death becomes a reasonable choice. Was Montesquieu right when he claimed that "men should be bewailed at their birth and not at their death"? (*Lettres Persanes*, 1721). Is that what happens in-between is bad, nothing to do with either of them? Was Aleksandr Solzhenitsyn right when affirmed that "nothing so bespeaks the current helplessness of our spirit, our intellectual disarray, as the loss of a clear and calm attitude toward death"? (*The Russian Question*, 1994). The greater his well-being, the deeper his chilling fear of death cuts into the soul of modern man. Many gifted people, after spending a lifetime searching for answers to life's lingering questions, came to the conclusion that there is no 'way out', no hope for an answer, and finally realized that death is the only 'solution'. The fact, nonetheless, is that we live in a "culture that can only value itself through the lexicon of death", to borrow a line from Ocean Vuong, author of *On Earth We're Briefly Gorgeous* (2019). Covid-19 has brought a tsunami of a change in that lexicon. It has brought out human helplessness in the face of death. Our designs of curing, preventing, and managing all diseases by the end of this century, and our dreams of impending immortality, sound way off the mark. Euphoric ideas like 'evolution of intelligent life beyond its currently human form and human limitations by means of the secular deployment of science and technology' suddenly sound far too simplistic or egoistical. And our messianic zeal to technologically alchemize our species from *Homo sapiens* to *Homo Deus* will have to take a back seat for some time, to allow us sheer survival as humans. Whatever it is and however we might characterize all this, the underlying assumption is something for which we have scant evidence: that life is better than death. These are all 'assumptions' to keep us alive, when we don't even know if we are actually "virtual beings in a computer simulation".[80] Such a vision is nothing new; it is very similar to the Vedantic concepts. In his celebrated work *Vivekachudamani*, Adi Sankaracharya, the great exponent of the Advaitic philosophy of India, proclaimed: *Brahma satyam jagat mithya, jivo brahmaiva naparah*—the Brahman alone is real, the world is the appearance [of Brahman]. But a practical man will answer: What or how does it make any difference to my daily existence? I still have to 'live' and 'die'... The paradox is that whatever the body needs to live—oxygen, food, a survivable temperature, water—are also ways to die, if the need goes too long unmet. Although death was always accepted as inevitable and although we never have had any clue about what life truly is, the mantle of the 'miracle of life' was culturally venerated. At the same time, an ever-growing number find the sheer mechanics of living so onerous, if not obnoxious, and feel, in the words of the philosopher Seneca, "sometimes, to live is an act of courage". Or, as another more recent philosopher Hannah

---

[80] Ananthaswamy, A. 2020. Do We Live in a Simulation? Chances Are about 50–50. *Scientific American*. 13 October 2020.

Arendt once (1952) wrote to a friend: "It would be wonderful to live, if only world history were not so awful". The 'awfulness' of the world did not deter too many, including Arendt who, following an accident, wrote, "I thought that life actually is quite beautiful and that I like to live a lot".[81]

And then again, we do have multitudes who want to live forever. Odd as it may sound, a principal motive for aspiring for immortality is that mortality is a given, not a choice; if we *are* really extended a choice, we might even want to choose death! In fact, that is what is now happening: what we may call 'deliberate death' is becoming an alternative to obligatory life. The revulsion and distaste attached to killing is not so spontaneous and overwhelming. A new human right is the 'right to die', the right to a safe space for you to decide to end your life as you like, without any ethical interference or moral guilt. One justification for mass migration suggested is that if the world cannot guarantee a life of dignity and humanity, it should at least provide a 'right to choose where to die'. Murder narrative is mainstream in pop culture; and after sex, sure to sell. There are many who, in the words of Thomas Ligotti, "despise the conspiracy of Lies for Life almost as much as they despise themselves for being a party to it" (*The Conspiracy Against the Human Race*, 2011), and for them death is the only honorable option. Anyone can be a Cain (the first son of Adam and Eve), who disowned his responsibility, justified it with his pain and fear, and became a callous, corrupt, and murderous anthropoid. But, by the same token, anyone, even if gentle, good, and god-fearing, can end up as an Abel (Cain's brother), a suitable candidate for killing.

The human psyche, as David Buss posits, has evolved with specialized adaptations whose function is to kill (*Evolutionary Psychology: the New Science of the Mind*, 2019). According to him, in the "cold calculus of evolution, killing is 'adaptive', and murder, 'advantageous'". He goes on to say, "The real mystery is not why killing has been so prevalent over our

[81] Giridharadas, A. 2021. Love the World Anyway. Anand Giridharadas in conversation with Ann Heberlein. *The.Ink*. 12 January 2021.

evolutionary history, but why killing has not been *more* prevalent". While we will never know precisely why, when and even how anyone of us can become suicidal or murderous, the truth today is that self-homicides and negligent homicides, morally if not legally, are fast reaching the tipping point. In fact, as Ingeborg Bachmann pronounces in the final lines of her 1971 book *Malina*, "I maintain that still today many people do not die but are murdered". Often, even suicide is murder in effect; there are more 'killers' in it than in most murders. Men have taken their life since antique times, but questions such as 'when is self-extinction morally excusable even if it is objectively wrong?' have persisted. That 'objectivity' is too subjective and situational for an easy answer. What has really happened is that suicide is being seen by many as a way out of what in Tibetan is called *ye tang che,* roughly translated as 'totally worn out', when life, as surgeons say, is seen as inoperable, a kind of killing in self-defense, and when homicide is seen as a way to resolve almost every interpersonal conflict, the final solution to any intractable impediment. Many experience the dilemma of an insufferable life and irrational clinging to life. A feeling that is well expressed in *The Old Woman's Story* of Voltaire's *Candide*: "For what could be more stupid than to go on carrying the burden that we always want to lay down? To loathe, and yet cling to, existence? In short, to cherish the serpent that devours us, until it has eaten our hearts?". Although homicides, particularly mass murders, capture the spotlight, the reality is that twice as many people worldwide die from suicide as from homicide or from car accidents. Another troubling study says that in USA, more military personnel are dying by suicide than dying in battle.

The Way Forward is the Way Inward

To truly make any sense of these trends and tendencies, we must look inwards and relate it to the war within, and outwardly improve our capacity to tend to one another—in the 'living experience of our everyday changeable being'. As Marcel Proust wrote, "Even with respect to the most insignificant things in life, none of us constitutes a material whole... our social personality is the creation of the minds of others" (*Swann's Way*, 1913). We should ceaselessly endeavor to, in Adam Smith's words, "feel much for others and little for ourselves... to restrain our selfish, and to indulge our benevolent affections" (*The Theory of Moral Sentiments*, 1759). We have to transmute *mitsein* ('being with others', in German) into *sorge*—instinctive care and concern for others.

We must fully grasp and absorb the pivotal point that all of us have the freedom to decide what kind of life we want to live: what the French call *nostalgie de la boue,* to live a simpler, downsized, or less-indulgent life or a selfish, complacent, and callous life. As it were, at the end of the day, we are, in George Orwell's words "Lost in a haunted wood", and "we have never been happy or good" (*Pleasure Spots*, 1946). We have never achieved any consensus on what we want to do with ourselves in a finite lifetime, on what is complete realization of human personality, or on what is the true content of, to quote Ocean Vuong again, "life worthy of our breath". Till recently, man used to think that to make something of oneself, work was how one did it. Even God-incarnate Krishna said he never stops working although He didn't have to. We want to build a 'world without work', to experience everything without experiencing it. We want our life's vocation to be an unending vacation. The issue is not either work or leisure; it is what kind of work and what do we do with time on our hands. Does it increase 'face time' or screen time, appease our material thirst or spiritual hunger? What we have to worry about is why a life soaked with material comforts and sensual delights has such power over our soul. For, as Thomas à Kempis says,[82] *Nolle consolari ab aliqua creatura magnae puritatis signum est*, that is, 'to desire no comfort from any creature is a sign of great purity'. The human body functions on the principle of *homeostasis*, a posture of stability and equilibrium, and that translates as resistance to any kind of about-turn. It is our body and what it has got used to, its urges and

---

[82] Thomas à Kempis. *The Imitation of Christ*, 1427.

cravings, and our inability to resist their allure, that is the principal cause of every pinprick and pestilence we face. As Jean Shepherd (*A Christmas Story*) says, "Our most profound urges come from within". But that offers us also hope against hope. And, after all, we are all, as Cornel West said, 'prisoners of hope'. The hope is that the same urges can also incarnate in better ways. It means that it is in our power to save the world.

We must draw a line between 'desire' as a generic force or energy, and 'desire' as a cankerworm in our life, as a 'manufactured impulse for material possessions'. It was such a desire that Wordsworth possibly referred to when he wrote the sonnet, *The World Is Too Much With Us* (1807), and the telling line, "We have given our hearts away, a sordid boon". To get a grip on the sordid boon, to resist the snares of consumption is not easy. We do not need austere asceticism, any more than one of, in Henry Wood's words, 'voluptuous self-indulgence'. In fact, the key to a wholesome life is equipoise and moderation, what in Greek is called *apatheia*. As Swedish philosopher Emanuel Swedenborg says, "If we would accept heaven's life, we need by all means to live in the world and to participate in its duties and affairs" (*Heaven and Hell*, 1758). Internally, the forces of goodness must be aided to become dominant in the war within. Externally, we need a sweeping swerve in technological development, which is presently oriented towards a bundle called DARQ (Distributed ledger technologies, Artificial intelligence, Extended reality, and Quantum computing). To that canon we must add radical life extension or in-person immortality. What is at issue is not their pursuit but what else is left behind. It has to be 'bottom up', not trickle down; ascending, not descending, need-based, not wish-fulfilment. Many thinkers like the economist Keynes have long believed that technological progress will turn a pie-in-the-sky into a reality, not a vision or dream. In a similar vein, Aleksandr Solzhenitsyn (*The Russian Question*, 1994) cautions us, "We must not simply lose ourselves in the mechanical flow of Progress, but strive to harness it in the interests of the human spirit; not to become the mere playthings of Progress, but rather to seek or expand ways of directing its might towards the perpetration of good". To paraphrase Gabriel Garcia, we have lost direction, both internally and externally, while losing ourselves in the solitude of our fearsome power (*One Hundred Years of Solitude*, 1967). Whether we like it or not, where our resources go is where our priorities lie, and we need what someone once dubbed as 'resource rebellion' to ensure that resource allocation becomes a subject of systemic social scrutiny. Alongside, we must reverse the locus of global technological power, 90% of which now rests, according to the UNESCO, in the hands of one-quarter of humanity. Technological change, the processes of invention, innovation and diffusion of technology, must be a part of contextual-change, and without contextual-change, there can be no consciousness-change. Consciousness-change, which means rekindling and enhancing the role of heart-intelligence and diminishing that of mind-intelligence, is no different from what scientists call 'reengineering human nature' as a way to eliminate our apocalyptic tendencies.

The powerhouse behind accelerated technological swagger is modern science. And yet it is the least regulated. Issues concerning what research to pursue, what social resources to devote to it, who should make such decisions, and how they should be made are not subject to any well-ordered scrutiny. Without any such scrutiny and starving many other worthier priorities for the masses, 'Big Science', 'Big Think', and 'Big Money' are joining forces and narrowing down the entire scientific effort around three big projects: artificial general intelligence (AGI), indefinite life extension, and, what we might describe as 'escape to outer space'. Some existential risk experts like Nick Bostrom, predict that success in controlling AI will result in "complete elimination of the boundaries separating human minds and AI" and in a "compassionate and jubilant use of humanity's cosmic endowment". If it is even close, that is awesome; the ultimate techno-utopia. But others warn that "humanity will never be able to control a super-intelligent artificial intelligence that could save or destroy humanity". As for 'project immortality', man has long treated death as 'our trouble, the human trouble', as James Baldwin called it, and overcoming it has been a holy grail since at least our remote past. Some, like Alex Zhavoronkov[83], say that human immortality might be found in the hands of artificial intelligence. We might also need AGI to achieve our third goal: space colonization. There are many philosophers and high-profile entrepreneurs like Amazon chairman Jeff Bezos and SpaceX CEO Elon Musk who say that since Planet Earth can no longer, thanks to our predation, be saved, we shouldn't be a Casabianca but jump the ship and migrate to the Moon or Mars. But there are others, like Bill Gates, who posit that it is a bad idea and there there's more important work to be done here on earth. The trouble is that their real quest is unaligned with other basic priorities, which ought to be at the top of any global egalitarian docket. And they siphon off scarce resources, financial and technical, from where they are needed most, like promising research that could make a significant effect on climate change, like turning carbon dioxide into fuel for everyday life, or making water from moisture in the air. While we must concede that what the *Humanist Manifesto I* (1933) describes as the 'equitable distribution of means of life' is a remote utopia, it is well within our power to remove morally distasteful disparities. For example, as Toby Ord notes, "As a species we spend more on ice-cream per year than we do on the mitigation of existential risk" (*The Precipice*, 2020). While we are fully aware that the industrial infrastructure is severely skewed, we should ensure that at least the spoils of the inherently exploitative industrial apparatus are divided fairly and justly. It has to be addressed at two levels: among the citizens of a country, and between countries. Just as the grossly disproportionate accumulation of wealth in the now-notorious 'One Percent' is morally repugnant, so should be the fact that, for instance, while Switzerland has an annual average per capita income of about $35,000, Mali has an average per capita income of less than

---

[83] Alex Zhavoronkov is Director of the International Aging Research Portfolio, and Director of the Biogerontology Research Foundation, UK.

$300. We cannot apply double-standards; alas, what is good for the goose cannot be bad for the gander; what is intolerable and unacceptable within a caring country cannot be otherwise globally; a man-drawn national border cannot negate what is right and what is iniquitous. If this vulgar variance extends to mortality versus immortality, as it will surely be, it will be even more combustible and repugnant. If the economic gap between rich people and rich countries, on the one hand, and the non-rich people and countries is radically reduced, the mortality gap will also shrink, which will then douse the simmering flames.

But it is always something else that we want, someone else we want to switch places with. What we tend to overlook is that, through millions of lives, everyone we have wanted to be, we have already been, and who we were, everyone else has been. Every life is *de novo* but nothing is 'original'; we are all copies of each other across time. In the words of Jorge Luis Borges (*The Immortal*, 1947), "over an infinitely long span of time, all things happen to all men"—to the good, the bad, and the bizarre. And everything is transitory, everyone in an earlier time was everyone else. There is nothing 'original' in life. There are no 'others'; *we were them*. In the lyrical language of Borges, "No one is someone; a single immortal man is all men. Like Cornelius Agrippa, I am god, hero, philosopher, demon, and world—which is a long-winded way of saying that I am not". That is why Buddhism says, "We should treat each person we encounter as if they are our beloved". There is never anything to lose and nothing to gain. And therefore, we must, as Yoda, the Jedi of *Star Wars* franchise says, "train ourselves to let go of everything we fear to lose"—even our own life. Our fear about losing life, what the Buddha characterized as 'clinging to life' is, according to him, as dangerous as any other form of ignorance.

To a large extent, the fulcrum of our murky moral universe is based on the inevitability of our mortality, the disorienting awareness that, in the words of Brian Doyle,[84] "we're here for a little window". But that very inevitability has only made life hostage to what Keats called 'negative capability', uncertainty. If we truly can live forever, who cares what we do to any other? And there is no guarantee that it will reap the fruits of not dying. In the words of James Joyce (*The Dead*, 1914) 'dismally with age', we may end up with no youth and with extended, not arrested, old age, something like the *Struldbruggs* (in Jonathan Swift's 1726 satirical novel *Gulliver's Travels*). The Struldbruggs are born seemingly normal, but are in fact immortal. Upon reaching the age of eighty, they become legally dead. Or, we may become like the protagonist of Mary Shelley's *The Mortal Immortal* (1833), who in the end discovers that, being immortal, he is cursed to endure eternal psychological torture, as everything he loves dies around him. Faced with the ennui of eternal life which itself, as Ludwig Wittgenstein says is "as much a riddle as our present life", our future generations might, as in Jorge Borges' story *The Immortal* (1947), seek to create an antidote that allows them to die. While most think that longevity is a blessing, not all long-lifers feel that way. Perilously, we might turn out to be like Tithonus (of Greek mythology), who achieved physical immortality but not eternal youth, and who later lamented, "Only cruel immortality consumes: I wither slowly in thine arms", and beseeched, "release me, and restore me to the ground".

Recent research tells us that even something so nondescript as what we eat can have a bearing on how it affects the fortunes of the fighting forces in the war within; some foods nourish positive emotions, while some others nourish negative emotions. The tedious minutiae of our rote tasks, could have a positive or negative ripple effect not only on the world but also on the war within. We could then become compassionate 'warriors' in real life, warriors who not only help everyone but refuse to hate anyone,

---

[84] Brian Doyle, author of *Mink River*, published in 2010 by Oregon State University Press, USA.

whose falchion is love and armor is cascading empathy, having the ability to put themselves not only in other people's shoes but also in their hearts.

But first, we must take a dispassionate look at what our current passions are. If we step up and look down on ourselves, what we see is swimming, mostly sinking, in a sea of money. To borrow the words of Karl Marx, there is no other nexus between man and man than naked self-interest, than callous 'cash payment'. Everything in life is an approach to make money. As Edgar Villanueva puts it, "Money is like water; it's a precious, life-giving resource… If we use it for sacred, life-giving, restorative purposes, it can be medicine" (*Decolonizing Wealth*, 2018). At least, ever since Judas Iscariot betrayed Jesus for thirty pieces of silver, we have known the baleful impact of money. It is through money, or funding, that much of moral compromising takes place. How, and how much, money is allocated for what purpose or project or even disease or desire-satiation is a direct reflection of the priority a society and a government attaches to it. A recent study reveals that "the simple idea of money changes the way we think— weakening every other social bond".[85] We only need to ensure that those who already are the casualties of our endless pursuit of economic growth are not pushed even lower. We must realize that although we justly feel a sense of shame about slavery in human history, our current approach and attitude toward economic immiseration and degradation are not so dramatically different, and so is our acceptance of grotesque inequities as the necessary price of a rising GDP. Rising GDP, at the expense of the natural capital, we mistakenly assume, is the only way we can assure the continuous supply of all the 'good things', not goodness, of life. The time has come for the world to move away from GDP, as a recent report on biodiversity suggests, towards "a more inclusive measure of wealth that accounts for nature as an asset".[86] The current coronavirus has shown, as

---

[85] Porter, E. 2013. How Money Affects Morality. *The New York Times*. 13 June 2013.

[86] Dasgupta, P. 2021. The Economics of Biodiversity: The Dasgupta Review. (London: HM Treasury).

the author of the report Partha Dasgupta points out, "what can happen when we don't do this".[87]

Man is the only animal that is not satisfied or happy with what it is. That dissatisfaction finds utterance in many ways, one of which is the inquiry of the meaning, and purpose, of life. The search for life's meaning or purpose has attracted much metaphysical, scientific, esoteric, and theological speculation throughout the history of human thought. The quest largely remains unfulfilled primarily because the very 'meaning of meaning' and 'purpose of purpose' are problematic. And it betrays anthropocentric arrogance, that we are entitled to be privy to all secrets of creation and the cosmos. Joseph Campbell said, "Life is without meaning. You bring the meaning to it". We interweave and interject 'meaning' to life through the myriad apparently 'meaningless' things we do day in and day out. Philip Appleman makes it practical and says, "Whatever we are, whatever we make of ourselves, is all we will ever have—and that, in its profound simplicity, is the meaning of life" (*Karma, Dharma, Pudding & Pie*, 2009). What all we can do, and should do, is to ensure that whatever and however we do anything has a beneficial bearing on yet another life—nothing taken; nothing added. If we focus on the good, then the cumulative effect can be overwhelming. One need not be a Bodhisattva to make the world a tiny bit better. And we don't have to be a soaring Saint Paul, and solemnly affirm, "I could wish that I myself were accursed and cut off from Christ for the sake of my brothers, my kinsmen according to the flesh".[88] It is enough to infuse every deed with what Buddhism calls 'loving kindness'. It only calls for renouncing the sense of ownership of things that we possess. In Jainism, there is a doctrine called *aparigraha*, meaning the absence of the "feeling of mine", as an essential step towards achieving liberation.

---

[87] Dasgupta, P. 2021. The Economics of Biodiversity: The Dasgupta Review. (London: HM Treasury).

[88] Romans 9:3.

One thing is for sure. We cannot make any sense, much less address the underlying causes, without framing it in its context. In many ways, context is content. The 'content of the context' of human life has rarely been put under greater pressure and tension than since the beginning of the year 2020, due to the changes deemed necessary to keep a deadly infection at bay. Life itself is, in the words of the Spanish philosopher and essayist José Ortega y Gasset, "a ceaseless, intense dialogue between oneself and one's environment". He also says, "I am myself plus my circumstance..." If we do good, the forces of good in the war will be stronger, and if we do bad, the forces of evil will gain an upper hand. Nothing we do goes in vain or without impact. Context is life, and life is not solid. It is fluid and constantly opens opportunities. It is close to Newton's Third Law, 'For every action, there is an equal and opposite reaction'. According to Hindu scriptures, *karma* is the predominant force and energy in the universe, outranking even *kala* (eternal time) and *mryuthyu* (death). So much of bitterness, hostility, animosity and envy is caused because we make everything too 'personal'; in fact, it is all karmic. Even those who torment, hurt and humiliate are playing their assigned *karmic* role; in fact, they end up getting the short end of the stick more than you. They deserve pity, even gratitude, not reprobation or revenge. Karma, contrary to popular understanding, is not fatalism or pre-determinism, much less does it deny free will, initiative or intent. According to the karma principle, everything that happens in the world is a consequence of a cause which itself becomes a cause. That is because every time you act, you create a 'birth of possibility', in this life or future lives. Karma doesn't have a schedule of outcome or upshot; you cannot outlast its reach or hoodwink it by any red herring. While we can't recast our karmic circumstances, we are not that helpless about our volitional response to them. That's the sphere where we have space for personal agency, ability to make choices in response to new and unforeseeable circumstances. If, for instance, we turn the other cheek, as Christ suggested, we can earn extra karmic credit. It also means that what happens to us is only partially determined by what we do to ourselves. It is also influenced by what others do; and vice versa. As Reinhold Niebuhr says, "Evil is not to be traced back to the individual but to the collective behavior of humanity" (*Moral Man and Immoral Society*, 1932).

While the individual dimension of karma is well publicized, its intra-family, intra-community, intra-national, and global implications are less well known. Every human being, possibly even every sentient being that shares the same living space and time, is karmically connected; it is not an accident or happenstance. As Thomas Mann says, "A man lives not only his personal life, as an individual, but also, consciously or unconsciously, the life of his epoch and his contemporaries" (*The Magic Mountain*, 1924). What happens we cannot overturn, but how we experience it we can change. Everything depends on how we experience and experiment with experience. But what is happening also is a reaction and recreation of an action in which we had collectively participated. That is up to each of us. This insight is of special relevance at the current troubled times, when so many feel not only endangered but also defenseless, and often ask 'why us' and 'why are we unable to see truths too terrible to recognize until it is hopelessly late', which in fact is another way of flagging the twin questions with which we began this labyrinthine odyssey—Why can't *I* be good? Why do *I* do bad?

By any reasonable reckoning, we have never been so close to the proverbial doomsday clock striking the midnight hour, and it is not because of the corona or the climate or nuclear crises, or of any bio-error or of man-machine dalliance gone bad, or any other still unknown assault on human civilization; it is because all signs say that we are on the verge of losing this war within, when evil might finally vanquish good, or cripple it beyond repair. For us to take decisive steps to arrest and reverse the fortunes of this war, we must go within and do what the Upanishads call *atma-vichara* (self-inquiry), an 'inner conversation', as a point of departure. It also means that we must realize that it is our worldly actions that determine our fates, and every deed has a fallout in more than one mode. There can be a fallout even from falling, if we adopt the Japanese adage, *Nana korobi ya oki* (fall seven times and get up after the eighth fall). We must also realize that we all carry a bigger burden than our own middling, mousy lives filled with myriad inane things. But each of them can trigger a 'butterfly effect' outwardly and tilt the war within. The way to still save ourselves is to begin at the lowest level of our daily physiologic existence, all the things we do day in and day out just to be alive and as a functioning society. What we need is the infusion of moral and spiritual dimensions into our daily doing. At the very least, in a critical mass of responsible, not always reasonable, global citizens. This is somewhat analogous to the 'herd immunity' to a pandemic. The principles of critical mass and herd immunity are of universal applicability, in the world within and the world outside, both for good and evil. One reason why we have never been able to reverse the *status quo* trend for so long is that even those who recognized the need could not concretize and operationalize that need. What the American Declaration of Independence (1776) proclaimed as 'the rectitude of the intentions' never had any tilting effect on the context and conduct of their own life. In other words, they, and we, mean well but do not know how to make it tick. What they missed and what is imperative is a substantive and practical launch pad for a lift-off. That has to be something that absorbs and preoccupies our daily life, our attention, our thoughts, our priorities, our 'wild and furious passions', to borrow Lincoln's words.[89] Both by elimination and affirmation, it is best encompassed in the triad of morality, money, and mortality. Other than these three, everything else, as Einstein said about the mind of God, is a detail, mere minutiae. To make sure that these 'M's play a constructive role in human affairs and positively

---

[89] Abraham Lincoln. *The Perpetuation of Our Political Institutions.* Opposition to Mob-Rule address before the Young Men's Lyceum of Springfield, Illinois, USA. 27 January 1838.

contribute to the war within, we need new terms of engagement, a fresh global conversation, and an original playbook.

Clearly, of the three, what ought to be upfront is money. As Ayad Akhtar says, "Money is the big story of our time", and our emblematic affliction is "our diseased relationship to money" (*Homeland Elegies*, 2020). For most people, everything crystallizes as 'getting rich'. It not only breaches every social barrier, but also, according to Yuval Noah Harari, enables us to acquire god-like powers and immortality (*Homo Deus: a Brief History of Tomorrow*, 2015). Way back, Karl Marx called money the "bond of all bonds" as well as "the universal agent of separation" (*Economic & Philosophic Manuscripts*, 1844). Everything assumes value only as money. We must arrive at a fresh *modus vivendi* with money. For, as Jacob Needleman says, "If we don't understand our relationship to money in this culture, then I think we're doomed" (*Money and the Meaning of Life*, 1991). The astonishing fact is that a huge slice of what is amiss with the world can be resolved, at least mitigated, if money is properly generated, allocated, and channeled. In one sense, as someone said, 'every billionaire is a policy failure'. And that failure is built into the paradigm of public policy-making; the billionaire is only incidental and illustrative.

While attempting to reconfigure morality, we must first remember that we live in a divisive world where man feels he is entitled to choose his own 'values', or even invent them to redeem his whim. Morality, in this setting, has to become an instrument to enhance our sense of inclusiveness, transcending gender, race, religion, and nationality. As Immanuel Kant emphasized, morality, above all, has to be practical, which means it must be intimate with what we do. Many of our communal ills stem from faulty public policymaking; it is a major impediment to any radical remaking. What we must do is to ensure that public policies are fully aligned with morality. At the heart of the arc of the moral universe, we must remember, lies justice; more pointedly, fairness. Everyone must get their fair share in a shared world, and everyone must be fairly rewarded and rebuked. What we must recognize is that there is no such thing as a level playing field, not even in nature, far less in the human world. That is why fairness along with justness becomes a moral imperative. Most of us are at home with being moral in the mind, and at best amoral in our actions, or being, in the phrase of Francine Prose, a 'more-or-less moral person', which translates as more 'less' than 'more'. More to the point, even to be 'more' and not 'less' of a moral being, morality cannot anymore be distanced from our attitude and treatment of other fellow-animals, and how we behave towards other animals.

The model for such behavior has to carry the spirit of an old Irish saying about trust: *Mo sheasamh ort lá na choise tinne*—'you are the place where I stand on the day when my feet are sore'. We must bear in mind that the human, although a mere speck on the great graph of time, has acquired the starry status of a geological and geographical force and is changing the geochemical makeup of the planet. We routinely read about rising seas, sinking cities, and advancing deserts without the slightest concern. We have also metamorphosed, as David Attenborough reminds us, the very anatomy of the animals and plants that live around us. [90] That gives a new context to everything human. The fact is that in our rush to be civilized, successful, and prosperous, we have mislaid our moral compass. The time is, to paraphrase Martin Luther King Jr., 'fiercely urgent', to fashion what Joanna Zylinska calls the "Minimal Ethics for the Anthropocene".[91] One moral quandary concerns what TS Eliot called 'provincialism of time' (*What Is a Classic*, 1944), which when extended forward means a failure to imagine the generations that will come after us, to take responsibly our responsibilities toward humans of the distant future. Another crucial caveat, in the context of our seemingly unstoppable urge to assimilate with the machine, is about *human* ethical

---

[90] Cited in the Foreword to: Dasgupta, P. 2021. The Economics of Biodiversity: The Dasgupta Review. (London: HM Treasury).

[91] Zylinska, J. 2014. Minimal Ethics for the Anthropocene. Open Humanities Press.

responsibility *vis a vis* that of 'machine-made' god-like humans. At the turn of the 21st century, another exigent issue is the age-old human quest to outlast mortality. The moral dimension is, should we allow now a situation to arise by which a miniscule of men become 'elite immortals' and the rest remain 'mere mortals'? What we should understand is that although deathless existence in a biological body is next to impossible, even aspirations like radical life extension or youthful-rejuvenation, or cryo-resurrection and mind-uploading will raise weighty ethical issues, to address which we do not have the mindset we need.

To sum up, as we meander into the 21st century and assuredly will face many civilizational threats—some say, to paraphrase Jean-Jacques Rousseau, that the biggest threat to human salvation is civilization itself—what we must address is a critical issue: man has become a bundle of paradoxes, too powerful and too enfeebled, too ambitious and too malicious. We must clearly understand that malice (the wish to will ill of others sans self-gain), and its twin sister, *schadenfreude* (the dark desire to see others suffer)—which Schopenhauer called 'devilish'—more than any other human attributes, are at the heart of human evil. Disconcertingly, it is not an acquired habit or the traits neither of a 'noble savage' nor of a 'civilized brute'. Indeed, that dark trait, researchers have found, is there even in some nine-month-old infants. It is hard to imagine how malice fits into the scheme of Nature/God in putting together the human 'package', not that of a carnivore. But what is heartening is that we are also equally capable of what in Buddhism is called *Mudita*,[92] pure joy unadulterated by self-interest, the ability to rejoice in the other's joy. It all amounts to this: human nature is neither, or both, good and bad, and therefore it is always safer to assume the good in others, which can either draw the best in them or allow us to have a good experience. Everything hinges on what we as humans do day in and day out routinely and reflexively, consciously

---

[92] *Mudita* is one of the four immeasurables (*apramana*) or sublime attitudes (*brahmavihara*) in Buddhism: *maitri*: loving kindness; *karuna*: compassion; *mudita*: joy; and *upeksa*: equanimity.

or unconsciously. We do not have to do any original; it is always what ordinary persons do during quotidian moments that can leave a lasting effect. It is the ordinary, the drab, dull daily stuff, that we disregard and disdain and expend much time and energy tying to be a stand-out, a hero or a martyr. In fact, the lives of most great men and women were ordinary and humdrum. Jesus, for instance, it is said, spent thirty years, a big chunk of his luminous life, in that way, the way of any of us. It is in this spirit that Pope Francis speaks of 'everyday holiness' and 'next-door saints'. The objectification of nature has implicitly led us towards the objectification of humanity. The source of the source is each and every one of us. We do things, but do we know who is the doer, and who propels or deters the doer when he does anything? This is particularly pertinent because the actions and silences of all of us can tilt the scales. We must move towards a total displacement of 'thinking' and 'thought' as the ultimate volition of human life. All good and bad things, our hopes and fears, dreams and nightmares, ideas of excellence and downfall, all we associate with thinking. The 20th-century Indian sage Ramana Maharshi simplified it all and said 'thought is the origin of sin'. If thinking inherently is tainted, how can anything that comes out of thinking be any good?

Even if we are all 'made out of meat',[93] we would still be 'New Meat', not only 'thinking meat', but also a more humane meat. We will move towards a mindset that allows us "to love without deceit, to think no evil, to bear no grudge, to be free from selfishness, to be innocent and straightforward". And, most of all, to be heart-driven, not head-dominated, in our everyday existence. We need what the Institute of Heart Math (USA) calls a 'Heart Revolution', that will enable and empower us to harness heart intelligence holistically. That is what we should aim at, not 'super intelligence', defined by Nick Bostrom as any intellect that greatly exceeds the cognitive performance of humans in virtually all domains of

---

[93] "They Are Made Out of Meat". Short story of Terry Benson, published in *Omni* magazine, 1991.

interest (*Superintelligence*, 2014), and which novelist Vernor Vinge called the 'ultimate weapon'. We need a sea change in the way we view and perceive our heart; it is not merely the organ or muscle that pumps blood and keeps us alive. It has an energy, memory, and intelligence of its own, connected with, but independent of, the brain. As the Institute of Heart Math puts it, "Your heart and brain are in constant communication—and your heart is doing much of the talking!" What we should tear ourselves away from is what we may call the 'mind-mindset', and the whole complex of thought and thinking, awareness and recognition, understanding and learning. The result of which is that although we think that it is our call to choose what we do, the reality is that "we are hallucinating all the time".[94] That is also the path of destruction. Only by breaking away from that mental stranglehold—which means not letting our consciousness be captive to our mind—can we put to fuller use our *intuitive impulse*, the capacity of understanding through direct insight, without rational analysis or discursive reason or empirical ratiocination. Immanuel Kant called it intellectual intuition, i.e., the capacity to intuit entities that are beyond the dimensions of time and space, hence beyond our experience. It is this innate potentiality, variously called sixth sense, inner sensing, or inner insight, that has slipped into a state of atrophy, which we need to awaken and energize for us to be able to overcome our inveterate inabilities—why can't we do good; why we do bad. Science is throwing its hat in the ring. They have announced that a machine they call the "Ramanujan Machine" is "trying to replace the mathematical intuition of great mathematicians…"

Let us not forget what Athenagoras of Athens says in *Supplicatio Pro Christianis*: "The devil, when he purports any evil against man, first perverts his mind". It means that both for God and the devil, the mind is the favorite medium to get at man. And for the mind, the machine will become the medium. Some fear that this medium will then come to be

---

[94] Seth, A. 2018. Reality Isn't Real: We Are Hallucinating All the Time. *The Atlantic*. 30 November 2018.

the master. One good thing that the machine has done is to force us to really confront the question, 'What really is the 'human niche' that we must persevere and sustain and save and bear any burden for?' The fact is, as Augustin Fuentes puts it, "It's messy to be human, but it's really fascinating". The point is not that an intelligent machine is fated to be bad; what is bad is to look up to it as the way to synthesize and unify all our likes and dislikes. We want to abandon responsibility, but augment our power; we are not predictable but we want to *predict* everything about ourselves for profit; we want to transgress the confines of our capabilities but not sell our soul in exchange. However smart or moral a machine we might make it to be, it cannot cater to such a wish-list. On the other hand, it is possible that it exacerbates the fundamental—and fraught—dichotomy in our consumer-consumed civilization, in which, in Margaret Atwood's words, we are "converted into waste by the things we acquire", and in which a miniscule minority, one percent, consumes more than the bottom fifty percent, whose lives are devalued by society, and also "produce more than twice the carbon that the poorest fifty percent do".[95] At the end of the day, to really set right what is askew in the world, we must learn to look at them through the moral spectrum. That is the only way we can overcome the salad bowl of inertia, inclinations, inhibitions, and impediments that deter us from doing what is needful.

The triad of 'M's have not stood still; they also evolved along with the rest. They cannot also be separated from how the world is presently structured and fractured, colored and corrupted. There have always been those whom Thorstein Veblen called the *Leisure Class*, who lead a lazy life, and there have always been several shades of toiling classes, for whom being lazy is equal to death by starvation. The clash between the two was what Marx called 'class struggle'. It is always the former—the 'world's most optimized inhabitants'—that will continue to prosper whatever happens to the earth. That is not only their conviction but also the call of the play.

---

[95] McKibben, B. 2020. Where We Stand On Climate. *The New Yorker*. 11 December 2020.

They are the ones whom the rest ape. Even the morality we all aspire is the morality of that 'inhabitants' class, its "class interests and its class feelings of superiority". And then, we have to work out a way to deal with what we might term as mob morality, how immorally 'moral' men behave under the cover of mob anonymity, and under the spell of unprincipled mass leaders and megalomaniacs. One of the timeless dilemmas that sensitive people wrestled with is how to lead a righteous life in a society that is not righteous. What they did not, and we still do not, realize sufficiently, is that, as Meister Eckhart said, "truth is within his own ground; not beyond it". It is that ground that we must till and plow, and where we must plant the seed and nourish the sampling. For a 'true man', there is no other way to make society truly caring. We need a new conversation on how to ensure that our actions and reactions relevant to the three 'M's of our lives pave the way to a new beginning, or the end of the beginning. This book presents a mélange of ideas, and insights, options and opportunities, to make it possible for the good in us to prevail over the evil in this war within.

The Legend of the
Cherokee's Two Wolves—
Its Topicality Today

<hr>

The Triad of Worlds We Live In

All of us talk routinely and reflexively of the world we live in as if it is a standalone, homogenous, harmonious entity. We actually *live* in three parallel, yet interdependent worlds. And our inability to harmonize the three worlds is the source of much misery. The *first* is the world as another name for Planet Earth—seen as a pale blue dot from space—which harbors and houses over seven billion humans, and many more billions of nonhumans. It is a dark, dreary, and dangerous world that catches our eye and engages our attention, but we never truly believe we are a part of it, that what happens to it is of any relevance to our life. Practically speaking, we don't live in one big world. We live in a collection of small worlds. The *second* is the world of near and dear—family, friends, neighbors, and foes. This is the world that truly matters, and yet we are affected by what happens in the first world. The way we have tried to overcome this ambivalence, this irksome inconvenience, true to our genius, is to have it both ways: to be caring and cooperative towards a few, the ever-shrinking near and dear, and be competitive and callous towards the rest. Caring for the few, as the Dalai Lama noted, is 'emotional attachment', not genuine compassion. As he puts it, "true compassion is universal in scope"—one might add, not subject to reciprocity. The Dalai Lama goes on: "The rationale for universal compassion is based on the same principle of spiritual democracy. It is the recognition of the fact that every living being has an equal right to and desire for happiness... Compassion and universal responsibility require a commitment to personal sacrifice and the neglect of egotistical desires". Jesus said, "You must be compassionate, just as your Father is compassionate". And compassion is simply returning a favor, a *quid pro quo*, if it is shown only to those who are 'good' to us. True compassion comes into play when it is extended to those who do 'harm' to us. In the karmic, if not cosmic, sense, those who harm others, 'suffer' more than the others do. Human nature is such that if we do (or think we do) good to other people, it is natural to expect recognition, if not gratitude, from them. And when we do not get it, as it so often happens, we feel hurt, even resentful. And that sours our own mood and mind and affects our future responses to similar situations. Expectation always leads to disappointment, and it is very hard for a person of average abilities to do anything, particularly an act of altruism, without expecting something in return, even a simple and sincere 'thank you'. Scriptures and sages tell us that we should try to transcend that spiritual limitation. Prof. Iswar Chandra Vidyasagar, a philosopher, reformer, and educationist, whom Sage Ramakrishna himself hailed as compassionate, was once informed that someone was abusing him. Prof. Vidyasagar reportedly answered, "Why so? I do not remember having done any good to him". Compassion is not only for others; we need to be compassionate, at least considerate towards our own selves. Too often people try to cope with their suffering with low self-esteem or harbor a sense of inadequacy and failure. They fall into patterns of stressful and destructive self-loathing which just multiplies into misery. Self-compassion is different from self-love, which is injurious to others; compassion, wherever it is directed, can only do good. It is also different from random acts of kindness; they lull us into thinking that we are good, that it balances our 'bad'; which might even embolden us to be more brazen. Compassion essentially is a state of sublime consciousness, and once we cultivate it in our whole mindset, our behavior and personality changes. We do not need to become a Buddha or Christ or even a Gandhi to be compassionate. At its core must be the dictum that our lives and those of all beings are connected as in a giant web spread right across the planet and indeed beyond. If we can imbibe the sense that we are all made of the same stuff, subject to the same natural processes, all sailing in the same existential boat, we will naturally feel compassion towards all other life and forms of life. As the Buddha sings in the *Karaniya Metta Sutta*: "Have that mind for all the world, get rid of lies and pride, a mother's mind for her baby, her love, but now unbounded". It is relatively easy to accept this intellectually, feel good about ourselves and stay stranded in the smug status quo. For it to have any practical effect it has to become our reflex reaction.

The *third* and the most important, is the *world within*, our inner world, invisible, impervious, and impenetrable. This is the world where everything originates. As the famed author and occultist Madame Blavatsky says, "We see that every external motion, action, gesture, whether voluntary or mechanical, organic or mental, is produced and *preceded* by internal feeling or emotion, will or volition, and thought or mind" (*The Secret Doctrine*, 1888). All our problems as well as solutions are within this world. All our vulnerabilities and strengths are sourced in this within. All that happens in the first world is really *ex post facto*. What we do is implementation, not really 'doing'. Although the world outside, the phenomenal world is the same geographical zone of activity, different people perceive it differently. For some, the world is wondrous and the people are good, while for others, it is, in Arthur Schopenhauer's words, 'such a miserable and melancholy world', where the people are deceitful and sinful. It is so, because the outer world is the projection of our *inner* world. But somehow, we see ourselves apart, and separate. The paradox is that everything is globalized in this world but not our mindset. We stay connected regardless of distance or culture, but lose touch with our own inner or deeper selves. Everything any of us does affects everyone else, and yet we all behave as if we are an island unto ourselves. Another pivotal issue we have to address is how to harmonize the two contradictions: while we have evolved to live locally, we are living 'globally'. As Roman philosopher Seneca said, "Each of us dwell, in effect, in two communities—the local community of our birth, and the community of human argument and aspiration that is truly great and truly common" (*De Otio*, 62 CE).

Deep down we just believe that the fate of the earth is not our fate; and even if it is, we will *somehow* survive it, triumphant amidst the smoldering ruins and burning *ghats* of a dying earth. That is the headwater of all that is amiss with humanity today. It is this facile, if not false, faith that lets us go to sleep at night, and do all the sundry silly things the morning after and feel good. And that is why the second world is the real world we actually care about, because everyone in this world is but an extension of 'I, me, and mine'. It is from this world that we derive our sense of identity, or sorrow and well-being, rather than from the first world or the third. The lives in the second world crisscross ours, give us joy or sorrow, delight or despair, make life tolerable or toxic, meaningful or malignant. It is what happens in this world that seduces us to suicide, and impels us to homicide. What is upsetting about death, in fact, is the prospect of getting separated from the second world, not the first, universal world. The third world is the inner world, the most consequential and the most meaningful. It is this world that Matshona Dhliwayo calls the 'greatest temple in the universe' (*Lalibela's Wise Man*, 2014). Both the first and second worlds are but its reflections and extensions. But our inner world is invisible, and yet, as George Eliot says (*Middlemarch*), "the true seeing is within". The biggest change man has to make, is a paradigm shift in his preoccupation and focus from the external to the internal, from the without to the within, from outer space to the inner space, and, most of all, shift his focus from the wars outside to the war within his own consciousness. The world within is the world of our consciousness, and the 'war' that rages is for gaining control of its commanding heights.

The paradox is that there is no consensus on the definition of what constitutes this 'third world', (except that it is not the much-talked-about Third World, a term used until recently to designate the economically underdeveloped countries of Asia, Africa, and Latin America). This is not a geographical or physical world; it is the *spiritual* world. Although we used to think that it is exclusive to the human world, many scholars and researchers are now positing that it is inherent not only in the animal kingdom, but also in the vegetable and mineral kingdoms, although human consciousness is higher than that of others. And that spiritual growth calls for attaining higher levels of consciousness. Consciousness is both universal and unique; unites and separates. All of us are fragments or sparks of the divine or cosmic consciousness. And yet, as individual forms of life, we all have our particular consciousness specific to each of us. The dissolution of the particular into the universal or cosmic consciousness is the ultimate spiritual goal. Views, however, vary on where we are consciousness-wise at this juncture in our history. Some say that although everything appears dark, grim, gloomy, and depressing, there are tell-tale signs that we are actually poised at the dawn of a global or planetary consciousness. From the other end, others argue that all the stomach-turning things happening in the world, perpetrated by us humans, indicate how depraved and debased human consciousness is. If that were so, how does one explain the good things people still do? In truth, both are true. Our individual consciousness houses all our emotions, feelings, and inclinations and dispositions and passions and, depending on their intrinsic nature, they all fall into two camps or sides or opposing sets of forces: good and bad, darkness and light, constructive and destructive, *raga* (attachment) and *dvesha* (aversion), positive and negative, righteousness and wickedness, altruism and selfishness, mind and heart. And the opposing forces battle for control of the consciousness. We do good when the forces of goodness attain an upper hand, and bad when the bad adversary dominates. The good, the bad, the ghastly that happens in the world is simply the external manifestation of this war, and it has its ebbs and flows, and fluctuations and swings. It is an intense and fierce struggle for control and conquest of this planet and the human consciousness. In spiritual terms, the fight is between our two 'selves', the higher self and the lower self. And the final goal is not to 'defeat' or eliminate one or the other, the good or the evil, the raga or the dvesha, but to transcend them. That is what the Bhagavad Gita suggests—*raga dvesha viyuktaihi*, transcending the opposites—as the way to cultivate tranquility and divine grace. But in the intermediate state in which we live, the 'fight' goes on. What is striking is that nothing grabs our adrenaline more than war; it brings out man's true nature—good and bad, noble and ignoble, heroic and horrendous. And yet, we are utterly oblivious and unaware of the deterministic of all wars within. In the words of the Christian evangelist Billy Graham, "The wars among the nations on earth are mere popgun affairs compared to the fierceness of battle in the spiritual unseen world. This invisible spiritual conflict is waged around us incessantly and unremittingly". It is our consistent and persistent failure to recognize and pay sufficient heed to this greatest of all wars, the war within, that is the root cause of all our troubles and problems, and for all the venom, virulence, and violence in the world that causes so much despair. This explains the stubborn persistence of organized violence in the human world. War-making is a major aspect of modern life, and research indicates that this has been the case for the past several millenniums. In recent decades, numerous anthropological studies have presented compelling evidence that interpersonal violence and warfare, in varying degrees, have been an integral part of humanity's history. Current studies suggest that some of the earliest humans did engage in organized violence that appears as approximations, forms of, or analogues for what we now view as warfare. Some scholars even suggest that it could have been a significant driver of human evolution.

As for the *war within*, we really don't know when it began—estimates vary from two million years to three thousand years. Many scriptures have referred to the evil within, and the paramount need to fight it, and some saints have lamented their inability to do what is right, but no one has painted it in its true colors. We have been waging all sorts of wars for several centuries, but few, if any, have realized that the most important of them all is going on right under our noses, inside the citadel of our own consciousness. We have long wondered why we behave so badly at times, but never even suspected that the cause as well as the remedy is in the sanctum of our own soul. It is a matter of everyday frustration that we are often paralyzed into passivity in showcasing qualities like what the Buddhists call 'loving kindness and compassion' in stressful situations, but it never occurred to us that it is because these very qualities are on the losing side of the war within. Human transformation has for millenniums been the aim of our spiritual *sadhana* (practice), but it always gave us the slip because we chose to ignore the fact that true transformation must rise, like the Phoenix, from the ruins of the war within. When breaking news tells us of a bloody massacre somewhere in the world, we ask, like an alien up in the sky, 'what is happening to humankind?', but it never crosses our mind that it is the ascendancy of this very mind in our consciousness that is responsible. And so, the capacious charade goes on: we get on with the myriad mundane things of our meandering lives, always surprised, shocked, and saddened, but feel helpless even as the forces of anarchy and evil gain strength, fed by our own actions. The answer to the question why we do nothing individually, even as a blind man can see that the climate crisis is real and potentially capable of making the planet uninhabitable, is that without consciousness-change, climate change, like the ill-fated *Titanic*, is headed towards its own iceberg—our willful blindness.

All too often, we feel overwhelmed and besieged by what life entails, and we get stricken with a sinking feeling, like a raft let loose in a stormy sea. It is because our gaze, attention, and energy are wrongly directed. We gaze at the stars instead of 'seeing within'; we voyage to outer space, instead of 'going within'; we marshal all our forces to wage all kinds of wars, driven mainly by ego, avarice, and malice, instead of directing out attention to the mother of all wars, the *War Within*. And this war, unlike other wars, has two frontlines: consciousness inside and context outside. We really do not know when this war began. Some say it was there all along, and that it gained speed and shape only with modern man. Others say it began when human evolution evolved to the present self-aware level—what Julian Jaynes (1976) calls the 'breakdown of bicameralism'—about three thousand years ago. But the fact is, whether it was a war or not, the struggle or fight between two sets of intrinsically inimical forces, good and evil, light and darkness has been a constant through the ages. To win this war—which is to facilitate the ascendancy of the forces under the rubric of good over those of evil—we need to induce and orchestrate a radical modification of the character and content of our consciousness in the contemporary human way of life.

Forward—Outward or Inward?

Framed differently, the question is this: is the way forward *outward* or *inward*? Do we turn our gaze and energy to engage with the universe within, or do we exploit and enjoy the world without? Almost instinctively, we view them as separate, even alternatives or opposites. The idea that everything in nature comes in pairs of opposites permeates Greek philosophy too. The most prominent is the Table of Opposites of Pythagoras, which, among other items, includes good and evil and light and darkness. Similar examples are 'day and night' in Heraclitus' philosophic theory, 'justice and injustice' in Anaximander's, and 'love and strife' in Empedocles' philosophy. The paradox is that both opposites are two primal cosmic energies, two poles which are opposite but, at the same time, complementary to each other and which are both manifestations of the one and only reality. How to harmonize the two without destroying either is the challenge we face, which is at the heart of the war within. We tend to think that science deals with the world 'outside', and spirituality with the realm 'within'. We assume that the within is a given, but unknowable unknown, about which we can do little. But the outside, we feel, is within reach, which we can mold and manipulate to our advantage at will, to make human presence on earth eternal and unchallenged. The fact is that they—the worlds within and without—are holistically connected, even functionally interdependent; neither can exist without the other. And the world within is a veritable gold mine of all that we seek and long for. In the Indian epic Mahabharata, queen Gandhari, who willingly marries the blind king Dhritarashtra, chooses to blindfold her own eyes for the rest of her life, to show her oneness with her husband. From that point, she does not see the world without, but she receives the "choice blessings of the world within" and acquires great spiritual powers, strong enough to throw a curse on Lord Krishna himself. The macrocosm is within the microcosm, as much as the microcosm is within the macrocosm. That is the central message from the Upanishads. Swami Vivekananda explained: "The microcosm and the macrocosm are built on the same plan. Just as the individual soul is encased in the living body, so is the universal Soul in the Living *Prakriti* [nature]—the objective universe". The inward–outward dichotomy is also used to define the man–God interrelationship. Meister Eckhart wrote, "The more God is in all things, the more He is outside them; the more He is within, the more without". Everything that comes out is but an extension, reflection, and projection of what is already inside. And the 'already inside' is itself an outcome of an internal struggle. We may think that only wars of the world are real, but spiritual warfare too is very real.

Warfare happens every day, all the time inside us. Whether we believe it or not, all of us are in a state of war. Eknath Easwaran says, "Spiritual life too is a battle. Mystics call it the war within; the clash between what is spiritual in us and what is selfish, between the forces of goodness and the powers of destruction that clash incessantly in the human heart". He also says that the subject of the great epic Bhagavad Gita is "the war within, the struggle for self-mastery that every human being must wage if he or she is to emerge from life victorious".

The arena, the theater of operations, where we can find any leads to solve our problems can only be within the microcosm—the individual man. WB Yeats wrote in his poem *Cuchulain's Fight with the Sea*, "I only ask what way my journey lies". Jalal ad-Din Rumi said, "Everything in the universe is within you. Ask all from yourself". But the outward-to-inward journey is more complex; it requires more effort. For, how we live in the world outside influences what goes on inside. The inward journey has been characterized as the longest journey, the path to God, the internal pilgrimage, etc. The inward is the world beyond perception, the world of intuition, emotion, and feeling, the world of seekers and noble souls. The destination is the *nihitam guhayam,* the One hidden in the 'cave of the heart', the *Atman,* the Self. And the obstacles are the senses and 'mind-body-identification'. In the Bhagavad Gita, Lord Krishna draws the analogy of a tortoise to convey the message. He says, "When, again, as a tortoise draws in on all sides its limbs, he withdraws his senses from the objects of sense, then is his understanding well poised".[96] Just as our brain and body are connected, so are our inside and outside. We are fairly clear that what appears as the outside is the phenomenal world in which we exist, work, play, live, and die. The conundrum is that while we must undertake a journey inward, we do not know the way; we only know the way outward, but it leads nowhere. We must transcend our robot-like existence that devours all our energy and attention, even imagination,

---

[96] Besant, A. 1977. Bhagavad-Gita (2.58). Chennai, India: Theosophical Publishing House. p.39.

mostly just to stay alive, to fulfill our obligations, to earn a living, to raise a family, to have fun. In the end, we feel only inadequate, going from crisis to crisis, while time ticks away to an end that ends it all. Most thoughtful people concur that what mankind needs is a cathartic cleansing of consciousness. With our consciousness composed of different stages or levels, some say we are now at the stage that manifests as the 'me-first', materialistic, and aggressive behavior; but there are signs that we are on the threshold of a leap up the ladder to a consciousness driven by 'trans-rational intuition'. Scientists tell us that man is certainly at the same time the most aggressive and altruistic animal. In other words, different individuals, or the same individual at different times, can respond differently to different situations, and temptations and provocations. It is said, "Evolution didn't just shape us to be violent, or peaceful, it shaped us to respond flexibly, adaptively, to different circumstances, and to risk violence when it made adaptive sense to do so. We need to understand what those circumstances are if we want to change things".[97] If we want to tame human aggression, we have to create appropriate circumstances. Many might argue that the circumstances we are shaping will make us more aggressive; others opine that once the consciousness threshold is crossed, man could become a more introspective, tolerant, socially sensitive, and environmentally harmonious person. When that threshold is reached, consciousness does not dissolve; it is the *limits* that dissolve. The final stage, reached by prophets like Jesus, Muhammad, the Buddha and Mahavira, by mystics like St. Teresa and St. John of the Cross, by masters like Ramakrishna Paramahansa, and by teachers like Sankara and Swami Vivekananda, is when we are able to erase the boundary between the creator and creation, between one living being and another living being, and reach a level at which humanity itself becomes one tribe, living in harmony on Sacred Earth. We might indeed

---

[97] Elizabeth Cashdan, professor of anthropology at the University of Utah, USA. Cited in: Whipps, H. 2009. The Evolution of Human Aggression. LiveScience. 25 Feb 2009. Retrieved from: <https://www.livescience.com/5333-evolution-human-aggression.html>.

all have clairvoyant consciousness, dormant but extant, with which the living can talk to the dead. While we can speculate about the evolution of aggression of the human, the two critical factors that everything hinges on are consciousness and circumstance.

Our chief living limitation is our instinctive interpretation of our own selves as limited and lone beings. It is our inability to comprehend the import of the Upanishadic mahavakya, *Tat tvam asi*, (Thou art that), and come to terms with what Martin Buber[98] called the '*Ich und Du*' (I and Thou) relationship. We think, feel, and behave as autonomous individuals; all pleasure and pain, happiness and misery is experienced by our standalone selves. However, most religions tell us this is the greatest misconception. The truth is that everything is united, everything is connected, nothing is separate, and the substratum, the ground underneath is all divine. What we have to overcome is not a malfunctioning brain or a wayward mind or even a corrupted consciousness; it is to move into a different realm of reality. The realm we are comfortable with is the one that is physical, observable, measurable, and repeatable; in short, borne of the scientific method. We have ignored the spiritual realm. We possess all the pieces of the jigsaw puzzle but it is so huge that we never see it as whole.[99] And we wonder why. Could it be because of the brain that nature has given us? The brain—the 'three pounds of strange computational material found within our skulls'—is the master of the body. For happiness and harmony, it should work in tandem with the body, but for over a million years of our evolutionary struggle for survival, the left-brain, which is the seat of what we call reason and logic, became the dominant part, and the right-brain, the source of emotion, intuition, love, and empathy, became a passive

---

[98] *Martin Buber.* Wikipedia: The Free Encyclopedia. Wikimedia Foundation. Retrieved 23 Mar 2016. Buber's *Ich und Du* was published in 1923, and first translated from German to English in 1937.

[99] *Martin Buber.* Wikipedia: The Free Encyclopedia. Wikimedia Foundation. Retrieved 23 Mar 2016. Buber's *Ich und Du* was published in 1923, and first translated from German to English in 1937.

passenger. We are now poised at a momentous crossroads. The kind of intelligence we will nurture, and towards what direction and purpose, will eventually shape human destiny. Intelligence is the one thing that separates man and other species, and man from man, and contributes to making us how successful we are.

We have two autonomous but inter-reinforcing sources of energy, memory, and intelligence, centered around the mind and heart. Until recently, it was the heart that was the dominant partner, and man was a happy and harmonious being. For reasons not quite clear, the mind acquired ascendency, the heart went into eclipse and all our troubles started. Such a view is no longer confined to scriptural thought; it is now emerging as a scientific possibility. Julian Jaynes called the dual-centered human consciousness a bicameral mind. We all know that we have something that we have come to call 'consciousness', but we do not know what it really is and how it operationally relates with the brain, mind, and heart. Yet another hypothesis is that we all have a *Laurel and Hardy* type of consciousness, two different selves that constantly spar with each other. In addition, we also have, according to this view, a third person inside, a robot, who (or which) performs all repetitive tasks of life.[100] Some argue that we all have hidden, dormant occult powers. These are more pronounced in some people, and were possessed by our ancestors, but have been lost as they were no longer needed. While we live in the visible physical world, there is another invisible, 'normal, original, eternal, spirit' world.[101] Our ancestors were in constant contact with the spirit world, and literally conversed with the gods. The complete severance of this communication is responsible for our diminished human lives. Rudolf Steiner even says that if we do not get closer to the world of spirits, "something completely different from what ought to happen will happen to the earth".

---

[100] Wilson, C. 2010. Beyond the Occult. London, UK: Watkins Publishing. First South Asian Edition. p.87.

[101] Kardec, A. 1857. The Spirits Book (Le Livre des Esprits).

As if we are not sufficiently befuddled, we are also told that what appears remote and marginal is "often what the soul inwardly needs".[102] But then, some researchers tell us, about 'the power of thinking without thinking',[103] that more often than not, right decisions are taken not after deliberative thought, but by instinct and blind feeling. Chesterton wrote that you can only know truth with logic if you have already found it *without* it. Whether we rely on intelligence or intuition, the question that arises is that if life's road, in the harrowed phrase of Emily Bronte, 'winds uphill all the way', a Sisyphean struggle, then why not quickly slide down and end it all? To whom should we turn for help—the 'you', the 'stranger', the 'robot', the 'hibernating heart', the 'hidden self'?—and for what purpose, and how? Does the solution to all our problems, personal and civilizational, lie in harnessing our hidden powers, described as 'a sign of our evolutionary potential'?[104] And if so, how? How do we untie the knots that hold us back? If we want to turn our lives around and become modern-day mini-mystics or miniature-mahatmas, or simply men without malice, what is the road map?

Consciousness-change and Contextual-change

The real suffering, and its only solution, is embedded within each of us. And, *each of us* requires *each one of us*. The deepest secret of sentient life, particularly human, is very simple. We can achieve everything, fulfill every desire, and dream, not directly but through a detour; not explicitly but implicitly, through the medium of another person. Anything done solely for self-gain is pyrrhic; anything we do for another's well-being is a win-win; you benefit more than the beneficiary. Only by sharing can we become

---

[102] Steiner, R. 1918. The Dead Are With Us. Lecture on 10 February 1918. Nuremberg, Germany.

[103] Gladwell, M. 2007. Blink: the Power of Thinking Without Thinking.

[104] Wilson, C. 2010. Beyond the Occult. London, UK: Watkins Publishing. First South Asian Edition. p.501.

whole; and make life less difficult to someone else, anyone from spouse to stranger. All our life, we search for a meaningful life when the 'elephant' is next to us. We seek the divine everywhere when our true identity is the divine within, the immortal aspect of our mortal existence, the *Atman* as the Upanishads call it. It is something that we cannot 'see'. There is a growing realization in the world today, especially in the New Age movement, that the only way to avert a cataclysmic catastrophe is a gradual shift in global consciousness, that without such a paradigm shift nothing else will work, nothing else will save us... Before we even ponder over such weighty issues, it is important to offer some cautionary caveats. Like in all issues relative to the future of *Homo sapiens*, it is possible, even highly probable, that all our best answers are tantamount to tilting at windmills; for the truth is beyond our mind-mediated capacity of perception. The capacity we need is to be able to 'see things, ourselves, other people... differently', *à la* Beau Lotto.[105] But this much is still true: whatever might possibly happen in the future is contingent and congruent upon the direction of the transformation not of the world around us, but of our *inner* life—a process that spiritualists call 'consecration'. And just as in worldly life we don't win or lose, but live, so it is with our life within. We cannot survive either victory or defeat, triumph or capitulation. What we should aim at is a constructive stalemate, a favorable deadlock. All creativity is transformation. In fact, without transformation there is no life. The key question is transformation from what to what, and how. While we are witness to and passive participants of external transformation, we are wholly clueless and utterly unaware of what goes on inside us, and that results in a disconnect between the two: external transformation and internal transformation. As a direct consequence, many of us try to deal with this 'disconnect' by resorting to all kinds of distractions and amusement. The American writer Scott Fitzgerald portrayed the 1920s as a decade that began with 'the general decision to be amused'. This applies

---

[105] Lotto, B. 2017. Deviate: the Science of Seeing Differently. London, UK: Weidenfeld & Nicolson.

even more sharply to the 21st century. What is important to note is that these distractions and delusions do not end at amusing or entertaining us; they act as nutrients to our internal destructive passions, and feed the 'wrong' army in the war within.

One of our biggest obstacles to bringing about a holistic approach to address the challenges of our time is that, although we talk of one humanity and one world, we all exist in our own personalized worlds, which are specific and special to each individual, a fraction of humanity. As the Mexican saying goes, *cada cabeza es un mundo* ('every head is a different world'). In fact, it is the head that gives form and shape to everyone's world. And that is the chief problem man faces. We mistake it for an answer, whereas it is really a question. It is the main handicap and hindrance to better the human condition, and stands between morality and man. Perhaps the greatest delusionary illusion is to think and act as if there is an unbridgeable chasm between our life's inside and outside. The fact is, for something to happen outside in the external world, that activity has to be caused by something inside in our internal world, and vice versa.

The war within is also the answer to the question why, despite being essentially a spiritual being, man has become an economic animal. If we can change the direction of our desires, it will change the direction of human effort and creative power. We will then be able to radically alter not only the context of our life, but even the content of our consciousness. However, the 'consciousness-content' cannot be changed unless the 'context-content' is changed. And then again, what does God, up from the sky or deep inside each of us, think of all this? While it is sheer stupidity or utter naivety to rule out any possibility, a note of caution will be in order. Logically then, we should all somehow cling to life, hang on for a quarter century, by which time, it is expected that people will start lives that could last a thousand years or more. The down-to-earth reality, however, is far more modest and matter of fact: so far, whatever science has done in this field is to prevent premature deaths and thus increase the average life span;

it has not really extended our actual life span, which is generally believed to be 120 years, even by a single year.[106] The irony that eludes our acumen is that on the one hand, man, unable to come to terms with the demands of modern life, is struggling to find reasons *not* to die, and, on the other hand, science is dangling the carrot of immortality before us. Perhaps the greatest indictment of contemporary life is that so many are finding it easier to end life than to continue living. If ever the era of immortality does descend, we might well see a reversal of roles; just as we now long for immortality, men then might yearn for mortality.

What we are outside impacts on what happens inside, and what goes on within our consciousness makes us who we are. Most of us live outside and strive to achieve some goal, some ideal, through our external effort. But the truth is that there is nothing 'out there' unless it already is 'in here', within the confines of our consciousness. We may not know exactly what consciousness is and its link with the brain and mind, but we do know that it is, in large measure, the difference between being alive and being dead; and that it is what both unifies and differentiates us as living beings. If we want compassion to be our compass in navigating through life, we need a compassion-dominated consciousness, and for that we need to nurture a compassionate context of life. What we need right now is a new compass to set our direction and steer us through the stormy seas of our own consciousness. And, it is important to note that it carries some basic evolutionary implications. Natural selection has been a governing principle in creation for over four billion years. As Elizabeth Kolbert points out in her book, *The Sixth Extinction: An Unnatural History* (2014), whether we intend to do it or not, we are deciding which evolutionary pathways will be shut off forever, and which can be left open to flourish. We are moving towards what is being described as 'evolution by intelligent direction'.[107]

---

[106] Harari, Y.N. 2015. Homo Deus: a Brief History of Tomorrow. London, UK: Harvill Secker. p.25.

[107] Peter Diamandis, founder and chairman of the X Prize Foundation.

We are also being told to brace ourselves for the seismic possibility that the human, or whatever remains of him, is about to transcend Darwin, and that evolution will be, in the future, mediated by man, not by natural selection, which has held sway for over three billion years. What does it all amount to? And what does that mean for the much-talked-about *New Man of the New Millennium*? If the species has been static on the evolutionary scale, since the monkey became a man, and if an equally seismic man-mediated change that rivals such an event is coming soon, how should we react and, more importantly, how should we try to influence such a change? If we are approaching a tipping point in which all things that were hitherto impossible suddenly become commonplace, and if everything we wish we could actually make it happen, then are we yet again eating another forbidden fruit? And does this prove or disprove the all-knowing, all-powerful Almighty? Whichever answer appeals to whoever, the stark fact of the matter is that mankind is tottering on a balancing beam, and there is a more than a fair chance that it is about to get thrown off the beam. And man is not even sure what is down below.

The scary thing is that while the outside world is brimming with hair-raising events, profound mutations are happening *inside* our consciousness, even as we go about living, working, mating, multiplying, murdering, and, most of all, making money. And that entails much more than going to work every day and getting a periodic paycheck to buy groceries and gadgets; it has an enormous ecological cost. Even spiritually we are all at sea, as uncertainty meets us at every step. Is mortality the sinful fruit of our Biblical fallen nature? Or is it a golden gift of life, the envy of the angels, or an epiphany liberating us from life's *fait accompli*? All this rumination within trickles down to three matter-of-fact matters: world-weary as we might well be, how do we live so that life is worth its whole? And, on the individual level, as long as *I* am alive, how should *I* relate with other sentient beings who are anyhow as alive as I am, both in its limited and larger sense? And then, what is this '*I am*' that is so intrusive and insolent, at once threatened and vulnerable? So, who is that 'I' (or *me* or *mine*) that we so pathetically and pathologically cling to as sentient beings? According to the Vedanta school of Indian philosophy, all troubles start the moment we utter the 'I'; everything else is an illusion.

If there is one common thread between all religions and most cultures, it is the rarity and sanctity of human life. It is based on the premise that life is priceless and the human is special, closest to the divine. Scriptural injunctions like the Jewish Talmud say, for example, that since all mankind is descended from a single person, taking a life is like destroying an entire world, while saving a life is like saving an entire world. But these have largely ceased to be serious restraints to taking a life… While we are, on the one hand, trying to achieve breakthroughs in living without ageing, and living as long as we wish to, without regard to cost and consequence, we seem, on the other hand, to have lost our nerve and self-confidence, if not self-belief. Such is the depth of our self-belief that we have, for all practical purposes, given up on ourselves and our own internal power, and cast our lot with external powers, be it artificial intelligence or thinking computers or robots or androids or cyborgs, to help us out. And it is not science-fiction—about 4000 Swedes are already 'cyborgs', part human and part machine. Implanted in their hands is a tiny identity chip, which they can use instead of ID cards or credit cards. We have cognitively concluded that without hooking up with an external contrivance we will not be able to achieve anything. The surprising thing is that every time we have to believe something, say God, we want proof, but when it comes to technologies like artificial intelligence, we trust them even if we don't understand how they actually work. And although we associate proof with rationality, not everything can be proven true or false. In Kurt Godel's words, "You'll never be able to prove every true result… you'll never be able to prove every result that is true in your system". The fact is that facts on their own don't tell you much; in fact, they can lead you astray. It is only when coupled with what you desire and with whatever gives you pleasure or pain, that they can guide your behavior. That is why it is so important to desire the right desire, and want the righteous want. In real life, the dividing lines between proof, fact, opinion, and truth overlap and crisscross. It is important not to underestimate the power of hatred, like love, in the world and within all of us. It gives, albeit depraved, a sense of purpose larger than life, of working for the greater good. Purpose is highly personal and subjective, and yet it always develops in a social milieu and a consciousness-context. To have a right purpose requires a right mindset and that requires the right balance and mix in our consciousness. It means that what we need now is not a cognitive but a 'consciousness revolution', powered by both cognition and intuition, mind and heart in the *right* combination. While the two have to work in harmony, not in hostility, we must make sure the command and controls are with the heart. A sprinkling of brilliant minds can vest us with promethean powers, but a few beautiful hearts are not enough to ensure that we are worthy of having them. The new word to put us in our proper place is that humans are organic algorithms.

Literally everything around us today runs on *algorithms*. They power the internet, make all online searching possible, they direct our email, work silently behind the scenes when we use our GPS systems, and so on. Smartphone apps, social media, software… none of these things would function without algorithms. Altruism itself is based on algorithmic calculation of cost and expected payoffs, which are vital for self-survival. The humble algorithm is now being anointed as the New Almighty of the techno-religion, omnipotent, omniscient, and invisible but all-pervasive. As Yuval Harari puts it, "More than a century after Nietzsche pronounced Him dead, God seems to be making a comeback. But this is probably a mirage. Despite all the talk of Islamic fundamentalism and Christian revival, God is dead—it just takes a while to get rid of the body".[108]

---

[108] Harari, Y. 2016. Salvation by Algorithm: God, Technology and the New 21st-Century Religions. *The New Statesman*, 9 Sept 2016.

The Power of the Heart

The power to effect a consciousness revolution must rise from *within*. And that 'power' is none other than our own heart. We learn early in life that it is good to have a kind and caring heart—and it feels good, too. The intuitive intelligence of the heart could tilt the scales in the war within. The spiritual story of the 21st century will be, at a deeper level, the drawing and redrawing of the battle lines of the head and heart, between what you know and what you feel in the war within, of how *Homo sapiens* is trying to broker a kind of détente between the two, to ensure the survival of both but in a different blend. We live in a world where the logic of the head is at odds with the emotion of the heart. For a wholesome and harmonious life, we need to listen to both the heart and the head, but too often, the voice of the head almost silences that of the heart. We are now pretty much focused on our head, or brain, which James Watson[109] called the 'grandest biological frontier, the most complex thing we have yet discovered in our universe'. While pretty much ignoring, and taking for granted, the even grander frontier—our heart. The relatively new concept of 'coherence' is emerging, pioneered by institutions like the HeartMath Institute;[110] it is a highly efficient state in which all of the body's systems, in particular the heart and mind, work in sync, ensuring that the whole of us is more than the sum of our parts. To be fully human, we must ensure the development of the heart and the head. It is in this spirit and with this objective that initiatives like 'activating the global heart' are being taken to bring about a shift in the content of global consciousness, a work in progress. In his work *The Celestine Prophecy*, James Redfield, for example, wrote that 'over the past half century, a new consciousness has come to the human world'.

---

[109] James D. Watson, American molecular biologist, geneticist and zoologist, is best known as one of the co-discoverers of the structure of DNA (1953), along with Francis Crick. They were awarded the 1962 Nobel Prize in Physiology or Medicine.

[110] HeartMath Institute, USA. <https://www.heartmath.org/research/science-of-the-heart/coherence/>.

We need to blend both our strengths and weaknesses in the right proportion to have the right consciousness. The renowned 20th-century Indian philosopher Jiddu Krishnamurti said, "Intelligence comes into being when the mind, heart, and body are really in harmony".[111] He also underlined the utter inadequacy of thought and thinking. He believed that it was thought that gave us religion, and it is thinking that separates us as individuals from one another. But to overcome the impediment of their insufficiency, we don't have to abdicate thinking and eliminate the mind. What we need is a new balance and baseline in our consciousness between the two primary sources of intelligence and energy—the mind and the heart. We must also bear in mind that everything in the cosmos, from trees to humans, is energetically connected. But like in every situation and between any two things, there cannot be perfect equality; one or the other has to be a dominant partner even if it constantly changes. And it applies to the head and heart, too. We have to make a kind of choice no man has ever been called upon or required to make: which of the two must be at the commanding heights of our consciousness: the head or the heart? Science is working in both directions, although the bulk of the effort is brain-centered. That has to change; science must have a greater heart-centric focus. Only then can we achieve what we glibly call a paradigm shift, and move towards what some mystics call transcendental consciousness, or cosmic consciousness, which induces awe, supreme joy and the highest, unalloyed felicity, free from pain, sorrow, and fear. It is, in its effect, a divine consciousness, a state of sublime spirituality attained by prophets, ancient rishis and great saints and sages. The Upanishads proclaim it as all-embracing, one that keeps the stars, the sun, the moon... all in their place in a state of close communion. Most of us cannot attain that state, but we can certainly move towards it in different degrees. That is the kind of consciousness-change that mankind should strive towards. Only that will enable and empower us to see ourselves differently about our place on the planet, and only then we can alter the causal course of

---

[111] Krishnamurti, J. 1973. The Awakening of Intelligence. USA: Harper.

human creativity. If we do that, and if we do let the heart control the mind, then 'we are off to the next galaxy, both inward and outward'[112], and we will almost permanently prevail in the perennial war within. Man by himself is incomplete for that task. In Hindu scriptures like the *Vishnu Purana*, it is said that the final or tenth avatar of Lord Vishnu, called the *Kalki* avatar, will not only restore dharma to its rightful place on earth but also awaken the minds of those who live at that time. Our age is that time, and it could mean that the advent of the next divine manifest on earth could well entail and result in a profound consciousness-change. That is because, unlike in earlier divine avatars, evil on earth is not personified in some of us. As Nwaocha Ogechukwu says, "No one can deny that each one of us has an aspect of the devil within us" (*The Secret Behind the Cross and Crucifix*, 2009). But for God to restore dharma on earth, He cannot simply slay modern-day *rakshasas* (demons), which most of us are in different degrees. He has to help us win the war within, and that will lead to a consciousness-change. And that is the only way to what the ancient Chinese philosopher Lao Tzu called, "the introduction of higher dimensions of consciousness into our awareness", which theosophist Annie Besant compared to the snake shedding its skin and the butterfly emerging from its chrysalis.

As a species we are at a critical crossroads and have to make a decisive directional choice between two divergent paths. The *Katha* Upanishad speaks of the two-fold path available to mankind: the *Pravritti marga* (path of material and bodily pleasures), and the *Nivritti marga* (path of goodness and righteousness). We can frame it differently for the 21st century: today's *pravritti* is augmentation of cognitive intelligence through artificial intelligence (AI). And, *nivritti* is exploring and energizing the awesome but dormant power of the heart's intuitive intelligence. AI is now clearly at the cutting edge of our creativity (and big business, too), whereas we know very little about the heart as a source of intelligence and energy

---

[112] Quote by Gabriel Iqbal. Retrieved from <https://www.goodreads.com/author/quotes/10787600.Gabriel_Iqbal>. Gabriel Iqbal is author of the book *Heart Intelligence.*

independent of, or in tandem with, the brain. Heart intelligence is 'the flow of intuitive awareness and inner guidance we experience when the mind and emotions are brought into coherent alignment with the heart'.[113] The inner dynamic working of the deep consciousness is altogether different from the dynamics of the rational mind, which we are familiar with. We have been conditioned to perform all our cognitive, analytical, and synthesizing activities of knowledge at the rational level. This conditioning is so deep that we have forgotten the faculty of intuition that we possess inside our heart intelligence. That is why our choices and decisions are so skewed. Recent cutting-edge research suggests that the "heart also is an access point to a source of wisdom and intelligence that we can call upon to live our lives with more balance, greater creativity, and enhanced intuitive capacities"[114] Both the brain and that thumping organ in our body are powerful tools that not only sustain life, but help us experience the world in a profound way at a deeper level. A proper alignment of the heart and mind can help us make better decisions and live more balanced and peaceful lives. And that calls for a fundamental change in the content and balance of our consciousness. Consciousness is the master key, and every crisis the world faces—political, economic, climatic, social—is but a reflection of a 'crisis of consciousness'. It is, in Jiddu Krishnamurti's words, "A crisis that cannot anymore accept the old norms, the old patterns, the ancient traditions. And considering what the world is now with all their ill will and destructive brutality, aggression, and so on, man is still as he was: brutal, violent, aggressive, acquisitive, competitive, and he has built a society along these lines".[115] When Pope

---

[113] HeartMath Institute, California, USA. Research FAQs. <https://www.heartmath.org/support/faqs/research/>.

[114] HeartMath Institute. 2015. Science of the Heart: Exploring the Role of the Heart in Human Performance. Volume 2. California, USA: HeartMath Institute. < https://www.heartmath.org/research/science-of-the-heart/>.

[115] Cited in the blog post *Jiddu Krishnamurti—a Radical Transformation of the Mind*, on 8 Mar 2009. Retrieved from <https://thecriticalthinker.wordpress.com/2009/03/08/krishnamurti-mind/>.

Francis said that the "ecological crisis is also a summons to profound interior conversion",[116] he meant consciousness-change, a fundamental shift in the command and content of our consciousness. Climate change is more than ecological crisis; it a mirror to what is wrong with the human way of life.

Nothing deters us from dreaming to be the masters of the universe, of birth and death, of brain and body, and willing to be, as Thoreau once said, 'the tools of our tools'. Some may not flinch from death, but they still want to make our lives free from fear, worry, pain, and anxiety. The fundamental question this generation of humans must ask itself is, what must we desire or hope to have? For hope is no longer so harmless, and desire can be decisively destructive. Earlier, in the main, our dreams and desires, hopes and aspirations and ambitions were largely individual-centric and local, and our failures and setbacks were individualistic and isolated and the fallout was also limited and contained. To meet, to really connect, and to encounter another as deeply as possible—this has been an abiding and enduring human aspiration. Now, we can have the unlimited ability to technologically communicate, combine, connect, and cooperate on a species-scale. But that immense 'ability' to better the human condition largely remains untapped. But it is not merely technical or technological; it is spiritual too. In Karen Armstrong's words, "We urgently need to examine received ideas and assumptions, look beneath the sound-bites of the news to the complex realities that are tearing our world apart, realizing, at a profound level, that we share the planet not with inferiors but equals".[117] What we ought to strive towards is consciousness-to-consciousness, and heart-to-heart communion, not mind-to-mind communication and microchip-implants.

To arrest the drift and drag, and to change the course of our civilization, we need another internal revolution: a consciousness-revolution, an inner

---

[116] Pope Francis. 2015. Encyclical Letter *Laudato Si': On Care for our Common Home*. The Vatican, Rome, Italy.

[117] Statement by Karen Armstrong, author of books like The Case for God, 2008, and 'Three steps to a compassionate life, 2010, on being bestowed with the 2017 Princess of Asturias Award for Social Sciences; 31 May 2017.

alchemy that allows us to go beyond the boundary of thinking itself and restores or reawakens the role of heart intelligence. The very evolution that led to this impasse has to be re-directed within. We have to contain the predominance of our mind in molding the way we live and that requires drastically diminishing the mind's internal monopoly. For that, we need an internal counterweight, which can only be the heart in its role as a major source of energy, memory, and intelligence. The real reason why we have failed to make any breakthrough in the face of problems that threaten our very future—like climate change, terrorism, moral paralysis, runaway mechanization, materialism, and militarism—is our abysmal inability to take cognizance of the fact that there is a whole universe within, and that what happens there has a decisive bearing on what happens in the world in which we are born into, to live and to die. Spiritual literature is replete with words like 'inner world', inner self, power within, inner seeking, inner awakening, inner journey, and so on. We have been repeatedly told that we can find everything we search for if we can reach inward into our heart: truth, strength, love, hope, happiness. And inward is not a direction or depth but a dimension. As Rainer Rilke said, 'the only journey is the one within'. For Rumi, we enter 'a mine of rubies and bathe in the splendor of our own light'. All such are noble thoughts and wise advice, but the reality is that we are stranded at the gates of our own skin.

The Evil Within

While we externalize the clash between good and evil, it actually is an incestuous affair. As Carl Jung puts it, "Nothing is so apt to challenge our self-awareness and alertness as being at war with oneself."[118] Even if we do win all external wars, it will be a vacuous victory; it would be, as the Bible

---

[118] Source: Collected Works of Carl Jung (1936). 6:964 (Psychological Types).

says, tantamount to losing the soul.[119] Among our contemporary great thinkers who have pondered long and hard over this war, the one that springs instantly to mind is Aleksandr Solzhenitsyn. In his monumental 1973 work, *The Gulag Archipelago*, he brings out its immediate context and its intricate complexity, and writes, "If only it were all so simple! If only there were evil people somewhere insidiously committing evil deeds, and it were necessary only to separate them from the rest of us and destroy them!" And he goes on, "In my most evil moments, I was convinced that I was doing good; and I was well supplied with systematic arguments. And it was only when I lay there on the rotting prison straw that I sensed within myself the first stirrings of good. Gradually it was disclosed to me that the line separating good and evil passes not through states, nor between classes, nor between political parties either—but right through every human heart, and through all human hearts. This line shifts. Inside us, it oscillates with the years. And even within hearts overwhelmed by evil, one small bridgehead of good is retained; and even in the best of all hearts, there remains… an un-uprooted small corner of evil. Since then, I have come to understand the truth of all the religions of the world. They struggle with the *evil inside a human being* (inside every human being). It is impossible to expel evil from the world in its entirety but it is possible to constrict it within each person".[120]

These are very weighty and wise words. We can constrict the evil within each of us only if we can positively influence the war within. However, we have almost convinced ourselves that if we do not want to end up on the scrapheap of scapegoats, or be labelled as a loser, we must at the very least acquiesce to evil. Once we allow ourselves to wallow in that line of thought, the temptation becomes too much to resist to cover up for all our misdeeds; 'necessary' becomes 'necessity'. Such a necessity is the

---

[119] Mark 8:36. For what shall it profit a man, if he shall gain the whole world, and lose his own soul?

[120] Solzhenitsyn, A. 1973. The Gulag Archipelago. p.312.

necessary evil that even if we behave badly towards other people, we still think we are 'good' people. Our moral nonchalance and ethical apathy to what happens around us—which is unfair, unjust, exploitative—and our inability to instinctively or impulsively respond to others' suffering, has become so ingrained in daily life that it has taken a tragic toll on human personality. Thomas Hobbes tellingly wrote that 'all in their natural condition are possessed of the will to injure others, to tyrannize over other men; each has thus to fear the other'. And by ignoring the within, we are injuring ourselves, putting our well-being, even our health, at risk. It is now even being said that 'cancer is thus a breakdown from within'.[121] It means that not only evil, but illness too is within. A Rwandan proverb reminds us, 'You can out-distance that which is running after you, but not what is running inside you'. The world outside is the periphery, but the epicenter is within. We can control the periphery if we control the center. What we do on the outside influences what happens inside, but it is the center that prevails. We talk of good people and bad people, and that if we can get rid of the baddies, the problem would get resolved and the world will become a place of peace and harmony. One actually wishes there are identifiable bad people; it would then be easy to exterminate them like what we did with smallpox and polio. Alas, that is not only too simplistic but also false. We know that all of us are both good and bad at different times, or to different people at the same time. And we do not always feel bad about being bad to a person who is not considered bad. Our idea of someone being good or bad hinges purely on how that person behaves towards us, not on what others think. The burden of our suffering often is to 'suffer' others. If everything about morality is so sliding, slippery and subjective, or as-you-like-it, how then can we know how we're doing, and if we cannot, how can we become better? Contrary to what Spinoza tells us that 'to act in conformity with virtue is to act according to the guidance

---

[121] Dasgupta, A. 2015. Lessons from Russalana: In Search of Transformative Thinking. New Delhi, India: Harper Collins. p.140.

of reason…', it is a good that is common to all men, and can be equally possessed by all, in so far as they are of the same nature. And contrary to what TS Eliot said, "So far as we are human, what we do must be either evil or good; so far as we do evil or good, we are human; and it is better, in a paradoxical way, to do evil than to do nothing: at least, we exist",[122] we do both 'good' and 'evil', and evil today is so stomach-turning that doing something to combat evil is better than doing nothing. The accent here is on 'doing', not 'being'. It simply means that every time we do anything, we must try to do the good thing that is good for our soul and does no harm to anyone else. But to do that does not depend on 'us'—the breathing, walking person who stares back at us with a smirk in the mirror. It depends on the *war within*, inside our own deepest depths. The truth of the matter is that inside each of us "Dragons are there, and there are also lions; there are poisonous beasts and all the treasures of evil. But there too is God, the angels, the life and the kingdom, the light and the apostles, the heavenly cities and the treasuries of grace—all things are there".[123]

We must bear in mind that this is not something metaphorical or symbolic or figurative that we can ignore or condescendingly nod our head and do nothing about. Starkly put, everything we do in our life, agreeable and disagreeable, good, bad, ugly, has an effect on the war within. In the language of worldly war, they are the supplies and logistical support that gives the wherewithal to both sides to wage the war. This war is as literal, real, actual, and authentic as any other on the ground; if any, it is even more tangible, as it underpins every other war. It is not a 'star war', or war of the worlds, or some remote tribal war about which we can, in the comfort of distance, read in the papers or see on a screen, be entertained or get our adrenalin worked up, and feel smug that we are not on the

---

[122] Source: T S Eliot's 1930 essay on Baudelaire.

[123] St. Macarius on the Heart. Cited in blogpost *From Under the Rubble* on 26 May 2011. Glory to God for All Things. Retrieved from <https://fatherstephen.wordpress.com/tag/solzhenitsyn/>.

frontline or have to bear the collateral consequences like in the external wars. Everything about this war is about us; the place, the fighting, the forces, the fallout, they are all *us*. This war rages inside each of us with every breath we take, all the time, without a lull or break, relentless, remorseless, with no shut-down at sundown. And more ominously, every shift in the course, and the flow and every turn of the tide impacts on us in every thought, word or act that we entertain or engage in. Every happening or activity in what we tend to call 'our everyday life' affects the war. It determines who we are and what and how we do, and what we create and for what purpose. We tend to think that 'life' is different from our 'everyday life'. We want our life to be beautiful, but lead everyday lives in ugliness, pettiness, and perfidy. We view everyday life as some kind of a prison and yet we crave for eternal life of the same genre. Our within is both a 'black hole' and a 'war zone'. The black hole inside each of us is more impenetrable and more difficult to get into than any in the cosmos. The perplexing part is that, unlike in any other war, we have to take sides in this war; help one side any way we could, but we cannot let the other side get annihilated. God can sit on the sidelines with a smug; that is why he is He and we are not. Nothing happens to Him, everything happens to us. All our problems arise because, for a long time, the 'other side'—the evil within—has gained dominance. There are clear tell-tale signs. Some of these are the steady surge in senseless suicides, cutting across all ages, particularly children, the casualness of homicides, mass murders, and suicide-bombings. Every religion has projected its own vision of God and we have had so many religious wars—some people even blame organized religion for most of history's killings, and Christianity alone is blamed for the deaths of some 17 million people[124]—but what is needed now is a change in our perception of and posture towards God. Scriptures and sages have told us to treat God as our savior, refuge, and shelter, and to

---

[124] Source: Isn't Religion to Blame for Most of History's Killings? Retrieved from <http://www.provethebible.net/T2-Objec/G-0101.htm>.

surrender to Him wholly—called *prapatti* or *saranagati* in the Vaishnava tradition of Hinduism—and absolutely, but now we want Him to submit to our 'strength' and we ask 'clever' questions such as 'what has God done lately for me?'. This line of thought is closer to what the great anarchist Mikhail Bakunin said—"If God really existed, it would be necessary to abolish Him"—than to Voltaire's aphorism, "If God did not exist, it would be necessary to invent Him". We turn to god-men and gadgets to help us out, not to God. With them we have more patience, and even faith, than God. All this is due to the fact that, wittingly or unwittingly, both by what we do and (perhaps even more) by what we don't do, we are doing the opposite of what we want to do—lending support to the endogenous forces of immorality, wickedness, and evil. What we should constantly strive to do is to support the nobler part of us so as to empower it to have an upper hand over our nastier side. Henry Miller wrote, "Every day we slaughter our finest impulses". We slaughter by constantly singing the '*sutra* of success', which usually translates into academic excellence, professional progress, and making a lot of money. Success is also associated with control and power, and we act on the premise that 'every increase of power means an increase of progress'. Sometimes our success might be similar to what Mary Shelley wrote about Victor Frankenstein's success in creating a monster: "Success would terrify the artist; he would rush away from his odious handywork, horror-stricken. He would hope that, left to itself, the slight spark of life which he had communicated would fade; that this thing, which had received such imperfect animation, would subside into dead matter".[125] But like Frankenstein, we too cannot escape from the 'success of success'. We can succeed and fail, and fail and succeed, but we can never really know, in either case, if we are failing or succeeding. That is because both are relative and contextual. Our obsession with success is

---

[125] Source: Frankenstein (Curran, S., ed.). 2009. Mary Shelley's Introduction to the 1831 edition of Frankenstein. Romantic Circles. <https://www.rc.umd.edu/editions/frankenstein/1831v1/intro>.

so overpowering that when failure—the antithesis of what success stands for—stares us in the face, be it a term test in school, or in keeping a job or in love, and the whole world crumbles, life itself becomes both worthless and wearisome and the sutra turns out to be one for self-destruction. The success sutra is exacting a terrible price from society. The lead character in Greg Egan's story *The Infinite Assassin* (*Axiomatic*, 1991) proudly defines himself as "'I' am those who survive and succeed. The rest are someone else". That 'rest', that 'someone else' is, above all, the stranger within, the alien inside. But success is a measure as decided by others, which we ourselves deploy when dealing with others' success. We must also bear in mind another little-noticed factor. It is about what we take for granted almost routinely: everyday existence; what it could do to us; its grind and drudgery, what it entails, how much of our psychic and physical energy it extracts. In modern society, an individual cannot see himself, as Albert Camus wrote, beyond the routine and the ritual. All life is nothing but so many 'everydays'; every new dawn a new beginning. Everyday has a name, a particular day of the week, and a number in the calendar; the day and date is the setting for every triumph, the mundane and the magical. Nature gives so many chances to relive our lives; it makes every morning a new birth, to start all over again, and to die when we sleep. And no matter what we do, or don't, the war goes on.

The war within is not only a war for the control of our consciousness; it is also *within* the consciousness. In fact, they are the two aspects of the same war. The fight is really between 'mind-controlled consciousness' and 'heart-incubated consciousness'. This war is crucial for mind-control, and crucial for the cathartic cleansing of our inner cosmos. And for better behavior and for a world in harmony with itself. Unlike external wars, the aim cannot be to ensure permanent victory or total defeat of either of the two 'blood-brothers'. The human genus cannot afford the luxury of total and comprehensive victory of either of the two. Were that to happen, sooner or later, the human will be extinct. Not only do we need love, compassion, generosity, altruism but also things like anger, aggression, avarice, at the proper time and place. If they are not necessary, they wouldn't be there in the first place. Duality is not necessarily hostility. We have the tendency to view and label things either 'good' or 'bad', and wish to get rid of the 'bad'. They are as much a part of us as our 'better' ones. They are essential for the existence of the other. Without chaos there can be no order; without darkness we cannot experience light. In fact, even the so-called negatives, if rightly redirected, can do us a world of good. If we are all and only good inside, then too there will be trouble. What's good may not always be good, and what's bad may not always be bad in the world outside. On that most can assent. Some say that 'being kind and caring is a good thing—as long as the person you are kind and caring towards deserves your kindness'. Being forgiving may produce contentment—except when the forgiven has no plans to make amends. Even that may sound sensible. But in the crucible of give-and-take living, we find it very difficult to forget our hurts and forgive our tormentors. However, as Jack Kornfield puts it, not-forgiving is tantamount to 'giving up all hope of a better past'. In that sense, forgiveness is really not about someone's hurtful behavior; it is about our own relationship with our past. All this sophistry misses a central moral point. Why do some people go out of the way to help someone whom they hardly know, and why do many others pretend not to see or turn a Nelson's eye?

The tragedy of our life is that while it might well be possible to live a life without *consciously* helping anyone, it is simply impossible to live without hurting, intentionally or unintentionally, anyone anytime. All of us, at some time or other, hurt someone or the other, almost routinely and almost every day. We need to forgive and be forgiven. A withering glance, a wounding word, even killing one's own self can hurt another human being. It can happen anywhere, at home or at work. Anyone who has suffered a grievous injury knows that when our inner world is disrupted, it is difficult to concentrate on anything other than the person who caused it.

Forgiveness is easy because it is unilateral, an act of compassion towards the person who, not you, has to pay the price. The good we feel about ourselves, many psychological studies have shown, is tremendous. But in practice, we find it very hard to forget or to forgive. And that includes forgiving ourselves, which is sometimes harder than forgiving someone else. Instead of forgiving, we play the blame-game. In fact, it is easier to forgive than to forget; for forgiveness comes from the heart, and forgetting comes from the mind. Indeed, the heart is the fountain not only of forgiveness but also of love, kindness, and most of all, of mercy. If we can manifest these qualities in our life, we will also be strengthening the virtuous forces in the war within. If, for example, as Pope Francis implored, mercy—which he described as the ultimate and supreme act by which God comes to meet us—becomes 'the basis of all our efforts',[126] then the very context of our daily life will become compassionate. The opposite of compassion, we must remember, is not cruelty; it is complacency, which is what afflicts the most 'good'. Sometimes we face questions such as these: Can we be compassionate without taking sides in a dispute? In other words, can we be compassionate for both sides? And does that amount to encouraging evil? A thorny issue that all of us, even God, face, is how to balance mercy and justice, and which assumes paramountcy, in the infinite possible variations of human life. Mercy too at a point becomes unjust. Jesus, when asked how often one should forgive, said, up to 'seventy times seven'.[127] Lord Krishna, in the Mahabharata, promised that he will forgive Sisupala ninety-nine times, and slayed him the hundredth time. Simply put, what we do and what happens has a huge bearing on what happens after death. This message comes out strongly in what has been called the *Myth of Er* in the last chapter of Plato's *Republic*. Socrates says that not only do justice

---

[126] Source: Ivereigh, A. 2015. Pope Presents Curia With List of Virtues to Counter Temptations. Mercatornet. 30 Dec 2015. Retrieved from <http://www.mercatornet.com/above/view/pope-presents-curia-with-list-of-virtues-to-counter-temptations/17391>.
[127] Matthew 18:22.

and justness, and injustice and unjustness, and good and bad, play a huge role after death, but also implies that Er was chosen to be the messenger to humanity about what he has seen take place between death and new birth. In the words of Socrates, "For each in turn of the unjust things they had done and for each in turn of the people they had wronged, they paid the penalty ten times over, once in every century of their journey... But if they had done good deeds and had become just and pious, they were rewarded according to the same scale".[128]

We can also see the war within in the form of a clash between mercy and justice, or intuition and intellect. Einstein once said, "The intuitive mind is a sacred gift and the rational mind is a faithful servant. We have created a society that honors the servant and has forgotten the gift". That again is a fallout of the Internal War. What we need is harmony and positive balance in the consciousness. If we can shift the center of gravity of our consciousness away from intellect to intuition, our vibration begins to change; we begin to feel greater levels of peace and well-being in our life. If we can induce such a shift, as it were, we will begin to realize that we are a powerful spirit, experiencing 'being human' for a period of time, and not a human being striving for a spiritual experience. The stakes are simple but stark: whether the human continues to be the most malicious creature that ever walked on earth until he implodes or immolates and cripples earth itself, or if he will mend course through a 'conscious' consciousness-change and becomes a benign being, a soothing, spiritual presence on earth. Many great thinkers have long recognized that imperative, and some have predicted an impending leap in human consciousness. In 1974, the American professor of psychology Dr. Clare W Graves wrote an article for *The Futurist* magazine, titled *Human Nature Prepares for a Momentous Leap*, in which he described it as "The most difficult, but at the same time the most exciting transition the human race has faced to date. It is not merely

---

[128] Plato. Republic. [Translated by G.M.A. Grube; revised by C.D.C. Reeve. 1992. Indiana, USA: Hackett Publishing.].

a transition to a new level of existence but the start of a new movement in the symphony of human history".[129] Some predict what Terence McKenna called *The Archaic Revival*, of the emergence of a 'Global Tribe'. Everything else other than consciousness-change, the shape and form it will take, are but mere details. But then, as is said, often the devil is in the detail. Those details are our daily deeds, what Coleridge describes as the "petty things of daily life".[130] As for 'God', man's mind has effectively rendered him an opportunistic option; no longer a necessary nuisance. We have turned the aura of divine sanction to whip up our darker urges, and we have come to believe that if we are pious, we do not need to be pure at heart, that if we are devout, we do not have to be decent, and that if we try to get closer to God, we can be callous to human suffering. Nobody wants to suffer; everyone shuns it except those who see it as a way to constantly seek God. In the Mahabharata, the mother of the virtuous Pandavas, *Kunti*, prays to Lord Krishna to bless her with perpetual sorrow, as she realizes that if sorrow deserted her, she would cease to seek Him. It brings to mind what Keats said about sorrow: "But cheerly, cheerly, She loves me dearly; She is so constant to me, and so kind: I would deceive her, And so leave her, But ah! she is so constant and so kind... But now of all the world I love thee best" (*Ode to Sorrow in Endymion*, 1818).

Once we recognize and accept and come to terms with this bedrock reality of this war within, and its implications and impact on our life, all contradictions, confusion, and conundrums will dry up. Our task will then become very simple and straightforward: to do all we can to help the kinder and gentler better-half be the dominant partner. The ebbs and flows of the war are so continuous and shifting that we become unsure of everything because our fortunes and misfortunes reflect the state this war at that time. That keeps us always in an ambiguous state, always on the

---

[129] Graves, C.W. 1974. Human Nature Prepares for a Momentous Leap. The Futurist. Retrieved from <http://www.clarewgraves.com/articles_content/1974_Futurist/1974_Futurist.html>.

[130] Coleridge, S.T. 1798. The Rime of the Ancient Mariner.

edge, and prevents us from making up our mind and to act upon what we even know to be the right thing. To illustrate, even assuming that 'being moral' is good for our own well-being, we are plagued with nagging questions. Is it universal and timeless or is it subject to time and space? And if it is both or neither, how does one distinguish the timeless from the time-bound, and the perennial from the particular? Does a 'higher' moral end justify 'lesser' immorality? Or, in *dharmic* terms, should we sacrifice the lesser dharma that is enjoined upon fewer people at the altar of the greater dharma that contributes to the cause of the greater good? This is the question that emerges out of the Indian epic Mahabharata. So much scholasticism has accumulated on this subject that there is a whole winnow of metaphysical knowledge, generally called moral philosophy or ethics, that deals with questions such as the right and wrong of what we do and how we ought to live our lives. And it is so closely interwoven with religion that morality without religion is deemed not only dangerous but also blasphemous. The entrenched belief is that God either crafted the moral sense during creation, or inspired religion to show us the path to morality. There are others who argue that there is nothing divine about morality, that habit is purely a human expediency and an atheist can be equally, if not more, moral than a theist.

The Three 'M's and the War Within

While consciousness-change entails altering the current content and character of our consciousness so that the very dynamics that drive our thinking, feeling, and experiencing change, contextual-change encompasses change in the way we create our living context. In that context, at this tumultuous time, the three most important constituent parts are the triad of the three 'M's—morality, money, and mortality. Unless we induce and orchestrate a paradigm shift in our conception and understanding of what they ought to mean in modern life, we will continue to lose the war within. On all three fronts, we need to go back to the drawing board, so to speak, to break out of the box and turn the three obsessions into openings and opportunities to tilt the scales in the war within. These are so intricately embedded in human consciousness that there is nothing we can do without the underpinning of one or two or all the three. Of the three, it is the magnetic might of money that is now at the frontline of both human transformation and planetary destruction. And the time has come to comprehensively rethink its role in human destiny. Invented as a means of exchange, money has no intrinsic value, but allows us to ascribe relative values to all things. Money is more portable, more durable, more easily exchanged and hence more sought after than other goods. It is almost a cliché to say that time is money, but time is also life, and we ought to demur at putting a price on our own lives. Money's very pervasiveness and transformative power also makes it a translucent instrument, a spiritual tool. Money, righteously earned and shared, can make the world so much better. There is no doubt that money makes the world go round. The deterministic role of money was long foreseen in scriptures. In detailing the traits of the age of *Kali Yuga*, it was written several millenniums ago that: "In the Kali Yuga, people will seek only money. Only the richest will have the power. People without money will be their slaves". And even more tellingly, "The leaders of the state will no longer protect the people, but plunder the citizenry through excessive taxation". There is hardly a moment in our life when money ceases to be a factor in earning, saving, spending and even more in thinking. We will have to rack our brains to think of anything bereft of a money angle. And there is hardly a crime without a money-motive, and money is a big factor in many suicides, even homicides, that occur these days. It is man-made but it has become the most finite of all finite resources and everyone is short of it, individuals, businesses, countries and the material world.

Money is hydra-headed, each head sensitive to the purpose and circumstance. It is salary when an employer compensates you for your work, wages for your sweat; dowry if a father pays it to get his daughter married; dividend if a company pays it to a shareholder; interest if a bank pays you for keeping your money; donation if it is given to charity; ransom if given to kidnappers; bribe if given for illegal favors; alimony if it figures in a divorce, and so on. In multiple ways, we discriminate race, caste, color, religion, ethnicity, but they all vanish if one has enough money. It gives respectability to everything we seek, and every position and power—political, social, economic—comes within reach. Making money do what we want, and not doing what it tries to make us do is morality. In reality, man is now marginalizing morality and trying to overcome mortality. When one does not have money, the only other alternative, as some are discovering, is to go back to the body; use it to trade for money to live, and to make a living. Mortality has been called the ultimate leveler in human life; that all men are finally reconciled in death. That whatever we achieve or fail to achieve, rich or poor, powerful or powerless, acclaimed or anonymous, everyone will end up the same way, become a cold corpse, which the living hasten to destroy lest it linger and not let us live. Money is now threatening to undermine that central tenet. If you are really rich you can afford to extend your life span far more than that of others, if not to become immortal. Money can *make* man do anything, even murder one's own near and dear, a spouse, one's own child, a friend. And money by itself can *do* almost anything, can empower a life of dignity, erase social deprivation, even save a life; or make us greedy and gluttonous, erode sensitivity and compassion. Money and murder are increasingly getting interconnected, and no relationship is immune, intimate or professional. Spouses have killed each other, children their parents, friends their friends, business associates their colleagues, and so on, when greed turned deadly. What are called 'dowry deaths' and 'contract killings' are murders for money. The insatiability of money is such that no one feels he has enough to satisfy his desires, dreams, and delights. The limit that worries our mind is not things like limits to growth. Everyone feels 'limited' by money—individuals, the ultra-rich to the dirt-poor, corporations, even nation-states.

It is at the heart of every crisis we face, environmental, economic, and moral. It is to have *more* money that we put poison into the air we breathe, into the water we drink, and into the food we eat, and at the same time to become immortal. Fritjof Capra makes a telling point when he says, "We accept ever-increasing rates of cancer rather than investigate how the chemical industry poisons our food to increase its profits".[131] And yet, it is but a tool, an instrument, a means, and a medium, although of late we have made it an end in itself.

Money occupies our mind, but it doesn't have a mind of its own, at least not yet. As of now, the master is the mind, what Swami Vivekananda described as a demon-possessed, scorpion-bitten, drunken monkey. Buddhism uses the psychological metaphor of 'monkey-mind'. Adi Sankaracharya, in his famous poem *Bhajagovindam*, called it *mudhamati*, the foolish mind. It is such a monkey that controls our consciousness, and is at the helm of our lives. If our mindset, or as some like to say, 'mindsight', remains frozen about the three 'M's, and if consciousness remains static, then both changes—consciousness or contextual—will remain static. Because, if we do not learn to deal with them differently, one might say *spiritually*, then it makes no difference what else we can do. We must also at once note another dimension. It is that the very place and position of man in the cosmos has fundamentally changed. The human is no longer merely another biological being. He is now an 'ecological serial killer',[132] 'the deadliest force in the annals of biology',[133] a geological force. And humans are "running geologic history backward, and at high speed".[134] In biologist Edward Wilson's words, man is a "geophysical force, swiftly changing the atmosphere and climate as well as the composition of the world's fauna and

[131] Capra, F. 1984. The Turning Point: Science, Society, and the Rising Culture. Bantam. Reissue Edition (1 Aug 1984).

[132] Harari, Y.N. 2013. Sapiens: A Brief History of Humankind. Vintage. p.74.

[133] Harari, Y.N. 2013. Sapiens: A Brief History of Humankind. Vintage. p.82.

[134] Kolbert, E. The Sixth Extinction: An Unnatural History. New York, USA: Henry Holt.

flora". That is happening alongside another important happening. That very force that made man such a force has also biologically enfeebled him, as compared with his ancestors,[135] and the trend appears to be accelerating. For instance, we are told, today's children are growing weaker as computers replace outdoor activity.[136] Not only our bodies but our brains too will become weaker with computers and other gadgets doing much of what we used to do before, and they will leave us even stupider.[137] The irony is that we are trying to become more efficient decision-makers and aiming to go 'beyond the brain' and, at the same time, the brain has come to the conclusion that being 'beyond' in situ is too much of a bother and, in line with man's lure of short-cuts, it is easier to go external. And that also fulfills another craving of the human—the urge to mate or merge with, or dissolve into something or someone like the divine or the beloved. Now, we say the divine and the beloved are too troublesome, too opinionated, can be too demanding, and in any case, life is short and we have no time to waste on such loony pursuits. As a rebound and as an extension of our materialistic mindset, that urge is manifesting as the machine. For, unlike the beloved, we can embrace the machine without being rebuffed, and unlike the 'divine', we can insult it without inviting its wrath.

The ultimate spiritual aim and end of all life, even creation, is unity, merger, and dissolution, to lose one's distinctive identity. It manifests in many ways both spiritually and sensually. Prophets and wise men aim at 'dissolution' to serve humankind. Some call transcendence spiritual

---

[135] Source: How Modern Humans Have Become Weaklings Compared With Our Ancient Ancestors Who Could Outrun and Outlift today's Top Athletes. *Daily Mail Online*. 28 Apr 2014. Retrieved from <https://www.dailymail.co.uk/sciencetech/article-2614780/How-FARMERS-fitter-athletes-Human-strength-speed-peaked-7-300-years-ago-declining-rapidly.html>.

[136] Source: Children Growing Weaker as Computers Replace Outdoor Activity. *The Guardian International Edition*. 21 May 2011. Retrieved from <http://www.theguardian.com/society/2011/may/21/children-weaker-computers-replace-activity>.

[137] Source: How Today's Computers Weaken Our Brain. *The New Yorker*. 9 Sep 2013. Retrieved from <http://www.newyorker.com/tech/elements/how-todays-computers-weaken-our-brain>.

dissolution. The 5ᵗʰ-century Chinese philosopher Lieh-Tzu said that division and differentiation are the processes by which things are created. Since things are emerging and dissolving all the time, you cannot specify the point when this division will stop. Indeed, death is dissolution; we dissolve, or merge into the elements. One such sublime experience while we are alive is what we call 'being in love'—we say things like 'I am you; we are the same one'; 'I am thee also now. You are me now'. We just want to dissolve, merge or vanish into the one we are in love with. Man's ultimate goal is the same: to dissolve into the divine. Indeed, that is the purpose of human birth, which, therefore, makes it very important not to waste it, or leave it empty-handed. Modern man, exasperated with his fellow-humans and disenchanted with the divine, has fallen in love with his own child: the machine, much like *Pygmalion*, the Greek mythological figure. That process is called *whole brain emulation* (WBE) or mind-uploading—simulating a human brain in a computer with enough detail that the simulation becomes, for all practical purposes, a perfect copy and experiences consciousness. Pope Francis described this as turning human beings into 'ghosts trapped inside machines'. The apprehension that people might actually fall in love with their smart pet appliances like responsive-robots, with whom or with which they spend far greater amounts of time each day than with humans, is now being taken seriously by psychologists and social scientists. Incredible as it may seem, according to one study, men cannot stay away from their smartphones for more than 21 seconds, while that time-lag is 57 seconds for women. John Lennon once said, "If everyone demanded peace instead of television sets, then there will be peace". Now, we should substitute the smartphone for a TV set. And we tend to think that peace is for politicians to worry about, not us. But the truth is that what we demand depends on what happens in the world *within*.

Technology is also messing up all the three 'M's and pushing humanity headlong into murky, unchartered waters. Death is thus far the final finality, and must be dealt with first among the three. It is also at the frontline of the scientific agenda. It is to confront and defy nature and negate the three things that nature has ordained for all animate life on earth: decay, disease, and death. That we cannot escape it is exemplified by the lives of prophets. A particularly good one is the life of the Buddha. On his way to becoming a Buddha, he conquered the mighty *Mara*, which actually means killer, liberating himself from the frailties and forces within him that rendered him mortal, and yet he too suffered the pangs of old age, and finally died from disease. Even Lord Krishna, revered as the complete personification of godhead, died stricken by the arrow of a hunter due to mistaken identity or, as some say, to pay for an adharmic act in his previous incarnation as Rama... Science is, in effect, saying that what avatars and prophets and sages could not surmount, *science* can. Not only that, we can have it both ways: we can be both, 'be dead' and 'be alive', and even if a loved one is clinically dead, we can virtually keep that person alive in a machine and be able to interact with him or her, whenever we want! It is also claimed that "Avatars would be created using a process called *photogrammetry*, which can accurately reconstruct a virtual three-dimensional shape of a human being from existing photographs and video. Computer voice synthesis will take into account local and regional accents to deliver a more accurate representation of what they sounded like. The digital lifeform would also be linked up to social networks and large databases so they would be kept up to date with their relative's activities and could communicate with them about their day".[138] All this is still science-fiction, but by now we should be wary of such stuff; they can surprise and show up. But all this once again raises the question: What constitutes a 'person', and which of that is to be 'uploaded'? Are we a clump of molecules moving and interacting in a way to create what we call '*Homo*

---

[138] Simon McKeown, quoted in the post *Can the Internet Make Loved Ones 'Immortal'?* by Denyse O'Leary on 4 Nov 2015. Retrieved from <Mercatornet, http://www.mercatornet.com/connecting/view/can-the-internet-make-loved-ones-immortal/17119#sthash.Pr7rcqbO.dpu>.

sapiens', 'brain', 'personality', or 'you', or is there an unknown X-factor? What about consciousness? Will that be transference or transformation?

The Cherokee's Two Wolves

But no new moral reconstitution will even remotely become probable unless we go *within* and shift the fluctuating fortunes of the war within, the greatest, the longest and the most fateful of all wars. The idea that even as we fight external wars, we ourselves are a war zone, that two sides of our own psyche fight for supremacy, has long been a part of ancient wisdom and indigenous folklore. Notable among these is a Cherokee story, in which a grandfather tells his grandson that inside each of us, a constant battle goes on between two wolves. He says that one 'wolf' is *Evil*: it is anger, jealousy, greed, malice, resentment, inferiority, lies, and ego. The other 'wolf' is *Good*: it is joy, peace, love, hope, humanity, kindness, empathy, and truth. Hearing this, the boy ponders for a while and asks which wolf will eventually win. The grandpa replies, "The one you feed". In another version, the grandpa says, "If you feed them right, both will win", because a starving wolf will become more dangerous, but "make sure the 'good wolf' is fed more". This is how the battle unfolds in our 'within'. We feed the wolves inside us by the way we live, the way we relate with other living beings, and that in turn, depends on who calls the shots inside us. We must realize that every day we make choices, important choices that are liable to be overlooked as being trivial—and these choices define us; they constitute the 'feed' to the wolves. They are a statement of who we choose to be in this life and what impact we will have on the world around us. Philosophers like Marcus Cicero put it differently: "The enemy is within the gates; it is with our own luxury, our own folly, our own criminality that we have to contend". We are left bewildered by our own behavior. We could discuss and debate on moral principles and ethical objectivity and on how to anchor our conduct, and if that should be the greatest good of the greatest numbers or by the application of a universal litmus test, or by balancing conflicting moral obligations and duties. That is futile, as we have known all along, because the methods and means we mobilize for the task are themselves inadequate, even improper. That is why most of our choices and decisions are flawed. For, the real choices and decisions would already have been made in the cosmos within before we get down to it. It is like trying to put a Band-Aid on an internal bleed, or closing the stable door after the horses have bolted.

If we are to find a way forward and make man a better being and even to make earth a less-endangered planet, we must shift our gaze within and recognize that the most seminal of all struggles is in our own self. The nearest yet farthest space is inner space; the most impenetrable barrier is the periphery of our very body. The tragedy is that we all have the answers to all our questions within ourselves; it is just that we haven't learnt how to get in touch yet. It is like starving, while the food we need is in a locked room next door, and the key lost in the ruins nearby. We have to find the lost key or break through the wall. For that, we must *go within*. A Buddhist saying goes, 'Look within, thou art the Buddha'. Marcus Aurelius said, "Look within. Within is the fountain of the good, and it will ever bubble up, if thou wilt ever dig". To dig within or, in Yeats' poetic phrase, 'entering into the abyss of himself', or in the words of Tennyson, 'temple-cave of thine own self', is a recurrent refrain, and a central message in all religions. Jalal ad-Din Rumi described it as the 'long journey into yourself'; and for the poet-philosopher Iqbal, it was to 'pass from matter to spirit'. Carl Jung said, "Your vision becomes clear when you look inside your heart. Who looks outside, dreams. Who looks inside, awakens". Many simply call it a spiritual journey, the journey which, as human beings, we are expected to go on, a journey not to go somewhere but, in Aldous Huxley's words, "in the dissipation of one's own ignorance concerning one's self and life", which is "the finding of God as a coming to one's self". It is only through such a journey that we can achieve the greatest of all conquests, the conquest of the self, and the highest of all freedoms, the freedom of one who has overcome himself. It is only through such a venture that it will become possible to, as ancient wisdom exhorts us, 'rouse thyself by thyself'. It is only by undertaking, at least consciously choosing to go within that we can discover the kind of alchemy we need most of all, the ability to cleanse our consciousness.

Some evolved souls experience divinity by cultivating what has been called a 'two-fold existence'. Swami Mukteswar, the guru of Paramahansa Yogananda, explains that "Saints who realize their divinity even while in the flesh know a similar two-fold existence. Conscientiously engaging in earthly work, they yet remain immersed in an inward beatitude". He described the interior of our being as an 'Eden within'. It is also the darkest and brightest of places; dark as it harbors all our negative impulses, and bright as it not only offers a home to our positive feelings and emotions but also to the Almighty. According to the Upanishads, transcending the bounds of knowledge into the realm of realization is the spiritual journey man is born to embark upon. In effect, this means overcoming or overpowering the hold of the brain/mind over our consciousness. This is the trick or prank that nature has played on us. On the one hand, it has given us the marvel of a brain, which has enabled and empowered us to outflank, outsmart, and prevail over physically much stronger species. On the other hand, it has ensured that our overwhelming dependence on this very marvel keeps us confined to those very bounds of knowledge that we should cross to fully realize human potential. And, as William James noted, we live 'half-awake' and 'habitually fail to use powers of various sort'.

The Quicksand Within the War Within

The war within, unlike other wars that end at a certain time with a victor and a vanquished, is a continuous continuum, and will never come to a definitive closure. It is a war with millions of mini-wars, or little battles that are fought every day, every hour or every minute, in which there is a transient winner. Such is the level of our ignorance that what we are surmising about the war within is actually internalizing what is happening in the world outside. That is the basis for the premise that it is an epic struggle between good and evil. We may not know much but we do know enough to know that what goes on deep down inside, shapes what we are, and how we behave, and it has a vital bearing on what goes on in the world beyond our bodies. It is this war that decides if we will rise up to our noblest potential or go down to the lowest, meanest depths. What we call our 'behavior' is purely a reflection, indeed a mirror image, of the seesaw battles with fluctuating fortunes. How we behave, how we act and react are all mini-manifestations of the state of the war at that point and time. We do not see the battles or the rubble; we don't feel it or experience it; we hear no rumblings of guns blazing, or the shouts of the winner or the screams of the loser. Life goes on with innumerable chores and choices, delights and disappointments, triumphs and tragedies and all the while we think these are all our doings—of our free will, or of Fate or God. Yes, they do play a part, pull a string or two in the *karmic kathputli* (the karmic puppets), but they do that in the internal theater. All that we witness in the world—all the terrible horrors, insanity, cruelty, terrorism—are but a display of the state of the war within and the perpetrators. And all the wars, conflicts, wickedness, and viciousness in the world are but sparks and skirmishes in comparison with this insidious internal incinerator. Being at war has been the state of the world. According to one estimate, during the last 3,000 years, the world has been at peace for only 240 years; that is less than 10% of the time. This is but an enlarged reflection and extension of the internal war. We must understand that there is no question of winning this internal war. We need the negative as much as the positive to continue to exist within us to survive in the world outside. The ideal state of this war is a state of stalemate, with the virtuous forces having an edge in most of the daily battles within the war. If we somehow manage to ensure that the good that is in us prevails in these mini-wars, then all the intractable problems we are grappling with will become manageable.

The universe within we variously call mind, consciousness, sub-consciousness, soul inside, and so on. The locus and focus of our effort has to be in that bounded but limitless space. That space is also sometimes compared to dry quicksand; every step we take to get out gets us deeper down. As Jess Scott says, "It was alarming, how humans could spend entire lifetimes engaged in all kinds of activities, without getting any closer to knowing who they really were, inside" (*The Other Side of Life*). Without such cathartic cleansing and churning and looking within, we cannot morph the fundamentals of what it entails to be human on earth. We cannot go forward on any of the problems and issues, or mend our behavior unless we recognize that the greatest and most tenacious of all wars is taking place right within each of us, and we are barely even conscious of it. Even 'external' wars and natural disasters are brought about by the inner vibratory balance of good and evil being disturbed by an ascendancy of harmful vibrations and resultant human actions. If we can rectify and restore the inner equilibrium in each of us, or at least in a critical mass of mankind, then such outbreaks will be far fewer. But we need minimal but sufficient numbers to succeed, to change the direction of human endeavor. Swami Vivekananda said, "A few heart-whole, sincere, and energetic men and women can do more in a year than a mob in a century". How many are those 'few', and what the threshold is, crossing which unleashes an unstoppable momentum, we do not know, and perhaps will never know. That 'threshold' can be any of us, and so we must believe and behave. There is also an important change in the dynamics which we must take note of. Human evolution has entered a new phase, a new direction: the blurring of the boundary between individual and community. Henceforth, things can get done, problems get resolved only through men living in tandem for the common good. Even the next avatar, the cosmic savior, might be a conglomerate, not an individual entity. The Buddhist monk and author Thich Nhat Hanh in fact foresees that "It is possible that the next Buddha will not take the form of an individual. The next Buddha may take the form of a community—a community practicing understanding and loving kindness, a community practicing mindful living. This may be the most important thing we can do for the survival of the earth". An individual is necessary but not sufficient for human transformation.

The most negative of all—the main malaise of man—is malice, which is the most destructive of all emotions, distinct from envy and jealousy, and perhaps the only truly unique thing about this animal. There is nothing 'self', or even selfish about malice; it is all about 'others'; wishing them ill without any self-gain; capable of feeling unhappy about others' happiness; of rejoicing in another's misfortune. In that sense, unless we can get rid of the malice in our mind, we are not even equal to other animals emotionally. It has been reported that recent neurological research has revealed that in many individuals, the amygdala and its associated systems in the brain, which are responsible for the negative emotions are becoming prominently enlarged, at the expense of other areas such as the hypothalamus, which is responsible for people's sense of well-being and happiness. We have always had within both the negative as well as the positive emotions like love, kindness, tenderness, compassion, sharing, solidarity, and connection to others. But they were for long in large measure evenly matched, in a state of balance. It is the breaking of the balance, which started a few millenniums ago, that marked the beginning of corruption of the human condition, alienation from nature and solidification of the sense of separateness. The tragedy is that although, as neuroscience tells us, our brain's very design makes it sociable, inexorably drawn into an intimate brain-to-brain linkup whenever we engage with another person, our competitive culture has come to identify our very identity with separateness. In a practical sense, we have different bodies; therefore, we are 'separate'. There is inevitably some distance between any two of us, but that gives an opportunity to share the space in between. But it has become a crippling disability that deters complementing each other. We exist, work, and live always with other people, but we have not found a way to build bridges between being 'near each other' and being 'together'.

The madness and mayhem on this planet is largely due to our inability to achieve a balance within, and with, ourselves. For a more harmonious and happier human being, the restoration of this balance is an imperative. For better human behavior, we have to ensure that the 'positive' emotions prevail in the process of decision-making. The only way for that is to alter the course of this eternal internal war. Outwardly, the war within manifests as a moral injury or trauma, which is the clutch of the throat, twitch in the stomach, which we feel whenever we violate what each of us considers right or wrong. But we quickly put it away, lest it become too bothersome. That, in turn, translates into the plethora of ills that we experience in everyday life: indifference, intolerance, injustice, callousness, cruelty. All or some of them have existed in human society from time immemorial, but never before have all found a safe haven at the same time in our within, nor has their virulence been so scorching. The war is fought not only between two forces; its influence and impact are also two-fold. The war, and the myriad battles within, affects, even determines the content of our consciousness as well as our earthly conduct. And, on the side, we can influence the course of the war through our will and behavior.

Technology and the War Within

Whether technology *per se* is ethically inert or morally malevolent, its power and potential has other implicit consequences that we barely take note of. The anti-technology mass murderer Theodore Kaczynski (also known as the *Unabomber*) explained in his manifesto: "Due to improved techniques the elite will have greater control over the masses; and because human work will no longer be necessary, the masses will be superfluous, a useless burden on the system. If the elite are ruthless, they may simply decide to exterminate the mass of humanity. If they are humane, they may use propaganda or other psychological or biological techniques to reduce the birth rate until the mass of humanity becomes extinct, leaving the world to the elite". That scenario is certainly a possibility; so are potential risks in technological advances and frontier technologies like genetic re-engineering, nuclear power, and so on. But there are dangers in the current 'low' technologies also, indeed even in primitive technologies. How we use any technology, or any technique or tool, depends on who the user is, and how that technology or tool is harnessed. To be fair, there are a number of thoughtful and spiritual persons who think that modern science-based technology could do wonders to mankind and that the much-dreaded 'marriage' of man and machine might be for the mutual good. The Dalai Lama recently quipped, probably in a lighter vein, that he would not rule out the possibility of one day reincarnating as a computer! He says that man is also a 'machine with a consciousness'. Now, if a man-made machine, with man's help, acquires something akin to what we describe as consciousness—ability to feel emotions, for example—then will it transform into a 'living entity' like any of us? The question is not if technology, like everything in the universe is God's creation, and therefore spiritual. And not also, as the Dalai Lama says, that man too is a conscious machine. Both assumptions and inferences might be true or false; it does not matter much. The essential question is: what kind of 'consciousness' might it have and how does it get it? If it is from man (probably), and if its consciousness is anything like what man has now (most likely), then we are doubly-doomed. What kind of machines we might make and how we put them to use all depends on the state of human consciousness, particularly of those who are on the frontline of scientific research and spiritual search. We know that technology has not only been the defining force behind the military-industrial complex, but it has also unrecognizably altered the character of war and made the enemy-land (there is no such thing as warzone anymore) into a theater of massacre, an open-ended graveyard, a smoldering giant burning *ghat*. Even spirituality can be a negative force, if it is practiced by the wrong people.

Everything we do, even how we harness human creativity, depends on the state of the war within. A huge chunk of that creativity is currently manifesting itself not in the arts or letters, literature or painting, but in technology. The debate whether technology is double-edged or not, boon or bane, will never be settled. What is increasingly becoming apparent is that human consciousness, at the level at which it is operating, seems more hospitable to its negative power because consciousness itself is corrupted. As a result, technology is being put to use for elitist and divisive and destructive purposes. It is widening the chasm between plutocracy and the people, the elite and the masses to such an extent that some say that a no-holds-barred global class struggle is inevitable, spearheaded this time not by the working class but by the middle class. We are living at a time when people are seriously saying that "there is not a single aspect that doesn't have the potential to be totally transformed by these technologies of the future". The decisive impact that technology will make on our future hinges on the epic struggle inside us. Our tireless and ceaseless endeavor should be to reinforce and strengthen the positive forces like love, caring, compassion, sharing, humility, gratefulness, tolerance, and temperance that are caught in that struggle in our consciousness. Some say that the real combatants are gods: "There are gods at war within each of us. They battle for the throne of our hearts, and much is at stake". This is why idolatry is the most discussed problem in the entire Bible. Behind every such struggle that you and I have is a false god that is winning the war in our lives. Don't give in to the myth that gods are only statues that people of 'other' cultures or people of 'long ago' worshipped. Pleasure, romance, sex, money, and power are just a few of the gods that vie for our allegiance in today's society. Loss of self-control, both as individuals and as a species, has always been man's biggest problem, but never more needed or absent than now. It is at the root of all problems, from casual sex to catastrophic climate change, gluttony to global warming, broken homes to social breakdown. No one seems to be in control over their lives, emotions, feelings, desires, dreams, and drives. The less control we have within, the more we need it outside. And that lack of inner control is at the core of concern about our behavior. But there are some who worry what might happen if we are able to gain control over ourselves, that is, if we are able to intervene, meddle, and manipulate what goes on inside our consciousness. If we are free to make ourselves however we wish to be, if we are able to modify our motivations, what would we do? If we have the power, on whose side in the war within would we tilt towards? Would we become more 'humanely' human or more 'inhumanly' human, more compassionate or more callous?

The bottom line is that our *behavior*—which in practical terms means the kind of things we do to stay alive, to share the living space on earth with fellow-beings; to make a living, to amuse and entertain ourselves, to compete and to progress—defies our claim to be a rational race, or as the species with a *carte blanche* direct from God to rule over all life on earth. The irony, and tragedy, is that no other species and no other man of any other time, has been more 'busy' than the man of this day and age, with all the dazzling add-ons at his elbow. Yet his life, after it is done with 'being busy', is more barren and bereft of meaning than of anyone before. Man has long wrestled with this question: Life being 'given'—a blend of divine beauty, brutality, and barbarism—what then should I do with myself? Carl Jung agonized over this question in his autobiography *Memories, Dreams, Reflections*. He wrote, "I know only that I was born and exist, and it seems to me that I have been carried along. I exist on the foundation of something I do not know. In spite of all uncertainties, I feel a solidity underlying all existence and a continuity in my mode of being". He quotes Lao Tzu, "All are clear, I alone am clouded", and interprets it as Lao Tzu being a man with superior "insight who has seen and experienced worth and worthlessness, and who at the end of his life desires to return into his own being, into the eternal unknowable meaning". He ends with a hope: "Life is—or has—meaning and meaninglessness. I cherish the anxious hope that meaning will preponderate and win the battle". The battle, or the war, is in his own being, his 'within'. If Jung, with his great insight into the human psyche, was left with nothing more than 'anxious hope', what hope do *we* have?

Many, particularly the very young, often referred to as Gen-Y, are experiencing the pangs of the terrifying gravity of inner emptiness, the unbearable lightness of heavy hopelessness, the dreary drudgery of making a living. And many feel, looking at the coarseness of contemporary society, a numbing sense of moral despair at the enticing trappings of our soul-less civilization. We are more on the move than moving towards where it matters. We produce to discard, and what we consume does no good to anyone. We take and take, and take everything that appeals to our senses; we give no thought to how what we 'take' comes from, from where, and what it entails. If it is in the market, and if we have money, nothing else matters. How many fellow-humans are exploited, how much child-laborers are involved, how many trees are cut, and how many animals are tortured and slaughtered to get the things we 'take' from the marketplace or the shelves of a store, we give no thought to. Our clothes, fine or cheap, are our second skin and reflect our personal sense of style, taste, personality, culture, and even beliefs and values. But do we know, or care to know, how and where they are made? It is a huge industry, and the world clothing and textile industry (clothing, textiles, footwear, and luxury goods) generates several trillions of dollars annually, backstopped by sweatshop labor of women and children in poor countries or in totalitarian states, who work long hours in toxic environments at abysmally low wages. Fast fashion is the second biggest polluter in the world, second only to oil. We don't see them and we don't know them and we don't care. We feel good wearing 'sweat-and-blood-soaked' fancy clothes, and we have enough money to get them, and that is all that matters. The moral alibi is that that which is not within the immediacy of our knowing we cannot be held accountable for. Everything is a matter of marketing on mass media. Everything that happens, and even every image of horror, has to compete not only with other horrors, but also with images of consumer goods, toothpaste, cameras, luxury houses, etc. Because our attention span is limited, and sometimes seconds on the fleeting screen can cost millions, the image must grab our eye and mind instantly or else the money goes bad and all in vain. Repetitive exposure to such viewing has a numbing effect, and we need, each time— the sponsors and the marketing-gurus, who specialize in the production and specialization of such an image know that—more gripping and more horrific horrors. And watching them is when we relax, enjoy and be entertained! Distance mass production and mass marketing gives us the cover not to think of the process of production—where, how, and by whom an item is made—and of the attendant moral and ecological costs, and then we think that what stands between the image of an item and us is only money (if we have it we can get it), and the moral aspect gets marginalized.

Court of Conscience

It is again the mind that chooses how to put technology to use. The same robot that can be used in warfare can also enable a paralyzed man to lead a life of dignity. Since many remote areas of the globe lack all-weather access, scientists have invented transportation systems that use electric autonomous flying machines to deliver medicines, food, goods and supplies wherever they are needed. The message down the ages and across the oceans is always the same: everything in nature and everything man can make could be used constructively for the common good or destructively for collective doom. It is the make-up and mix, character and content of human intelligence that is the arbiter. The problem is not with either scripture or science, culture or civilization. It is in the nature of the beast, intelligence. And one of the drawbacks in our left-brain intelligence has been its inability to break the barriers between different religions, philosophy, and science and to inject what Abraham Maslow called 'being values', or meta-values, into other attributes like logic, devoutness, sincerity, passion, and fervor. That is how the religious personality can live in comfort with cruelty and callousness towards other people, and an honorable and upright scientist can, in 'good conscience' make weapons that kill thousands of people whose names and identities he will never even know. And the rest of us can lead normal lives with multiple personalities, which allows us to use a mask to cover our inconvenient faces! We are living in unsettling times and our mind-driven consciousness has annihilated, or abolished, what we used to call our 'conscience'. No one considers he is accountable, in Gandhi's phrase, to the highest court of conscience. We feel no moral pricks, hear no voices, no tugs of our gut; and it is not because it is all 'quiet on the inner front', but because all our seeking, all of our journey, our hunger for adventure is outwards and upwards. After all, we only want a good life, good sleep, a good career, good recreation and live eternally even if we are already dead within.

And we have failed to notice that what we are searching for in the universe is right within the 'inner universe': within our own selves. Ancient traditions and many religions have long told us that our heart and our gut are independent (though interconnected) sources of intuitive intelligence, which many animals too have, but which have become comatose for hundreds, if not thousands, of years. Scientists say that there are more neurons in our gut than anywhere else except within the brain, signifying that it is more than a place of ingestion, digestion, and excretion. The gut, along with the heart is called the 'intuitive brain'; these two organs are separate but are holistically connected with the brain in our head. If we can somehow awaken and activate them—the heart and the gut—they can, along with the brain, bring about the right blend in our intelligence. We have chosen to set aside the 'help' available within and we have lost the dart of longing love. What our creativity is laboring upon is to harness the machine to overcome the inadequacies of our brain-incubated intelligence. The rationale that is often offered is that the human brain is increasingly unable to cope with the complexity and contradictions, range and scope of factors that need to be harmonized for sound decision-making in the contemporary context, and, as a result, we have little choice but to rely on computers to supplement or even supplant human intelligence. One believes that computer systems that have access to, and are able to store, analyze and process, mountains of data almost instantly and objectively, can be better at decision-making than humans with their foibles, prejudices and with their tendency to look at every issue through the prism of personal benefit. The fact, they say, is that most people are severely limited in terms of the amount of information they could process at any particular moment in time, and are unable to carry out the mental operations necessary to make calibrated decisions. While that is a reasonable inference, the question is: are computer-aided or computer-made decisions truly objective non-human decisions? Some experts say 'not necessarily'; they say that it is wrong to think that computers are neutral. Algorithms can reflect the biases of their creators, which means they too are subject to the same limitations of human decision-making capabilities. This means that whether it is scientific activity or political problem-solving or computer-aided calibration, the orchestrator is the brain, and the intended purpose of insulating or marginalizing our choices and decisions from the weaknesses and vagaries of our brain/mind will not be achieved. That again means that if we want to improve human problem-solving capabilities we have to induce and orchestrate a paradigm shift in the very infrastructure of our intelligence that drives our lives. And such a shift has to happen within generations.

In embarking on this adventure, we must also realize that what we call intelligence is not the monopoly of man. Every creature, from ant to ape, from a plant to a dolphin has its own insignia of intelligence that is unique to that form of life, created in its own world, called *Umwelt*. There are as many umwelts out there as there are organisms, perhaps even many more, although they all share the same environment. We 'think' that we are the most intelligent, an assumption increasingly in question. It is now reported that crows, ravens, and rooks possess higher intelligence. We do not know about other creatures but man has multiple intelligences. We wrongly identify 'being gifted' with having a high intelligence quotient (IQ). So prized is the IQ that even one-year-olds are being subjected to tests to determine their score, so as to enhance it as a way to stay or succeed in the endless, self-defeating, or pointless pursuit. We want our kids to be smart, in fact smarter than others, as we believe that that will empower them to prevail in our highly competitive world. The key factor in life, we have come to believe, is to be 'smarter' than others. And we credit our very survival as a species to that single attribute. For many millenniums, we humans have considered ourselves superior primarily due to our large brains and our ability to reason, that we humans are exceptional by virtue, that we are the 'smartest in the animal kingdom'. It has been believed that human superiority is the decisive definition of man's place in nature and that it is ingrained in the genetic code of all of us. Even Aristotle, whom the *Encyclopedia Britannica* called the first genuine scientist in history, echoed this view and wrote that nature had made animals for mankind, 'both for his service and his food', and 'there is no such thing as virtue in the case of a god, any more than there is vice or virtue in the case of a beast: divine goodness is something more exalted than virtue, and bestial badness is different in kind from vice'. Spanish philosopher Ortega Gasset reassures us that "the greatest and most moral homage we can pay to certain animals on certain occasions is to kill them". If killing is a way to pay homage—it may well be so, from nature's point of view—then why not humans? And that, incidentally, is what we are doing!

There are different voices too about human uniqueness. Some say that we might not be as smart as we think, and that animals can have cognitive faculties that are superior to those of human beings, and that "the fact that they may not understand us, while we do not understand them, does not mean our intelligences are at different levels; they are just of different kinds".[139] If further substantiated—and even if not generically more intelligent, if it can be established that our animal-cousins can do some tasks more 'efficiently' than human animals—this could be one of the most sobering of spiritual revelations. Even more far-reaching and profound, it indicates the desired direction of evolution of human thought. It is to focus our attention on ways to bridge the abyss between human and non-human animals, to learn to treat them as full-fledged forms of life, like our own kin and kindred, not inferior beings deprived of all the feelings, emotions, pain, empathy, and camaraderie that we humans are capable of. That is another path to realize and 'know' God, the common Father and creator.

Whether or not we are the most intelligent and smartest of all animals, cognitively or functionally, is not really germane to the instant point. It is that our current brand of intelligence, which is left-brain incubated, is a big part of the problem, and not the solution. At its most basic level, it has not enabled us to cooperate and complement each other, at least to simply 'get along' with each other. What we need to do, and what we should do to our kids, is not to deepen our extant intelligence, but to broaden it to include others like emotional, interpersonal, social, and spiritual intelligences. The fact is this—which particular 'intelligence' dominates at any point determines what kind of 'world' we create, live in, experience, even imagine. Change of intelligence changes everything. In our case, it is the intelligence of the brain/mind that dominates us and the world of our experience, marginalizing others like emotional and spiritual intelligences. But it was not always so and it need not be forever. So, if we want to change the world for the better, we have to change the brand of our intelligence that drives our lives. It is not a matter of becoming *more* intelligent; it is about being *differently* intelligent. And that source

---

[139] Prof. Maciej Henneberg, quoted in 'Humans Not Smarter Than Animals, Just Different, Experts Say'. Phys.Org. University of Adelaide, Australia. 4 Dec 2013. Retrieved from <https://phys.org/news/2013-12-humans-smarter-animals-experts.html>.

of 'differently' must be *in situ*, germinated within our own selves, not exogenously or artificially, but outside the ambit of what we call the mind. The measure of how intelligent we are—our intelligence quotient—is what essentially differentiates man from man, the upshot of whatever we do as conscious beings. While a high IQ has obvious advantages in the human world, the idea that higher IQ is better, and that a certain level of IQ is required to achieve certain goals in life, has been proven wrong again and again. Ironically, a very low IQ, too, can be a life-saving alibi; it can literally save one from the gallows. Whether it is high or low, intelligence has come to mean the difference between success and failure, recognition and ridicule, genius and garden-type. Most of all, intelligence is prized for its problem-identification-solving capacity. The basic assumption is that our intelligence enables us to assemble and analyze all relevant facts, to take into consideration all the pertinent factors, and allows us to frame and make right choices for the right course of action. At this pivotal point in human history—which itself is a chronicle of human bungling and faux pas, and of the attempts made to cover them up, where many are aghast at what man has wrought on earth and where he is headed—it is this dimension that calls for careful study and reflection. First, we must recognize that the scope for our choice-making is very narrow. On the really important issues we have no choice. We have no choice over our earthly arrival: to whom we are born to or the place and time of our birth. We have no choice over the birth of our progeny. We have no choice over the time and place, even the way, of our earthly departure: death. And yet all our life we try to ward it off; and sometimes to embrace. If death is predetermined then does our drive towards physical immortality, tantamount to divine defiance, a dare to nature?

Even within this meager 'menu', the actual choices we make are highly circumscribed and conditioned; they appear as choices, but we are, in reality, the executors, the instruments. Choices make us more than we make them, and over time, we *become* what the real choice-makers want us to be. Jean-Paul Sartre simply said, "We are our choices". We make a choice among the choices offered to us, and they themselves are loaded. What is not on the table doesn't really exist, and the table itself is so crowded with such pseudo choices that the difference between them is actually, 'Twixt Tweedle-dum and Tweedle-dee'. Still, every choice has a ripple effect, both on our character and, something we scarcely are conscious of, on society.

The most worrisome aspect is that we have turned out to be, with all these caveats, poor choice-makers and problem-solvers. In fact, we tend to identify intelligence with problem-solving capabilities and we tend to believe that the better we are at problem-solving the more intelligent we are. Problem-solvers are usually highly regarded and rewarded. Yet the fact is that all through our history, problem-solving has been our weakest spot: skewed-prioritization, flawed decision-making, faulty harmonizing of competing demands. It is this that has led to all the problems we have faced, all the wars that we have waged, all the misery we have endured as a species. If we want more harmonious humankind and a more stable world, the 'problem' about problem-solving has to be addressed. The real problem is that often we cannot even agree on what the problem is; let alone how to resolve it. Basically, the problem is that our brain, more precisely the left-brain, consists of many specialized units designed by the process of evolution by natural selection for fragmented tasks. While these modules occasionally work together cooperatively and seamlessly, they don't do so always, resulting in impossibly conflicting beliefs, vacillations between patience and impulsiveness, transgressions of our self-supposed moral imperatives, and pompous views of ourselves. We have always been reasonably good at narrow advocacy and compartmental conception, and weak on holistic thinking, integration, and harmonization. In modern times it has gotten worse, because today's problems are more complex and convoluted, requiring precisely those very skills we lack or we do not possess in sufficient measure. To the point that we are unable to agree on what needs to be done to address any of our issues, what Shakespeare called 'sea of troubles'—political, social, economic, technological, environmental, psychological, and cultural. For example, what we see around us is chaos, creeping shadows, darkness, and horrors, but what we cannot make sense of is what the mute message is. We are lost in the darkness, but whether it is the darkness before dawn or the darkness at the midnight of the new moon, whether or not the darkness is of the 'maternal womb of a new consciousness', or of the chilling confines of a cold coffin, we can only surmise.

That mankind is on the threshold of an epic transition, we all concur. The trouble is that we are confused if what we see and experience in the world presages the dawn of a Utopia or the dim darkness of a Dystopia. Views vary if, as many fear, we are experiencing the death-throes of impending self-extinction or the faint birth-pangs of a new 'Axial Age' of 'spiritual unfoldment', which could lead to a profound consciousness-change or when 'singularity' comes calling. Human brains are chipped, or linked to computers, and a kind of man–machine merger is occurring. All three different scenarios appear, all are plausible, but there is no way to tell which one will be the winner. Here again, it depends on who, or which attributes, prevail in the war within. During the long length of human pre-history, our brain and our emotions were by and large, in tune, in a state of subtle balance. That balance was between what we call 'positive' or 'negative'. Our negative emotions such as anger, fear, anxiety, hate, and aggression were used for survival and hunting, and for the defense of the group or community against predators and rivals. They were entrenched and embedded within long after their need was not so strong, and have become more powerful through the inputs received from the outside world. The positive emotions such as love, kindness, compassion, and solidarity to others were brought to bear as a means to synergy in the community. And they have become weaker as they were starved of the nutrients from the external world. The principal reason for much of the aggression, wretchedness, wickedness, and hatred, which seem to be on the rise every day, is the growing ascendancy of the negative forces in the war within.

Every religion has recognized and warned us of this war within. Zoroastrianism calls it a war between the god of light and the god of darkness, and it advocates the simple formula of 'good thoughts, good words and good deeds'. Its founder Zoroaster was, in the words of Tagore, the "first man who gave a definitely moral character and direction to religion and at the same time preached the doctrine of monotheism which offered an eternal foundation of reality to goodness as an ideal of perfection".[140] And he showed the path of freedom to man, the freedom of moral choice. Christianity describes the 'war' as a fight between God and Satan. However one might view it or call it, deep inside all of us there is a struggle, tension, fight or war, which determines how we act or react, how we behave. There is in everyone a Dr. Jekyll and a Mr. Hyde; and perhaps many Jekylls and Hydes, particular to every situation and relationship. The 'universe' is within and the forces are internal, but the stakes are universal. It is not confined to the well-being and liberation of each of us; it directly and decisively affects the whole of humanity and the fate of the earth. The fact of the matter is that if we cannot control what happens inside, we cannot control what happens outside. A suicide is also an outcome of the war within. When some people say that something 'broke inside', what they mean is that they lost the battle, and that, in turn, led to ending it all. The irony is that while we have no qualms about species self-destruction, we have always been ambiguous about individual self-destruction. Our stance has wildly wavered between noble, heroic, and honorable, to mortal sin, heinous crime or cowardly act, between an 'act of genius' and a 'form of insanity'. On the species-scale not many agonize, because the individual mind cares as much or as little about the human as any other. The war is within, so are the barriers. Rumi wrote, "Your task is not to seek for love, but merely to seek and find all the barriers within yourself that you have

---

[140] Tagore, R. 2012. The Religion of Man. India: Niyogi Books. p.68.

built against it". The chief barrier is our own mind. Joseph Campbell said, "The ultimate dragon is within you".

All wars, between individuals or tribes or nations, are within our own selves, and we have to win that war for the future evolution of mankind. The Preamble to the Constitution of UNESCO declares that "since wars begin in the minds of men, it is in the minds of men that the defenses of peace must be constructed". Those 'defenses' have to be erected within. War, it has even been said, is a "biological necessity of the first importance... not only a biological law but a moral obligation... an indispensable factor in civilization".[141] Similarly, "War is not a pathology that with proper hygiene and treatment can be wholly prevented. War is a natural condition of the State, which was organized in order to be an effective instrument of violence on behalf of society. Wars are like deaths, which, while they can be postponed, will come when they will come and cannot be finally avoided".[142] At the outset of the First World War, Thomas Mann wrote, "Is not peace an element of civil corruption and war purification, a liberation, an enormous hope?"

All wars of all sorts, in the ultimate reckoning, are about 'control'. It is our irresistible urge for control, to prevail, to dominate, to impose our will that consumes our lives and causes so much misery and mayhem in the world. Control gives the feeling of power and satiates the desire for power; it allows us to humiliate and to feel superior. We want to control through knowledge, through privilege and position. In every relationship, there is an element of control. Through control, we exploit each other and it is innate to every dimension of the human way of life. The fact of the matter is that we virtually cannot live without exploiting someone or the other sometime or the other; at least we should not heap humiliation— the feeling of being put down, being made to feel less than one feels

---

[141] von Bernhardi, F.A.J. 1911. Germany And the Next War.

[142] Bobbitt, P. 2003. The Shield of Achilles: War, Peace, and the Course of History. New York, USA: Anchor.

oneself to be—not rob others of their dignity, not invade and violate their personal space. Deep inside our psyche, almost everyone harbors 'humiliation'. Wayne Koestenbaum (*Humiliation*, 2011) says, "I have lived with humiliation all my life, as I think all human beings do". WH Auden wrote in his work *In Solitude for Company*, "Almost all of our relationships begin and most of them continue as forms of mutual exploitation, a mental or physical barter, to be terminated when one or both parties run out of goods". What Donald Klein calls *The Humiliation Dynamic* is, in his words, "a pervasive and all too often destructive influence in the behavior of individuals, groups, organizations, and nations... from an early age, inescapable". As Klein puts it, it is not only the 'experience' of humiliation but also the 'fear of humiliation' that dominates human lives. It is implicit in every relationship of mutual-dependency. The fact is that there are many things we do in life which serve no purpose or self-interest except to humiliate others and get some kick out of it. Essentially it is a show of power, of sadism. It can be belittling and berating, the browbeating of the defenseless. It can be as simple or innocuous as raising one's voice, finding fault, admonishing, giving a dirty look, a withering glance; anything that hurts or injures another person's self-respect and sensitivity is humiliation. And much of it comes from the near and dear; more from the near than the dear. Prolonged proximity removes the veneer we hide behind and oftentimes brings out the worst in us. We become naked not only in the bathroom or bedroom, but also in the immediacy of intimacy and that can rob one of respect. Power corrupts more when the other person seems powerless. Imposing our will on anyone, even if for 'their own good' can trigger a feeling of humiliation. Gandhi said, "It has always been a mystery to me how men can feel themselves honored by the humiliation of their fellow beings". But there is a catch here. Sometimes we may be thinking we are honoring someone by our actions while in fact we are humiliating that person. Gandhi himself is a paradox. He imposed his will on others including his wife, and in one instance, coerced her to clean toilets. He might have been nobly motivated, but was he right to make someone do what they did not want to do? Perhaps there is no perfect answer. We do impose our will on someone or the other, at some time or other, knowingly or unknowingly, for good or bad reasons. If no one tries to control anyone else, does not impose their will on others, there will be no conflicts, no exploitation, no violence, and no wars. But that is as much an ideal as a violence-free world. The difference is that while violence is inherent in nature, *à la* the big fish eats the small fish, control seems to be endemic to the human species. Perhaps with few exceptions, other animals kill their prey primarily for food, not to seek to control or humiliate or hurt for their own sake. But exploitation, like violence, need not be only physical or materialistic. It can be—indeed is more—psychological, mental, emotional.

Our Two 'Hearts' and the War Within

The question about the morality of war has long been discussed. Morality is a crucial dimension of human life. We have long agonized over what we ought to do, should do, must not do, or may do, to make our life fulfilling and at the same time, make sure that it does not jeopardize others' lives. Is 'morality' man-made, a social convenience and necessity, or is it a divine injunction? If so, where is it codified and what is its irreducible essence? What is moral behavior and when is it morally right to do wrong things? Is a religious person inherently 'moral'? Should any war, which necessarily is violent and involves mass killing and maiming, be deemed moral, immoral, amoral, or evil? It has been said that 'morality has no place in the assessment of war'; or perhaps, more factually, we can say: morality, by definition and design, has no place in war. And hence the question of 'assessment' does not arise. In fact, one might say that man invented war precisely to abandon morality of every kind; to give license to evil of every imagination. But almost all religions that do not condemn war *per se*, sanction war, if not glorify it, in certain circumstances. There is also an implied sense that wars, which essentially entail the sudden death of large numbers of human beings, are necessary as a way, or the only way, to maintain the life-balance on earth. It is a part of the package of 'being human', nature's ruse to counter the human survival capacity. Basically, war is really a composite of two of our worst traits: avarice and aggression in an organized and virulent form. Some have argued that human beings, especially men, are inherently violent and, while this violence is repressed in normal society, it needs the occasional outlet provided by war. When we are not actually at war, our inherent urges like avarice, aggression, and violence get exposed in other non-war-like ways, no less lethal and more embedded in our daily life. Many have suggested that war-making is fundamentally cultural, imbibed by nurture rather than nature. Still, we cannot say it is another animal instinct; like that of a tiger, who needs to kill to live. It means that it is not germane to being human but is now as much human as anything else. What is intrinsic is the war within. The 19th-century Tibetan Lama Jamgon Kongtrul characterized the war thus: "From the outside, we appear to be genuine *dharma* practitioners; on the inside, our minds have not blended with the dharma. We conceal our afflictions (called *klesas* in Sanskrit) inside like a poisonous snake. Yet, when difficult situations arise, the hidden faults of a poor practitioner come to light". In fact, the 'war without' has become such a huge part of human history because the wrong side is winning the war within.

What incubates inside is 'perception' and what happens outside is 'behavior'; both of which influence each other reciprocally and simultaneously. What we perceive is what we become. The ancient rishi *Ashtavakra* says, "The reason why we grow old, age, and die is we see other people grow old, ageing, and dying. And what we see we become". Our predicament is that we do not know exactly what goes on inside us, but we do know that some kind of turmoil is constantly at work. We seem pulled by different forces, even from outside we can sense it and feel it; as if someone other than 'we' is calling the shots. We do not know exactly how but we do know that our brain, body, and behavior are connected and even our heart. We use almost involuntary expressions like 'I just feel that way'; I am in two minds; I have the gut feeling; I hear voices within or an inner voice; and I cannot prove it but I believe it, etc.—all symbolic of the war within. When Hermann Hesse said [he listens to] 'the teachings my blood whispers to me', he was referring to a voice from within. When we say 'I doubt it', it could well be someone suggesting what we call a 'second opinion'. When we say 'I am not so sure', it could be a word of caution offered by a more sober internal impulse. The trouble is that the inner voice talks to us in a soft whisper, and we cannot hear it in the downpour of the din of modern life. That is why many mystics and saints stay silent, to be able to listen to what the Bible calls the "still, small voice within". Our external wars are bloody events interspersed with periods of peace, or *absence* of a war. The war within is a continuum, without any interregnum or interruption, sometimes intense and fierce, and sometimes subdued and subtle, but always involuntary and effortless. If we do not know who is fighting whom and what the rules of warfare are, how can we take sides or try to influence the outcome? But, maybe, it is extreme naiveté to think of the inner struggle as a fight or war, in the sense in which these words occur in the external world. Both imply that one side must vanquish or destroy or decimate the other side, the opponent, and that we would be better off if we manage to eliminate the 'bad' side. This is a unique kind of war that should not conclude with a total victory or defeat of either of the two; that would be a greater catastrophe than the war itself. Both sides, the 'good' and the 'bad' have legitimate roles to play as they are the two sides of the *dwanda*, and it would be a catastrophe if one side manages to totally wipe out the other. Indeed, one might even say that one can derive creative power from the tension of the opposites, from the dialectics of dwanda. What has gone awry and what needs to be promoted is 'cooperative co-existence' and inner harmony. This brings up the timeless question: why do humans fight when they can share and live in a spirit of synergy? Is it biological or evolutionary? We fight because we don't like sharing, whether it is sharing food or shelter, fame or fortune, success or glory. It is this inability to partake that is at the root of all friction, conflict, and war in the world. We want to possess, own everything. Our mind likes exclusivity, not inclusiveness.

Kurukshetra—Arjuna's War Within

An analogy often invoked to mirror the war within is the great *Kurukshetra* war in the Indian epic Mahabharata. This war, which lasted 18 days, took place at a place in North India called *Kurukshetra*. What is unique about this war is that it happened in the direct presence of the Divine, Lord Krishna, the only perfect incarnation of Lord Vishnu. It resulted in all that horrific bloodshed, killing of a brother by a brother, of a student by a teacher, of a grandson by a grandfather, not to speak of tens of thousands of others. It was a war that not even Lord Krishna could prevent, although it is open to question whether really He could not or did not want to prevent. In the very end, Krishna asks Arjuna: "O Dhananjaya! Conqueror of wealth, have you heard it with an attentive mind? Have your ignorance and illusions been dispelled?" Of course, Arjuna said 'yes'. It is important to recognize that what dispelled Arjuna's moral qualms about fighting was not the answers and arguments of Krishna, but ultimately the absolute and unconditional surrender of his ego at the Lord's feet. It is also important to digest the truth that Krishna's real target audience was not just Arjuna, but all humanity for all times. The goal of Krishna's discourse was not only to induce Arjuna to win his war within, but also to help *us* win our own inner spiritual wars.

The Kurukshetra war offered an opportunity to Lord Krishna to propound the great Bhagavad Gita, which has served as a beacon and balm for tens of millions of people, some of whom, paradoxically, were pacifists like Tolstoy and Thoreau and Emerson. Thoreau called it the 'First of Books'. Gandhi said, "I have received more nourishment from the Gita than my body has from my mother's milk". Tens of thousands, including the *Narayana sena* (Krishna's own army), were killed, through means fair and foul. Here is an important moral issue worth noting. Krishna gave His own army to the evil Duryodhana, when the latter, along with Arjuna, came to seek Krishna's help. The intriguing question is, why didn't Krishna refuse to provide any assistance, and say that He would only help the righteous side? The answers to such questions are that there are no absolutes, even when it comes to good or evil, and one must choose sometimes among conflicting compulsions. The right course for one person might not be the right one for another person in the same circumstance. And it is possible that for the same question there could be more than one right answer, which is what quantum physics now tells us. Each one must decide for oneself. That is why, it is so important to have the right consciousness, and that is why, consciousness-change is so important for correct decision-making.

The moral message is that whether we do good or bad, it is the motive and purpose that matters, and it has to be done regardless of whatever consequences, good or bad, that might follow. To a limited extent, it does mean that the question of end versus means has to be resolved contextually, governed by the overarching principle that the larger good should prevail over the lesser need. That was why the grandsire and 'godly' Bhishma, who was duty-bound, fought for the evil side and justified his own 'unfair' defeat as his penance, and as necessary for the safety of Hastinapura, his motherland. It was Bhishma, not only Krishna, who could have prevented the war had he forsaken his vow of obeying whoever sat on the throne of Hastinapura. Bhishma held his personal honor higher than what was best for society. That was why, despite being a great man and despite having the gift of choosing his own death, he had to experience such a painful death, lying on a bed of arrows for 58 days, with the arrows protruding from his own body. Bhishma's moral quandary holds lessons for us. It means in our own daily life, where we all play limited roles, as employees or workers, in large organizations, we are still morally responsible for the final outcome, based among others on our own contribution and work. It means who you work for is as important, if not more, as what you actually do. In other words, even if you have no control over what you do, whatever you do in your own narrow niche carries moral accountability.

It was said that where there is dharma, there is Krishna, and where Krishna is, there is victory. The Kurukshetra, both in mythology and in the popular mind, symbolizes the victory of dharma or righteousness and justice over adharma, evil and injustice. The first verse of the Gita refers to the Kurukshetra as the *dharma-kshetra*, or the 'field of dharma'. One wonders how a place of war, bloodshed, and massacre can be called a holy place. The implication is that nothing is either good or evil *per se*, nothing is sacred or sinful on its own. Everything is relative, contextual; even mass killing. It is the intent and the purpose that determine what it is. But then, who determines? In the minds of both opponents waging the war, it was justified and necessary; or else there would have been no war. And it does mean that at times the ends do justify the means. And Kurukshetra was not just the location of the brutal carnage. It was also the birthplace of the Bhagavad Gita, about which the great Adi Sankara said, "From a clear knowledge of the Bhagavad Gita, all the goals of human existence become fulfilled". Albert Einstein said, "I have made the Bhagavad Gita the main source of my inspiration and guide for the purpose of scientific investigations and formation of my theories". In turn, it was expounded by Lord Krishna to help the prince Arjuna to win his own war within— between, on the one hand, the forces of doubt, despair, demoralization, apathy, and moral ambivalence, and, on the other hand, the forces of resoluteness, decisiveness, ethical duty, and moral clarity—so that he could wage and win the war between dharma and adharma, between good and evil, in the external world.

Gandhi referred to the Gita as "An allegory in which the battlefield is the soul, and Arjuna, man's higher impulses struggling against evil".

Swami Vivekananda further remarked, "This Kurukshetra war is only an allegory. When we sum up its esoteric significance, it means the war which is constantly going on within man between the tendencies of good and evil". We must remember that all the characters are flawed one way or the other, and the war is not for the triumph of flawless good over absolute evil, but of the lesser evil over the greater evil. And as Carl Jung noted, "In the last resort there is no good that cannot produce evil, and no evil that cannot produce good". Inside each one of us there is a Kurukshetra; and all the characters in that epic are also within each of us: a Dhritarashtra (willfully blinded by *moha*, undue attachment), a Duryodhana (knowing what is right, but unable to resist the wrong due to jealousy), a *Sakuni* (scheming and trying to settle scores), a *Karna* (noble at heart, but ruined by misplaced loyalty), an *Arjuna* (righteous but wavering), a *Dharmaraja* (noble but vulnerable), a *Kunti* (virtuous but fearful of society), a *Draupadi* (who was born through fire, whose humiliations act as a trigger for the battle of Kurukshetra). And perhaps a mini-Krishna, too. No character is flawless, just as no human can be. Which particular character, or a mix of characteristics, manifests at what time is hard to tell. At the end of the Kurukshetra, what remained was a despondent Dharmaraja, the decimated Kauravas, the bereaved Pandavas, a 'cursed' Krishna—and a river of blood. And Krishna justified all that, and even the use of unfair means, for the triumph of dharma. It is sometimes said that great wars take place to reduce what is called *bhoobharam*, the burden of Mother Earth. If that be the case, and if a horrendous war like the Kurukshetra was required then, in the *Dwapara Yuga*, what might be needed now, in this *Kali Yuga*, the most immoral of all yugas, with most of over 7.7 billion humans choosing the path of *preyas* (pleasure) over the path of *sreyas* (goodness)?

The archetypal meaning is that within each of us a battle rages between selfish impulses that ignore the claims of justice and justness, and a realization that ultimately, we are all connected in a unity that embraces all humanity and the whole world. Arjuna is our conscious mind, which must make the choice of how we will live. The wicked cousins are our impulses to self-centeredness, lust for wealth and avarice, and anger and hatred. Krishna is the divine essence within us, our higher Self, which is always available to rein in the horses of our feelings and thoughts, and to guide us in the battle of life, if we will only surrender and seek that help. It tells us that we each have within ourselves the answers to all our questions and confusions. We only have to call upon that inner power to discover who we are, what we can trust, and how we should act. Sri Aurobindo compared Arjuna to a 'struggling human soul'. The Kurukshetra must be viewed as a gripping and gory battle between dharma and adharma, good and righteousness and evil. Just as the Pandavas and the Kauravas were first cousins, so are our inherent tendencies. Like the Kurukshetra, our war within too is a fratricidal war, both are endogenous and both are legitimate. In the spiritual sense, as Swami Nikhilananda says, "Arjuna represents the individual soul, and Sri Krishna the Supreme Soul dwelling in every heart. Arjuna's chariot is the body. The blind king Dhritarashtra is the mind under the spell of ignorance, and his hundred sons are man's numerous evil tendencies. The battle, a perennial one, is between the power of good and the power of evil. The warrior who listens to the advice of the Lord speaking from within will triumph in this battle and attain the Highest Good". At the end of the battle, the 'evil' Kauravas were defeated and destroyed and the 'virtuous' Pandavas, led by Yudhishthira ascended the throne of the Hastinapura kingdom. In that battle, the real hero or the *Sutradhari* is Lord Krishna, who, without himself bearing arms guides the Pandavas to victory through a variety of ruses. How do we apply that principle to our time and age? We face two moral imperatives. On the one hand, we do see raw and ravenous evil even in our daily lives; on the other hand, our moral choice-making has become extremely complex with competing priorities and claims: family, professional, social, national, economic, ecological, religious, and so on. The human mind has never been good at harmonizing conflicting obligations; it is now all at sea. The more perilous development is that we are unable even to separate evil from good. Thomas Merton says, "The greatest temptations are not those that solicit our consent to obvious sin, but those that offer us great evils masking as the greatest goods".[143] And the self-righteousness of individuals, races, religions, and nations is the primary source of a lot of evil. Our righteousness about self-righteousness is awesome, blinds us to others' righteousness, and breeds conceit and callousness and robs us of a robust sense of guilt. We must also not forget that 'it is the evil that lies in ourselves that is ever least tolerant of the evil that lies in others'. The inference we should draw from our history is that much of evil has been committed not by those people who wallow in evil, but by those convinced of their own righteousness and equally of the evil of their victims.

We experience this phenomenon in our own lives. That is how we are able to carry on with our lives while hurting, humiliating, and trampling over other people. If we are convinced of the righteousness of our own unrighteous actions, then we feel no guilt; indeed, we think we are the 'victims' while we are the oppressors. The other aspect, often underemphasized, is what is called 'institutional evil', committed by conscientious individuals as a part of or on behalf of, institutions in legitimate discharge of their duties. A recent post explains: "Institutions seem to be set up to put pressure on underpaid district managers, to make cheating easy, and to make it easy for the corporations to turn a blind eye to what's going on. The culpability of the whole is greater than the sum of the culpabilities of the parts".[144] A huge slice of contemporary evil is in this category, and the institution that ranks first is the State itself. The workplace, more than the home, is the locus of evil, and the institutional evil, more than the explicit individual evil, is the instrument. Although everyone condemns evil, most also agree that an evil-free world

---

[143] Merton, T. No Man Is An Island.

[144] Source: Opiniatrety: Half- to Quarter-Baked Thoughts. Blogpost of Matt Weiner, 6 Apr 2004. Retrieved from <http://mattweiner.net/blog/archives/000180.html>.

is impossible. After his 'experience with God', Dr. Eben Alexander wrote, "Evil was present in all the other universes as well, but only in the tiniest trace amounts because without it free will was impossible, and without free will there could be no growth—no forward movement, no chance for us to become what God longed for us to be. Horrible and all-powerful as evil sometimes seemed to be in a world like ours, in the larger picture love was overwhelmingly dominant, and it would ultimately be triumphant".[145]

There are three important differences between the battle at Kurukshetra and our own war within. One, while the war of the Mahabharata was an eighteen-day bloody battle, the war that wages in us is a continuum, without a break; it is in fact a chain of billions of battles. Two, as there is no final end, so is there no final victor or vanquished. It is a seesaw battle, with fluctuating fortunes, and with different 'victors' even every day and in every situation. Three, there is no Krishna to guide and help the Pandavas of our consciousness. And just as without Krishna the Pandavas would have been defeated, so is it now. There is another troubling outcome of the Kurukshetra that we should not ignore, but out of which it is difficult to draw any clear message. In one sense, there was no victor; no one was 'happy'. King Yudhishthira went into deep depression after realizing the carnage the war caused, including the killing of his own elder brother Karna (he did not know then). And the real finale of the war was not the coronation of Yudhishthira but the destruction of the entire clan of Lord Krishna himself by their own hand, caused by a curse of the queen Gandhari, the mother of the 'evil' Duryodhana and his ninety-nine brothers. So, if the war was nothing but wholesale killing, not only of the evil forces but also of the dharmic or virtuous, then what does it mean and what lessons should we learn from it? At one point, Krishna justifies the massacre as necessary to lighten the burden on *Bhoomata*, that is, Mother Earth. So, was it evil people who constituted the 'burden'? And if so, why

---

[145] Alexander, E. 2012. Proof of Heaven: A Neurosurgeon's Journey Into the Afterlife. New York, USA: Simon & Schuster.

was it that the righteous too had to be sacrificed? And if it was simply a question of reduction of human numbers, which was minuscule at that time as compared with present times, should we welcome another war or a nuclear Armageddon? Some scholars even say that the world's macabre fascination with nuclear war is just the latest repeat in a series of blunders that human technology seems obsessed with repeating, and many of today's deserts were the pre-historic battlefields of 'nuclear' wars. Perhaps, dreaded weapons such as the *Brahmastra* were actually nuclear warheads, at least what we very recently termed weapons of mass destruction. Without such weapons, it would be highly unlikely that in eighteen days, millions could be killed with swords and primitive arrows.

Whether or not any of this is true, the point to ponder over is this: if the Almighty—about whom the Quran says, "To him belongs what is in the heavens and what is in the earth. He is the Lofty, the Mighty"—was at that time 'directly' and 'physically' present and still a wholesale slaughter was unavoidable to restore the moral balance on earth, what about now, with over seven billion humans hell bent on destroying nature and directly endangering earth, the very Bhoomata to save which Krishna said the great massacre was needed? The Mahabharata war, it was said, was caused by Duryodhana's greed, jealousy, and hatred of the Pandavas. Those three attributes, plus malice, are now running amok on earth and have seeped into the deepest crevices of human consciousness, and have fundamentally altered the human psyche itself. And this time around, Mother Earth herself is in the direct line of fire. The fact is that none can tell if we are all, each of us in our daily lives and in the minutest choices we make every day, simply playing our deemed parts towards a pre-ordained end, as everyone in the Mahabharata did. Could it be that, like then, so now, there are no villains (or everyone is) and no heroes (or perhaps everyone is)? If everyone is playing a pre-ordained part, whether that part was a reward or penalty for what we did before or what Fate ordained for us as a part of a Cosmic Play, what can we do now, except to play that part as well as we are supposed to and derive as much pleasure as we are allowed to have? It means that we should do everything 'professionally', and not take anything 'personal' too personally.

Of Head and Heart

The real problem that has thwarted all attempts towards finding a *modus operandi* for human transformation is that the human is neither inherently moral nor rational. Had it been otherwise, the world would have been a different place. Rationality in broad terms is to hold ourselves answerable to the relentless rigor of logic and evidence, even when it is uncomfortable to do so. When we are rational, we try to avoid our natural biases and preferences, like paying heed only to evidence that supports our preferred options or selfish interests. We have long claimed uniqueness on both fronts. Morality is about the character of our actions and how they affect other people. Being moral is to shift the focus of concern from the self to another, not to do to others what you wouldn't want done to you. And to always factor in the larger cause and common good. Neither being rational or irrational is a sufficient test of human character. Our boast has long been that 'Other creatures may have wings or claws or sharper eyes, but none... have this unique power of reason, not even a weak or low variety of it. We alone have science, morality, and philosophy, and through them wisdom, for we alone are rational'.[146] But science itself also says that "There are inherent limits to logic that can't be resolved, and they bedevil our minds too".[147] And we associate 'reason' with 'reasonableness'. But as Shaw rued, "The reasonable man adapts himself to the world. The unreasonable man adapts the world to himself. All progress depends upon the unreasonable man. All my life I have refused to be reasonable". Adapting the world to

---

[146] Baier, K. 1995. The Rational and Moral Order: The Social Roots of Reason and Morality. The Paul Carus Lectures 18. Chicago, USA: Open Court. p.27.

[147] Yanofsky, N.S. 2013. The Outer Limits of Reason: What Science, Mathematics, and Logic Cannot Tell Us. USA: MIT Press.

yourself swimming upstream can be stimulating and challenging, but then we will have very little to do with being unrighteous.

Much as we might squirm and wiggle, even a cursory glance at the human cannot but fail to tell us that we are both selfish and self-destructive, if we are not otherwise restrained and influenced. We do not even know, as intelligent individuals, how we will react if tempted or provoked beyond an invisible threshold. If we had been rational, we would not have had, for example, the climate crisis, nor would we have, just to make some more money, polluted and poisoned the air we breathe, the water we drink and the food we eat. If we had been 'naturally' moral, we would not have had sadists and mass murderers like Elizabeth Bathory (the inspiration for *Dracula*), Talat Pasha (the architect of the Armenian massacre), Attila the Hun, Genghis Khan, Caligula, Ivan the Terrible, Adolf Hitler, Joseph Stalin, Mao Zedong, Pol Pot, and so on. They were human; had the same body and brain and heart, crafted from the same timbre, made of the same flesh, blood, and bone; capable of similar emotions and feelings. It is because evil is banal. And there are no moral conundrums or revulsions, and what concerns us is legal correctness, not moral character. It is because human nature is 'ordinarily' obnoxious and inordinately irrational, that human behavior is so unpredictable and so revolting and man so ungovernable. The philosopher Immanuel Kant argued that it might well be possible to govern a society of devils if they were rational and clear about their long-term self-interest. The point is that we are not devils (at least not all the time) nor are we angels; nor dogs or dolphins, or elephants or eagles. It takes us away from the right path to human fulfillment for us to try to describe, depict, and define the human by any single attribute or predisposition. That is why the human is so fascinating and frustrating, and even frightening. We are all a bit and blend of everything—divine, diabolic, rational, whimsical, intuitive, intelligent, noble, moral, immoral, evil. Everything that is in the cosmos we have within each of us. In the words of Rudolf Steiner, "For what lies inside the human being is the whole spiritual cosmos in condensed form. In our inner organism we have an image of the entire cosmos".

The tragedy is that man is nothing but *mind* —and *mind* is the principal problem. Instead of addressing this problem we struggle with the problems created by the mind. The way to address is to dilute, if not erase, its grip and hold on human consciousness. That 'way', that source is also within each of us, a part of what constitutes the human package, in our heart. Contrary to what we usually assume, the human heart is not only an awesomely powerful pump but also a tremendous source of energy and intelligence. Every day you are alive, your heart creates enough energy to power a truck for 20 miles of driving. Your heart pumps blood to almost all of your cells, quite a feat considering there are about 75 trillion of them. During a normal life span, the heart will pump about 1. 5 million barrels of blood, enough to fill about 200 train tank cars. The first heart, a tiny group of cells, begins to beat as early as when a pregnancy is in its fourth week. Humans form an emotional brain long before a rational one, and a beating heart forms before either. Heart intelligence is really the source of emotional intelligence. The heart has its own independent complex nervous system known as the 'brain in the heart'. Its 'intelligence' is independent of, but constantly in communication with, the brain, and is the source of much that is good about us. Heart intelligence is the flow of awareness, understanding and intuition we experience when the mind and emotions are brought into coherent alignment with the heart. Antoine de Saint-Exupéry said, "It is only with the heart that one can see rightly; what is essential is invisible to the eye". It validates the idea that people can be smart in a way that doesn't have anything to do with IQ scores.

What we should worry about is not only how to avoid a heart attack, but equally how to make our hearts rule our lives, or at least have a greater say in what goes on inside us. For, as Blaise Pascal said, "the heart has its reasons which reason knows not". And as an extension it implies that if we can learn to listen to those reasons, or rumblings, we can become less confrontational and more caring in making choices in our lives. However new research is indicating that intelligence and intuition are heightened when we learn to listen more deeply to our own heart. It's through learning how to decipher messages we receive from our heart that we gain the keen perception needed to effectively manage our emotions in the midst of life's challenges. The more we learn to listen to and follow our heart intelligence, the more educated, balanced, and coherent our emotions become. Without the guiding influence of the heart, we easily fall prey to reactive emotions such as insecurity, anger, fear, and blame as well as other energy-draining reactions and behaviors. Such wisdom can be now validated or legitimized by emerging science, but mystics have always known that true intelligence is a blending of head and heart, of thought and feeling. Our heart needs the help of our head to generate and act on more skillful emotions. Our head needs our heart to remind us that what's really important in life is putting an end to suffering. Intelligence has to be holistic and the next phase of human evolution must include this dimension. Then alone can we live as 'we are one another' and be able not to 'stop at our skin'.

The heart is now emerging as a key to a better human future. The beginning is to shed the sense that the heart is simply a superb hydraulic pump that pushes blood through the arteries, capillaries, and veins to deliver oxygen and nutrient-rich blood to the tissues of the body, and to evacuate waste products. Recent research indicates that it is not merely a pump and that our heart is more intelligent than the brain. It means that those feelings we have are 'intelligent' feelings and that strengthens the fact of all of us having inherent psychic abilities and intuition. If we could shed our brain-fixation and tap more of our 'heart intelligence' we might make more headway. Contrary to what we assume, the organ of intellect was not always known to be the brain. In fact, for long, there were two competing views regarding where the intellect resided in the body: the brain or the heart. Even Aristotle argued for a cardiocentric (heart-centered) model, that the heart is in fact the primary organ of intelligence. In this, he differed from his teacher Plato, who subscribed to the encephalocentric (brain-centered) model, and who posited that the "eyes, ears, tongue, hands, and feet act in accordance with the discernment of the brain". It is the heart, not the brain, which is the major energetic organ of organization and integration of the human body; physical and spiritual energy link up in the inner heart.[148] Our heart, in fact, has its own nervous system where the neurons are connected differently and more elaborately than elsewhere in the body, and while they are capable of detecting circulating chemicals sent from the brain and other organs, they operate independently in their own right. Having its own mini-brain is the reason why heart transplants work, given the fact that severed nerve connections do not reconnect in a different body. Furthermore, this elaborate nervous center in the heart has more functions than simply regulating the electrical activities of the heart to keep it pumping. It is interesting to note that while the heart can be influenced by messages sent from the brain, it doesn't necessarily obey them all the time. Furthermore, the heart's mini-brain can send its own signals to the brain and exercise its influence on it. Charlie Chaplin, who wrote a beautiful poem on turning seventy[149] which, *inter alia*, said, "When I started loving myself, I recognized that my thinking can make me miserable and sick. When I requested for my heart forces, my mind got an important partner. Today, I call this connection heart wisdom". And lest we forget, "connections are made with the heart, not the tongue"—nor with the mind.

"Perhaps the heart path represents a different way of interacting with the world than our current brain-dominated approach, a path many of us might want to explore and one that is based on sensing the energy that resonates within every one, than always trying to master and control

---

[148] Source: Seltzer, A. The Heart and Its Energy. Chabad.org. Retrieved from <http://www.chabad.org/kabbalah/article_cdo/aid/380377/jewish/The-Heart-and-Its-Energy.htm>.

[149] A poem by Charlie Chaplin written on his 70th birthday, on 16 Apr 1959.

things, people and cosmos".[150] We have to review our ideas of intention, intelligence and intuition. The French philosopher Henri Bergson, for example, posited that intuition is deeper than intellect, and said that the next human quality to develop is intuition. The theosophist Annie Besant brought in the spiritual dimension and said that intellect has to be "Subordinated to the higher spiritual quality, which realizes the unity in diversity and therefore comes to realize the divine Self in man. That is the next step forward, looking at consciousness". [151] And that way we could accelerate both *consciousness*-change and *contextual* change. The great Indian sage Sri Aurobindo declared that for "man to come face to face with the realization of all that has remained his dream and his aspiration through the ages, [he must] emerge into a higher stage of consciousness". Such a higher stage of consciousness has to be in a state of better balance between the mind and the heart, between brain-based intelligence and heart-intelligence.

"Cardio-energy not only maintains the very interactive cellular structures of the body, but interacts with other hearts and energy systems as well, creating an ever-increasing unity of ever more complex systems of energies which are constantly in communication and interaction with each other. Therefore, it is the individual heart which receives from outside itself, sources of information its related mind organ cannot access on its own, and in turn, transmits information to other hearts multiplied exponentially by the countless sources of cardio-L energy which contribute to its own wisdom. In so doing, the individual heart becomes a microcosm of the larger macrocosm of cardio-energy of which it is a part, and to which it contributes, thus, in a most significant manner, participating in the creation of its own reality. This notion of the 'wisdom of the heart',

[150] Pearsall, P. 1998. The Heart's Code: Tapping the Wisdom and Power of Our Heart Energy. New York, USA: Broadway Books.
[151] Besant, A. 1916. The Coming Race. Adyar Pamphlets. Lecture delivered at the Theosophical Conference held at Chittoor on 17 March 1916. Theosophical Publishing House. Adyar, Chennai, India. Retrieved from <http://hpb.narod.ru/ComingRaceAB.html>.

not only in the sense of what the heart knows and intuits, but also from where and to where its wisdom travels, and with what effect, is a central theme in Kabbala and Hasidism".[152]

It is also suggested that "It would be a serious mistake to view congestive heart failure and its treatment merely from the materialist perspective of physical organ dysfunction. Rather, such ailments of the heart must also be understood within the context of the heart's very own L energy and therefore, and most importantly, from the perspective of the heart's own energetic and spiritual effects upon itself". Some, like Rabbi Nachman, "Speak not only of the role of the heart in terms of one's own health, but also that, the good thoughts in the heart are the good inclination, through which good deeds and attributes are revealed. This is a formation for good. Thus, when a person thinks good thoughts, he purifies the Space of Creation".[153]

If we can manage to harmonize the three independent but interconnected intelligences that we have—mental (IQ or left brain), emotional (EQ, or, right brain), and heart (HQ)—then, and only then, can we change what and how we think and feel. Without such change, our behavior will not change and we will not win the war within. Only by that harmonization can we truly improve the quality of decision-making. Only then can we "foster a new level of understanding of the phenomena of life in the biological sciences, and enable physicians to rediscover the human being which, all too often, many feel they have lost".[154]

---

[152] Source: Seltzer, A. The Heart and Its Energy. Chabad.org. Retrieved from <http://www.chabad.org/kabbalah/article_cdo/aid/380377/jewish/The-Heart-and-Its-Energy.htm>.

[153] Source: Seltzer, A. The Heart and Its Energy. Chabad.org. Retrieved from <http://www.chabad.org/kabbalah/article_cdo/aid/380377/jewish/The-Heart-and-Its-Energy.htm>.

[154] Marinelli, R., Fuerst, B., van der Zee, H., McGinn, A., Marinelli, W. 1995. The Heart Is Not a Pump: A Refutation of the Pressure Propulsion Premise of Heart Function. Fall-Winter 1995 Issue [Vol.5, No.1] of Frontier Perspectives, the journal of the Center for Frontier Sciences at Temple University in Philadelphia, USA. Retrieved from <https://www.rsarchive.org/RelArtic/Marinelli/>.

Conclusion

The question why humans kill one another so needlessly has tormented the minds of philosophers, sociologists, and psychologists. Why is peaceful, amicable, and constructive conflict resolution so difficult in daily life? Why has diversity, instead of enrichment, become so divisive and destructive? Will we be ever able to make sense of human behavior and truly understand the human condition? Are we innately violent, as Thomas Hobbes hypothesized in the 1650s, or is our bearing and mien influenced more by nature, as Jean-Jacques Rousseau theorized a century later? Can we ever become truly moral beings?

That many saints and mahatmas have confessed to these failings should only enhance, not diminish their saintliness. We have long lived with the agony of the good-versus-evil affliction and how to resolve it. The great philosopher Nikolai Berdyaev wrote, "There is a deadly pain in the very distinction of good and evil, of the valuable and the worthless. We cannot rest in the thought that that distinction is ultimate... we cannot bear to be faced forever with the distinction between good and evil" (*The Destiny of Man*, 1931). What we have not sufficiently recognized is that our behavior, whether we do good or evil depends on what happens within our consciousness, which in turn is in a state of war between these very forces: good and evil. Although recent studies do suggest that there are "good grounds for believing that we are intrinsically more violent than the average mammal", we should not forget that we are also, on the other extreme, equally capable of supreme sacrifice and highest altruism. Fact is that if there is evil within, there is goodness too. Along with 'selfish' genes we are also hard-wired for empathy and compassion. That is why we are also the most complex form of life on earth. Our range of emotions are far wider and most exist as pairs of opposites, love and hate, cruelty and compassion, indifference and empathy, malice and altruism, etc. Our consciousness is also more evolved and that makes it more of a player in our lives than of other species. The result is that co-existence of 'pairs of opposites' in our consciousness turns into conflict, and conflict into a confrontation, and confrontation into a no-holds-barred war between two sets of forces, dharma (righteousness) and adharma (wickedness). And this *War* is all that matters, all there is to do. To win the war, rather, more to the point, help the forces of good to prevail in this war, we have to do good in our daily life, helping and not hurting, and by ensuring that whatever gets into our body through our senses is wholesome for the forces of righteousness. In other words, the war within can be won by leading a virtuous or dharmic life. But the conundrum is that to lead such a life we have to win the war within. It is a two-way process and we have to work on both fronts at the same time. Internally we must learn how to enhance the role of the heart intelligence and externally by performing our actions and activities in the spirit of what the Bhagavad Gita calls *nishkama karma*, to do one's actions without expectation of any reward. Expectation not only causes disappointment, but also colors and corrupts the action and the result. Freed from self-interest, our actions automatically become righteous. In turn, they become suitable to serve as feed for the forces of goodness. In short, the doctrine of nishkama karma not only sanitizes our external life but also helps us to win the war within.

To sum up, to win this war, we need to adopt the following nine-point agenda: (1) recognize, at the level of our collective awareness, that there is a whole world within; (2) recognize that the most consequential and the most important of all wars is taking place in that world; (3) recognize that all our current problems and hopes and dreams for our future hinge on how the war wages and its ebbs and flows; (4) recognize that although invisible and inaccessible, we must find a way to intervene in this war and help the 'good wolf'; (5) recognize that the only tangible way to do so is by changing our mindset and our behavior; (6) recognize that for that we need the twin changes: *consciousness-change* and *contextual-change*; (7) recognize that our comatose heart-intelligence has to be awakened in our consciousness as part of such a change; (8) recognize that to bring about the required change in our context of life, we have to follow the spirit of the doctrine of *nishkama karma* in our daily life; (9) recognize that given the way and extent the triad of the three 'M's—morality, money and mortality—shadows and dominates our lives, our particular attention has to be bestowed on these subjects.

Money—*Maya*, *Mara*, and *Moksha*—All-in-One

Money, *Homo economicus*, and *Homo consumens*

Money's precise moment of birth might be diffused and difficult to pinpoint, but its might is unmistakable. And yet it has always been vilified: the Bible says that the 'love of money is the root of evil'; Sophocles said that 'of all vile things current on earth, none is as vile as money'. Be that as it may, money is the only thing to which we will never say no. The paradox and potential of money is that, like river of Heraclitus, it constantly moves while remaining the same, making it a means for the pursuit of non-economic values. And it can reduce, as Georg Simmel suggests in his *The Philosophy of Money* (1900), the highest and lowest values to the same basic form. In contemporary human society, we measure, almost reflexively, virtually every activity in terms of money. In fact, some suggest that money became necessary following the inefficiency of barter—of trading one good for another—because "finding someone who has the item you want and is willing to exchange that item for something you have is both difficult and time-consuming". It can be seen as a 'lubricant', the measure of values that facilitate the free exchange of goods and services, and evens out the pitfalls of simple barter. It is at once a master key and a magic wand, the ultimate illusion (*maya*), the ultimate temptation (*mara*) and the ultimate liberator (*moksha*). Money, positioned at the center of the human mindset, asks, 'If everything has a price, does nothing have a value?' There are those now who say 'money is truth', and 'truth is a commodity'.

Most of us want plenty of money to have a good life and to join the ranks of those that Thorstein Veblen (1899) called the *Leisure Class*, and of those who indulge in what is called *invidious* consumption (the ostentatious consumption of goods that is meant to provoke the envy of other people) and *conspicuous* consumption (spending money to buy goods and services for their own sake). Coincidentally, these are also preponderantly the now-notorious 'One Percent' which owns more than half of the world's wealth; even worse, about 0.01% of that one percent have grown even more wealthy. They are the ones, the new class or new nobility. It was this 'nobility' that George Bernard Shaw once alluded to when he wrote, "We are the real aristocracy in the world. The aristocracy of money". As Scott Fitzgerald said, "The rich are different from you and me" (*The Great Gatsby*, 1925). Everything that happens, happens differently to them. And, as they say, always 'when the going gets tough, the rich build oases'. The political and economic system is so rigged in favor of the rich that what is imperative is not more equitable redistribution of income and wealth, but restructuring of the rules to create a more just power paradigm. Although money is much maligned, and rightly so, the reality is also that the same 'tainted' money can ameliorate the daily lives of hundreds of millions of people. More fundamentally, we should introspect how something that is man-made has been allowed to occupy such a suffocating sway in human society that it dwarfs everything else as a want, and for want of which the mental and physical well-being of billions gets stunted. We should introspect why no one, a person or a business or a nation, or even the world at large, has 'enough' money to do what they need to do. There is almost no crime or sin that is not somehow connected with money. Money now is central to our mindset. It raises a moot question: who, between mind and money, is corrupting whom?

At the core of our love of wanton wealth is the belief that with a lot of money we can do pretty much anything we want and escape any consequences. Other than malice, it is money that separates us from other animals. Mind coupled with money is like a man-eater; and without it, it is a toothless tiger. Recent research has shown that thinking about money undermines our sense of social connectedness. Obscene opulence adds social isolation to what is described as the psychological solipsism of power. Whether or not money can buy everything, the fact is, as Emerson said, it costs too much. Money, or its abysmal absence is what now stands between health and illness, and life and death of millions. In times of major health crises such as Covid-19 (2020), when there is a global lockdown, money becomes a major determinant. The debate is about how to choose between 'lives' and 'livelihoods', about how many, and whose, deaths are acceptable to reopen the economy. Which is the lesser evil: let a certain class of people die of poverty or starvation, or restart the economic engine and risk the lives of another class? Money, contingent on how it is put to use, can also resolve or reinforce the climate crisis. Anticipating—or hoping—for the best, some are exploring the best means for making money off the changing contours of the planet. Glaring inequities in income and wealth have become not only in their own right a serious threat to social stability, but also they have aggravated every other threat. Money sugarcoats everything, including murder; in fact, it has become a major incentive for killing. Money, someone said, is its own country; with enough of it, you live the same everywhere. Money rides roughshod over sex, qualms, restraints, or relationships. Some experts are beginning to see a link between inequality and rates of homicide, and find that inequality predicts homicide rates "better than any other variable".[155] The *perception* that it can, makes money

---

[155] Daly, M. 2017. Killing the Competition: Economic Inequality and Homicide. New York, USA: Routledge.

matter the most. Money too is at the heart of the crisis of morality. There is a general belief that all money tends to corrupt, and that absolute money corrupts absolutely. The point of departure is this: the world has transited from a *modus vivendi*, where most of humanity had no need of money at all, to a *modus operandi* in which much of mankind struggles to survive on extremely small amounts of money. This 'transition' has profoundly altered the role and place of money in human life. The moral perils of being rich were made clear in many scriptures. The Book of James warns the rich: "The wages you failed to pay the workers who mowed your fields are crying out against you. The cries of the harvesters have reached the ears of the Lord Almighty. You have lived on earth in luxury and self-indulgence. You have fattened your hearts in the day of slaughter..." Money is now the median and measure of success, fame and fortune. Whether or not money can buy happiness—a subject on which many have said much—it certainly has much to do with our acute anxiety, high levels of stress, and the rat-race, a metaphor for our modern life of Sisyphean struggle without satisfaction, sometimes described as the dog-eats-dog culture.[156] And money is the fulcrum of the market economy, which philosopher Michael Sandal says has turned into 'market society'. The dynamics of this society are seriously distorted, resulting in intolerable injustice. As a recent Oxfam report shows, in several countries, wage inequality has increased and the share of labor compensation in GDP has declined because profits have increased more rapidly than wages. While the income share of the top 1% has grown substantially, many others have not shared in the goodies of economic growth. And much of decision-making, personal to business and national—is not economic, and the result is that money crowds out motility in our everyday life. The use of money as the primary, often the only, measure of success puts enormous pressure on even those who are not directly involved to toe the party line, to echo the chorus. Everyone

---

[156] The original and more accurate Latin phrase *'canis caninam non est'* translates as 'a dog doesn't eat dog's flesh'.

wants to make more money, and the means or methods are untouchables. As a result, more and more people are cheating each other to make more and more money. In his classic book, *The Consolation of Philosophy* (CE 524) the ancient Roman philosopher Anicius Boethius said, "No man is rich who shakes and groans convinced that he needs more". That really means we have yet to have a 'rich man'. And, money will always be in short supply because it is created as an interest-bearing debt, which means there will always be more debt than money in the world. The conundrum is that 'more money means more debt', and debt is misdirected as it is now feeding evil. We are actually bound hand and foot by what David Graeber calls 'morality of debt': "the way that financial imperatives constantly try to reduce us all, despite ourselves, to the equivalent of pillagers, eyeing the world simply for what can be turned into money" (*Debt: The First 5000 Years*, 2011). Graeber even argues that debt came before barter or money or credit in human civilization.

Money is the one thing having which nothing else is needed, and not having which makes everything else valueless and vain. There is almost nothing man does these days without the shadow of money looming over. Its hold on man now is vice-like and vicious. For reasons still unclear, money seems to draw out of us some of our worst traits like greed, envy, jealousy, and malice. Some say money corrupts; others, that it is *man* who corrupts money. Some argue that money is only "a tool of exchange, which can't exist unless there are goods produced and men able to produce them, and therefore it is neither virtue nor evil". Some say that it is the instrument of the strong to exploit the weak; others say that it offers a chance to become strong by virtue of intellectual exercise and effort. Some say it exacerbates inequality and unfairness; others, that it gives inherent value and worth. Essentially, it is money that separates the so-called One-Percent—the ultra-rich—and the rest. It is money that could keep you healthier and live longer, maybe even make you immortal. Money is power in its barest sense. The British historian and essayist Thomas

Carlyle described its power in the following words: "Whoso has sixpence is sovereign (to the length of sixpence) over all men; commands cooks to feed him, philosophers to teach him, kings to mount guard over him—to the length of sixpence".[157] But what is indisputable is that money's essential character has changed from exchange to enrichment, from a means to obtain the basic needs of life, to it becoming an end in itself. And, perhaps above all, it has turned man essentially into a consumer, which has bred a culture of instant gratification and one-upmanship. There is lot of money to be made on 'body-upgradation', the latest fashion-statement. We are being sold on the need to upgrade all parts of ourselves, all at once, including parts that we did not previously know that needed upgrading. According to one estimate, the so-called self-improvement industry rakes in ten billion dollars a year. Money is the most pressing moral issue now. If we can handle money well, and do not allow it to mess with our mind, much of the rancor, friction, and violence in the world will become manageable. Everyone thinks that to make or earn money to feed a family, for example, nothing is bad or immoral, even cold-blooded murder. For instance, in some parts of India, anybody can be a contract killer, including a mother of seven, a science graduate, or a property dealer. How desperate they are and for how little they are willing to do a terrible deed is indicated by the fact that the money in question, for a 'killing contract' was a mere forty-nine thousand Indian rupees (less than $700). For some others, hired-killing is a moral short-cut to get rich, a snapshot of collapsing social norms and value of life. In other words, both the need and lure of money can trigger a mercenary and murderous response in us; if we can get it right with money, everything else will fall into place. With the rise of *Homo economicus* as the primary human persona, the emblem and analogue of human values, everything else, even health, has taken a back seat. Recently, the Director General of the World Health Organization (WHO) warned the world that putting economic interests over public

---

[157] Carlyle, T. 1831. Sartor Resartus: The Life and Opinions of Herr Teufelsdrockh.

health is leading the world towards three gradual health disasters: climate change, the failure of more and more antibiotic drugs, and the increase in so-called lifestyle diseases caused by poor diet and exercise. Overtaking them all is the current Covid-19 existential crisis. It has highlighted once again how it is virtually impossible to live without money. It has brought out the paradoxes inherent in modern human society. We can't live without money; to make money we must work; work requires human 'social' interaction; that interaction can threaten human life; if you work, your life is at stake, and if you don't, you will die anyway, through starvation, or go mad in isolation; no one, not even the state, can break this lethal cycle. Economics, materialism, and money have become synonymous.

And much of the way we entertain and amuse ourselves, and almost all of sport, is about big, if not dark money. From *Homo economicus*, we have turned into what Erich Fromm called *Homo consumens*—a total consumer in a paradise conceived as an infinite warehouse, "where everyone can buy something new every day, buy everything he wants and even a little more than the one next door to him, but transfigures us into an empty cipher—anxious, passive, profoundly discontented and bored".[158] That gnawing feeling of deep discontent is spreading to all human inventions and institutions that have been painstakingly built up and which hold humanity together—family, community, marriage, markets, traditions, state, religion, etc., foundationally altering our social and moral life. Whether it is *Homo economicus* or *Homo consumens*, the bedrock of the identity is money. What we give value to is how much money we earn regardless of how much we are left with to do things that give us comfort, convenience and control over other people. As the Chinese statesman Deng Xiaoping famously said, "It doesn't matter if a cat is black or white, so long as it catches mice". We don't care who the ruler is, what system of governance there is, or what 'ism' it follows. All that we want is to have

---

[158] Cited in: Moore, C. 2017. Moral Materialism. <http://www.plough.com/en/topics/justice/social-justice/moral-materialism>. Retrieved 12 Feb 2017.

plenty of money in our bulging pockets to get all the material goodies we see on the screen and on the shopping malls. It increasingly appears that ethical behavior and efficient markets are rarely compatible, a point implicit in what Adam Smith said in *The Wealth of Nations* (1776): "It is not from the benevolence of the butcher, the brewer, or the baker that we expect our dinner, but from their regard to their own interest". With all the euphoria surrounding free markets, which really is an oxymoron, there is a growing sense as articulated by thinkers like Michael Sandel that markets alone cannot define a just society, that there are moral limits to markets. The fact is that markets "do not just produce what we really want, they also produce what we want according to our monkey-on-the-shoulder tastes".[159] Well, we know what a monkey does whether it is on the back or the shoulder, or in the mind!

The difference lies in a mix of 'more' and 'less'. In earlier days, people led simpler lives, with limited wants and with more of a moral mindset. That made people generally 'more' hesitant to appease the monkey in, or on, them. And then their reach was limited to the local store and they were 'less' subject to temptations like seductive ads on TV. And those who had more money did not feel the need to buy more things. Earlier, wealth was finite, primarily spread and exchanged, and having it in excess was considered sinful. Generosity and charity were associated with wealth earned through righteous means and through *swadharma*, doing one's own dharma. People were generally open about their wealth and worth but they did not flaunt it. Now people are more open about their sex lives than about their wealth. The hypnotic effect of money and wealth was foretold in the scriptures in the context of describing the effects of the *Kali Yuga*, the most immoral of all ages. They describe the effect and attraction of money in these terms: "Men will devote themselves to earning money;

---

[159] Sunstein, C.R. 2015. Why Free Markets Make Fools of Us [Review of *Phishing for Phools: The Economics of Manipulation and Deception* by George A. Akerlof and Robert J.Shiller, Princeton University Press.]. The New York Review of Books, USA. 22 Oct 2015.

the richest will hold power. Wealth alone will be considered the sign of a man's good birth, proper behavior and fine qualities. Property alone will confer rank; wealth will be the only source of devotion".

The fundamental transformation came when the mind married money, as it were; when money was turned into a major fault line in human life— the divisive line between the haves and the have-nots. It came into being, as Aristotle noted, when the various necessities of human life could not be easily carried about and people agreed to employ in their dealings something that was intrinsically useful and easily applicable to the activities of life, like iron or silver. The value of the metal was first measured by weight and later, to avoid the trouble of weighing and to make its value obvious at sight, kings and governments devised coin money. It has come a long way since. Its primary purpose of exchange was sidelined and money became a symbol of social status and a major means for separation, discrimination, and exploitation. But unlike in a barter economy where savings and investment were very difficult, modern money—paper currency and the bank note—opened the doors to economic growth. By itself, paper money has no value; it rests on trust and it offers fluidity, flexibility and for the creative mind opportunities for speculation, savings and investment. Of all the things in the world, it became the most sought-after possession: to obtain, protect and keep money, people go to extraordinary lengths. They plan and scheme and use every subterfuge; they steal and kill for it; they expend more time, energy and effort for its sake than for any other purpose. Much of a person's life consists of no more than earning, saving, and spending money; and the remainder of his life is spent caring, tending, and preserving the possessions purchased. No sacrifice, no relationship or human bond is spared when it comes to making money. Alan Greenspan, a former chairman of the American Federal Reserve Board quotes a friend as saying 'I understand the history of money. When I get some, it is soon history'. With it, man is a monarch; without it, subhuman. With money in abundance, man can overcome natural or inherited limitations; but without it, one can scarcely obtain what is needed to be wholly human. Just as man has evolved, so has the character and color of money. Moderation and the middle path have given way to gluttony and greed. There are those who have come to believe that striving for inner balance and tranquility will erode their competitive ability, who see a dichotomy between being wise and worldly-wise.

The Epiphany of Modern Man—Money

Somerset Maugham famously said, "Money is like a sixth sense without which you cannot make complete use of the other five". Voltaire put it differently when he said that when it is a question of money, everybody is of the same religion. Thomas Jefferson said that money, not morality is the principle of commercial nations.

Cicero said that endless money forms the sinews of war. Indeed violence, warfare, and wealth are intimately connected. Men are violent for money and money makes violence possible. Money is both the tool and the purpose of violence. Money is a principal factor in most of suicides and homicides, not only among the poor and poorer regions of the world but also in affluent societies. Glyn Davies in his *A History of Money from Ancient Times to the Present Day* (1994) writes that 'ever since the invention of coins, monetary and military history have been interconnected to a degree that is both depressing and surprising.' He even paraphrases Clausewitz's famous dictum and refers to war as the continuation of monetary policy by other means, quoting 18th-century William Davenant: "Nowadays that prince who can best find money to pay his army is surest of success". Davies concludes that the military ratchet was the most important single influence in raising prices and reducing the value of money in the past one thousand years, and for most of that time, debasement was the most common, but not the only way, of strengthening the sinews of war. Whether it is making love or war, some mavericks say that "we are evolving unto a society with much in common with that of insects: ants, termites, hornets, etc. Something analogous to social behavior makes us swarm in towns and cities like ants in their dark colonies". The instinct that compels us to behave like that, the theory continues, is money, which is "to us what genes are to ants", and which "will govern human evolution in the future more than DNA". Selfish economics rather than selfish genes govern human evolution; in the richer nations, "we are no longer evolving according to the principles of natural selection", and "we have swapped our life-giving queen for cash". If money is the root of all evil, the human race has greedily sold its soul to the Devil. There is little doubt that money, much like technology, has had a transformational effect on the human condition. By empowering man to acquire convenience, comfort, and gadgets for every need, money, together with technology, has made man a 'soft species' and eroded considerably the strength and resilience of the human organism. And technology is also raising money-made moral issues. For example, who should a driverless car choose to kill in order to save its passengers: a money-less man in rags or an executive in a business suit? How should we program for such an eventuality?

The very fact that our desires often transgress the bounds of biology or balance of life on earth, and that our social life goes beyond the demands of sheer survival, requires a medium to harmonize and optimize the diverse capacities of human society and makes synergy socially possible. That was the origin of what we call 'money', initially designed as a medium of exchange of products, services and talents, facilitating human interfacing, an input into the making of an orderly, if not an egalitarian, society. The transformation of money from what it was intended into what it has become—our all-consuming passion—is perhaps the single most destabilizing development in human history; it has created not only a new class, but even a new breed of men. Money is more than the coin, paper or plastic to acquire goods and services. Money is linked to complex emotions, feelings, and behaviors. It has a huge influence on what we call 'quality of life' and on the pursuit of the three Cs and Ps that consume much of human life—comfort, convenience, and control; pleasure, profit, and power.

Mind and Money

The mind invented money but, in turn, is enslaved by its own invention. The mind views and relates to the entire world of life through the prism, and prison, of money. Money is broadly defined as 'any marketable good or token trusted by a society to be used as a store of value, a medium of exchange, and a unit of account'. Glyn Davies defines it as anything that is widely used for making payments and accounting for debts and credits. Money has been called many things by many wise and 'otherwise' men: like muck, not good unless spread (Francis Bacon); like manure, which spreads around does a lot of good, but piled up in one place, stinks like hell (Clint Murchison Jr); the most important thing in life (Bernard Shaw); equally important to those who have it and who don't (JK Galbraith); one of the great inventions of mankind (Alan Greenspan); and a myriad more. Since prehistoric times all sorts of things have been used as money. Davies says that money did not have a single origin but developed independently in many different parts of the world.

Today, scholars say that money's origin had little to do with trading, as popularly believed, but arose in a social setting, possibly as a method of punishment. Barter was probably the earliest form of human exchange when humans were essentially hunter-gatherers, fishermen, and farmers. Stone Age man, according to anthropological evidence, used precious metals as money. Silver was first used for coins in the Iron Age kingdom of Lydia (in the region of present-day Turkey) in 3 BCE. In Babylonia, a form of rudimentary banking was prevalent. In 118 BCE, banknotes in the form of leather money appeared in China and in 800 CE, printed paper currency also appeared. According to Marco Polo, the Mongols adopted the bank note as legal tender, i.e., it was a capital offense to refuse them as payment. Only in the 17th century did coinage become standardized and certified. Paper money, first in fiduciary form (which promises to pay specified amounts in gold and silver), and later in its own right (where the paper did not promise payment in some other form), became the mainstay of money in the late 18th and early 19th centuries.

In our tumultuous times, it is becoming increasingly difficult for laymen to decide how they should react to research on ethical issues like human immortality. Money has much to do with it. Firstly, money is flowing into attendant research at the expense of far more important and urgent provision of basic needs for billions of people. Second, the fruits of that research will not be equally accessible. It is being openly said that by the year 2050, man can become technologically immortal but that only the rich will be able to afford that immortality. In other words, it will be money which will be the deciding factor on who has to die and who doesn't have to. That, in turn, could create one more source of tension, friction, and divide, and it could easily reach the boiling point. Already many are saying that the next apocalypse might be economic, not ecological or nuclear; that the current grotesque global inequality—just eight men own the same wealth as the poorest half of the world—is unsustainable and morally abhorrent. It appears so offensive to any semblance of justness, which is central to morality, that not overturning it would be tantamount to inciting evil. But secretly we all want to be, and hope we will be, sooner than later, one of that One-Percent, and so we watch and wait for our day. This along with large privatizations has fueled the rise of wealth inequality among individuals. By any reckoning, we are living in the times of the ultra-rich, a second gilded age in which a shimmering surface masks crony capitalism, serious social problems, and crass corruption. As Umair Haque[160] puts it, capitalism has turned life into money. Money, then, is 'made' and 'owned' by the super-rich, who make the rest do or acquire things that are even injurious, and whose sole goal is to make much more money, money that they are running out of ideas on how to spend for pleasure. Some are saying that this could prove, in the long term, to

---

[160] Haque, U. 2021. The Great Leap the Human Race Needs to Make This Century. *Medium Daily Digest*, 2 January 2021.

be more of a trigger for an existential threat than climate change or any pandemic. It could lead to a so-called 'revolt of the rest', or a war between the mass of mortals and the miniscule of 'immortals'. While there can be no perfect equality in any human institution or relationship in any walk of life, the present situation in which a CEO earns more than a thousand times compared with his employee, clearly violates every canon of fairness and fair play. But then, whose morality is it anyway, of the master or slave, of the rich or the poor? The CEO thinks it is moral because he has earned it by leading the company, and he has not cheated anyone. The worker thinks it is obscene because the value of his work for the company is much more than the glaring gap indicates. But perceptions are important and there is growing groundswell that we are at a flash point and that sooner than later, the non-rich will revolt and when that happens it could dwarf all earlier revolutions in its intensity and destruction.

Money—*Maya*, *Mara*, and *Moksha*

The issue is not whether or not some sort of money is necessary for human life. It is both necessary and noxious; it depends on how we earn it, how much we retain of it, and how we disperse and dispose of it. Indeed, the discovery or invention of money has been described as arguably one of the greatest, on par with fire and the wheel. All religions recognize the need for it, but they also warn us to be wary of excessive attachment to it. On the one hand, they treat it as a blessing, a blessing that God wants to bestow upon us in plentitude. On the other hand, they describe it as an obstacle to faith, and a mortal menace. At the same time, scriptures also talk of 'spiritualized wealth', and of money as a 'divine tool'. The key is to ensure that it flows in the right direction—without stagnating, or being used for obscene ostentation—and that it is put to use as an instrument to lift the lives of the impoverished millions dying for want of dignity.

Money that is made at the expense of others gets tainted, because it is energetically used in an egocentric, selfish way. No money is too small to make some life-saving difference to someone or the other. One of the *purusharthas* (human aspirations) in Hindu philosophy is *artha*, or material wealth. *Artha* means that which is an asset or that which is meaningful. Most important, it must be acquired or possessed in a righteous way, which also means not hurting or harming others and not unjustly depriving others of what is their moral due. The question is what the quest for money makes of us, and what it makes us do. In its material sense, it provides the wherewithal to enable people, families, institutions societies, and nations to have the basic material needs of life. Yet, money and wealth can also offer humanity more than existential value. Rightly conceived and understood, it can improve the human condition and even bring joy, beauty, and leisure to life. Lack of money can impoverish life, enfeeble the body, denude dignity and make human life a living hell. On the other hand, if wealth becomes an unprincipled obsession placed above our duties to God and society, it becomes perverted and devoid of its power for the good. Money in some form or the other has always been a legitimately important and moral factor in human life. The Quran says, "How excellent wealth is! Through it, I protect my honor and get closer to my Lord". The Bible does not call money the root of evil; it is the love of it or obsession with it that leads to evil. What is new is the preeminence of that very love of, or obsession with money in human life, and its emergence as almost the sole means to achieve all human aims, aspirations, expectations—prosperity, well-being, security, control, comfort, power, fame, to be good, even to acquire a good after-life. We can no longer ignore money in any serious reflection of anything human—politics or philosophy, economics or ecology, science or spiritualism, morality or evil, mortality or immortality. The villain is not money, it is the mind. Technology, as a medium of the mind, has accentuated the evil that the love of money can do. Only the rich can afford life-extension technologies, at least in the short term. From pocket money to pensions, making a living to standard of living, savoring the good life to the joys of philanthropy, obscene opulence to abysmal poverty, conspicuous consumption to pragmatism, it is all about money.

Money creates problems when we do not have it, and yet, even more problems when we *do* have it. Money has become a major test of human character. How we 'manage' when we do not have it, and how we 'behave' when we have it, speaks a lot about our moral mettle. Money makes us both master and slave. Our power over money is real only inasmuch as we are able to understand its power over us. For centuries, if not millenniums, man has sought to digest the essence of money. Philosophers and economists, statesmen, writers, even poets, have written about money. It has been acclaimed and cursed; dreamed of and disparaged. Money is capable of creating and destroying, of uniting and dismembering. Like God, if we have money in our corner nothing and no one else is needed; for we can 'get' everything else with it. It can be exhilarating, intoxicating, magical and mesmerizing. It can make people both partners and parasites and can impact the fate of individuals and whole nations. Here comes the unfortunate bit: what was meant as a medium of exchange has turned man himself into a medium—to make money. Those who possess money are in fact possessed by it, overcome by the passion to multiply it by any means and at any cost. And this change, unless corrected, could destroy human society. The crisis in the global financial system is but a symptom. The time has come to face up to the fact that any agenda for human transformation must include how to change the way money is perceived, generated, and utilized. A great virtue of money as a commodity is that it simplifies and facilitates one of the greatest requisites of spiritual life: sharing and giving. If money is properly shared and spread, there would be, for example, no extreme poverty in the world. When it comes to rousing our conscience, statistics have lost their sting and pinch. Yet they provide useful insights. The World Bank says that at least 80% of humanity lives on less than $10 a day. According to UNICEF, about 22,000 children die each day due to poverty. And they die quietly in some of the poorest villages on earth, far removed from the scrutiny and the conscience of the world. Being meek and weak in life makes these dying multitudes even more invisible in death. And, according to Oxfam, the surge of $762 billion in the wealth of the world's 2,043 billionaires, in the year 2017, was enough money to end 'global extreme poverty seven times over'.[161] Another shocking statistic is that only 5% of all new income from global growth trickles down to the poorest 60%. Grim and bad as it might seem, it also offers a ray of hope. Never before did so many people need so little to lead healthier lives, and never before could so few people do so much for so many. Money's very concentration makes it easier to diffuse it in the right direction, with the maximum effect. What is needed is consciousness-change in these billionaires.

Try as we might, it is hard to understand money's grip and gravity, and to fathom how it came to be the building block of human happiness, the fulcrum around which human life revolves. We can understand the lure of sex, or of power, or pursuit of pleasure, or fear of death; all of which are somehow related to biology and human nature. How could money grow to be such a sinister shadow under which we spend all our brief time on earth and waste all our energy? It looks as if money is the ultimate temptation to drag us down to our doom, to bring to the surface our darkest instincts. Money plays the role of both *Maya*, the Vedantic illusion (the euphoric feeling that with money we need nothing else), and the Buddhist *Mara*, as it tempts us to follow the unrighteous path to acquire, amass, and enjoy wealth. The truly intriguing, even exciting, thing is that in this very area of darkness, it can be a source of liberating light. The much-derided material wealth can also be a means for *Moksha*, not in the sense of breaking an individual's cycle of birth and rebirth or death to death, but in helping each other to break out of their cycle of misery and dehumanization. It

---

[161] Oxfam. 2018. Reward Work, Not Wealth. Oxfam Briefing Paper January 2018. <https://www.oxfam.org/sites/www.oxfam.org/files/file_attachments/bp-reward-work-not-wealth-220118-summ-en.pdf>

is so essential, its absence can cripple life to such a degree, that providing the means to acquire it to the truly needy can become transformative and benefit the 'giver' more than the 'taker'. Although baneful in its effect on the mind, it can also be a conduit for compassion. 'Blessed are those who have money; for they have the power to make the everyday lives of so many so much better'. John D Rockefeller, one of the richest and most philanthropic men of modern times, expressed it aptly: "God gave me my money... I believe the power to make money is a gift from God, to be developed and used to the best of our ability for the good of mankind. Having been endowed with the gift I possess, I believe it is my duty to make money and still more money and to use the money I make for the good of my fellow man according to the dictates of my conscience". This Rockefeller quote was described as a kind of partnership between God and Mammon. Mammon lords over the accumulating department, and God over the giving and spending department. It also means that different rules govern the two departments. Rockefeller himself was described as 'money mad, money mad, sane in every other respect but money mad'.[162] He didn't pay much heed to means and morals while becoming very, very rich but channeled a good bit of it for charity. How do we rate him as a 'moral man'? Was the world better off or worse off with Rockefeller as he was, lock, stock, and barrel? The fundamental fact does not change: wealth righteously earned and shared generously can help lift many lives; wealth, ill-gotten and unshared, is corrosive. Although we tend to conflate the two, wealth is not another name for money. Wealth is fundamental and is the stuff we need to live: food, clothes, shelter, gadgets, travel, land, and so on.

One can have wealth without having money. Wealth is as old as human history. Far older, in fact; even ants have wealth. Money in its current dominating form is but a comparatively recent invention. Leave alone money, making wealth is not the only way to get rich. In fact, for a huge chunk of human history it was not even the most common way. Until a

---

[162] Statement attributed to US Senator Mark Hanna.

few centuries ago, the main sources of wealth were mines, slaves and serfs, land, and cattle, and the means to acquire them were by inheritance, marriage, conquest or confiscation. Money gives the false feel of easy access to pleasure, power, and pelf. It makes us feel powerful and paves the path to possessing power.

The Many Faces of Money

The baneful influence of money on humanity was foretold in Hindu scriptures like the Mahabharata, Srimad Bhagavatam, and the Ramayana. In Srimad Bhagavatam, for example, Sage Suka says, "In the Kali Yuga, wealth alone will be the criterion of pedigree, morality and merit". And 'merit' is not so meritorious, and 'meritocracy' has come to be, according to Daniel Markovits, "exactly what it was conceived to resist: a mechanism for the concentration and dynastic transmission of wealth and privilege across generations" (*The Meritocracy Trap*, 2019). In the Mahabharata, Sage Markandeya tells King Yudhishthira: "… and wedded to avarice and wrath and ignorance and lust, men will entertain animosities towards one another, desiring to take one another's lives". Taking another life is now no longer as forbidding as it was in the blood-soaked 20th century. The dilemma with money is that while its abundance can corrupt the mind, its extreme absence can cripple life and deny dignity, an essential attribute of the human condition. DH Lawrence wrote, "money poisons you when you've got it and starves you when you haven't".[163] Bob Dylan crooned, "while money doesn't talk, it swears".[164] But its hypnotic spell also contains a silver lining. It has, on the one hand, deepened the ill effects of the love of money; no relationship, no moral scruple, no sensitivity is immune to its lure; no crime or sin is unthinkable. In contemporary society, we have bestowed almost godly powers upon money, and whilst money's necessity

---

[163] Lawrence, D.H. 1928. Lady Chatterley's Lover.

[164] Dylan, Bob. 1965. *It's Alright, Ma* (I am only bleeding).

makes it irreplaceable and universal, it is its deification that makes it a 'religion'. However, in religious terms, money and wealth *per se* are not always deemed bad or evil. In Hinduism, the consort of Lord Vishnu is Lakshmi, the goddess of wealth and money.[165] The important point is that money and wealth are viewed in a broader context than in pure monetary terms. They are 'sacred' too, and even Lord Vishnu needed wealth to get himself a wife on earth and had to borrow it from Kubera, the God of wealth.

Apart from its magnetic lure, and because it is deemed so vital for human life, money also attracts many superstitions. There are superstitions surrounding every aspect of money, from getting it to saving it. Some rose from plain old-fashioned common sense while others were rituals based on natural phenomenon that were seen to be omens, auspicious and ominous. There are even conflicting superstitions, depending on the culture. In Argentina, finding money in the street is considered extremely lucky. As long as you never spend it, it will bring you more money. But in Trinidad and Tobago, finding money in the street could bring evil spirits into your home. In some countries like Greece, it is believed that money attracts money and so it is bad luck to completely empty one's pocket or wallet. The ancient Greeks threw coins into their wells to keep them from going dry. In Japan, snakes are viewed as symbols of prosperity and therefore purses made with white snakeskin are popular. The ancient art of *Feng Shui* advocates several practices to make money. In England, putting money in new clothes is supposed to bring good luck. According to Mexican tradition, making a cross on the floor after picking up 'found money' will bring even more money. In some countries even bubbles in a cup of coffee or tea are associated with money; elsewhere, if a bee lands

---

[165] The eight secondary manifestations of Lakshmi, called the 'Ashta Lakshmi' are: *Adi* (primeval) Lakshmi; *Dhana* or *aishwarya* (money or prosperity) Lakshmi; *Dhanya* (grain or agricultural produce) Lakshmi; *Gaja* (elephant or giver of animal wealth) Lakshmi; *Santana* (giver of progeny) Lakshmi; *Veera* or *dhairya* (valor or courage) Lakshmi; *Vijaya* (victorious) Lakshmi.

on your hand it indicates wealth is on its way to you. Or, if you write with green ink, profits will flow from your hand.

The impact of money goes beyond what we can do with it, what it can buy or procure; it defines life itself, feeds our ego, vanity, and viciousness. Money breaks all moral barriers. We might serenade *à la* The Beatles that 'money can't buy me love', but the fact is it is so vital for life, it could even prompt some to take lives in its name. There is almost no crime without a money trail; all crime is, in the end, crime for gain—personal, national or international. There is growing recognition that controlling money flow is the key to controlling crime. On the other hand, it also became an easily available instrument to better people's lives. The good thing about money is that we do not need a lot of money to do good; even small amounts, properly channeled, can make a significant difference. The same amount can have a varied impact on different people; for some marginal, and for some others life-saving. Properly channeled, money can be a powerful 'compassionate' conduit to alleviate pain, suffering, and misery in the world. It can be a boon and a bane, a blessing or a curse, contingent on how we come to possess it and spread it. One could even go the extent of saying that a person's moral stature is more enhanced if he makes every effort to earn lots of money righteously than if he chooses to eschew any contact with money, even if it were possible. But it is moot if the choice is between earning money unrighteously and using it righteously, or not making any effort to earn any money and not spending any money to help others.

We may fitfully fantasize about transforming human society into a *Shambala* or *Shangri-La*, an *El Dorado* or Utopia, but the crucial challenge before man is to move from the mind-dominated mindset of 'money-mindedness' towards a more just social order and 'spiritual alchemy', which, in the words of Karen-Claire Voss, is "a form of illumination, a means of transmutation, a method for experiencing levels of reality that are not ordinarily accessible, since they exist beyond the level of everyday reality". It is to fundamentally alter the coordinates that drive human consciousness. What becomes unmistakably clear, as we struggle with the pressures, pitfalls, and pulls of modern life, is that the Rubicon that man has to cross is reason itself, what TE Lawrence called 'thought-riddled nature' (*Seven Pillars of Wisdom*). The Sufi saint Jalal ad-Din Rumi said that "it is reason that has destroyed the reputation of the intellect". It is with a blend of inductive reasoning (from the specific to the general) and deductive reasoning (from the general to the specific) that we think through, to deliberate, to deduct, to distinguish the real from the unreal, good from evil, to judge and evaluate the ethical. But the conundrum is that reason is not good enough to *reason* about reason. It does not allow us to be reasonable; it tries to exclude every other source of thought; it makes us feel so smug and sanctimonious, so human-centric.

Money—from *Summum malum* to *Summum bonum*

We all know that money is not only the most valued thing in the world, but human life itself would not be possible without money. On the other hand, although as the Greek philosopher Protagoras said—'Man is the measure of all things: of the things that are, that they are, of the things that are not, that they are not'—money certainly is the measure of everything human, and its 'non-existence' makes human life functionally meaningless. It, above everything else, is responsible for the moral meltdown of man. We also know that for the sake of more money there is nothing man will not do, no barriers he will not cross, no relationship beyond sundering, no crime too heinous. But money, in essence, is only a medium and a tool. It will, like a carriage, take us wherever we want to go, but it will not replace man as the driver. It will give us the wherewithal to satisfy our desires, but it will not *create* our desires. Money gives material shape to the principle that men who wish to deal with one another, must deal by trade and give value for value. When we accept money as a return for our effort, we do so only on the assumption that we will be able to exchange it for the product of the effort of others.

Money cannot purchase happiness nor can the lack of it lead to unhappiness. It is also a question of degree. Daniel Goleman says, "The rich may experience more pleasure than the poor but also require more pleasure to be equally satisfied".[166] It is the mind that makes the difference. As Ayn Rand puts it in *Atlas Shrugged* (1957), "Money will always remain an effect and refuse to replace you as the cause. Money is the product of virtue, but it will not give you virtue and it will not redeem your vices". And, "Money is so noble a medium that is does not compete with guns and it does not make terms with brutality". She goes on, "So long as men live together on earth and need means to deal with one another—their only substitute, if they abandon money, is the muzzle of a gun". It is the mind, not money, that calls the shots. It is the way the mind manipulates money that is responsible for the ills ascribed to money, such as the skewed distribution of wealth. For example, it has been reported that 'the bottom half of the world's population owns the same as the richest 85 people in the world'.[167] The real problem is that money becomes baneful if it flows in the wrong direction, from workers to non-workers, from the poor to the rich, from the creative to the noncreative. The reality is that the creators are often impoverished and much of the money is held by the work of others, not their own. Money itself would be good if it were our servant, not the master as it is for most of us. Money itself would be a great social stabilizer if it represented goods, labors, and creativity, but it does not.

But strange as it may seem, in this immoral age, money can be made sacred too. It could become a potent moral tool and spiritual bridge. Contrary to popular belief, money *per se* is not innately evil or dirty. It is the mind that matters. Money can be anything: power, freedom, temptation, provocation, the root of all evil, the sum of all blessings. If we use it for

---

[166] Goleman, D. 2007. Social Intelligence: the New Science of Human Relationships. USA: Bantam.

[167] Oxfam. 2014.Working for the Few: Political Capture and Economic Inequality. 178 Oxfam Briefing Paper – Summary.

the right purpose, it is moral. We must separate earning from spending; just because the money we possess is lawfully earned does not mean we can spend it as we wish for our wants. We must view money too like morality and mortality, indeed like everything else in the contemporary social context, which includes the stark reality of abysmal poverty and awful living conditions of over a billion people. And money alone, in whoever's hands it might be in, and however little or large, can alleviate, if not erase poverty. And making money should not be seen simply as a zero-sum game. We must revive the spirit of philanthropists like Andrew Carnegie, who maintained that 'no man can become rich without himself enriching others'. In this regard, the rich and poor are alike. The rich can do more but, no one is too poor to help someone poorer or in greater need. Joseph Murphy says, "I like money, I love it, I use it wisely, constructively, and judiciously. Money is constantly circulating in life. I release it with joy, and it returns to me multiplied in a wonderful way". For the *rich* to do more, we need to loosen the grip of what is called 'lifestyle money', money we dispense with to conform and maintain our comparative style of living, and the attitudes, activities and habits that come with it. Indeed much, if not most, of our money goes in that direction, consumed by what is expected of us by the industry and advertisers. We are unremittingly bombarded with endless images that are trying to convince us that we're not good enough as we are. The message that comes across is straightforward: "As you are, you suck, and you need to be different to not suck. Here, get this product and you won't suck anymore".[168] The need to live up to our lifestyle leaves very little. For money to serve the social good, we must free ourselves from the assumptions and expectations of a good life. But then, some tricky issues crop up. For example, is it okay to rob a bank and distribute the money to the poor? Is corruption justified if we give the money to charity? What takes precedence, righteous earning or righteous sharing? Do ends justify the

---

[168] Archon, S. 2020. To Sell You Happiness, They First Make You Feel Like Shit. The Unbounded Spirit.

means insofar as money is concerned? Buddhism lays stress on what it calls 'Right Livelihood', which implies that we cannot work for or participate in socially harmful activities. In any case, its very pervasive indispensability—no one can live without any money—offers an opening. If morally earned and properly channeled, it can make a life-or-death difference; it can lift the poor from the margins of deprivation and destitution to a life of decency and dignity. Through money, at this time in history, one could do more good to more people than through most other means. In other words, we now have a window of an opportunity to transform money from *summum malum* (the greatest evil) to *summum bonum* (the greatest good). If we can succeed in this effort, the world will be transformed from what Thomas Hobbes called *bellum omnium contra omnes*—the state of 'war against all', of every man against every man, which is the condition of current society—into a happier and harmonious place.

The source and the use of money demands the highest judgmental skills. It has come to be unjust and exploitative because of the way we 'make it' and mobilize it and marshal it. In the process, our negative passions come into play, like greed, avarice, and malice. These have dominated our mind-driven consciousness and, unless we change the composite of our consciousness, money cannot become a force for the good. The result is a human society aptly described by Ayn Rand: "When you see that trading is done, not by consent, but by compulsion—when you see that in order to produce, you need to obtain permission from men who produce nothing—when you see that money is flowing to those who deal, not in goods, but in favors—when you see that men get richer by graft and by pull than by work, and your laws don't protect you against them, but protect them against you—when you see corruption being rewarded and honesty becoming a self-sacrifice—you may know that your society is doomed".[169] But if we can somehow bring to bear on our personality

---

[169] Rand, A. 1957. Atlas Shrugged. USA: Random House. [Francisco d'Anconia's 'money speech'].

our positive passions like compassion, sharing, sensitivity, and justness, then money too can become a creative power. We must also bear a central fact: throughout our lives, we do myriad things as members of society, and, despite our best efforts, we can never be sure that what we receive is proportionate to our effort and inputs, that our share is just and that we are not living on someone else's labor, and that our rewards are not ill-gotten. Many theories have been put forth by social scientists on how to ensure fairness in distributing gains from social cooperation but none of them have proved beyond leaks and misapplication. The simplest way is to constantly and consciously make every effort in every context and situation to give more than what we get, to always be on the lookout for even the most trivial opportunities to help and heal, and not let go any such openings, regardless of who the recipient, or the occasion, might be. And the simple fact is that there is no other way; nothing else works to give us a sense worthiness and fulfillment—and to solve every problem the world faces—than giving, caring, empathy, compassion, going beyond ourselves and our family, crossing out of our comfort zone to serve others. Let God, not you, be the judge whether they deserve or not. Thank God that He has given you the mind and means to give. That is His gift. The good thing about giving is that you do not need to have anything; you have yourself and that is more 'givable' than anything else. To love, you need to give, but to give, you do not need even love. We simply need to have a heart.

The Great Moral Issue of Our Age—
Money Management

The medium of money and the act of making profit sanitize any ill effects of what goes on in an office or shop floor or boardroom. If we want to raise the bar of morality in human society, we must not exclude any place from moral responsibility. Adding insult to injury, so to speak, the fact also is that most people do not like, let alone enjoy, what they do to make money. In other words, they get no joy in this world and are accountable in the afterworld. We must also address what has come to be known as the 'doctrine of lesser evil', that sometimes we have to deliberately choose an alternative that violates our own moral sensitivity and do things against the grain, as the only other choice would be to condone or allow something more horrible to happen. For example, suppose the state has in its custody a suspect who has information about a horrific act, and does not reveal it despite cajoling and persuasion. Would the state be morally justified in torturing him? While it is true that often choices are between different grays, not between white and black or good and evil, we must not forget that the lesser evil is also evil and that we are morally culpable. It also underscores the truism that there are no absolutes in nature, not even in morality. Each case has to be judged on its own merit in a given context.

A big chunk of extant human effort is to do what the ancient Indian sage Yagnavalkya (in the *Brihadaranyaka* Upanishad) told his wife Maitreyi cannot be done—buy immortality with money. Scott Fitzgerald famously said, 'Let me tell you about the very rich. They are different from you and me...' They are different not only because they have more money, which enables them to live differently and live in 'refinement, utmost refinement, total refinement' as Siddhartha Gautama described his life before his awakening, they even think differently of death! They are different from the rest but they are also different from each other in the way they see, gain, and use their wealth. Although money has a corrosive effect on human consciousness, money can also make a difference between a life of dignity and a life of indignity and degradation. Being very poor can rob a person of what it takes to be human. And the very rich can lift the very poor from that subhuman state. Not doing so can be as sinful as slow murder. That is why all religions extol charity. Charity is not meant only for the rich; it is sharing, and sharing can be done by everyone, even the poor because there is always someone else richer and poorer than us. Every one of us is both rich and poor, or neither rich nor poor; there is always another 'richer' or 'poorer' than us. And it is more true if we expand the ambit beyond money. And then, as Sinclair Lewis says, "there never will be a time when there won't be a large proportion of people who feel poor no matter how much they have" (*It Can't Happen Here*, 1935). No one can become rich only through solitary effort, or because they believe that they are the most deserving of them all. For the very process entails unequal and disproportionate effort. In that sense it is a reasonable assumption to go by that no one is rich because he has righteously earned it and charity is not giving but giving back; it is paying back in money what we borrowed in kind, as sweat and skill, time and energy of other people.

There have always been economic gaps, and some have had more money than others, and men have always desired to live in the lap of luxury. Today, the gap between the rich and the poor is becoming wider and sharper than perhaps ever before, which could become a major source of social tension. While much of the world grappled with soaring unemployment and plunging growth, the wealthiest 500 people on the planet added $1.8 trillion to their combined net worth in 2020. That 31% jump is the biggest yearly gain in the history of the Bloomberg Billionaires Index, a daily ranking of the world's richest people. Human experience over millenniums has shown that human ingenuity is far better at creating wealth than sharing and distributing it. In 2011, *The Economist* magazine, usually an ardent advocate of economic growth as the panacea for the ills of humankind, identified this issue as a primary trigger for global instability. In its special report, it noted that there are more high-net-worth-individuals and millionaires than Australians in the world. About 1,000 billionaires happen to control one-third of global assets; the richest 1% of adults control 43% of the world's assets; the wealthiest 10% have 83%, and the bottom 50% have only 2%. Those at the bottom, particularly those at the 'bottom of the bottom', the absolute poor, the marginalized, the downtrodden, the oppressed, are those who lead lives that deny them the full biological human potential, and yet it is they who allow the rest to lead human lives. The leisure class and the mainstream mass and the middle class depend on the marginalized, for the goods and services that backstop their luxury, leisure, entertainment, even to live in their opulent homes. The growing gap between the leisure class and the working class has widened social divisions. It has given rise to those, particularly in the rural areas, what are called left-wing-extremists, who argue that those at the top are rank exploiters and cruel predators and that only through violence would it be possible to endow, enable, and empower those at the bottom and restore a better economic balance in human society. Their aim is to overthrow the tyranny of plutocracy and install the reign of the proletariat. Because of the widening gap, on the one hand, and because the poor are now able to actually see through mass media how the rich lead their lives at their expense, their creed is increasingly finding favor with the rest of the bottom in many countries. If money continues to play the same deterministic role in human affairs, and the new class of the Nouveau Riche, which includes national and transnational corporations, continues to control the levers of economic and political power, there can be little doubt the economic divide of the world could become a source of catastrophic conflict in this century.

There is another downside to this division. With sheer bodily survival and subsistence consuming so much labor, effort, and time, the human has long dreamed of leisure as the route to *nirvana*, allowing him to do more worthwhile things that are good for his soul. We commonly identify affluence with luxury, luxury with leisure, leisure with entertainment, and entertainment as a way to eclipse our misery. In the contemporary society, nothing holds our attention except what comes to us as entertainment. Entertainment is today's enlightenment. It gobbles up almost all the time left after making a living, all the time released by traveling faster, and working with, even being replaced by, a machine. For entertainment stimulates; and without stimulation, our mind wanders away, looking for something more juicy. We watch the news only if it is entertaining and graphic. A celebrity or high-class murder is the perfect fix—in one go we have glamour, sex, violence, and mystery. Earlier, people used to dread natural disasters as their lives and homes would be in danger. Now, secure in the thought that we are insulated and insured, the excitement begins the moment we hear of any impending storm or cyclone; we are even inwardly disappointed if it passes by without event. The real tragedy of human life is that we are at sea both in the state of work and at leisure; in earning a livelihood and in enjoying leisure. The Mahabharata reminds us that *kala* (time) 'cooks' all beings. As life ebbs and every passing moment brings us closer to death, the cosmic question crops up: after biology is done with, what should a living being do with every waking minute of earthly life? Since nothing is purposeless, what did nature intend when it created the human form of life? The affluent have luxury but little leisure, and no time other than to make more money and to keep it safe, not even the time to enjoy the luxury, let alone provide food for the soul. They are not worried about their own growth; they want their money to grow. While money appreciates, morality depreciates. Topmost on the menu of what parents want to leave behind to their kids is money in its various avatars. What we now have is a desire for the lap of luxury. The kind of things that some want—and have—are outlandish and obscene, not only when compared to the poor and deprived, but also in terms of what it means to the earth. Morality apart, that kind of human life, albeit limited to a tiny minority of men, carries not only serious economic implications but also potentially perilous ecological, environmental, and civilizational consequences. In one sense, the milieu of their lives is not human anymore. The rest are 'doubly-disadvantaged'—they do not get to share the spoils, yet they pay the price. This leads to bitterness, hatred, and violence. The irony, and tragedy, is that in our craving for the luxuries of life we are compromising and corrupting the necessities of life. What the poet Edward Young said of kingdoms applies equally to civilizations, and perhaps to species—on the soft bed of luxury most kingdoms have expired. That very perceptive philosopher Thoreau also puts it well: "Most of the luxuries and many so-called comforts of life are not only *not* indispensable, but are positive hindrances to the elevation of mankind".

We can erode but not erase economic inequity, let alone inequality. Another name for inequality is diversity, the backbone of nature. We cannot bridge the so-called development divide or eliminate the exhibition of obscene opulence if we treat the issue only in economic or political terms. Even conceding that perfect economic equality is impossible and that that inequality is a part of diversity, the fact in its extreme forms has a pernicious effect on societies, "eroding trust, increasing anxiety and illness, ... encouraging excessive consumption".[170] And, that "for each of eleven different health and social problems: physical health, mental health, drug abuse, education, imprisonment, obesity, social mobility, trust and community life, violence, teenage pregnancies, and child well-being, outcomes are significantly worse in more unequal rich countries".[171] Inequality is bad both for the very rich and the poor, and for the in-betweens. It is bad for the rich as it robs them of their capacity for empathy. It is bad for the poor because their minimum material needs overwhelm everything else, distorting their priorities and diminishing their human potential. But the more important point is that, even if we want to, we do not have the means, or the methods, by which we can justly apportion the fruits of any common labor in any collective work. Let alone put to practice the Marxist maxim 'from each according to his ability, to each according to his need'. It is also because the nature and quality of labor of different constituent persons is so different that it is not possible to objectively weigh their contributions; and if we cannot do that, how can we determine their 'fair bite' of the collective pie? But still, no one can say that a CEO getting

---

[170] Pickett, K. and Wilkinson, R. 2009. The Spirit Level: Why More Equal Societies Almost Always Do Better. London, UK: Allen Lane.

[171] Pickett, K. and Wilkinson, R. 2009. The Spirit Level: Why More Equal Societies Almost Always Do Better. London, UK: Allen Lane.

a hundred times more than an employee, at a time when money is what matters most, is not socially incendiary and morally repugnant.

Even if one practices the adage 'frugality is morality', the essential point is that what we do with money—quantum being immaterial, and the poor not excluded—and how we earn it and live with its tantalizing presence or paralyzing absence, is the true test of morality. Money has also a critical bearing on man's two other, in the words of Prof. Darshan Singh Maini, "cruel despoilers of life's bounties and largesse":[172] sex and power. Sex has a strange power over us. It is a great leveler like death, and breaks through all barriers of gender, age, relationship, blood ties, position, and privilege. No one is an untouchable when it comes to sex. A master would not even touch a slave or share a meal with her, but is eager to engage her in the most intimate exchange and seduction. A billionaire would not care to glance at a destitute, but if she is deemed 'desirable', he would pay anything to buy her body. Where is the hypocrisy? Is this nature's way to ensure that sex never gets outdated or outclassed by any other power or temptation, including money? We have come to believe that with enough money we can control everyone, buy anything and anyone, barter everything—from virginity to maternity; from societal adulation to angelic immortality. In a sense, wanting to be good and not wanting to be dead are natural desires; it is money that makes man a monkey, makes him do things he would not otherwise be tempted or possibly be persuaded to do. And money accentuates the veneer of vanity that clouds our vision. Although money has come to play a deterministic—maybe even terminal—role in human affairs, its power of seduction has long been recognized. The *Panchatantra*, the ancient Indian text long considered a *nitisastra* or text book of wise conduct and good behavior, says, "Money causes pain in getting; In the keeping, stress and fretting; Pain in loss and pain in spending; Damn the

---

[172] Darshan Singh, M. 2002. Power, Money and Nexus: a Freudian Nexus. India: *The Sunday Tribune*. 26 May 2002.

trouble never ending". [173] Money can only get what money can buy—not happiness, not sleep, not wisdom. The Panchatantra also says, "No treasure equals charity; Content is perfect wealth; No gem compares with character; No wish fulfilled, with health".[174] The Bible says that 'The love of money is the root of all evil'. Christ elaborated, "It is easier for a camel to pass through a needle than for a rich man to pass through the gates of heaven",[175] and "If you want to be perfect, go and sell all your possessions and give the money to the poor". And again, "No one can serve two masters, for either he will hate the one and love the other; or else he will be devoted to one and despise the other. You cannot serve both God and Mammon".[176] It is not that all rich are all evil; it is that money must be righteously earned and it is that those with a lot of money are more likely to expend much of their energies towards protecting their riches and their expansion.

Yet, despite their different trajectories and governing dynamics, man has been able to maintain, until the advent of modernity, some kind or semblance of balance between the triad of his three deepest desires—to be moral, to make money, and to ease into immortality. Each was able to hold its own and assert its own legitimacy, without inordinately or improperly encroaching on the other's psychic space. Man's desire to be moral did not stifle his desire to be materially well-off; his desire for material well-being, in a large measure, was morally moderate; and his desire to be death-less was not overly influenced by his moral or monetary standing. It is this balance or symmetry that is now seriously disturbed and distorted. For men of this century, *moksha* or liberation comes down to one thing: to

[173] Cited in: Chalapathi Rao, I.V. 2007. Culture Capsules: Living Through Changing Times. Hyderabad, India: Sri Yabaluri Raghavaiah Memorial Trust. p.67-68.

[174] Cited in: Beck, S. 2006. Ethics of Civilization. Volume 2: India and Southeast Asia to 1800. Literature of India. Retrieved from <http://www.san.beck.org/EC12-Literature.html#4>.

[175] Matthew 19:24.

[176] Matthew 6:19–21,24.

be free from the hypnotic hold of money and thus be able to share it. Put differently, without freedom from money, or rather from the things that money lets us afford, no other freedom is of much use on the spiritual path. Indeed, it is becoming clearer with every passing day that the economic, environmental, and social problems of the world are, at their very core, moral issues that need to be addressed at the micro level; not only at the individual level, but even at the microcosmic level of the mundane chores of daily life. At the root of morality is money. In one sense, we have made morality mortal, and mortality amoral, and money the metaphor for man. The minimal goal, the benchmark, so to speak, has to be that we must be able to lead full and productive lives, work for a living, raise a family and savor the goodness of life without worshipping wealth, exploiting each other, trying to cheat death, exterminating other forms of life and ravaging nature. And in so doing, we must let the *Buddha*, inside the womb of each of us, come to life.

Money, it has also been said, has "the power to blind us even to our better selves".[177] Marx, in his *Economic and Philosophical Manuscripts* (1844), gives the dialectical and existential perspective. Among other things, he writes that "By possessing the *property* of buying everything, by possessing the property of appropriating all objects, *money* is thus the *object* of eminent possession. The universality of *its property* is the omnipotence of its being. It is therefore regarded as omnipotent... Money is the procurer between man's need and the object, between his life and his means of life. But *that which* mediates my life for me, also *mediates* the existence of other people for me. For me it is the *other* person". Marx calls money the '*distorting* power' both against the individual and against the bonds of society, etc., which claim to be *entities* in themselves. It transforms fidelity into infidelity, love into hate, hate into love, virtue into vice, vice into virtue, servant into master, master into servant, idiocy into intelligence, and

---

[177] Heffernan, M. 2011. Wilful Blindness: Why We Ignore the Obvious at Our Peril. London, UK: Simon & Schuster. p.4.

intelligence into idiocy. He says again, "That which is for me the medium of money—that for which I can pay (i.e., which money can buy)—that am *I myself*, the possessor of money. The extent of the power of money is the extent of my power. Money's properties are my—the possessor's—properties and essential powers. Thus, what I *am* and *am capable of* is by no means determined by my individuality". He further says, "Money is the supreme good; therefore, its possessor is good. Money, besides, saves me the trouble of being dishonest: I am therefore presumed honest…" Marx, citing Shakespeare, calls money the 'visible divinity', that it has the ability to transform all human and natural properties into their contraries; and that it is 'the common whore, the common procurer of people and nations'. He then asks, "If money is the bond binding me to *human* life, binding society to me, connecting me with nature and man, is not money the bond of all bonds?" Although Marx writes intensely about money, albeit tinged with an implicit warning, perhaps the most euphoric description of money comes from the pen of Ayn Rand, who writes, in her magnum opus *Atlas Shrugged*, that money is 'the barometer of a society's virtue', 'the creation of the best power within you and your passkey to trade your effort for the effort of the best among men'. Ayn Rand says that "Money rests on the axiom that every man is the owner of the mind and his effort". That "When you accept money as payment for your effort, you do so only on the condition that you will exchange it for the product of the effort of others… your wallet is your statement of hope that somewhere in the world around you, there are men who will not default on that moral principle, which is the root of money". Further, according to her, "Money demands of the recognition that men must work for their own benefit, not for their own injury, for their gain, not their loss—the recognition that they are not the beasts of burden, born to carry the weight of your misery—that you must offer them values, not wounds—that the common bond among men is not the exchange of suffering, but the exchange of goods. Money demands that you sell not your weakness for men's stupidity, but your talent for their reason..." For Rand, 'money is the product of virtue, but it will not give you virtue and it will not redeem your vices'. She sums up the positivist view and says, "Until and unless you discover that money is the root of all good, you ask for your own destruction. When money ceases to be the tool by which men deal with one another, then men become the tools of men... Run for your life from any man who tells you that money is evil. That sentence is the leper's bell of an approaching looter. So long as men live together on earth and need means to deal with each other—their only substitute, if they abandon money is the muzzle of a gun". She adds, "But money demands of you the highest virtues, if you wish to make it or keep it", and proclaims that the proudest distinction of Americans is the coining of the phrase 'to make money', which she says 'holds the essence of human morality'. Rand is breathtaking and makes one breathless too. If all that she says is true, man, at least an American, must have become an angel by now, and the Western World, at least America, a land fit for gods. That it hasn't happened nor is it likely to should give us some food for thought.

That kind of thought is articulated by those scholars and spiritualists who have chronicled, what they call, the perils of money. The reality is that, as the writer Louisa May Alcott put it, "Money is the root of all evil, and yet it is such a useful root that we cannot get on without it any more than we can without potatoes". John Stuart Mill once said that money is a machinery for doing quickly and commodiously, what would be done, though less quickly and commodiously, without it. Metals have been used as money throughout history. They became useful when the various necessities of life could not be effectively carried out, and, as a result, societies agreed to deploy in their dealings with each other something that is innately useful and easily applicable. The value of the metal was in the beginning measured by weight, but, over time, rulers or sovereigns put stamps upon it to avoid the headache of weighing it, and to make the value recognizable on sight. While money always played an important role in human civilization—metallic money was in use over 2,000 years before the birth of Christ—its power increased enormously with the advent of paper money in the late 18th century and since then man has not been the same. It fuelled the contemporary culture of consumption and a mindset of materialism. The arrival of electronic money and what is called e-commerce in the late 20th century unhinged money from the constraints of space and time. Money has transformed human personality more than any other single factor. It became the sole criteria for judging a person's worth and success in life. The pervasive influence—mostly negative—of money and materialism on human psychology is well documented in a recent book called *The High Price of Materialism* by Tim Kasser.[178] Kasser offers a scientific explanation of how materialistic values affect our everyday happiness, but also makes the point that the effect is not only on the psychological well-being of man but also on his physical health.

Money, Body, and Brain

In today's world, the underscoring belief is that nothing and no one is without a price tag, in cash or kind; nothing we can summon is beyond barter for pleasure and progress. The driving force is money. A growing number are turning to their bodies to earn extra money, or to make both ends meet, not as a last resort but as an easy option. Today's utilitarian man argues: why must we exclude, as a resource, the body that is the only thing we unquestionably own, and over which no one else can lay a claim? If one can 'morally' and legally sell or mortgage our brains to make a living, which is what much of what we call 'work' or doing a 'job' is, why can't we sell or put to use our own body and its parts to make a living? In the age of 'marketing' for money, specific parts are marketed for cash. For instance, in Japan, one advertising agency paid young women for *thigh-vertising*—wearing a temporary product tattoo on the bare skin between the hem of a short-skirt and the top of a knee-sock. Then, an enterprising

---

[178] Kasser, T. 2002. The High Price of Materialism. USA: A Bradford Book.

young man in America launched *Lease Your Body*, to entice good-looking people to 'lease' space on their bodies to advertise and market commercial products. Of course, there are innumerable other ways in which one could market his or her body for a living—selling one's hair, sperm or eggs, breast milk, bone marrow and blood, renting a womb, modeling naked, etc. We generally consider that some of these practices, particularly prostitution, to 'make a living' as signs of moral degeneration, but we are soft and silent when it comes to selling one's skills and souls, talent and ingenuity for the sake of promoting armaments, alcohol, cigarettes, and drugs. It means that the body is sacred and the brain is secular. In fact, we can do more harm by lending or leasing our brain for the wrong purposes than the body. Body vending primarily affects the individual whereas brain misuse impacts on society itself. It is very difficult to inject morality into this matrix. One could forcefully argue that there is nothing wrong, that the individuals are only making use of whatever nature has endowed them with. They are harming or hurting no one. If anyone suffers, it is only they, and society cannot have double standards between brain and body. The critical ingredients in whatever work we do are intent, sincerity, honesty, diligence and being useful and helpful, not harmful.

After all, it is with the body that athletes and sportsmen earn money and glory, by being auctioned to represent or play for the highest bidder in games such as cricket. Then again, if selling sex is the culprit, what about marrying for money? Many sell their body, and arguably their soul and autonomy, in an institution like marriage. It is also said that 'prostitution' is not simply selling sex; it includes any action that compromises one's beliefs and values to obtain another thing whether money, security, or even a promotion. The other view can be that all religions prohibit the use of sex for a living. This view holds that the sex organ is not like any other organ, that sexual intimacy is of a different genre than any other human interfacing, that commercial sex is often exploitative and that, as it is associated with procreation, it is sacred. For long, experts have debated why the human race is so aggressive, bloodthirsty, and kill-happy. Is the 'villain' the gene, our hormones, or the environment? Why do we destroy that which gives us shelter and which keeps us alive, the earth? Why do we starve ourselves and build weapons that kill us all many times over? Are we diabolic, or demented or deranged? Contrary to what one might infer from today's horrific cruelty, massacres, and mayhem, the idea that humans are peaceable by nature and corrupted by modern institution, has always found a voice in authors and intellectuals. Take, for example, José Ortega Gasset ('War is not an instinct but an invention'), or Stephen Jay Gould ('*Homo sapiens* is not an evil or destructive species'), or Ashley Montagu ('Biological studies lend support to the ethic of universal brotherhood'). There are some scientists who say that, in the ultimate test of altruism, "we are better at putting ourselves in other's shoes than we used to be", and that we are actually more evil in the cause of antiquated morality (e.g., religious morality) than from "amoral predation and conquest".[179]

The Good That Money Can Do

In essence, and in its effect, money is power, the most powerful and potentially polluting of all. If the power of money cannot be wished away, what do we do? Should we use all our energy, attention, and activism to curb and contain its role and influence, or can we turn it around and use it as an instrument for doing good, to help others in dire need, to use it as a social leveler. Whether we like it or not, we have to acknowledge money's magnetic hold on the human mind and yet strive to see how to salvage some time and synergy for our spiritual growth. We do not have to choose whether it is the root of evil or a necessary evil, a divine gift or the devil's ploy—it may be all or none. We don't have to agree with the assertion that

---

[179] Waldron, J. 2012. A Cheerful View of Mass Violence. Review of Steven Pinker's book *The Better Angels of our Nature: Why Violence Has Declined*. The New York Review of Books. USA. 12 Jan 2012.

"Until and unless you discover that money is the root of all good, you will ask for your own destruction. When money ceases to be the tool by which men deal with one another, then men become the tools of men".[180] One of the more important questions is: in a world controlled by money, how can we make or earn it rightfully or *dharmically*, and spend and spread it bearing in mind that much of what we come to have is invariably more than our moral right? To make money moral, it must flow in the right direction; it must be shared and spread. Is the Robin Hood way, the moral way? That is, the redistribution of wealth, what most governments are supposed to do under the cover of legality.

Money is now the measure, motive, metaphor, and means of everything we do, desire, and dream of in life. It is also a measure of self-worth and self-respect. As an *ABBA* lyric intones, 'Money, money, money; always sunny in a rich man's world'.[181] In the poor man's world, its lack is marked by the three deadly 'D's: desperation, deprivation, and death. In fact, there is no such thing as rich man or poor man *per se*; everyone is both richer and poorer than someone else. And then nobody wants to be who we come to call a rich man. As Pablo Picasso once said, "I want to live like a poor man with money". But that doesn't change the fact that our fascination with wealth knows no bounds, with some even being addicted to wealth. People have confessed that earning bulging bonuses running into millions of dollars causes something similar to an alcohol or drug addiction, prompting rage and an uncontrollable desire for more, risking to destroy themselves and their companies rather than be satisfied with the millions or billions they already have. Money does indeed make the world go round but most of us want the best of both; we don't want to be rich and be the subject of envy, derision, and disdain but, as Pablo Picasso quipped, we want to 'live as a poor man with lots of money'. Although it is

---

[180] Rand, A. 1957. Atlas Shrugged. USA: Random House. [Francisco d'Anconia's 'money speech']

[181] Lyrics from the 1976 song *Money, Money, Money*, by the Swedish pop group ABBA.

impossible to define the rich, and although we want to have what the rich have, we don't want to be 'different from you and me', which is how Scott Fitzgerald famously described the very rich.[182] As for living like the very poor, we would rather die. We would rather be a Gabriel Garcia Marquez, who said, "No, not rich. I am a poor man with money, which is not the same thing". What he implied is that he wanted to have his cake and eat it too; exercise power without responsibility. Money has many functions, purposes and attractions. But it is most irresistible as power, in its essence and in its effect.

Money and the mind are made for each other; together they are playing havoc on human life. Money and commerce have become the analogies through which all our human experiences are mediated. In a 2010 survey in the USA, some 77% of the youngest people polled said they are more concerned about outliving their money in retirement than about death itself.[183] The make-or-break importance we attach to money was foreseen. In the Hindu scripture Srimad Bhagavatam, it is written that 'a person will be judged unholy if he does not have money, and hypocrisy will be accepted as virtue'. Whether or not it is the love, or lack, of money that is at the root of evil, the reality is that we don't own money anymore; *money* owns us. Money is the bedrock of materialism; the backbone of capitalism; indeed, the essential to any economic 'ism'. It is the measure of meaningfulness, of well-being, of good feeling; of health and happiness; but not necessarily of goodness or of a virtuous life. Socrates said, "I tell you that virtue is not given by money, but that from virtue comes money and every other good of man, public as well as private". Money has, left to its own genius, had a baneful influence on morality. Possessing, earning, amassing, even spending it, is so overpowering that anything that comes in its way is brushed aside. A study revealed that "as a person's levels of wealth

---

[182] Fitzgerald, S. 1926. The Rich Boy. [All the Sad Young Men].

[183] Davies, L.A. 2013. Agenomics: Trivializing Death. Retrieved from <http://agenomics. ca/2013/09/trivializing-death/>

increase, their feelings of compassion and empathy go down, and their feelings of entitlement, of deservingness, and their ideology of self-interest increases…", and that "wealthier individuals are more likely to moralize greed and self-interest as favorable, less likely to be pro-social, and more likely to cheat and break laws if it behooves them".[184] The findings of the study also revealed that "People who make less are more generous… on the larger scale… Rich people are more likely to ignore pedestrians… Poverty impedes cognitive function".[185] Another study indicates that 'more money makes people act less human or, at least less humane'.[186] As one writer put it, "Money can weaken even the firmest ethical backbone. Money sows the seeds of mistrust. It ends friendships. Experiments have found that it encourages us to lie and cheat".[187] The simple idea of money changes the way we think—weakening every other social bond.[188] As Marx remarked, "Money, then, appears as the enemy of man and social bonds that pretend to self-subsistence".

We have to bring into our economic thinking the moral dimension. To be moral, money must move from the affluent to the middle class, and from the middle class to the lower class. One way could be to inject what was once known as *georgism* (also known as geoism and geonomics), which is an 'economic philosophy holding that the economic value derived from natural resources and natural opportunities should belong equally to all residents of a community, but that people own the value they create'.[189] That philosophy attracted great thinkers like John Locke, Spinoza, and

[184] Gross, J. 2013. Six Studies on How Money Affects the Mind. TedxMarin talk by Paul Piff. Retrieved from <http://blog.ted.com/2013/12/20/6-studies-of-money-and-the-mind/>

[185] Gross, J. 2013. Six Studies on How Money Affects the Mind. TedxMarin talk by Paul Piff. Retrieved from <http://blog.ted.com/2013/12/20/6-studies-of-money-and-the-mind/>

[186] Miller, L. 2012. The Money-Empathy Gap. *New York*, 1 July 2012.

[187] Porter, E. 2013. How Money Affects Morality. *The New York Times*, 13 June 2013.

[188] Porter, E. 2013. How Money Affects Morality. *The New York Times*, 13 June 2013.

[189] *Georgism*. Wikipedia: The Free Encyclopedia. Wikimedia Foundation. Retrieved 26 Apr 2014.

Tolstoy. It relies 'on principles of land rights and public finance which attempt to integrate economic efficiency with social justice'.[190] It is based on the premise that many of the problems that beset society, such as poverty, inequality, and economic booms and busts, could be attributed to the private ownership of land, the necessary resource. It is in this light that in *Progress and Poverty*[191] Henry George argued, "We must make land common property", and he drew a distinction between common and collective property. Such ideas are worth a serious look at a time when there is heightened alarm about economic inequality, so starkly brought to light by the Oxfam report mentioned earlier: the 'world's richest 1% control half of global wealth'. Those eight men now own the same amount of wealth as the 3.6 billion people who make up the poorest half of humanity. Such revelations might have sparked a revolt, if not revolution, in our better, more moral times, but now we are too numbed even to react.

Killing Kids for Money

Spurred by his insatiable desire for money, man conceals within himself a sinister 'mass murderer', who does not directly kill with a knife or a bullet, but who is capable of far greater damage to the human spirit and vitality. Such is this murderer who deliberately, methodically, and single-mindedly pollutes, poisons, and adulterates the food we eat, the water we drink, and the air we breathe. He does this, not to make a living, but to make *more money*, to earn more profit. The reference, obviously, is to the ever-increasing use of chemical agents in the foodstuffs we consume. Fruits like mangoes are ripened with ammonia; vegetables are treated with carcinogenic pesticides; chicken and cattle are injected with overdoses

---

[190] *Georgism*. Wikipedia: The Free Encyclopedia. Wikimedia Foundation. Retrieved 26 Apr 2014.

[191] *Progress and Poverty*. The Free Encyclopedia. Wikimedia Foundation. Retrieved 26 Apr 2014. [Progress and Poverty: An Inquiry into the Cause of Industrial Depressions and of Increase of Want with Increase of Wealth: The Remedy, published in 1879 by Henry George.].

of antibiotics; fish is preserved with formaldehyde (the chemical used to embalm corpses); spices are mixed with dung, sand, and saw dust... From fruits to vegetables, from milk to sodas, from clarified butter to edible oils, from wheat flour to pulses, from spices to sweets, even the medicines we take, chances are that we are consuming products that are injurious to our health, in effect, slow poison. Food that is supposed to give us nourishment has now become the source of our enfeeblement and endangerment; so is the air we breathe and the water we drink. In some countries, what passes for milk, which school books describe as complete food, contains high levels of urea, detergents, and cheap edible oil. For the record, let it be said that no other species deliberately feeds its offspring food that it knows is putrid. Only human beings would not hesitate to do anything for profit, for money. The poison we put into everything we ingest is also consumed by our children and grandchildren, which means that, for money, we don't mind maiming or murdering the ones we profess to love the most, and for whom we will sacrifice anything, and for whose sake we earn that very money.

Whose job is it to see such things don't happen? The 'rulers', of course. But power is what motivates them to do *nothing* about it. The general public are helpless as they have no alternatives to eating, breathing, and drinking whatever is made available in the marketplace. They are too much in love with the good life; and while on other issues of far less import they organize, agitate, and manage to change the perpetrating system, in this case they are apathetic, refusing to believe and to act decisively and collectively. And while they are prepared to pay exorbitant prices for luxuries and fine goods, in the case of food and water they want affordable prices, forcing the producer to choose adulteration over authenticity, poison over purity. So, everyone has a stake in this: the producers profit and consumers enjoy lower prices. Everyone makes a 'ritual' protest but is not prepared to fight or make any sacrifice; we are all both villains and victims. It is like death: everyone thinks that they are somehow untouched and only others will get affected. Yet another example of willful blindness of the consequences; and blind faith in their personal invulnerability. These synthetic chemicals contribute to subtle and gradual dysfunction in the human body. They not only cause slow and more painful death to far more people than rampage killers, they also jeopardize their vitality because an enfeebled generation cannot but beget more enfeebled offspring, and endanger the next generation. Adulteration, like adultery, is time-tested; it is a very old practice for profit. But it used to be relatively innocuous, like mixing water with milk, adding lower-grade oil with more expensive oil, and so on. Today, however, harmful chemicals are mixed with foodstuffs as a way to spend less and to earn more. Then, it was cheating; now, it is mass murder or 'generational genocide'. Synthetic chemicals, or what Randall Fitzgerald (*The Hundred-Year Lie*)[192] calls 'chemical synergies', that is, the combinations of these chemicals stored in our bodies, are major sources of mass murder or mutilation. Modern man lives and dies in a cocoon of chemicals; almost everywhere he lives and everything he inhales and intakes is laced with such synergies, which are now embedded into the mainstream of the food chain and are integral to and inseparable from leading what we have come to call 'civilized life'.

The mind created money to manipulate, if not to enslave, man. To ensure that man will never become a true moral creature. The original functions of money were both revolutionary in character and evolutionary in its utility. Revolutionary, as man discovered that, through money, his excess energy of one day could be used for another day or could be preserved over a length of time. It became an evolutionary instrument in bringing men to act together and create a social collective of economic energy. Money is a symbol of human energy. It organizes that energy and its movement across the society in time and space. It is created by the individual's trust in the other individual and in the collective. But the

[192] Fitzgerald, R. 2006. The Hundred-Year Lie: How Food and Medicine Are Destroying Your Health. USA: Dutton.

mind has the power to make money 'good' if used for a good purpose, and 'bad' if used wrongly. The fact is that our obsession with money has loosened the strings that connect one human being to another. It incubates and induces an intoxicating sense of independence, an arrogant euphoria of autonomy and makes us believe that if we have it in amplitude we become 'complete' and life will be under control. From the earliest times, money in some form or another has been central to organized living. Over millenniums, money has reflected the changes in habitat of human society; but it also helped bring about these changes. Increasingly, money shapes the foreign and economic policies of all governments. There is little that man is not willing to compromise—from virginity to marital fidelity, friendship to patriotism, personal honor to professional probity—for money. The dilemma is that with money we are subverted, and without it the world will descend into chaotic disorder. The fact is that in spite of its antiquity and ubiquity, its rightful place and proper management has eluded the ingenuity of the human mind. It has become synonymous with pleasure, pride, and power. Throughout history, the people who have had most power have almost always been rich. It has developed into a principal means of human-to-human interfacing, the glue that holds human society together. The economist Alfred Marshall maintained that the history of money is synonymous with the history of civilization. The smooth functioning of the money economy enables society to raise its standard of living by increasing production and equitable distribution through the medium of exchange. Money is central to the processes of production, consumption, distribution, and purchasing power. It makes people believe that they are free as long as they have the supposed freedom to consume and money to pay for it. It is through money that we satiate our greed, avarice, and ambition. Will Rogers sums it up well: Too many people spend money they haven't earned, to buy things they don't want, to impress people they don't like.

The extent to which money has come to dominate human life is such that the way we think and relate with money is now a tool and touchstone to find out who we really are at our core. What we do with money, and how we live with money's pervasive presence, tells a lot about our values and essence. Money is all there is—medium and measure; means and end; symbol and substance of life. We love it (when we have it) and we hate it (when we don't). Money is often perceived as a lifeless object separated from people; in reality, it is man-made, imbued with the collective spirit of the living and the dead. It is also an 'instrument of collective memory'. Money has its own character, in the sense of having particular attributes, especially moral and ethical, which differentiate a person, a group or a thing from another. Over time, and more sharply in modern times, it has radically changed the personality of man; but in so doing it changed its own character. In the humdrum of everyday life, we often find ourselves asking the question: how can we juxtapose money and morality in the same sentence and not come face to face with an ethical contradiction? As the Indian guru Osho put it, "Either you will be consumed by your desires or you have to consume your desires". While it is true that a wholly contented man is a dead man, and that it is discontent that fuels creativity, it is also true that it is avarice that turns man into a menace. Socrates said that one who is not content with what he has is not likely to be content with what he would like to have.

Money, Poverty, and Morality

The question that arises is this: Is it morally okay to play Robin Hood, to rob the rich and give to the poor? Does it make a moral difference how we earn the money if we spread it properly in society? The Mahabharata gives an answer. Vidura, the erudite and wise minister, tells his king: "O King Dhritarashtra, one should never think of earning material wealth through wrong means like falsehood, bribery, corruption or stealing, not to speak of practicing such evils. Wrongly earned money pollutes its possessor to such an extent that all the activities done with such sinful wealth result in harmful troubles. Even praiseworthy acts like charity and worship, and sacrifices done with such sinful income, produce undesirable results. No amount of purification can set right the defects of ill-begotten wealth". The Bible[193] says, "Ill-gotten gains do not profit/But righteousness delivers from death; He who profits illicitly troubles his own house/But he who sows righteousness gets a true reward; Bread obtained by falsehood is sweet to a man/But afterward his mouth will be filled with gravel; The getting of treasures by a lying tongue is a fleeting vapor, the pursuit of death". But if we are confronted with a choice between ill-gotten wealth well spent, and well-earned wealth ill spent, how should we choose? Does the critical importance of money in today's world sanitize how it is earned if that money saves or gives dignity to other lives? In any event, how money is allocated and utilized in the future, both individually and collectively, will become a major moral matter. And the glaring fact is that our priorities are pretty distorted. We are spending trillions of dollars on big-ticket items like immortality, artificial intelligence and the Internet Of Things (IOT), and too little on global health and sanitation. The other question is: what is ill-gotten wealth? Does it concern only how we make money, or does it include how we inherit it or how the one who gives us money for services rendered earns it? Is an employee morally responsible for how his employer generates the money he gets? In other words, are the means marginal in matters of money as long as the end is worthy and socially relevant? Does tainted money become holy if offered to the divine or for charity, and absolve them of the sin of acquiring illicit money, or at least lessen the severity of sin? One can also argue that the larger good—helping the needy who otherwise might be impoverished and incapacitated for want of purchasing power—justifies or overshadows the evil of money made unethically, which could also tantamount to depriving others of what they might have ethically earned.

A person who suffers from poverty might have been less sad, angry or revengeful if poverty did not exist amidst plenty. The fact that poverty

---

[193] Proverbs 10:2; 11:18; 20:17; 21:6.

co-exists with affluence has made its victims not only sad but also angry with the wider sociopolitical power structure that determines the kind of life they lead. At the same time, of all typologies of suffering, it is economic suffering that is also the easiest to mitigate or eliminate. The existence of extreme poverty and luxurious living and income disparities is not only unjust but also immoral. It is 'economic justice' that stands at the frontline of social justice. Elizabeth Ann Seton simplified it: "Live simply that others might simply live".[194] 'Simply' means a life of simplicity, frugality, and moderation, with a mindset that it enables others, less fortunate, to live likewise. As the writer Stuart Wilde said, "Poverty is restriction and as such, it is the greatest injustice you can perpetrate upon yourself". Economics absorbs such a huge slice of our life that one must come to believe (to paraphrase Martin Luther King Jr.) that economic injustice anywhere is a threat to human dignity anywhere. Our instinctive tendency is to have as little to do with things that disturb us; we banish them from our lives, homes, and even thoughts. Poverty is also a problem of money: it is caused by lack of and maldistribution of money; and it can be ameliorated by both a bottom-up and trickle-down approach, by the empowerment of the poor and by public policies that transfer money from the top to the bottom. The rich view the presence of the poor as a law-and-order problem, a potential peril to their well-earned affluence and market-value of their homes. The 'not-rich' and 'not-poor' are united in the view that cohabitation with the poor means a problem of sanitation, public health, and 'bad company'. John Stuart Mill wrote way back in the 18th century that a distinctive mark of the 'modern age' is the determination to put far away from our sight anything ugly, disturbing, and disagreeable we find. That is one way not to feel threatened, or not to feel any sense of shame or guilt; out of sight is out of mind; out of mind is to be rid of culpability. The god-fearing, pious people would rather leave the poor to God; who are *we*, they say,

---

[194] Seton, E.A.B. (1774–1821) was the first native-born citizen of the USA to be canonized by the Roman Catholic Church.

to intervene where *He* does not? Global poverty is also a critical factor in good governance. Confucius said, "In a country well governed, poverty is something to be ashamed of. In a country badly governed, wealth is something to be ashamed of". When both abject poverty and obscene opulence coexist and we go about our lives unruffled and unfazed, as we all do, it is a clear indication that something is awfully out of joint in our consciousness.

For Gandhi, the poor were *daridra-narayana* (*daridra* means poor, and *Narayana*, God). Swami Vivekananda said, "So long as the millions live in hunger and ignorance, I hold every person a traitor who, having been educated at their expense, pays not the least heed to them". Our current approach to poverty alleviation, as William Easterly writes, is 'based on a technocratic illusion: the belief that poverty is a purely technical problem amenable to such technical solutions as fertilizers, antibiotics, or nutritional supplements'.[195] To make any headway we must view the problem of inequity and injustice as a virulent virus in human society.

The earliest form of money that we are exposed to is *pocket* money. Parents intend their children to learn the basics of money management, but this soon becomes a slippery slope and a sense of entitlement gets embedded in their psyche. Educational experts say that there has probably been no aspect of family life that has been the cause of greater strain and stress than the problem of the child and his money. The last thing a dying man is supposed to do is distribute the wealth of a lifetime to his progeny by a will, so that, hopefully, they won't kill each other fighting over it! Some even put away money for their funeral, lest their kids short-change them and deny them their due. Life between birth and death is spent under the shadow of money. Money has become the measure of man. Philosophers like Seneca might have held that a great fortune is a great slavery; but most men today would prefer that kind of slavery. Benjamin

---

[195] Easterly, W. 2013. *The Tyranny of Experts: Economists, Dictators, and the Forgotten Rights of the Poor.* New York, USA: Basic Books.

Franklin might have said 'man does not possess wealth, wealth possesses him', but most prefer being so possessed. Schopenhauer said, "Money is human happiness *in abstracto*; consequently, he who is no longer capable of happiness *in concreto* sets his whole heart on money".[196] Money and 'more' are synonymous. From a beggar to a billionaire, the endless desire is to have more of money. Thomas Jefferson said, "Money, not morality is the principle of commercial nations". Jean-Jacques Rousseau described wealthy men even more harshly: "The rich are like ravening wolves, who, having once tasted human flesh, henceforth desire and devour only men".

Scriptures generally view money like flesh, as an impediment to spiritual progress, and all saints have shown not only detachment but also disdain towards money. The Hindu concept of *artha* or wealth emphasizes that money must be earned, stored, and spent dharmically, i.e., through righteous means. Money may be neutral in its nature but it is either good or bad in relation to how it is generated, garnered, and expended. In that sense, money is energy; money is power; and money is a form of life-energy (*prana*) contained in paper, coins, silver, or traditionally and most importantly, in gold. The underlying philosophy is that bad money can never do good deeds; nor can good money used wrongly reap right results. Good money is righteous money, derived from a righteous source, earned by helping, not hurting, people; by serving, not cheating, people; by making people happy, not adding to their misery. Bad money does bad things; it is money earned through the making or selling of harmful things like alcohol, arms, cigarettes, and drugs, and through bribes and taking more than one's legitimate share. The 2,000-year-old spiritual classic *Thirukkural*, written in Tamil by the South Indian saint Thiruvalluvar, distills the basic tenets of dharmic money: "The worst poverty of worthy men is more worthwhile than the wildest wealth amassed in wicked ways. What tears gain will go by tears. Though it begins with loss, in the end

---

[196] Lapham, L.H. 1988. Money and Class in America, Notes and Observations on Our Civil Religion. New York, USA: Weidenfeld & Nicolson. p.9.

goodness gives many good things. Protecting the country by wrongly garnered wealth is like preserving water in an unbaked pot of clay. Riches acquired by mindful means, in a manner that harms no one, will bring both piety and pleasure. Wealth acquired without compassion and love is to be eschewed, not embraced. Finding delight in defrauding others yields the fruit of undying suffering when those delights ripen.[197] Even after two millenniums, human ingenuity cannot do any better than this to codify a more moral way of handling money.

Another equally ethical and morally progressive view of money is advocated in Islam. Its perspective on banking and lending best symbolizes this view. As one article put it, "For millions of Muslims, banks are institutions to be avoided. Islam is a religion that keeps believers from the teller's window. Their Islamic beliefs prevent them from dealings that involve usury or interest (*riba*)". The Quran explicitly prohibits interest or *riba* on money lent. The Islamic view of money is based on interesting principles: any predetermined payment over and above the actual amount of principal is prohibited; contrary to modern banking, the lender (the provider of capital), and the borrower (the user of capital) must equally share in the profits or losses arising out of the enterprise, what we call shareholders or stakeholders; uncertainty, risk, and speculation (*gharar*) is also prohibited; and, perhaps the most important, capital or investments should only support practices or products that are not forbidden or discouraged by Islam.[198] Worth emulating also is *zakat*, a form of alms-giving, treated in Islam as a religious obligation or tax, which, by Quranic ranking, is next after prayer (*salat*) in importance. While no amount is specified, the customary practice is that the amount of zakat paid on capital assets (e.g., money) is 2.5%. Islam is not the only religion that

---

[197] Cited in: Hinduism Today. 2016. Good Money, Bad Money. Satguru Sivaya Subramuniyaswami. Retrieved from <http://www.hinduismtoday.com/modules/ smartsection/item.php?itemid=4857>.

[198] Source: Principles of Islamic Banking. *Nida'ul Islam*. November–December, 1995.

advocates such an altruistic approach. The Hindu *Bhagavata Purana* says that a sixth of one's wealth must be given away to the less fortunate. This will take the soul to the next level on the spiritual path. If we want to fundamentally alter the modern 'context of life', the world must move towards this path. Whether it is the Katha Upanishad, or the Bhagavata purana, or the Tamil classic Thirukkural or the Quran, the message is therefore the same. Money should be earned and used only in permissible ways; money is not an end but a moral means for moral ends, meant for communal good. In the Bible, it is said that 'the love of money is the root of evil; wisely channeled, it can root out, at least outflank, evil'. Man cannot worship God and Mammon at the same time. Brian Hathaway, in his article *Money and the Kingdom of God* says, "If the overarching theme of Christ's message was the Kingdom of God, then the single most talked about topic within that theme is our use of money and possessions. Any attempt to live within the principles of God's Kingdom will bring us face to face with this topic and will shine a spotlight on our attitudes towards money and possessions".[199]

It is a truism to say that it is the bond of money that connects man to man in the contemporary world; the difference between one country and society to another is only a matter of degree. Scott Fitzgerald, author of *The Great Gatsby*, said the rich are different from other people. But they are different only because they are rich. If we become rich too, we would be no different by way of what we do. When the inherent avarice of our mind and the magnetism of money come together, it changes the state of our consciousness. An incisive and stimulating snapshot of this phenomenon is drawn in the book *Money and Class in America* by Lewis H. Lapham, the editor of *Harper's Magazine* and a thoughtful commentator. Although it is an exposé of the American love affair with money, and some statements appear rather apocalyptic, it reflects broadly money's sway over

---

[199] Hathaway, B. Money and the Kingdom of God. Retrieved from < http://www.reality.org. nz/articles/28/28-hathaway.php>.

man's mind today: "The avarice of the rich testifies not to the fulfillment of their appetite but to the failure of their imagination... In increasingly somnambulist state of mind, they discover themselves herded into a gilded cage from which they find it increasingly hard to escape. It isn't money itself that causes trouble; but the use of money as votive offering and pagan ointment. Imagining that they can be transformed into gods, they find themselves changed into dwarfs".[200] The gilded allusion is from Edith Wharton who describes the asylum of wealth as a gilded cage, "sumptuous in its décor but stupefying in its vacuity".[201] According to Lapham, "In a rich man's culture, the wisdom of the rich consists of what the rich wish to hear and think about themselves. The protocols of wealth govern the distribution of society's awards and punishments. People seeking redress for their grievances or compensation for their sorrow have no choice but to translate their grief into a specific sum of money, people come to be valued for the money they command, not for their deeds or character... people who define their lives as functions of their wealth display their affection, or rather the lack of it, by withholding both the substance and the symbolism of money". Lapham traces the effect of money on the arts and humanities that shape man's sensitivity. He says, "A good author is a rich author and a rich author is a good author... The romance of the artist as an impoverished seer no longer commands belief... The phrase 'poor artist' stands revealed as a contradiction in terms... The definition of money as the sublime good... results in the depreciation of all values that do not pay. What is moral is what returns a profit, and satisfies the judgment of the bottom line. Freedom comes to be defined in practice... as the freedom to exploit... gives rise to a system that puts a premium on crime, encourages the placid acquiescence of the dishonest

---

[200] Lapham, L.H. 1988. Money and Class in America, Notes and Observations on Our Civil Religion. New York, USA: Weidenfeld & Nicolson. p.7, p.27.

[201] Lapham, L.H. 1988. Money and Class in America, Notes and Observations on Our Civil Religion. New York, USA: Weidenfeld & Nicolson. p.30.

thought or deal, sustains the routine hypocrisy of politics and proclaims as inviolate the economic savagery otherwise known as the free market or freedom under capitalism". Many thoughtful commentators now are suggesting that one possible cause for the new-found love of what is dismissed as superstition and 'unscientific', religion, is a rejection of the modern capitalism-centric society.

Morality and Money

It is important to make everyone feel that there is more than money that can act as incentive to human betterment. Right now, what is moral in business is what returns a profit. Under the rules of a society that cannot distinguish between profit and profiteering, between money defined as necessity and money defined as luxury, murder is occasionally obligatory and always permissible.[202] By and large, the rich have the temperament of lizards, and their indifference to other people's joy or sorrow has always been evident. Among all the emotions, the rich have the least talent for love. It is possible to love, say, one's dog, but a human being presents a more difficult problem.[203] Assigned at an early age to the care of servants, surrounded through most of their lives by enemies who they mistake for friends, the children of the rich tend to become orphans.[204] The man besotted by a faith in money believes that if it can buy everything worth having—that if it can prolong life, win elections, relieve suffering, make hydrogen bombs, declare war, hire assassins, and so on—then surely it can grant him the patents of respect and triumph over so small as death. Despite the miracles of modern science, 'we feel the glory of revelation only when presented

---

[202] Lapham, L.H. 1988. Money and Class in America, Notes and Observations on Our Civil Religion. New York, USA: Weidenfeld & Nicolson. p.93.

[203] Lapham, L.H. 1988. Money and Class in America, Notes and Observations on Our Civil Religion. New York, USA: Weidenfeld & Nicolson. p.224.

[204] Lapham, L.H. 1988. Money and Class in America, Notes and Observations on Our Civil Religion. New York, USA: Weidenfeld & Nicolson. p.156.

with the embodiment of unutterable wealth'. Lapham compares American society to others and says, "The restlessness of American experience lends to money a greater power than it enjoys in less mobile societies. Not that money doesn't occupy a high place in England, India, or the Soviet Union, but in those less liquid climates, it doesn't work quite so many wonders and transformations".[205] Objects (or individuals) retain their value only insofar as they represent money. Lapham almost demonizes the rich: "The substitution of money for all other value becomes so complete as to change them, if not into gold, at least into stone. To describe the rich as people is to make a mistake with the language. Rich nouns or pronouns perhaps, not people. The rich tend to identify themselves with a sum of money and by so doing they relinquish most of their claims to their own community.[206] He goes on to say that "the obsession with money dulls the capacity for feeling and thought I think can be accepted as an axiom requiring no further argument".[207] Much of the critique of Lapham and his ilk centers around the culture and context of the lives of the rich. If that is all that there is to it, we can groan and bemoan and say a few sorry words and get on with our not-so-rich, 'thank-god-for-that' lives. But we have no such camouflage. Money casts its shadow over a much wider humanity than the rich, practically the entirety of humankind. For the poor, almost one out of three, money is the essential means to feed, clothe, and shelter the body or dependent bodies, and to lead a life of dignity. It is the effect of money on the huge and growing middle class that is of mounting concern. It is due to the corrosive influence of money, that the middle class, which traditionally in all societies had been a moral bastion, is now, with its large

---

[205] Lapham, L.H. 1988. Money and Class in America, Notes and Observations on Our Civil Religion. New York, USA: Weidenfeld & Nicolson. p.78.

[206] Lapham, L.H. 1988. Money and Class in America, Notes and Observations on Our Civil Religion. New York, USA: Weidenfeld & Nicolson. p.222.

[207] Lapham, L.H. 1988. Money and Class in America, Notes and Observations on Our Civil Religion. New York, USA: Weidenfeld & Nicolson. p.219.

numbers, in the vanguard of the moral decline of modern societies. Money and consumerism have a noxious nexus.

Money feeds, Lapham asserts, the appetite for consumerism; and consumerism in turn increases the thirst and need for money. Together they erode the moral insides of man. The need for a certain sum of money for a certain standard of living becomes overpowering enough to overcome the moral means of making 'both ends meet'. The lure of obscene opulence becomes irresistible to all but the morally most stubborn. For some people, having and spending money becomes an emotional and psychological irreplaceable; any diminution or deprivation can unhinge them emotionally. The character of money also changes according to those who possess it—inherited or acquired, easy or earned. Inherited wealth with few exceptions is more morally debilitating. Usually, not having undergone the travails of making money, the inheritors tend to spend it in ways that are personally and socially destructive. It induces a mindset of license, laxity, and lasciviousness. The caution and circumspection associated with old-fashioned frugality and need-based living becomes a casualty. An illustrative, possibly apocryphal story is told in America about John D. Rockefeller, the founder of the Rockefeller business empire and his son. Whenever the father came to New York he used to stay in a rather spartan hotel. When the son came, he used to stay across the street but in a far more luxurious and expensive hotel. The father was asked about this telling difference. He supposedly replied, 'Because I stay in a place like this, he could stay in a place like that'.

In America, when the mantra was 'greed is good' in the 1980s, there were three 'Michaels' who epitomized quick and stunning success and fabulous riches—Michael Jackson, the pop star; Michael Jordan, the basketball wizard; and Michael Milken, the Wall Street insider trader who later went to prison. They had three things in common: youth, genius, and luck. Of the three, only Michael Jordan remained a role model largely unaffected by the adulation and awesome affluence. Making good in the entertainment business always meant big money. A close second is sports. Given the pressures and frustrations of modern life, many people turn to a favorite sport for emotional escape and to transport them to another world where someone else is under pressure. Seeing movies one gets proxy pleasure; watching sport one achieves vicarious excellence. The problem is not only the accrual of easy money but also the mixing of our ideas of a celebrity and a role model, 'goodness of life' and the 'good life'. Those who attain intellectual or ethical excellence by the lives they lead, their creativity and legacy, serving as a candle in the dark, are hardly noticed, much less rewarded. They ought to be the real role models for the young and restless, and society should do everything possible to facilitate that process. Artist, writers, and musicians languish in obscure poverty, while a sportsperson barely out of his or her twenties is extolled and idolized by society and showered with gifts and goodies. It is not so much the lionizing of sportspersons that is the problem. The message that comes out is that social recognition can be obtained only through such sports. Even more, many of these sports icons, because of the wealth they control, lead lifestyles that are far from worthy of emulation and adoption. But in the public mind, their lifestyles and their achievements are indistinguishable. The result is while their fans rarely achieve their idol's professional success, they copy their lifestyles. In its raw essence, our adulation of movie stars and sportsmen is our fixation with money.

Precisely because man is mortal and could be dead the next minute, property becomes, next to progeny, the means to permanence. Property gives him a feeling, even if fleeting, of security in this life, and it gives him a piece of immortality. But the downside of security is daunting. As the British political theorist Harold Laski said, "Those who have security often luxuriate in a life devoid of meaning; and those who are poor can sometimes know the rarest things that life can offer... Those who have security may, in fact, live a life as solid and as pointless as the ugly mahogany with which they are surrounded. But at least their existence is freed from the specter of fear (of poverty)".[208] To live a life of dignity, society gives one no choice except to acquire property, movable or immovable. And, like in most other things in life, man loses the balance and property becomes the end and the means, the purpose and the process. Soon, instead of him owning property, property begins to own him. Private property is the heart of capitalism. Some even say we live in an 'Age of Intellectual Property'. The American Constitution guarantees, along with the right of liberty, the right of property which, some say "has contributed more to the growth of civilization than any other institution established by the human race".[209] Others like Russell say, "It is the preoccupation with possession, more than anything else, that prevents men from living freely and nobly". Freud said that by abolishing private property, one takes away the human love of aggression. And Plato wrote in his *Republic* that no one should possess any private property, if it can possibly be avoided; secondly, no one should have a dwelling or storehouse into which all have not the right to enter. But Aristotle, his disciple, said that it is not the possessions but the desires of mankind that require to be equalized. Aristotle was right that property is only a means to fulfill desire, but possession of property also whets and whips desire. Property may be inanimate but not neutral. Plato did not condemn property, only private property. He underestimated human ingenuity. Public property, if anything were to be really called that, does not fare much better with the public mind; the arbiters of that kind of property are 'public people with private minds'. Their public position offers easier access and a shortcut to possession of unearned property. It seems to be that in the proximity of property, morality runs away from the mind. The Bible says that it is harder for men who trust riches 'to enter the Kingdom of God'; and Oscar Wilde said that in the interest of the rich

---

[208] Laski, H.J. 1925. A Grammar of Politics. London, UK: George Allen & Unwin Ltd. pp.173,174.

[209] Cited in: William Howard Taft Quotes. William H. Taft, 27th President of USA (1909-13). Retrieved from <http://thinkexist.com/quotes/william_howard_taft/>

we must get rid of property. To both the rich would say 'Thanks, but we would rather keep our riches and take our chances'.

One of the minor mysteries of human life is that we all know we are transitory in this world but still we want to 'own', to 'possess', everything we come into contact with—whether it is a spouse or child or an employee, a piece of earth, or a house, even God. In fact, as Erich Fromm[210] pointed out, modern man gives more importance to 'having' than 'being'. So many battles and wars are fought over ownership of land. Rousseau wrote that "The first man who, having enclosed a piece of ground, bethought himself of saying *This is mine*, and found people simple enough to believe him, was the real founder of civil society. From how many crimes, wars and murders, from how many horrors and misfortunes might not any one have saved mankind, by pulling up the stakes, or filling up the ditch, and crying to his fellows, 'Beware of listening to this impostor; you are undone if you once forget that the fruits of the earth belong to us all, and the earth itself to nobody'".[211] But Rousseau goes on to add, "But there is great probability that things had then already come to such a pitch, that they could no longer continue as they were; for the idea of property depends on many prior ideas, which could only be acquired successively, and cannot have been formed all at once in the human mind". Kingdoms, empires, and nation states, the rich and the poor, are all defined, and constrained, by ownership. It is through this kind of ownership that most people make much money because, as they say, land appreciates, which means if you hoard it, its value only increases over time. The urge to own is insatiable and insidious. John Steinbeck says "If a man owns a little property, that property is him, it's part of him, and it's like him… The property is the man, stronger than he is. And he is small, not big. Only his possessions are

---

[210] Fromm, E. 1976. To Have or To Be?

[211] Rousseau, J-J. 1754. Discourse on the Origin and Basis of Inequality Among Men. Retrieved from <https://www.marxists.org/reference/subject/economics/rousseau/inequality/ch02.htm>.

big—and he's the servant of his property".[212] We own, and ceaselessly want to own, everything: land, house, goods, gadgets, and people. Actually, you can only buy and sell the rights to use; you can't actually own. But the idea of servitude, fidelity, loyalty, love, and even employment comes from ownership. People owe you their time, skills, attention, and exclusivity. When these are shared with someone else, we say we were 'betrayed'. And that leads to possessiveness, jealousy and, as in love, to bloody revenge. The words 'my' and 'mine' imply we own something. All our life is spent 'owning' and 'being owned'. In reality, we don't own anything that we cannot part with; that thing owns us. And in truth, we don't even own ourselves; we owe so much to so many people that very little is left to ourselves. But perhaps in death alone we finally own something, some property—at least in the traditions in which the dead are buried—a tiny piece of barren earth, which is all ours, whose price ironically appreciates over time, but is of no use to us, the dead.

And the question of property is inseparable from money; they are interchangeable. Without money there can be no property, and without property money is useless. Money lets us own and possess property and property multiplies money. Money lets us own not only physical property like land, buildings, and goods but even people. French anarchist philosopher Pierre-Joseph Proudhon described property as theft, because no one can own anything without depriving something, even a person, from someone who needs it more. Our passion for property, for ownership, and for possession, which are linked, has now taken a new dimension with our craze for the machine. It is the new status symbol—what machine we own, whether or not we need it or even know how to harness it. We are zealous, if not jealous, about our gadgets, appliances, and mechanical add-ons. We are almost, if not actually, in love with them and in love everything is fair or foul. And, as in love, it is fair not only to keep what we have, but to get what another has, if we take a fancy for it.

---

[212] Steinbeck, J.E. 1939. The Grapes of Wrath.

Good Life, and Goodness of Life

No act happens in its own exalted solitude; more than one person is invariably involved or affected in everything that occurs, and the fallout, too, is a blend of the good and the bad. The problem comes when we want, in every situation, the good for ourselves, and the bad for others. Although we do not still know what kind of a life is a well-lived life, and what is a wasted life, the mantra in modern society is 'good life' and 'growth', with idioms like 'standard of life' and 'quality time' thrown in between. And money is central to them all. The fact is, as Anthon St. Maarten put it, modern society has generally 'lost the plot'. The place where we 'lost it' is not in the marketplace of materialism, as many commonly believe; it is within the confines of our own consciousness, when it came under the undue influence of our own mind. While we will perhaps never get any conclusive answers to all that we ask or seek to know, the time has come to do some soul-searching on questions such as: What is the true value and purpose of money? What is affordability? How do we judge the moral worth of our work? And, What is a life well spent or a life that is wasted?

To be alive is distinct from goodness of life, which again is different from good life. This differentiation is what distinguishes the human from other animals. To be alive on earth, one needs very few things from nature, and in that condition, entails more giving than taking. Except man, all other creatures instinctively lead that kind of life. That is how nature maintains its own overall equilibrium, and stays alive. Why nature or God gave a 'different' treatment to man and endowed him with the faculty of willful choice we do not know. Has it overestimated or underestimated man? How does it intend to make amends to its 'mistake'? One theory is that in the 'original' man, all his endowments, faculties, powers, and abilities were working in harmony with each other and his way of life was not very different from that of the rest. Somewhere, that 'harmony' was sundered and then man wanted more than 'to be alive', and 'money' came in handy. We came to believe that 'what we cannot be, our money can get for us'. And that money can offset whatever nature has denied us. It has come to mean more than what it can actually do, its value more than its worth. John Stuart Mill wrote, "Its worth is solely that of the things which it will buy… Yet the love of money is not only one of the strongest moving forces of human life, but money is, in many cases, desired in and for itself".[213] Psychologically speaking, it has been described as "our projection onto coins, bills, bank accounts, and other financial instruments of our beliefs, hopes, and fears about how those things will affect who we are, what will happen to us and how we will be treated by others or by ourselves…".[214] Put differently, "Because money is the solution to poverty, it can make us believe that we are impoverished only by lack of money. So, money becomes a kind of greedy symbol for anything and everything we might want".[215] Pope Francis, in one of his addresses, noted that many of the problems the world is facing are rooted "in our relationship with money, and our acceptance of its power over us and our society… The worship of the golden calf of old has found a new and heartless image in the cult of money and the dictatorship of an economy which is faceless and lacking any truly humane goal".[216] Human cognitive and creative capacities then crafted a civilized life, which also meant living well with material conveniences and comforts. With technology making inroads into our daily life, consumerism came into being. The cocktail of 'culture', 'civilization', and 'consumerism' is what we call *good life*. In the process, man changed from a net-taker to a polluter and predator, and increasingly, from a consumer to "consumer goods which can be used and

---

[213] Cited in: Trachtman, R. 1999. The Money Taboo: Its Effects in Everyday Life and in the Practice of Psychotherapy. *Clinical Social Work Journal*. Vol. 27, No.3.

[214] Trachtman, R. 1999. The Money Taboo: Its Effects in Everyday Life and in the Practice of Psychotherapy. *Clinical Social Work Journal*. Vol. 27, No.3 (Fall, 1999).

[215] Diane Barth, F. 2001. Money as a Tool for Negotiating Separateness and Connectedness in the Therapeutic Relationship. *Clinical Social Work Journal*. Vol. 29, No.1.

[216] Pope Francis. 2013. Address to the New Non-Resident Ambassadors to the Holy See: Kyrgyzstan, Antigua and Barbuda, Luxembourg, and Botswana. Clementine Hall, Vatican City. 16 May 2013.

thrown away".[217] To get the inputs needed to make earth fit for civilized human life—or good life—man has turned his greedy gaze and the tool of technology on earth and nature, even if it meant wrecking the very ecosystem, biodiversity, and environment that sustains life on earth.

The concept of what is 'good, or worthy, life' has changed over time. Initially it was the same or close to what we now call goodness of life. It was in this line of thought that Socrates said, "not life, but good life, is to be chiefly valued". The problem is that our 'values' are our valuables. Confucius said, "Consideration for others is the basic of a good life, a good society". Instead of consideration, we have callousness. Down the line in our own time, when Bertrand Russell wrote that a "good life is one inspired by love and guided by knowledge". Love, today, is bereft of two of its essential attributes, selflessness and sacrifice. It is the casualty of the *Kali Yuga*. And the knowledge we pursue is for power and privilege and to be successful. But for most humans, good life has come to mean lots of leisure, luxury, and lust, what Thomas Merton calls devoting ourselves to the 'cult of pleasure'.[218] It is not pleasure *per se* that is pernicious. The question is, *whose* pleasure? If it is directed at others, it can cleanse our soul. Gandhi said, "To give pleasure to a single heart by a single deed is better than a thousand heads bowing in prayer". Giving pleasure gives us pleasure but too often, as, Aldous Huxley said,[219] it is a way to exercise our power and to feel good about it. The four words 'money cannot buy happiness' is a cliché and conventional wisdom but, true to our times, even that is under attack. Richer people in any country are happier than the poorer people. Clearly, happiness levels are in positive correlation with the amount of wealth a

---

[217] Pope Francis. 2013. Address to the New Non-Resident Ambassadors to the Holy See: Kyrgyzstan, Antigua and Barbuda, Luxembourg, and Botswana. Clementine Hall, Vatican City. 16 May 2013.

[218] Merton, T. 1948. No Man Is An Island.

[219] Aldous Huxley in *After Many a Summer Dies the Swan* (1939): "For the Truth is that we are kind for the same reason as we are cruel, in order that we may enhance the sense of our own Power".

person accumulates, and, contrary to popular belief, happiness does not level off when the assets reach a certain threshold. We equate happiness with quality of life. What remains hazy is the true nature of happiness and how one can measure. One can also say that smarter spending can give us happiness.[220] Whatever 'smarter' is intended to be in this context, it is true that if altruistically used or spent, money does give happiness. If we can make others happy, the happiness we can and will obtain is immeasurable. One does not have to be a billionaire or Bill Gates; even the poorest can spend or share their money and give happiness to someone else.

The New Gilded Age and the Emergence of the One-Percent

In the days of yore, most gloomy forecasts for man's future came from religious texts, soothsayers, crystal gazers, and occultists. Modern man came to dismiss such end-of-the-world scenarios as mere mumbo jumbo. However, if science had for a long time predicted and promised 'happy days ahead'—that the human would live as long as he wished, and would be equal to a virtual 'god'—it, too, is now finding itself nodding its head in consonance with the Doomsday Brigade. Some scientists warn that modern civilization is heading for collapse within a matter of decades, due to growing economic instability and the pressure exerted on the planet by industry's unsustainable appetite for resources. People of the world are waking up to the rude realization that a select few extremely wealthy fellow-humans are enslaving the rest of us and even endangering the planet. Economic inequality is increasingly seen as a red flag, symbolized by the global gross distortion of capital, wealth, and income, and the rise of a new plutocracy dominated by the super-rich, or the *One Percent*, which some are calling the dawn, not of the Golden Age, but of the 'New

---

[220] Dunn, E. and Norton, M. 2014. Happy Money: the Science of Happier Spending. New York, USA: Simon & Schuster.

Gilded Age'. So glaring is the disparity that, for instance, in USA, the top 1% own 40% of the financial assets, and the top 10% own upwards of 85%. Moreover, while extreme inequality is fuelling climate change, the richest 1% of the world's population produces 175 times as much carbon dioxide per person as the bottom 10%, and the richest 10% produce fully half of all carbon emissions.[221] Money matters in everything, even in disproportionately being exposed to climate change and air pollution. The materialist menace might be a modern phenomenon but matter, as separate from spirit, has always been a part of the human condition. So has been the spiritual aspiration to be relieved from the coils of matter. It is that One-Percent that controls power and public policy making. That is the reason why governments are unresponsive to the plight of the poor, and contribute to culpable failure of the state and its laws which are tilted to favor the interests of the influential in society and are detrimental to the basic needs of the minorities and the marginalized, the homeless and the landless. The plutocracy that rules the world is not only leading to the accelerated extinction of other species, which, if unchecked, will make human life unsustainable on earth, but also to the casting away of vast sections of society to the vultures and wolves of penury, destitution, and deprivation.

Much of what we seek in life, much of what human life has long been associated with, is coded in one word: progress. Henry George wrote in his classic *Progress and Poverty*, "Many of the characteristics, actions, and emotions of man are exhibited by the lower animals. But man, no matter how low in the scale of humanity, has never yet been found destitute of one thing of which no animal shows the slightest trace, a clearly recognizable but almost undefinable something, which gives him

---

[221] Oxfam. 2015. Extreme Carbon Inequality: Why the Paris Climate Deal Must Put the Poorest, Lowest Emitting and Most Vulnerable People First. 2 Dec 2015. <https://www.oxfam.org/sites/www.oxfam.org/files/file_attachments/mb-extreme-carbon-inequality-021215-en.pdf>.

the power of improvement—which makes him the progressive animal".[222] But what denotes progress? In common usage, it signifies the movement forward, an improvement, or advancement towards a goal. What is the goal that humans should seek to reach? It is the improvement and advancement towards material well-being that is commonly construed as progress. Such identification has long been in the works but it took a decisive turn with the Industrial Revolution where we paid, and continue to pay, an apocalyptic price. Instead of trying to achieve 'moral' movement, we got ensnared in an insatiable, maybe insane, drive towards satiation of both inane and wanton wants. How to reverse the course and change the coordinates and compass is the central challenge. If we can meet this challenge, other challenges like climate change, social disintegration, and social and moral entropy will, at the least, lose their bite. We have to learn to radically refocus, redirect, realign our intellectual, psychic, scientific, technological, even spiritual resources to face up to the realities of the emergent world. And if we can do that no problem is insurmountable. We don't have to go back to the Stone Age or become neo-Luddites. But we must give up this craze for speed, smartphones, cyborgs, and endless automation, which exact a huge environmental cost. The more we rely on appliances the less capable we will become to act without them. And automation, it has been said, breeds automation, and human beings become optional, or unnecessary, to get human work done. How can the most 'intelligent' creature on earth be so stupid as to choose self-destruction through self-replacement? The answer comes from writer Sue Halpern: "the priorities are clear: money first, people second".[223] Put differently, we are prepared to downsize, de-skill, and de-dignify ourselves to empower companies and make businesses more profitable and the rich richer. But can we blame it all on money? What

---

[222] George, H. 1879. Progress and Poverty: An Inquiry Into the Cause of Industrial Depressions and of Increase of Want with Increase of Wealth: The Remedy.

[223] Halpern, S. 2014. How Robots & Algorithms Are Taking Over. Review of Nicholas Carr's book The Glass Cage: Automation and Us. *The New York Review of Books*. USA. 2 Apr 2014. p.28.

about our much-touted free will and freedom to make choices? Frankly, and really, we don't know.

One thing we need to get straight. We tend to think that the pervasive predatory role of money is a part of the modern malaise. The truth is that money or wealth was always integral to human existence, a kind of thorn in the flesh, an evil, but necessary nonetheless, like evil itself. The message from the scriptures is mixed. On the one hand, we came to terms with the reality that, as a social animal, we have to live with it. On the other hand, we also recognized its addictive, divisive, and corrupting character. The Gospel[224] says that Jesus cautioned his disciples about the seductive power of money and said, "It is easier for a camel to go through the eye of a needle, than for a rich man to enter the kingdom of God". And an ancient Hindu text, the classic *Arthashastra* by Kautilya (who is also known as Chanakya) states, *Dhanam moolam idham jagat*—'the world revolves around wealth'. This aphorism is much quoted and also equally misunderstood and misapplied to justify reverence for money. It actually conveys the contrary caution, that one should live for better ideals than for basal desires and worldly pleasures. But it is also important to learn that ancient wisdom and traditions also recognized the reality of money in human life, provided it is pursued righteously. Times and things have dramatically changed since the time of Kautilya, who is believed to have lived in the 3rd century BCE. But money remains supreme and unrestrained, if any, stronger and more intrusive and invasive. It has given birth to an assortment of 'isms' like materialism, consumerism, capitalism, communism, etc. And it has driven technology in the wrong direction, towards the mass production of goods, gadgets, and gizmos for the well-to-do and the tech-savvy bourgeoisie.

One of the greatest challenges we now face is to induce and orchestrate a sea change in our relationship with money. In fact, if we could develop the mindset and means to ensure that it is spread equitably and justly across

---

[224] Mark 10:25.

competing needs and priorities in the human population, it will give a tremendous boost to a fairer and far less fractious world. On the one hand, it will lift over a billion people out of acute poverty, and on the other hand, it will make it possible to do research and development on technologies that are currently still-born for want of funding, and which are critical to solve any nagging and pestering social problems like climate change, mass illiteracy, and ill health. We must move from grudging acceptance to recognition without reservations that it can do a world of good to the world. One of the hotly debated issues now is about a 'world without money', and how, and if, such a development will be a bane or a blessing. The hope is that such a world would be fairer, kinder, and gentler. There will be no rich or poor, and no money-power. It is hard to tell how such a utopian world might actualize. While other mechanisms like UBI (universal basic income) are worth intellectual pursuit, the more practical pursuit is to try to turn money around from the biblical root of evil to a 21st-century catalyst of social justice. We must believe that money and *moksha*, like science and spirituality, are not antagonistic but capable of coexisting. In other words, make as money as one can, but ensure that it is spread and shared as broadly and deeply as possible. And make sure it reaches those corners where it can flower the potential of the downtrodden and the dirt poor. Financial technologies can help bridge the gap between social mission and profit motive. Public policies and social norms must support activities that induce money to flow where it is needed the most, and turn society itself into what we may call a 'sharing society'. For that, fundamentally, the creation of money must be in public hands, not with private banks. Only then can money be channeled for social priorities like poverty alleviation and public health infrastructure, and for finding solutions to common problems like climate change. Money need not always be morally corrosive or socially disruptive; it can be morally uplifting and socially equalizing, if channeled properly. There are other motivators besides money, but money by its weight as a critical need in today's world can be a powerful inspiration. We need a new genre of social entrepreneurship that is capable of merging 'public purpose and private profit'. Along with the other two 'M's—morality and mortality—it is another, perhaps the most important, dimension of contextual-change. What is now perceived as an impediment has to be turned into an instrument for social empowerment. For the real obstacle to common good and human enhancement—which science is focusing all its energies upon through the medium of the machine—is not money, but our own unchecked mind. Still, at best, money is neutral; not the mind, which is both monkeyish and malicious. Money can do both good and bad, but as long as the mind dominates our consciousness, money is likely to do more harm than good. Technology is more 'misdirected'; it ignores the basic needs of the vast majority of mankind. We will continue the present system in which almost 97% of money in circulation in some advanced societies is created by private banks,[225] as it were, 'out of nothing' for private economic gain. If this continues, money can never become a moral agent. Money is too indispensable to be driven by money-making. Which means that without consciousness-change, we cannot expect much good to come out of money. In short, we must fundamentally change the place money occupies in our conscious mind as a giver of good things of life to a catalyst of an orderly and just human society. We need a critical mass for such a change, and that must come from the millennials who are tech-savvy, but morally adrift, wandering around, trying to find some meaning for why they are alive and what they should choose to do with their time. If that happens, the world will be a far better place, less fractious and more peaceful, less miserable and happier. And that will certainly make every human relationship and institution more stable and synergistic. More than anything else, it will greatly aid the forces of good and virtue in the war within.

---

[225] Martin Wolf, Chief Financial Editor of the *Financial Times*, UK. 9 November 2010: "The essence of the contemporary monetary system is creation of money, out of nothing, by private banks' often foolish lending."

Towards a New
Vocabulary of Morality

Malice and Morality

To be a 'moral species'—at least to be *known* as one—has long been one of man's enduring aspirations. And that has never been in sharper public glare, and at greater risk, than in our present times. We often spot, if not sport, what is called 'virtue signalling' without ethical intent and with more grandstanding than introspection. Today, a truly moral person is an oddity, if not an oxymoron. In the present world, we have to make more choices than ever before, and morality is increasingly being seen as just a matter of personal taste. The generation of emerging adults appears to have concluded that what is traditionally understood as 'moral', is an impediment to their pursuit of success and happiness. A slew of questions spring to mind. Is morality a force or an action and can it exist without a home or a host? Are we like the crooked timber that Immanuel Kant famously referred to, from which 'nothing entirely can be built'? What if the things we think or feel are good, are, in fact, *not* so good? And whose 'good' is it, anyway? Can a 'good' person do immoral things and still be good? How does one balance ends and means? What is the 'larger good' and in relation to what? Do we need to dirty our hands to do dirty work? Are good and evil entirely circumscribed by an event or individual or do they have an autonomous existence? Are they universal or particular to the human species? Are the rules of moral accountability specific to each species? And how about God; do we need Him as the source of all morality? Can one lead a moral life independent of a 'belief' in God? Can we do good for its own sake?

Regardless of answers to such troubling questions, most of us might tend to concur with what Sir Danvers Carew opined in RL Stevenson's *Dr Jekyll and Mr Hyde*: "No man could be as good as he looks... A man cannot destroy the savage in him by denying its impulses. The only way to get rid of a temptation is to yield to it". If we want to 'better our behavior'—despite all this—what is the litmus test? And 'better' in comparison to what and who in a world as psychotic as ours? Making the quandary even more murky, bereft of a moral compass and stricken with a comatose conscience, if one is determined, against all odds, to lead a moral life, one does not know what precisely to do or not do in practice. It is one reason why we behave so badly, and why we seem to be losing the war within—the war between the 'good' and 'evil'. Perhaps one practical way is the Benjamin Franklin way: to begin the day with the question: *What good shall I do this day?* And end the day asking oneself: *What good have I done today?*

The single most important obstacle has been the malice entrenched in our mind. Living in a brutal world like ours, one of the very few things that gives us some satisfaction and a hint of hope about our future is the belief that, although we arose from brutes, we are better—better because we think we can judge right and wrong, and therefore, that we are, or can be, more responsible and responsive in our earthly conduct. It is another matter that none of such assumptions are any longer accurate. We live in a morally ambiguous and ambivalent world, in which everyone wants to be moral, and most think they are, and yet morally macabre things continue to be done and no one feels responsible or remorseful. But to begin with, in such a compromised and corrupting world, what should one do to remain rooted to our moral moorings? How this has come about is a subject of scholarly discourse, whether it is hard-wired by nature or acquired through evolution. Some say that morality is simply an instinct just like sexual desire. Theologists like William Craig posit that, "If God does not exist, objective moral values and duties do not exist". Philosopher Patricia Churchland argues in her book *Braintrust* that it is a 'false dilemma' to claim that 'either God secures the moral law or morality is an illusion', because 'morality is grounded in our biology'. And atheists like Sam Harris attack both moral absolutism—that some things are absolutely right or wrong no matter the circumstances—and moral relativism—that moral or ethical statements, which vary from person to person, are all equally valid and no one's opinion of right and wrong is really better than any other. They propose that moral values are, in reality, moral facts, and as facts they can be scientifically understood by studying the brain and behavior. All this inevitably raises the matter of the problem of evil. In fact, it is a double problem of evil. Some ask: what is the essential nature of this evil and wounded world, and is there any way out of this woe and misery? From the other side, some ask: why should this essentially good world harbor any evil, and how can we live with it wholeheartedly? Is evil a perennial characteristic of finite existence, or are we responsible for the experience of evil? We must remember that, much as we might wish, we cannot get rid of evil. For, as Socrates said, "Evils, Theodorus, can never pass away; for there must always remain something which is antagonistic to good. Having no place among the gods in heaven, of necessity they hover around the mortal nature, and this earthly sphere". Science, which so far left such matters to religion and philosophy, is now trying to step in and make a difference. Recent research by neurologists like Michael Stone (*The Anatomy of Evil*, 2009) indicates that violent criminals have amygdalae (the region of the brain believed to play a key role in the emotions) that are smaller or that don't function properly. Views of people like Sam Harris and such findings are in sync with the current scientific chorus: everything—good, evil, empathy, compassion, aggression, love, addiction, even mind and consciousness—is simply a matter of our brain. If it is malstructured or malfunctioning, or the internal balance is disturbed, things go haywire and we misbehave. Other experts argue that our brain is a big part of us, but *we* are bigger than that. Indeed, our over-reliance on the brain, to the exclusion of everything else, in particular the heart, is what is inducing us to take the wrong route. If we want to strengthen and sharpen the kinder and gentler side of our personality, and make morality our default mode of choice-making, for example, we need to more than tamper with parts of our brain.

Whether man was born crooked or as a blank slate, or as a Noble Savage, or became a civilized brute, the fact is that man has always struggled to give birth to his 'Baby-Buddha' within. The 'birth' is a struggle because the wicked in us does not let it go. And we need morality precisely because we are not (wholly) moral. That for man to be wicked is easy and to be moral is difficult was recognized by all religions but with several nuances. That was why they all tried to pin us down to moral codes of conduct such as the Biblical Ten Commandments, the Seven Laws of Noah, and the Quranic Ten Instructions. By following and practicing these precepts and prohibitions, the expectation was that man would tread the moral path. While the very rationale of religious life was the assumption that it would keep man morally circumscribed, what has happened is that religious zealotry itself, down the ages, became a source of unspeakable evil and triggered the barbaric Crusades of the Middle Ages. And that continued through the ages, with some ups and some downs. Religion is closely associated with God, and God, through His every revelation, clearly instructed or implored man to lead a moral life and laid down the path to take. How then could religion itself rouse such intense emotions and feelings of intolerance, hatred, sadism, and blood thirstiness in the minds of millions of otherwise 'good' and 'god-fearing' people? Is there anything in the genre of religious knowledge that is tailor-made to arouse the worst in the human mind, subverting the good in us? Or has the evil inside us become so strong and virulent that it is looking for opportunities to express itself, and religious trigger is just one such opportunity? And does the current state of religious bloodletting reflect the waning fortunes of the good against the evil in the war within?

Although externally it has not always been so, morality, however weak, has always been a force for the good in the war within. Experts differ on the origins of morality. But it does appear that very early after his advent on earth, man realized that he needed the help of others around him simply to stay away from the throat of another animal. While it still did not mean they did not cut each other's throats, it did sow the seeds of morality. It is morality, not the bigness of the brain, that empowered man to outwit other much stronger and ferocious animals. Contrary to what is generally assumed, what allowed us to escape extinction was not the survival of the fittest, but as Darwin himself posited in his book *The Descent of Man*, it was the survival of the kindest. Darwin also wrote that natural selection favored the evolution of compassion, a statement of great contemporary significance. Morality evolved initially as a means to cooperate for the common good, and as a biological device to place the 'us' before the 'me' in small groups. We now need that too, not to survive, but to turn our individual energies into collective synergy. The moral axiom 'act so as to elicit the best in others and thereby in thyself' could serve as a point of departure. If we can do that, there are no limits to what we can accomplish. They say we are angels with only one wing, but that we can still fly by embracing each other. The choice is ours. It does not mean that we were not mean, malicious or murderous then; far from it. But it does mean that the moral sense in us became more manifest in response to the realization that it was the only way to prevail in those cut-throat conditions. Sadly, in today's cut-throat context of life, we have done a reversal: we have embraced the maxim of the 'survival of the smartest' in place of 'survival of the kindest'. And, instead of natural selection, it is now '*un*-natural selection'; fittest is smartest. And there is a growing concern that morality is in free fall, illustrated, for example, by the perception that Mammon matters more than morals. Some say that what we are facing is nothing less than a moral meltdown. Some are asking the agonizing question: have we come to such a perilous pass where morality has lost its raison d'être, lost the power, in and of itself, to motivate us towards good behavior? And, are morality and modernity an odd couple or inherently hostile forces? Is there any scope and space for a futurist in a terrified, compromised, morally-wounded world? What is the right moral option for a human being when he concludes that the world and the planet are safer without human presence? Does the present paradigm of modern life constitute the choice of what the Katha Upanishad called the primrose path of *preyas* (the pleasant), at the expense of *sreyas* (the good)? The path of preyas implies that any action that is pleasurable is good, to live his or her life in search of the next pleasurable thing, with no regard for attaining any higher purpose for his or her life. But then, the question arises: is it impossible to be good while leading a good life, a life of affluence, luxury, leisure? Some are posing 'the mother of all moral questions': do we, as a species that has done what it has for so long, have a moral right and legitimacy to inhabit this planet? What is the right moral thing for a human being to do in a world that seems to sink deeper and deeper into moral quagmire? We need a morality that is suitable to the future challenges and a force that deepens our interrelatedness and interdependence. While these issues do matter and need to be pondered over, we must not think that we are left only with a Hobson's choice between morality and modernity. Fact is both are indispensable and irreversible. We cannot reverse the tide of history and roll back modernity or allow morality to be the fall guy or a pushover. Actually, one could say that modernity already is passé and that we are living in a postmodern world. Clearly, morality too needs to be revisited and re-conceptualized to serve as a force for unity and sanity in a world which can only be characterized as a 'man-eats-man world'. If properly handled and guided, modernity, the fulcrum of which is technology, could be a huge help to strengthen the forces of morality within and without. But technology itself, or the *technosphere* as some describe it, now constitutes the widest crucible for morality and throws up new ethical challenges. Some thoughtful observers like Andrew Kimbrell see a "dramatic dichotomy between evil as it occurred in the social era of human history and evil as incarnated in the current technological sphere... the technosphere has created a technological, institutional plane on which 'the system' [not the individual] effectuates evil in circumstances where individuals and their emotions, ethics, or morals play no significant role".[226] It has nurtured a milieu in which, as Scott Peck (*The Road Less Travelled*, 1978) puts it across, modern evil is that which "one percent of the people cause, but in which 100 percent of us ordinary sinners participate through our everyday sins". He says that evil straddles the line between a personality disorder and spiritual disorder, and an evil person knows that they are doing evil, while a sociopath does not, even though their actions may be very similar. New dilemmas confront us. For example, who should we program an autonomous car to save: a pedestrian crossing the road, or the passenger in the car? And does it matter who the pedestrians are? Every technological advance invariably raises deep and wrenching moral issues, and it is not possible to have universal moral values because they are culture-sensitive. The more technology becomes autonomous, the greater is the need to design them properly. This coincidentally was underlined by the world's first robot citizen, *Sophia*. We must find a way to embed ethics into technology. And when robots increasingly replace humans, questions such as 'robot rights' will arise. As robots develop more advanced

---

[226] Kimbrell, A. 2000. Cold Evil: Technology and Modern Ethics. Annual E.F. Schumacher Lecture. Schumacher Center for a New Economics. Retrieved from <https://centerforneweconomics.org/publications/cold-evil-technology-and-modern-ethics/>.

artificial intelligence, empowering them to think and act like humans, new moral issues will arise. But for this, we do not have the consciousness necessary to direct technology for the long-term and for inter-generational justice and greater good. Similarly, morality can significantly offset many of the negative aspects of modernity. On the other hand, if misdirected, modernity could be a huge hindrance to making human life more moral. And morality, in its form and structure, is not sufficiently suitable to make the human world a humane world. What could make the difference is the war within.

The moral context today is vastly different from the times it helped small groups and tribes to cooperate for survival. Our brain cannot extend that necessity to the current global scale. The moral choices and dilemmas we have to make and face are vastly different. *WE* must bridge the gap between moral and social. What Nikolai Berdyaev said about spirituality equally applies to morality: "The question of bread for myself is a material question, but the question of bread for my neighbor is a spiritual question". We have to bring together the social and the spiritual. That is the way to contain the contagion of materialism. Concern is mounting that our materialistic mindset is not only leading to a destructive lifestyle but also creating mental problems. Recent studies link materialism to a variety of mental health issues, including anxiety and depression, with side-effects such as selfish attitudes and behaviors, putting kids particularly at risk. We now have to deal with and interact with nonhuman personas like robots, artificial intelligence (AI) systems, and cyborgs, and we have to make moral choices in relation to them. We not only need a new understanding of morality, we now need the tools to design and program it in a manner suitable to the digital age. The digital revolution has shrunk the world into an electronic village while, at the same time, widening the distance and distrust between man and man. It has also made raising kids 'with a conscience' more complex and difficult. But the ushering of a new morality must start with us. We cannot expect teenagers to lead lives of empathy if we ourselves do not lead such lives. We must first embody and exhibit the qualities we want the soon-to-be adults to show. *Be* the good we want our kids to be. *Show* the sharing we want them to imbibe. Early moral development is crucial for a moral society.

For, in the digital age, man is, at the same time, a solitary being and a social being. What technology has done is to make man both isolated and intertwined. It is even being boasted that technology will allow us to 'ditch speech and communicate using nothing but our thoughts' by 2050. As an isolated individual, living with minimal human touch, man's actions are more prone to be more self-centered and anti-social. But the impact of his decisions, distractions, and actions can be far reaching. We make myriad, mostly minute, choices in everyday life and they have moral ramifications. The context raises new ramifications but our consciousness has remained the same. The moral context cannot be separated from our overall living context, just as our moral behavior cannot be understood without juxtaposing it with our generic behavior and conduct. And like everything else, how we behave, morally or wickedly, is also an extension of what happens inside us, in the war within. Indeed, the two principal opponents in the war are morality and immorality, *dharma* and *adharma*. If morality and dharma are dominant, then we behave morally with love, kindness, and compassion. If they are on the wane, then our behavior will be tainted with avarice, aggression, hatred, and intolerance. If we want to avoid a moral meltdown, we need to make morality more compatible to the contemporary context.

Enlarging the Circle of Compassion

Our incapacity to factor in compassion into our daily life is a major contributory cause of our enfeeblement and the coarsening of contemporary human society. The two things we need to nurture and manifest in life are passion and compassion. We need to be passionate with compassion, and compassionate with our passions. Compassion in fact symbolizes the highest virtue. Through the sharing of suffering, we can help each other to become better beings. In the Bhagavad Gita, it is said that 'When [a man] sees all beings as equals in suffering or in joy because they are like himself, that man has grown perfect in yoga'. The principle of compassion lies at the heart of all religious and ethical and spiritual traditions, calling us to always treat all others as we wish to be treated ourselves, to strive ceaselessly to lighten the lives of others, to refrain from inflicting any sort of pain on all creatures. A telling and lofty example is an ancient practice in some old Russian towns. When a condemned criminal was carried off in a cart to execution, the people would follow behind, weeping for him. They would cry out to him, begging him to pray for them when he reached the 'other side'; even exclaiming that he went to die in their place—all being worthy of a death in one way or another; all being guilty.[227] It means that justice and compassion are not incompatible. What good is compassion if it is reserved for the virtuous? And what use is love if it is not reciprocal? And yet, even those who are reputed to be 'good' and 'decent' and even 'generous' among us have always found it difficult to make compassion a passion, that which gives us irresistible pleasure. It has always been a struggle and now more so than ever. As Jack Finley, the science fiction writer reminds us: "This is a time when it becomes harder and harder to continue telling yourself that we are still good people. We hate each other. And we're used to it". That 'hate' shows up in multiple ways, irritation, intolerance, anger, aggression, suicide, murder. Not being able to hate anyone anytime is a quality that human beings have yet to imbibe. It is said that, when asked for a summary of the Jewish religion in the most concise terms, the 1st-century Jewish leader Rabbi Hillel stated, "That which is hateful to you, do not do to your fellow. That is the whole Torah. The rest is the explanation; go and learn". The *Ishavasya* Upanishad says, "He who sees the entire world of animate and inanimate objects in himself,

---

[227] Fitzpatrick, S. 2015. Dostoevsky and the Glory of Guilt. *Crisis Magazine*, 1 Jun 2015.

and also sees himself in all animate and inanimate objects, because of this does not hate anyone".

That is a lofty ideal, but even without reaching such heights we can find no utility for hate. Hate is so wasteful, so utterly useless, that it is hard even to rationalize it. Martin Luther King Jr. said, "I have decided to stick with love; hate is too great a burden to bear". But that is a 'burden' in different degrees, shapes, and avatars that we all carry. Personal, religious, ethnic, and racial hatred is in the very air we breathe in and out today. Hate has become so acceptable in our language that we use this word without always intending it to be that. Even in ordinary conversation, we involuntarily say, 'I hate this' or 'I hate him'; even if it is really not in the sense of hatred, which is the intense desire to destroy another person, even if not necessary. It is malice in action. Even love, if unreciprocated or obstructed, can turn into murderous hatred. The way to counter it is to cultivate compassion, learn it like any other skill. Engaging with another individual without expecting anything frees one from the confines of 'separateness' and of one's ego. It is not only a spiritual *sadhana* but also a social imperative at this juncture in our troubled world. Einstein said, "Our task must be to free ourselves by widening our arc of compassion to embrace all living creatures and the whole of nature and its beauty". Compassion is more than helping people in distress or disability; more than generosity or mercy. As Mackie Ruka of New Zealand's Waitaha Maori tribe says, compassion is an act of power, of *transformative* power. It is our inability to harness that power that impoverishes us mentally and spiritually. We seem more capable of passion than compassion, of zealotry more than moderation. We need both passion and compassion, but we should try to be passionately compassionate, and compassionately passionate. When we are passionate or obsessed about something, like being in love, we become single-minded and driven, and everything else becomes secondary or non-existent. All related actions become involuntary and automatic. We must bring that state of mind to compassion.

For the theologian Matthew Fox, 'compassion, in its broadest sweep', is more than moral commandment, it is 'but a flow and overflow of the fullest human and divine energies'. It has been described as the 'keen awareness of the interdependence of all things (Thomas Merton); as 'the ultimate and most meaningful embodiment of emotional maturity'. It is through compassion that a person achieves the peak experiences and deepest reach in his search for self-fulfillment. Eckhart Tolle says, "Compassion is the awareness of a deep bond between yourself and all other creatures". All religions extol compassion as the highest value and virtue, both as a way to alleviate suffering and as a tool of salvation, *nirvana* or *moksha*. It is called *daya* in Hinduism, and *karuna* in Buddhism, although both terms are interchangeable. Compassion has been called the transcendental and experiential heart of the Buddha's teachings. It is one of the four tenets of the Buddhist doctrine of *Brahmavihara*: loving-kindness; compassion; empathetic joy; and equanimity. Compassion for all life, human and animal, is the very soul of Jainism. In fact, so identified is Buddhism with compassion, that the Buddha himself came to be known as the 'Compassionate One'. In Christianity too, compassion is given great importance. Jesus tells his listeners in the Sermon on the Mount, "Blessed are the merciful, for they shall obtain mercy". In the Parable of the Good Samaritan, he holds up to his followers the ideal of compassionate conduct. True Christian compassion, say the Gospels, should extend to all, even to the extent of loving one's enemies. As far as Islam is concerned, each of the 114 chapters of the Quran, with one exception, begins with the verse, "In the name of God, the Compassionate, the Merciful". The Arabic word for compassion is *rahmah*. A good Muslim has to commence each day, each prayer and each significant action by reciting *Bismillah ir-Rahman ir-Rahim*—invoking "God the Merciful and the Compassionate". In practical terms, compassion is two-pronged behavioral manifestation, one affirmative, the other avoidance: to help everyone who asks for or needs help; and not to hurt anyone by word or deed, if not in thought. That is the distilled wisdom, the backbone of all religions. Sin, it has been said, is hurting others unnecessarily; every other 'sin' is invented nonsense. The Dalai Lama said, "Our primary purpose in life is to help others. And if you can't help them, at least do not hurt them". It does not make a difference if one is a theist or an atheist. If we 'believe' in God, we are doing His work, as his proxy. And if we do not, if there is no God to help or protect the suffering, then there is all the more reason for another man to step up and help a fellow-man. Plato said, "Be kind, for everyone you meet is fighting a harder battle". We think that our 'battle' is the hardest because we cannot feel, or experience, the nature or the ferocity of the battles of others. We 'hurt' others and are wary of helping because of the 'mine–thine' mental divide, but which, Einstein told us, is 'an optical delusion of man's consciousness'. We forget that, as Herman Melville wrote, "our actions run as causes, and they come back to us as effects". It is not that most of us are incapable of being profoundly or compulsively compassionate; we are compassionate selectively and inconsistently. Many sensitive souls have long doubted whether true compassion exists at all in the human essence—or whether it is inherently rooted in self-interest. Our terrible, bloodstained, savage history gives no comfort. Indeed, the merciless message of human history is that, although man is capable of great good, he can be more easily seduced by unspeakable evil. Carl Jung wrote, "When [our shadow] appears… it is quite within the bounds of possibility for a man to recognize the relative evil of his nature, but it is a rare and shattering experience for him to gaze into the face of absolute evil".

We are all a blend of good and evil, malevolence and magnanimity, virtue and vice, and a host of other pairs of opposites. It is pointless to endlessly debate which is 'natural' and embedded, and which is not. If they are not natural or innate, they wouldn't be there in the first place. We are home to the noblest and vilest, sacred, and sordid, of emotions, feelings, and thoughts. Which of these, or a combination, comes out and affects behavior depends on the course of the war within. Compassion is not empathy or altruism, though the concepts are related. While empathy relates more generically to our ability to take the perspective of and feel the emotions of another human person, compassion is when those feelings and thoughts extend to a desire to help. Altruism, in turn, is the kind, benevolent behavior often prompted by feelings of compassion, though one can feel compassion without acting on it, and altruism is not always motivated by compassion. Although we tend to think that compassion or empathy or altruism are about 'giving' and being 'selfless', that is not always true. We gain far more than we give, both physically and spiritually. As the Dalai Lama puts it, 'the first beneficiary of compassion is always oneself'. He goes on, "If you want others to be happy, practice compassion. If you want to be happy, practice compassion". But we cannot be compassionate outside if there is no contentment inside. If we are discontented within, then we will try to find contentment outside, which means fulfilling desires. The focus will then be on that effort, not on helping or being compassionate towards others. In the modern world, most persons are trapped in a state of disquietedness, disaffection, alienation, and existential angst, and that is the reason why they find it so herculean to be compassionate in their behavior. It is because they are discontented with so many unfulfilled desires that they are so avaricious in their behavior; they want to find 'contentment within' by filling it up with material things. It is like trying to put out a fire by pouring fuel onto it. In compassion, one wholly gives, and is thankful for being given the opportunity to give.

Compassion is not only good for one's soul, but also for one's body. Recent studies of compassion reject the inevitability of self-interest. These studies support a view of the emotions as rational, functional, and adaptive. Compassion and benevolence and altruism, which are the hallmarks of all religions, this research suggests, are an evolved part of human nature, embedded in our brain and biology, and ready to be cultivated for the greater good. The study suggests that "the brain, then, seems wired up to respond to others' suffering—indeed, it makes us feel good when we can alleviate that suffering".[228] New research has shown that "when we feel compassion, our heart rate slows down, we secrete the bonding hormone oxytocin, and regions of the brain linked to empathy, caregiving, and feelings of pleasure light up, which often results in our wanting to approach and care for other people". They also indicate there is a biological basis for compassion, and there are physical benefits to practicing compassion— people who practice it produce 100% more DHEA, which is a hormone that counteracts the ageing process, and 23% less cortisol—the 'stress hormone'. They are in accordance with the view held by Charles Darwin that 'compassion and benevolence are an evolved part of human nature, an intrinsic part of our brain in particular, and biological system on the whole'. Studies indicate that "compassion is not simply a fickle or irrational emotion but rather an innate human response embedded into the folds of our brains". This "suggests that being compassionate causes a chemical reaction in the body that motivates us to be even more compassionate". Another research tells us that its findings "support the possibility that compassion and altruism can be viewed as trainable skills rather than stable traits". Specifically, they report that taking a course in compassion leads to increased engagement of certain neural systems, which prompts higher levels of altruistic behavior... Brain scans revealed a "pattern of neural changes" in those who had received compassion training, including "neural systems implicated in understanding the suffering of other people, executive and emotional control, and reward processing".

Cast Out the Beam Out of Thine Own Eye

Under what circumstances and conditions should an individual be refrained from what he chooses to do? Philosophers have long debated and differed on this question. Some have argued that it should only be when his

---

[228] Keltner, D., Marsh, J., and Smith, J.A. (eds.). 2010. The Compassionate Instinct: the Science of Human Goodness. New York, USA: W.W. Norton.

intended action is a potential threat to others. By extension, it means that an individual is the best judge of what is good for him and that no one else can be a surrogate. Others have expanded it to include the individual's own well-being, positing that, in point of fact, most people do not act, even if they do know, in their own interests, and tend to emphasize the short term over the long term, a premise that is the basis of much of social legislation. The question is: while legality can, to an extent, serve both purposes—prevent harm to others and protect an individual from himself—what about such 'behavior' of the species? Human behavior is now a grave and growing peril to the lives and interests of other species, in addition to its own. Albert Schweitzer paraphrased it aptly: "Man has the lost the capacity to foresee and to forestall. He will end up destroying the earth". Man is exhibiting three lethal tendencies: self-absorption, self-righteousness, and self-destruction. All three are interconnected and interdependent. We are so self-absorbed that every event in the world and in others' lives is judged by its effect on us. It is self-righteousness that makes us blind to our flaws and 'all-eyes' to others' lapses. The truth also is, as Rumi reminds us, "Many of the faults you see in others, dear reader, are your own nature reflected in them". Jesus exhorts us, "Thou hypocrite, first cast out the beam out of thine own eye; and then shalt thou see clearly to cast out the mote out of thy brother's eye".[229] Besides self-righteousness, we are single-minded to a fault about self-destruction; we leave nothing to chance in our drive to do things injurious to our well-being. We are, deliberately, and for something as ephemeral as profit, polluting the air we breathe, the food we eat, the rivers, the oceans, and filling the air with enough toxic fallout to put poison into our own children's bones. The eighteen-fold increase in the global economic output has not only deepened the divide between the elite and the masses, but also created the present environmental crisis, potentially cheating our children of their future. We are not even sparing the mighty oceans. It is said that our oceans are 30% more acidic than they

---

[229] Matthew 7:1–5 (King James Version).

were a bare thirty years ago. Scientists tell us that 'just the acidification of the oceans, by itself, is enough to wipe out life on this planet'. And that the acidification of the ocean today is proceeding on a greater and faster basis than anything that geologists can find in fossil records for the past 65 million years. Another existential risk, experts tell us, is the release into the atmosphere of methane. Its effect on global warming is 23 times more powerful than that of carbon dioxide, over the course of a century, and even worse in the short term of about 10 years. The National Science Foundation (USA) has recently warned that the "release of even a fraction of the methane stored in the [Arctic] shelf could trigger abrupt climate warming".[230] As if we haven't had enough of dire warnings, we are told that, of all things, jellyfish are 'taking over the oceans' which could accelerate climate change.[231]

None of such stuff scares us; it causes not a ripple in our smug consciousness, and nothing nudges us from our frenetic pursuit of the good things of life. All those warnings, however prescient or forbidding, might well be addressed to another species on another planet. It is doubtful if the authors of such reports themselves make any changes in their daily life. Clearly no other species is so hell-bent and clear-headed in this 'death-wish'. Over a million people every year take their own lives for reasons that are almost funny if only not so deadly. The World Health Organization (WHO) says that over the past 45 years, suicide rates have increased by 60% worldwide. Suicide is now one of the three leading causes of death among males between the ages 14 to 45. Children as young as six have reportedly killed themselves. What we are not sure is if this streak is constitutional or civilizational, a desperate cry for concern and affection, or some kind

---

[230] NSF (National Science Foundation). 2010. Methane Releases From Arctic Shelf May Be Much Larger and Faster Than Anticipated. National Science Foundation (NSF), USA. Press release 10-036. 4 Mar 2010.

[231] Flannery, T. 2013. They Are Taking Over! Review of Lisa-Ann Gershwin's book Stung! On Jellyfish Blooms and the Future of the Ocean. *The New York Review of Books*. USA. 26 Sep–9 Oct 2013. p.18.

of nature's revenge for our rapacious and predatory conduct. What can trigger murder or suicide, sadism or savagery, remains a mystery. While the majority relate to personal problems, frustrations, and provocations, some arise as a reaction to all that is wrong and wretched in the world. They reflect what Antigone tells the King of Thebes, Creone: "And if I have to die before my time, well, I count that a gain. When someone has to live the way I do, surrounded by so many evil things, how can she fail to find a benefit in death?"[232] Every 'suicider', potential or actual, might not look for a benefit in death; but they see no point in prolonging life the way it came to be. Theories abound, but the truth is that we just do not know why we go on living or when we think 'enough is enough'. But all this death-wish, and suicidal and murderous tendencies do not dull our unquenchable hunger for immortality, for a life not limited by the body. Man is not content to live within his natural limitations, but at the same time, he is systematically atrophying what nature has endowed him with. And the 'mystery' of what transpires within our own bodies as we go about living, or rather, dying, is deepening, even as our lives are turning more and more shallow. We do not know the 'why' of many things, and sometimes we ask 'why' when it ought to be 'why not'. Questioning reality as it appears to be is a human trait. The German mystic Angelus Silesius wrote, "The rose doth have no why; It blossoms without reason; Forgetful of itself, oblivious to our vision".[233] It might be oblivious of our vision, but we do know that at some deep depth under the largest organ of our physical body, our skin, there is some sort of melting pot that houses and harbors a host of things like thoughts, feelings, emotions, instincts, and impulses, but we do not know how they interface and interact and become understanding, comprehension, imagination, prejudice, analytical capacity, choice-selection, decision-making, etc. All those disparate but intertwined

---

[232] The tragedy *Antigone* by Sophocles.

[233] Crawford Flitch, J.E (tr.). 1932. A Selections from *The Cherubinic Wanderer* (1657) by Angelus Silesius. London, UK.

things collide, coalesce, and bubble up and gush out as 'behavior'. We talk of behavior as if it is some kind of a mystery wrapped in a riddle, something for psychologists to break their heads over. There is no unified theory of human behavior but, in practical terms, it is the way, or ways, we connect with and conduct ourselves relative to other people, to other creatures, to Mother Earth, to Nature, and to practically everything in the universe, seen and unseen. Our behavior is embodied in the myriad things we do in the normal course of every day—at home, at work, on the street and as a partner in multiple relationships. The *Maitri* Upanishad puts the subject in context: "As one acts and conducts himself, so does he become. The doer of good becomes good. The doer of evil becomes evil. One becomes virtuous by virtuous action, bad by bad action". Perhaps we will never know for sure why man does evil, which is different from not doing the right thing, but we can say that it is not at least always. As Plato's hypothesis implied, "Evil man is evil only through error, and if one free him from error, one will necessarily make him good". It depends on what is meant by 'evil' and by 'error'. Slitting someone's throat for not parting with a penny or raping a three-year-old child and strangling the child thereafter cannot be called an act of error. But no man is all 'evil' or all 'good'.

What is important in life is *what* is 'right' and what is 'wrong'; not *who* is right and who is wrong. And if we want to better our behavior, we need to put in place two things—sincere *abhyasa* (ceaseless effort) and *chitta suddhi* (purity of consciousness)—to ensure that in every circumstance, we 'give' more and 'take' less. For, every event is an amoral equation, every individual is at best an amoral time bomb; and every action is a pebble thrown into the cosmic ocean. And everyone deserves, indeed is entitled, to be treated well, including you by your own self. However much we might try, there is absolutely nothing we do, or can do, that does not involve or affect, directly or indirectly, another living being. We are all fellow-travelers and the safety and salvation of each of us hinges on the attitude and actions of others. That being the case, all that we need to do, or try to do to the best of our ability, is to ensure that our inevitable impact on others' lives is helpful, at least not hurtful. And if we cannot but hurt someone, we should make up for it by immediately thereafter helping another person. We are instinctively not much attuned to the happenings within, or to how our mind or consciousness works, or to whatever that lurks within us—out of sight, but all in the mind, one might say. We are only concerned about what we do outside, individually or as a group. But we *know* that the two—inside and outside, within and without—are connected, in a sense, mutually dependent and inseparable. While such a view until recently was the stuff of metaphysics and mysticism, emerging areas of science are coming round to this line of thought. As the physicist Jason Dispenza puts it, "We have been conditioned to believe that the external world is more real than the internal world. This new model of science says just the opposite. It says that what is happening within us will create what's happening outside of us". The external also influences the internal. Some scientists say that the neurobiological processes in our brain control our behavior, and some others say that it is the 'microbes residing symbiotically inside our bodies'.

Our goals in life cannot be divorced from the slew of obligations, responsibilities, and duties we have towards others, but at the same time, these cannot be allowed to become obstacles to realizing fulfillment. The question of 'duties' in life, direct or implicit, that we need to fulfill has long been a subject of thoughtful introspection as well as scriptural scrutiny. According to Vedic scriptures, an individual is born with three kinds of debts—*Deva-runa* (debt to God); *Rishi-runa* (debt to the sages, saints); and *Pitru-runa* (debt to one's parents, ancestors)—debts that must be repaid during his or her span of life. These debts are like mortgages on one's life, but not liabilities, as they constitute an attempt by the scriptures to create an awareness of one's duties and responsibilities. Special importance is given to one's debt to *Bhoomi Devi*, Mother Earth. On waking up in the morning, every Hindu is supposed to seek forgiveness through the prayer, *Samudra vasane devi; Parvata sthana mandite; Vishnu pathni namasthubhyam; Pada sparsam kshamasva mae*—'salutations to the divine consort of Lord Vishnu; who is clothed by the oceans; and is adorned prettily by the mountains; forgive me Mother for setting foot upon you'. The Hindu 'doctrine of duty as debt' is a very important dimension of human morality. What is significant is that it stretches the ambit of our duties and obligations beyond the immediacy or intimacy of terrestrial interpersonal relationships, and includes our duty to the dead who gave us life. Death does not terminate our duty or debt. During the *Bhadrapada* month of the traditional Hindu calendar, a specific period called *pitru-paksha* is set aside for ancestor-worship and veneration of the dead. During this fortnight, people donate food to the hungry in the hope that their ancestors will also be thus fed. The idea that a life on earth has an obligation not only to our fellow-humans but also to those who lived before us is a major contribution to moral philosophy and ethics. The premise is that repaying the debt to ancestors is as important as repaying the debt to God, nature, sages, and society.

Morality and Duty

Unlike the pre-industrial times, everything is work in the contemporary world; everything else is secondary; just being alive is so much work, often doing things you don't like. As the novelist Philip Roth said, "The road to hell is paved with works-in-progress". Almost everything we do is in pursuance of related duties, obligations, and responsibilities. Sometimes they complement each other, but more often they collide and clash, and that is when we fumble and falter. The human mind is singularly single-minded and narrow-minded. As Lovecraft put it, "The most merciful thing in the world, I think, is the inability of the human mind to correlate all its contents".[234] It is merciful because that way its maliciousness can

---

[234] Lovecraft, H.P. 1926. The Call of Cthulhu.

be more contained. It is good at advocacy and aggressive articulation but not reconciliation, renunciation, and harmonization. And we do not have universally or socially acceptable norms, models, modalities, and mechanisms. But choices have to be made, and we make not necessarily the right or most deserving choices, but the most expeditious, most pressing, and the softest ones. In the process, we not only morally err but also miss the big picture, and as Joel Primack said, 'without a big picture we are very small people'. Multiple roles compete for our attention, with time spent on one role often coming at the expense of time spent on another—sometimes creating a win–loss situation for the various roles. Additionally, recent research indicates that role-conflict and attendant spillovers can lead to stress, exhaustion, burn-out, and lower life satisfaction, not only for those of us experiencing the conflict, but also for others in our lives as well. In short, our exhaustion and conflict can spill over to others. We admire actors who play double or multiple roles in movies but all of us play more demanding roles, even if not consciously. The quality of our acting is not so much how we play any particular role, but in so doing how we do not compromise what is needed in playing other roles. If we are perfect in one particular identity, and neglect other identities and responsibilities, then overall we fare poorly. If and when we are finally judged, if we proclaim proudly 'I was a perfect parent', or a family man, the Cosmic Judge might counter and ask: "That was only a bit part; what about your social persona? And were you fully human and humane in the totality of human interconnectivity?"

We need to also bring a moral dimension to another of our most pressing identities, as a worker, an employee, a professional, as a means to make money, or make a living. The absence of this dimension lies at the source of much evil today. Most of us are privy to and participants in its furtherance, and we are all aware of this in different degrees. And we feel no pangs because of that magic word that sweeps away all sin: *duty*. Much of what we do in public these days is 'doing duty'. That is what we do all our life, doing our duty in multiple identities and capacities. More narrowly, it is what we do to make a living, to earn money. It devours much of the most active, productive part of our life, in our youth and adulthood, till we die, or till we 'retire'. Doing duty might have become a dubious, if not dirty, word now, the way we use it as an immoral cover, but the idea is not novel or new. Even mass murderers like Adolf Eichmann and extreme religious fanatics claim the same cover. It is linked to the concept of *karma yoga*, as well as to the doctrine of *nishkama karma*—doing one's duty or any work without attachment to the result; in its broadest sense, 'duty that *is due* to humanity, to our fellow men, and especially to all those who are disadvantaged and more helpless than we are ourselves'.

Duty is at the core of theosophy. One of the attributes we value most in contemporary life is professionalism, which can be broadly defined as performing whatever work we do with dedication, honesty, and diligence. And we cannot apply 'moral *exceptionalism*' to the workplace, on the plea that being professional requires doing any job regardless of how anyone else is affected. This is one of the most acute moral issues of our day: How to meld morality into what we do for a living? To what extent does our public persona and professional duty give a cover for moral transgressions? And that has a huge bearing not only on our private life but also on the war within. Work, doing one's duty, and professional life now consume and absorb so much of our living space, time, and energy, and impact on the lives of so many others that we cannot adopt different norms and standards of morality, for example, one for home and another for the workplace. Most people separate their work from their personal life and follow their professional code of conduct. To what extent it is driven wholly by professional considerations and how much of it is giving vent to their hidden inclinations is hard to tell. What is more important in today's world is what we may call public evil, or paid evil, that is, evil that comes from the workplace, be it a government office or a business or an organization or industry. This evil is far greater than purely personal evil, the evil we do off-duty. And moral offences that impact on the health and well-being of the community must attract more severe penalty than those that cause suffering to a few. For example, adulteration of food or drugs that harm the multitude must be dealt with greater severity than adultery. Moral offences like lying, cheating, and greed become far more injurious when perpetrated on the social scale. Cheating while building a bridge, for example, puts in danger the lives of thousands. We may even have to concede that morality is not confined to choice-making, but permeates our whole way of life from social life to sports, from education to entertainment, from how or where to channel technology, and how and where to spend money. Should one have babies? And, if so, how many? Such questions raise moral issues. And can we apply different standards to different places based on richness and poverty? Abortion is a moral issue. Some issues span geography and gender, and some questions span generations. If certain parts of the world like sub-Saharan Africa cannot sustain high fertility, why not encourage emigration to other parts that need more children? Some are even suggesting that some forms of sport, like American football (not only playing but even watching), and some kind of entertainment, like violent video games, should be branded unethical. The scope of morality must include actions necessary for saving the planet from our own toxic hands, that is, actions that are environment-friendly. The time has come for a 'new narrative' on climate change, which impels us to view anything done to protect the environment as moral and sacred, and anything that has the opposite effect as immoral and shameful. Conservation should be treated as consecration. There is growing realization that we have to change our perspective on the climate crisis from an economic or ecological matter to a moral issue. That is why it being called 'climate justice', and justice is a big chunk of morality. Climate justice is a vision to dissolve and alleviate the unequal burdens created by climate change on the poor and vulnerable. Philosophers like Mary Robinson characterize the climate change as a human rights issue and environmental justice. Water has to be given the holy tag, bearing in

mind the prediction that future wars will be *water wars*. The distinction
between social and spiritual needs has to be blurred.

Moral Crisis to Morality in Crisis

Instead of introspecting on those lines and exploring ways of retooling
our mindset, and cleansing our consciousness, we ask questions that can
be answered both in the affirmative and negative, to embrace questions
such as: Is the present plight of man an offshoot of the inner divinity in
eclipse or the death throes of a dying species? Is man 'born to be good' or
a hard-wired Good Samaritan, or, in the words of Paul Rusesabagina, the
Rwandan humanitarian hero, "a shark, just sleeping, lying on the bottom
of a sea, which can emerge any time and break a lot of boats"?[235] Moral
philosophers and perceptive people have long ruminated on issues such
as the evolution of human morality, the origins of virtue, and the link
between sexuality, morality, and mortality. Scholars and social scientists
have long debated who the authentic human is—egocentric or altruistic,
acquisitive or generous, parasitic or philanthropic—and, of late, the scope
has been broadened to include such questions as whether the present
behavioral crisis in modern society could be described as chosen blindness
or 'moral escapism'. We have long wondered about the origins and biology
of morality and about the raison-d'être of morality, just as much as we
have wondered about who we really are on the canvas of the cosmos, and
about the roles of genes and culture in shaping human personality. And
most of us agree with what Einstein said: "The most important human
endeavor is the striving for morality in our actions. Our inner balance
and even our very existence depend on it. Only morality in our actions

---

[235] Paul Rusesabagina, in an interview with Michel Martin, host of the show 'Talk of the
Nation' titled *'An Ordinary Man' Navigates Rwanda's Genocide*. 10 Apr 2006. National
Public Radio, Washington, USA. Retrieved from <https://www.npr.org/templates/story/
story.php?storyId=5334369>.

can give beauty and dignity to life".[236] Although we reflexively assume that 'good' is good, and 'bad' is bad, there have always been introspective individuals, not all 'bad', who pondered about why being good is 'good'. Sarada Devi, the spiritual consort of Sage Ramakrishna asked that if grief itself is a gift of God, then why can't we be bad and give that 'gift' to others? At a more fundamental level, the question is: Which is more 'moral' in terms of nature and natural selection? If we want to be moral and magnanimous, should we go beyond nature, as Thomas Huxley, for example, argued, or should we navigate a return to nature and try to emulate the ants, bees, and wasps? And what, in effect, constitutes a 'moral life'? Who does it benefit? How do we judge if an action is moral or not? Is goodness the same as morality and if so, good for what and for whom? These are timeless questions and many moral philosophers have extensively written about it. Generally, in lay language, we use the word *good* as the opposite of *bad*, and *moral* as the opposite of *evil*—and the test is our behavior. In actuality, we view all life as either being or doing good or bad. Although, in the very nature of human life, nothing is good in and by itself, and almost everything we do is a blend of both. Moreover, when we say something is good, it actually translates as good *for ourselves*. The primary, if not exclusive, focus has to be on personal piety, probity, integrity and on virtues like truthfulness, self-restraint, simplicity, loyalty, faithfulness, honesty, helpfulness, and adherence to codes of conduct and religious commandments.

Despite ups and downs from time to time, they have stood the test of time as measures of moral life. We must also bear in mind that our sense of morality, like human evolution itself, developed in a very local, confined world, and the intended beneficiary was the individual and that very limited world. But the world today is global and this contextual-change has dealt a mortal blow to morality. We need to bring forward the central

---

[236] Dukas, H., and Hoffmann, B. 2013. Albert Einstein, The Human Side. Glimpses from His Archives. New Jersey, USA: The Princeton University Press.

question: Being moral is to do what, and how does it help or hinder the common good? Now, it is hard to find something to do that has no global impact. When the moral context changes, the morality content too must change, in order to be relevant. We need to find new ways to judge what is moral and what is not, in the changed dynamics. That ought to thrust the whole of morality into the melting pot, and draw from it a fresh frame of reference. We should be repelled by the horrors of what the world abounds with—just as Emperor Ashoka, the third king of the Mauryan dynasty of India (322–185 BCE) was appalled by the horrors and cruelty of wars— and like him create a new 'infrastructure for moral living'. We don't need to discard the extant guidelines; we need to shift the focus and priorities so as to serve the emerging needs. What is good between two individuals or in the privacy of personal relationships, is no longer good enough to contribute to the good of society. In fact, a major moral issue now is how not to let our personal obligations towards our loved ones, and towards our professional call of duty, dilute or distract us from doing what is good for the commonwealth. This issue has now become more critical of the widening gap between what is required to lead a good life, to be a good family member and have a good career, and what is required to resolve serious social and global problems. We cannot treat everyone in our life alike and perfect impartiality is not humanly possible. At the same time, we have to exercise self-restraint to ensure that we are not overly influenced by such natural feelings and avoid to the maximum extent hurting other people. The thrust must be to support and serve social needs, so that an individual life becomes an input to address social problems, instead of being inimical. For long, what has been called *utilitarianism*—to choose a course of action that results in the greatest utility to the greatest number of people—has been viewed as a good moral yardstick. That has to be radically revisited since most people would like to lead a life of comfort, and what that entails has turned out to be hazardous to global health. Actually, while many of us think and often pride ourselves as leading passively moral lives, the fact is that the world is full of largely avoidable or significantly reducible suffering caused by our behavior, and the perilous state of the environment caused by the kind of lives we lead.

We cannot insult, ill-treat, and humiliate another person and think we are moral because we have not done anything to overtly harm him or her. We cannot harbor malice within and be moral in our behavior. We cannot be moral, mean, good, and greedy at the same time. Nor can we be rude and righteous at the same time; nor be pious and petty... And we cannot be deemed 'moral' unless we are 'just', and cannot separate the rudiments of a 'moral life' from our relationship with the divine, especially of others' faiths. And we cannot any more consider ourselves good unless our thoughts and emotions are devoid of guile, bile, and spite, and individual actions are driven by integrity and goodwill. We have been wrestling with these issues for ages and the time has come to raise a more fundamental question, to borrow the title of an article by Colin McGinn: *Is Just Thinking Enough?*[237] Although the context of McGinn's question was different, we can use the question to explore a much broader domain. 'Just' can mean either 'only', or it could be 'fair', 'right' and 'moral'. And can we be just and compassionate at the same time in the same situation? Some thinkers argue that if only we can get our thinking right and if we can boost more of our brain power, we can solve all our problems and the world would be a wondrous place; and they hope that science could show the way. While this is the mainstream modern view, others, even some scientists, demur and posit that thinking or rather the source of our thinking, the structure of our thought, an activity of brain/mind, is the central problem, and that unless we can find a way to remove the monopoly of our mind on human intentionality and our moral sense, we cannot exorcize the malaise and maladies that afflict mankind. It is a critical issue not only

---

[237] McGinn, C. 2010. Is Just Thinking Enough? Review of John R. Searle's book: Making the Social World: The Structure of Human Civilization. *The New York Review of Books*. USA. 11 Nov 2010.

for us, the current inhabitants of the earth, but also for future generations. For we are told that the human species, contrary to what we were led to believe, is still evolving biologically, which means that the construct and content of the future man can be influenced by the 'culture of our conduct' and the 'environment of our behavior'. This means that the milieu and minutiae of our mundane lives, how we relate with and treat other people and other creatures and how we use and misuse nature—the crux of morality—can become inherited attributes of future humans and shape the genetic mix and make-up of the human organism, and complete (or at least take forward) the unfinished evolutionary process. The time has come to broaden our narrow and individualistic conception of sin, and the idea that harming God's creation is tantamount to sin. The environment is at the heart of God's creation, and any action or non-action that leads to its contamination becomes a modern-day sin. In his encyclical *Laudato Si'*, Pope Francis, quoting Bartholomew, the spiritual father of the Eastern Orthodox Christians, said that the destruction, exploitation of the earth by humans has risen to the level of sin, and that we humans need to, as the Pope paraphrased, "replace consumption with sacrifice, greed with generosity, wastefulness with a spirit of sharing".

A growing number of thoughtful people are recognizing that what we call environmental, economic, or financial crisis is really a *values* crisis, a moral crisis. But we must take it beyond the point of a crisis to opportunity. It is not a question of ethics or personal morality. We need a new frame of reference, a new point of reference and a point of departure, a new reason to be moral. What is important at this juncture is to recognize that what 'being moral' has come to represent, is out of sync with what is necessary for social transformation, and to mend the human mold. And, to paraphrase Martin Luther King Jr., for the human moral arc to bend towards justice, we have to go down to the roots of what a 'moral life' ought to signify. When we say someone is moral or mean—and when we use terms like good and evil, right and wrong—we emphasize qualities such honesty, integrity, thrift, rectitude. It is anchored on the premise that each person has an intrinsic and singular worth, that he is an agent of his dedicated destiny, and that it is for *him* to choose between right and wrong and to suffer the consequences of his actions. The conclusion that philosopher Protagoras, as well as the sophists, drew was that there is nothing that is either right or wrong, but thinking it will make it so. Thinking is an attribute of the mind; everything is filtered through the human mind. Their understanding is different in the mind of a psychopath and in the mind of a priest. And sometimes we do wrong with the intent of doing good. Moral philosophy has long wrestled with the questions: Does the end justify the means, or can the right path take you to a wrong destination, the right end? Are consequences the ultimate basis of judging what is right and what is wrong? There are no *right* or *wrong* answers to these questions because there is no single right or wrong answer. As Epicurus once said, "Nothing was inherently good or bad. Something is only ethical or right if a person or society judges it to be so". In the end, the 'end' has to be what is beneficial, not baneful, to society and to sentient life, and does not make life more difficult for someone else. Scriptures send us mixed messages. Each time we have to struggle to make the correct calling. Ultimately, like everything else, it depends on the state of consciousness, more particularly if it is mind-driven or not.

Moral Gangrene and Unbridled Evil

We feel—we ought to feel at least—choked with the waste of moral effluvia, the spin-off of 'moral gangrene'. The horrific things that we see almost every day jolt even our slumbering sensibility, and we wonder if modern-day evil is no longer hiding behind the description of 'not being good', that of being the other side of the same coin. We wonder if it has audaciously acquired a life, a legitimacy, and a lethality of its own, and is now unstoppable and all-conquering. Afflicted with a 'plague', we look for a panacea and a pill. With a pandemic in the air, we want to survive with a closed nose or a mask. With a tornado howling outside each one of us, we think that our thatched roof will stay intact. But our crafty mind, afraid that we will blame it for all our malevolence and misery, throws up a seductive crumb: Have we all got it all horribly wrong? Are we missing the wood for the tree? And contrary to all that depressing detail the media highlights, are we, as some optimists argue, actually better placed than ever to act for the benefit of humanity as a whole? Do we believe that violence is on the wane, and a subtle spiritual renaissance is on the rise? We must also note that at the core of what has come to be called the New Age Movement, which seeks to harmonize science and spirituality, and mind, body and spirit, there is also a visceral, sometimes violent, reaction to the suffocating sweep of what we deem as good life. But, more fundamentally, it encompasses another deeper tenet, namely the thought that this life, this world, is not the entirety of existence, but merely one step in an infinite voyage; that our personal consciousness is but a fragmentary projection of a much greater wholeness. That the 'divinity' is 'within', intrinsic and all-pervasive. And that all forms of life, including animals and plants, have their own intrinsic value. That bait is what draws so many of the young and the restless, and today's dead-end kids to obscure metaphysical bookstores, to cults and gurus, swamis, lamas of all hues, spiritual workshops and seminars and meditation and mystical retreats. To go out of the way, to think out-of-the-box, has always been the way out in all turbulent times and in times of great change. That is at once a potential promise and a seductive peril, an opening and an obstruction. It could be a promise if we introduce greater clarity and make it more in tune with the tasks and challenges the world faces which require changes in our individual lifestyles. It could then be transformational in its depth and scope and melt away the malice and meanness, hatred and hubris that blight human life. On the other hand, it could be a peril if it is turned into a cover for pleasure pursuits by charlatans and charismatic self-seekers. Most of us are poised on what is called the 'hedonic treadmill' and have to keep walking, and keep making more money.

One can with equal passion posit both ways, as our very understanding of being better-off and what violence itself is, is blurred. For every moral misconduct or ethical impropriety our mind offers an excuse or an explanation and that enables us to lead normal lives. All this agonizing thought, in Thoreau's phrase 'quiet desperation', has given birth to a new branch of science called the 'science of morality'. Joseph Daleiden, Sam Harris, and Patricia Churchland, among others, have argued that society should now consider normative ethics as an important domain of science, and that it might be possible, using disciplines like neuropsychology and metaphysical naturalism, to outline a generic basis for moral life, or, to paraphrase JK Galbraith, to "search for a superior moral justification for selfishness", which is sometimes described as the epitome of all sins. But there are some who say that, contrary to popular perception, for a moral life, it is not only a matter of following moral principles and codes and applying them to daily life. It is, or ought to be, a process of determining what kind of humans we should be individually and collectively. Einstein, who described himself as an agnostic, said that without 'ethical culture', there is no salvation for humanity. The practical question is that while making choices and decisions in life, how do we differentiate the moral from the immoral, good from bad, right from wrong? Even from a purely selfish point of view, the problem often is that, as Rousseau said, "Our will is always for our own good but we do not always see what the good is". The new factor is not only *what* good, but *whose* good. Most agree that a moral or virtuous life too is a means. It is about the end that views vary widely, from honor (Homer), to justness (Plato), to happiness (Aristotle). Religions generally say that being moral or good is good for you to go to heaven, and it will be handy on Judgment Day. While by and large it was possible to describe and discuss, analyze, and find remedies and solutions to moral problems in earlier times, it does not seem possible now. The present crisis constitutes a different class, not different degree. In the contemporary context we do not know what is moral and what we need to do to be moral, and also if certain actions, under any conditions, should be deemed wrong, or if they *become* wrong because of their consequences. We are increasingly unsure if an individual is entitled to his 'moral space' which is sacrosanct and immune to others' invasion, and how to balance it with an increasingly elastic common good. But the essential question is: how best could we contribute to it? The answer is stunningly simple: whatever you are good in, do it for the common good. The problem also is that most of us really do not know what our signature strengths are; we are more aware of our failings and foibles. That requires a conscious and sustained work; it can emerge as an epiphany, a sudden revelation or incrementally, but we will know. Then the task is to channel and harness our strengths to service something that is higher and larger than your desires. We need to energize our energies, and also the moral context of human effort has radically changed. Every effort, however tiny and small, goes not in vain. *The Book of Golden Precepts* says, "Learn that no efforts, not the smallest—whether in the right or wrong direction—can vanish from the world of causes. Even wasted smoke remains not traceless".

The dilemma of human life is how one can be moral when all of us are potentially equally capable of doing both good and evil. And we have no way of foretelling what each of us might actually do under a similar temptation. Compounding the dilemma is another reality: we are all made of the same mud and mix but no one can ever be anyone else. As Zen master Kodo Sawaki said, "You can't even trade a single fart with the next guy". We might sometimes succeed in putting ourselves in someone's shoes but not *become* someone else. That 'jeopardy' becomes even more complex by juxtaposing another variable: in the words of Shannon Alder, "No two persons can learn something and experience it in the same way". As a result, we can never, ever, be certain how any of us will respond to any particular situation. Most of us are 'bad' because we have convinced ourselves that that is the only way we can survive. Another emerging factor is that the fountainheads of immorality and evil have shifted from primarily private behavior to public performance, to governance, and practiced by those who are supposed to be there to save us. The greatest evil is not now done in those sordid "dens of crime" that Dickens loved to depict. The locus is not even concentration camps and labor camps. There it was visible. Instead of Auschwitz we have Abu Ghraib. Instead of the Gulags, where people were worked to death, we have professionals; in the words of CS Lewis, "Quiet men with white collars and cut fingernails and smooth-shaven cheeks who do not need to raise their voices".[238] Those who don't flinch in dispensing death as a part of their duty, and are conceived, ordered, and managed in clean, carpeted, warmed, and well-lighted offices. These are not only, in Lewis' phrase "nasty business concerns" but, even more, in elegant White Houses, Downing Streets, Elysée Palaces, Kremlins, Zhongnanhais,[239] offices of secret services and nondescript offices of apparatchiks and bureaucrats. The State is now the chief source of evil, as much as those it vows to eliminate. It oppresses as much as it claims to protect, uses violence, fearless as it is lawful, brazen because there is no earthly higher power. Historically, in the interests of the common good, most people, including great philosophers like Plato, have exempted the State from the rigor of personal morality, and gave it, for example, the 'license to lie'. But it has now gone far and the common good is no longer the primary motive, which is now the interest of the ruling class, the politico-bureaucratic-business nexus. The Hobbesian premise that the State is necessarily evil to protect self-motivated individuals from other self-motivated individuals assumes that the rulers of the State have no vested interest other than ensuring fair play, and to protect the weak and vulnerable. That is no longer a valid presumption. There are some like

---

[238] Lewis, CS. 1942. The Screwtape Letters.

[239] The central headquarters for the Communist Party of China and the State Council (Central government) of the People's Republic of China.

David Graeber who even say that the State is a demonic force thwarting human freedom. Clearly it is a dangerous hyperbole since it ignores many positives that stem from the State. Without anything approximating a State what we call 'society' will implode in time.

Evil is not only globalized but it is also ghastly. It is globalized because its tentacles cut across all borders and have global reach. It is ghastly as we no longer have any moral safe havens. What were so far considered as safe even from evil, are now in its clasp. We read about mothers killing their own children, a father molesting his own daughter, a son killing his father for his job or for property, a *pujari* (temple priest) swindling temple treasure, a *swami* (holy man) sexually exploiting his disciples, and children slaughtered in their classrooms for the heck of it, people being blown up while in deep prayer in their places of worship, to avenge the affront to 'a' God and so on. Nothing is too intimate, sacred, or loathsome for evil. Every human, even divine relationship is now susceptible to its insidious influence. That is the awesome moral challenge mankind faces; to get a new understanding of the dynamics and dialectics of evil, bearing in mind that the very institution that is supposed to ensure security and justice, the State, is now a source of evil, and that the very branch of knowledge— religion—that is supposed to help us stay on the moral path, now incubates evil. Unless we comprehend how it works, we cannot contain or confront it. We cannot talk about the evil that the State is, in abstract terms, as if it is some distant third party. For, the fact is, as Karl Jaspers reminds us, "Everybody is responsible for the way he is governed". The State justifies every evil as a hard choice, unpleasant but unavoidable. Even the death of as many as 500,000 Iraqi children due to economic sanctions, designed to dent the will of a dictator, to make it so difficult for unarmed citizens to revolt, and do what the mighty 'sole superpower' could not do: overthrow the dictator. There are no moral qualms, no regret or remorse; the bottom line is that everything is justified to avoid bringing the body bags back home. Almost every State indulges, in varying depths of devilry and deviousness, in similar acts either at home to suppress dissent or to ensure internal security, or externally over weaker adversaries. Citizens, otherwise honorable, decent, god-fearing people, acquiesce, so long as it does not disturb their lives and those of their near and dear.

Morality and Modernity

Modernity, to which we sometimes ascribe many an unwelcome thing in our lives, is not the incubator of the internal war. The war is timeless, ageless, constant, and eternal. What distinguishes our 'times' from prehistoric times, is that while in those ages or *yugas* there was always a kind of stalemate or impasse, with no clear victor or vanquished, and with fluctuating and transitory fortunes between the opposing forces, it now appears that the tide is turning in favor of the forces of darkness and decadence. They are prevailing and winning most of the myriad mini-wars or battles that take place every time we choose to do something, or make decisions on any kind of mundane or momentous matter. It is, in effect, an invasion from within, and its every wish is our command. That could be the principal cause and source of much of the unease, disquiet, anger, anxiety, restiveness, rebelliousness, self-destructive impulses that so many of us sense. And that could be behind the gnawing gut-feeling that the world is, in Gandhi's words, poised on the 'threshold of a twilight',[240] that our lives are adrift like a reed in an ocean, that we are inexorably moving towards the edge of the abyss. Despite our feel-good culture and material affluence, we do feel that some malaise is afflicting mankind but we are clueless what it could be. We know we are lost in the dark woods, but we are uncertain how deep we are; we realize we are adrift but we are foxed about which way we should head; we agree that the present time is a huge historical hinge, but sense that history is slipping out of our hands. We yearn to find ourselves at a place like Shangri-La or in a time like the

---

[240] Phrase used in a letter that Gandhi wrote to Mahadev Desai in July 1918.

Golden Age, but what we do is to make a hell of our home. But, most of all, deep down, we also realize that, to arrest the drift and decline and decay, all of us and each one of us, must rise above ourselves from the "individualistic concerns to the broader concerns of humanity",[241] whose actions and habits could tilt the scales decisively. What we need above all is a clear appreciation of the behavioral drivers that paralyze humanity from changing its course from one headed towards a potential collapse of human industrial civilization, to one moving towards sustainable human behavior. A long time ago, the Buddha phrased the issue very well: "What is the appropriate behavior for a man or a woman in the midst of this world, where each person is clinging to his piece of debris? What's the proper salutation between people as they pass each other in this flood?" In short, how should one deal with and how much room must one give to another person on this crowded place called Earth while living one's own life? The real problem is that the way we 'understand' most often when we face moral choices, is wrong. We worry and fight for *rights*—all the way from human rights to conjugal rights—not how to do the 'right' thing. That good people do wrong things does not make the wrong any less wrong. We cannot any longer fall back on our conscience—called the vice-regent of God—to bail us out. As we live on in this society, actively taking on its spirit, our conscience gets more and more persuaded to go along to get along, to be realistic. In fact, our inability to get along, not to suffer each other, to accept, not tolerate, each other, to complement, not nibble, each other is the primary cause of suffering. Another cause is our inability to view society as a moral community, not a social conglomerate.

The growing power of the State, of globalization, of the ruthless randomness of terrorism, and of mass media adds a new dimension to morality. Anybody can be a victim; anybody can be deprived of dignity; anyone can become a refugee; anybody can be uprooted from their local milieu and support of traditional groups, family, friends, and neighbors. We

---

[241] Words of Martin Luther King Jr.

are living in times when sometimes only 'distant strangers' in cyberspace, watching flickering lights and fleeting images on a tiny screen, could become our saviors. Our neighbors might become strangers or enemies, impelled by caste, class, or religious zealotry, and strangers far away, whom we never even come to see or speak, can come to your aid on humanitarian grounds. It is through the arousal of global conscience, what Michael Ignatieff called "ethic of universal moral obligation among strangers" that, at times of need and peril, we could get help. Traditionally, morality has been personal and local, bounded within the family, tribe, community, religion, and nation. The idea of needing or helping strangers, showing compassion and seeking support, half-way across the globe, because we are all in the same leaking boat, to face the dangers of the day is new, but its time has come.

Morality, we are told, both binds and blinds: it binds us into groups, and blinds us to opposing groups and views. In today's world, morality is so adrift at sea that rarely does anyone admit even to one's own self that he is not moral, and if one does so, he intuitively lays the blame at someone else's door. If one is truly cornered, the escape route is to say that the other moral alternative is even worse. We have sought to replace our moral sense with moral reasoning. As Jonathan Haidt says, "We are just not very good at thinking open-mindedly about moral issues, so rationalist models end up being poor descriptions of actual moral psychology". In fact, what we face is not a moral crisis but a *morality in crisis*. Morality is in crisis because the very subject of morality, the human persona, has radically altered. Haidt says that today man is 90% chimp and 10% bee; the chimp representing selfishness, and the bee, sociability. We don't know what the blend was before, but today's mix is toxic. What is required at this point in human history is nothing short of a new conception and understanding of morality.

Morality is also in crisis because it has, on the one hand, become so fuzzy that we no longer can tell who is moral and who is not; and, on the other hand, almost everyone is compelled to be a participant, directly or indirectly, in immoral actions that hurt, humiliate, and harm other people. And technology has completely changed the moral context, making some obsolete, and raising new issues. Today, our temptations and provocations are different; how to handle them must also be different. We have to ask ourselves: if most of us are decent, caring and God-fearing, then from where is evil finding its sustenance and becoming stronger every day? If most of us are moral, even in the broadest sense, how come there is so much indifference, insensitivity, intolerance, indignity, bigotry, and pettiness in our world? Where is the 'good' going, leaving the world a planet where day after day horror after horror takes place? Our 'conceptual myopia' and moral ambiguity is a contributory cause. We posit that morality is time and space specific, that it has varied, and continues to vary, from culture to culture, and what is sinful in one context, is permissible in another. Hindu scriptures have long predicted the steep fall in moral conduct of man in the *Kali Yuga*, the age of darkness. If it were so, how can there be a moral crisis in human conduct? In short, is marginalized morality, or being essentially evil, the natural condition of the contemporary human?

The real problem we face is that we are unable even to know how to distinguish moral crisis from moral failure, moral masquerade, moral activism, and moral cowardice. Most of us fall into the category of cowards according to Confucius, for often we know what is right but do not adhere to it. Much of our morality is simply legal. If we get the law on our side, whether by conforming to it or by bending it, we feel we are invincible and we do not fear evil-doing. A Chinese proverb says, 'Laws control the lesser man; right conduct controls the greater one'. The importance of 'right conduct' is emphasized in both Buddhism and Jainism on the path of nirvana and moksha. But for right conduct we need the right consciousness. We have to bear in mind that while nature is, in and by itself, morally neutral, we must not see human morals as artificial, but as a legitimate part of the natural landscape. And given the fact that existence is nothing but a continuum of choices and chores, from the minute to the momentous, the question is: how do we inject the moral norm into normal life? If we cannot factor in morality or moral judgment into daily activity, our behavior will not change in the desired direction, and if that were to come to pass then both humankind and Planet Earth will remain gravely endangered. A good starting point, as a frame of reference, could be a Thoreau quote: "Do not be too moral. You may cheat yourself out of much life so. Aim above morality. Be not simply good, be good for something". That something can be many things; the connecting thread has to be to go beyond our own immediacy and importance. To rise 'above morality' is to rise above ourselves; to simply exchange places in every human situation; to put the common good ahead of personal pleasure. Much of the evil that happens in the world is in pursuit of pleasure, pride, sensuous satisfaction, selfish gratification, and sovereign ambition to lord over the world.

We succumb easily and fundamentally due to poverty of integrity, particularly in public life. But, like in the doctrine of dharma, conflicts and collisions crop up in the dust and din of competitive life. For example, how do we reconcile personal probity and professional integrity? And if one must choose between them, which one comes first?

We must also address another critical issue, which concerns situations such as conformity, obedience of 'superior orders', and simply doing what we are paid to do. So much wrong-doing, exploitation, suffering, and evil is occurring in today's world that it requires special attention. It is not a new issue. Historians have long pondered over it, particularly when horrific events like the Holocaust, genocides, and ethnic mass murders took place. How could a small group of people exercise the psychological and ideological power over otherwise ordinary people to allow killing, torture, etc.? Such questions are also part of the larger issue of 'why do we behave badly?', 'what do we get out of it?' But 'doing bad' for personal reasons, due to reasons like greed, passion, profit, or vengeance is different from committing unimaginable atrocities like organized massacres, exterminations, revenge rapes, religious barbarity, and ethnic conflicts. Do people do such things because deep within they want to? Or are they helpless, faced with an unacceptable alternative? Is it really necessary, or is it our appetite for more than our pound of flesh? Is it just conventional obedience or is it our deep and dark longing for guts, gore, and blood? Or, is it our inability to "make an omelet without wading thigh deep in the blood of chickens and wearing their entrails as a necklace".[242] We must also consider the issue of indirect or implicit moral culpability for the actions of other workers or employees in an organization, and for the acts of the institution itself. For instance, if you are an accountant in an arms factory, or in a company that makes pollutants and poisons which then get into the food we eat or consume, can you be considered culpable, even if only marginally and peripherally? Diffusion and division of labor does not dilute, not to say negate, our share in guilt for what the collective entity does. One could also posit that we have to bear our share of the moral consequences since whatever is the nature of our work, it constitutes an input into the overall work of the company or entity. On the other hand, it can also be argued that one's actions are in no way connected to the harmful things the company makes and therefore one is freed from all consequences.

The two practical principles ought to be: to avoid, if not minimize, any kind of harm to any sentient being; and to strive to do the 'greatest good to the greatest number'. For moral decision-making, what we need is the trigger of moral motivation. And for that, what we require to do is to engage not only our logical/reasoning and deductive cognitive capacities of our brain, but also the intuitive, emotional, and latent spiritual capacities that spring from the energy and intelligence of our heart. We have to nurture consciously and continually within each of us a moral mindset, a mindset or a consciousness that is not hostage to the mind and which

---

[242] Lawrence, M. 2012. King of Thorns. Book Two of The Broken Empire. New York, USA: Ace Books.

instinctively includes moral input into the process of decision-making. And we need to do it not only alone, but also collectively. Stray individuals or isolated groups, well-intentioned though they might be, are necessary but not sufficient. Most of us are moral sometime or the other, and some more often than others. Where we err is the lack of consistency. We need a critical mass for cultural change, which spreads not in a linear fashion but in a viral way. We need an elusive and indeterminate assemblage of men and women above an unknown threshold that, once crossed, generates self-propelling momentum, and positively infects minds like a pandemic. We must also face up to a fundamental fallacy. Like much else that is human, here too we apply double, or even multiple standards. Most of us, as Bertrand Russell noted, have two kinds of morality: one we preach but seldom practice; the other we practice but do not (dare) preach. We even accept, if not acquiesce to, the massacres of civilians as *jus bellum justum* (the just war doctrine). Although we might think that it is governments that fight wars, it is *we*, as primary stakeholders and shareholders, who are morally responsible. Although one might concede that some wars are ethically inevitable, the moral point also addresses when such wars should be brought to a close—what is called *jus post bellum* (justice after the war). Most politicians and decision-makers know more about when to start a war than how to wage it (*jus in bello*), than how and when to end it. As a result, they sow the seeds of more wars, as in the case of the First and Second World Wars. The circumstances that led to the latter are commonly attributed, among other things, to the harsh terms of the Treaty of Versailles of 1919, which brought an end to the First World War. And citizens, as 'owners' of governments, have a moral obligation to insure and ensure such fairness and humanness in a war.

We need a basket of rewards and penalties, incentives and disincentives to ensure that our individual actions contribute to the common good. Self-sanction is thus an implicit input for the common good. The specifics of shackles must also change in tune with changing times. At this juncture, we are by and large clinging to a moral code that no longer serves the purpose—which is to tame the 'natural' nature of man and make his participation in human society constructive, not destructive. Our understanding, even our cognizance of what is acceptable and unacceptable, what is appropriate and inappropriate, what is decent and deviant, what is good and what is bad, must mutate. It is because, with all their vulnerabilities and venality, most people want to play by the rules, as far as possible, and feel that they are decent people, and that their behavior is not immoral. And if our comprehension of morality remains static then our behavior will remain rooted in the current zone of comfort. If we do not believe that our way of life is socially injurious and morally offensive, then the best of us will stay the course, and avoid a course of behavioral mending and bending. We must bear in mind that in deciding what is moral, the simplest and safest choice is the 'larger good'. In the Mahabharata, the distinguished Vidura sums it up: "To save a family, abandon a man; to save the village, abandon a family; to save the country, abandon a village; to save the soul, abandon the earth".

On a parallel track, we have to design and nurture a new base and basis, a new fulcrum and foundation, a new paradigm and pattern, new rules and benchmarks of social adulation and opprobrium, recognition and rewards, adulation and ostracism, heroism and depravity. It must offer enough elbow room for individual initiative and self-interest, but must be subordinate to social interest, order, and justice. While we must strive towards a new moral platform, implicitly, unknowingly, and even unconsciously, we are already adopting a different moral (or immoral!) code in our behavior that condones things like lying, cheating, cursing, profanity in public, gossiping, groping, malicious conduct, causing intentional injury to others, and so on. But we still do not look at ourselves as 'bad' people. We are privy to and practice much of what we condemn by telling ourselves that these are 'social' evils, which have nothing to do with us. We lament the fall in values and standards, but adopt the same brand in our behavior;

we can do that because our mind protests: 'What can I do; it is systemic!' We remain trapped in our mind and in our behavior. We must become better before we can behave better, and we cannot become better unless we behave better. The silver lining is that there is also a yearning worldwide—cutting across continents, political or ideological leaning, and social and cultural identities—for a new, less materialistic, more moral mode of life that revolves around compassion.

Schadenfreude, the Modern Pandemic

Whichever way we might act or react contextually, man is essentially a pleasure-seeking animal; we instinctively yearn for pleasure and avoid pain. That does not stop us from mixing the two; deriving pleasure from pain, and pain from pleasure, and getting addicted to both, or to a blend of the two. Masochism (pain from pleasure) and melancholy (pleasure from being sad) are connected. It also often happens that, in life, one man's pleasure causes another man's pain. From the ancient Greeks, through 17th- and 18th-century British philosophers, to 20th-century psychologists, this hedonistic or pleasure principle has come to dominate efforts of scholars to understand people's motivation. Epicurean philosophy sprang from the attainment of pleasure, which was described as 'the beginning and the end of blessed life'. It is the basic motivational assumption of theories across all areas of psychology. While it is commonplace and conventional wisdom to say that we turn towards pleasure and turn away from pain, in actuality, human motivational behavior is more complex. Although we tend to view them as opposites, they are the two sides of the same coin. One can easily switch from one state to another. Alfred Hitchcock, the master of suspense, said, "Give them pleasure—the same pleasure they have when they wake up from a nightmare... Always make the audience suffer as much as possible". Scientists say that actually parts of the neural pathways for the two perceptions overlap. We are among the very few in nature who deliberately derive pleasure from others' pain. For us, it is not enough to succeed—others must fail. It is this twisted trait, our greatest moral failing, which has come to play a stellar role in contemporary life. From the Roman gladiatorial blood-and-gore combats to public hangings that people travelled from far to participate in, to our latest terrorist beheadings of hostages and the popularity of gruesome YouTube™ videos, we all show a voyeuristic streak of getting a kick out of others' torment. It is not only interesting but also titillating. This was what Edmund Burke possibly had in mind when he wrote, "There is no spectacle we so eagerly pursue as that of some uncommon and grievous calamity; so that whether the misfortune is before our eyes, or whether they are turned back to it in history, it always touches with delight".[243] Burke held that the pleasure we derive from others' suffering—our 'aesthetic pleasure in the terrifying'—was a 'brute and perverse fact of human nature'. The only thing we can question is the association with the brute: we are brutal, not brute-like, in our behavior.

The main message of all this is two-fold: one, increasingly, the main source of the appeal of competitive sport and the mainstay of entertainment is a shade of Schadenfreude; two, the participation, visually or vicariously, in acts of cruelty has become pleasurable, even necessary for man to face the drudgery and decadence, the ennui and emptiness of daily life. For, as author JK Rowling said, 'to hurt is as human as to breathe'.[244] That is perhaps why all of us should fervently put our hope in Tolstoy's words— "Here I am alive, and it's not my fault, so I have to try and get by as best I can without hurting anybody until death takes over" (*War and Peace*). A central feature of the pleasure-in-others'-misfortune notion is the belief that the other person *deserves* his or her misfortune. What is truly unsettling is that we cannot dismiss this phenomenon as an aberration, or dub people who entertain such thoughts as deviants or mentally twisted people. They are among us; they *too* are us. According to psychological scientist Erin

---

[243] Burke, E. 1844. A Philosophical Enquiry Into the Origin of Our Ideas of the Sublime and Beautiful. New York, USA: Harpers & Brothers.

[244] Rowling, JK. 2008. The Tales of Beedle the Bard.

Buckels, "Some find it hard to reconcile sadism with the concept of normal psychological functioning, but our findings show that sadistic tendencies among otherwise well-adjusted people must be acknowledged. These people aren't necessarily serial killers or sexual deviants but they gain some emotional benefit in causing or simply observing others' suffering".[245] Most of us watch movies with a lot of violence, killing, cruelty, and blood-letting. And when we read reports of some favorite celebrity getting into trouble our instinct is mostly wicked titillation, rarely empathy. Does it mean that deep within we are all infected by the malaise of Schadenfreude? One of the most basic conflicts in the human psyche is the friction between selfish impulses and self-control. When we see something good happening to someone else, many of us would stop and mutter to ourselves: *Why not me?!*

If God Does Not Exist...

In popular perception, God, morality, and religion are virtually inseparable and indistinguishable. The fact though is that they are not identical, but intertwined and interdependent. It is possible to believe in God without being religious, and to be independently moral without any kind of allegiance. There is no one 'God', although most agree on His attributes; and when it comes to worship, every religion depicts a different picture. There is no general definition of religion, or of what true religion is, and of what false religion is; nor is there any agreement relating to valid religious values. Nor even about what we mean by the truth of religion. Yet, what we conjure as 'religion' plays a huge part in human life. The same thing goes for morality, too; we cannot agree what it means; nor on any criteria to judge moral behavior. Even if we do not know most often what is right and what is wrong, we still want to be, or known to be wanting

---

[245] Cited in: Everyday Sadists Take Pleasure In Others' Pain. Association for Psychological Science (APS). 12 Sep 2013. Retrieved from <http://www.psychologicalscience.org/index. php/news/releases/everyday-sadists-take-pleasure-in-others-pain.html>.

to be, moral, good, upright, and so on. Without getting bogged down with questions such as when, how and why religion gained its foothold in human consciousness, we can safely say that it has been a part of historic human history. The same thing can be said with equal force about morality. We cannot pin a date of its entry or what need it was intended to fill. More important is the question how the three—God, morality, and religion—have affected each other. Some say that a principal purpose of religion is to enable man to lead a moral life. And that man stumbled upon morality as a way to survival as a tribe or community. If religion is understood to mean, in Alfred North Whitehead's words, "a system of general truths which have the effect of transforming character when they are sincerely held and vividly apprehended",[246] then one must conclude that it has not yielded the desired result; man remains untransformed, or one might say 'mis-transformed'.

Some say that religion is both necessary and sufficient to lay a moral foundation for an ethical life; some say that it necessary but not sufficient; others, that it has no need or place as a moral base. Some might be tempted even to argue that religion, or the way that it is put into practice, makes people dogmatic, intolerant, and that it actually subverts morality. Some scientists suggest that religious experiences shrink part of the brain, and some other studies show that 'having a strong religious belief acts as a buffer against anxiety', and that it has a calming, egalitarian effect. The fact is that the way such views are expressed bristle with value judgments, and it depends on what we consider as religious mindset, as distinct from any religion, and what we qualify as moral behavior. The essential question is what we might call religious outlook: Can we say that, 'if one is disposed to be good, religion helps'? And, on the other hand, 'if one is already drawn towards bad, would religion actually make that person more of a menace'? The way it is churning in our mind and the extent to which it is sundering the social fabric in the world, this is a vital issue to ponder over in the

---

[246] Whitehead, A.N. 1926. Religion In The Making. Lowell Lectures, 1926.

context of the war within. Which side is religion on? How are the religious people in the world influencing the endogenous war? Whom are they aiding and abetting? Are they, through their beliefs and behavior, pouring fuel onto the fire, or are they moderating and alleviating human passions like anger, avarice, and aggression that are so much in the play in today's world? Do religious traits and practices like prayer, pilgrimages, worship, and other rituals soften our ugly side, or do they make us feel intoxicated, condescending, special, superior, and safe, that our relationship with other people actually gets worse? While it is unfair and sweeping to say that religion makes people bad, or that it strengthens the evil inside us, what we cannot ignore is that, in the words of Blaise Pascal, "Men never do evil so completely and cheerfully as when they do it from religious conviction". Of all 'savageries', it is the religious kind that is hardest to understand. We cannot also ignore that religion has immense potential to make us confuse self-serving with serving God, confuse prayer with piety, self-righteousness with self-esteem.

It is unlikely that any new revelations or insights could be raised any more now. We will never have conclusive and universally accepted answers to questions such as whether God created man or not. Or, if He exists or not. Or, why He 'allows' evil in the world. The more pertinent point is that the 'idea' of God can play a transformational role in human life. Whitehead said that 'the purpose of God is the attainment of value in the temporal world'. The question of value is at the heart of morality. Whatever has been the impact and influence of religion on the human mind and human history, the fact is that many religions do have value frameworks regarding personal behavior in the form of *shastras* (laws), commandments and codes of conduct, meant to guide adherents in determining between right and wrong. These include the Triple Gems of Jainism, Judaism's Halacha, Islam's Sharia, Catholicism's Canon Law, Buddhism's Eight-fold Path, and Zoroastrianism's 'good thoughts, good words, and good deeds' concept, among others. These frameworks are outlined and interpreted by various sources such as holy books, oral and written traditions, and religious leaders. These have remained mainly in the domain or in religious and spiritual spheres, but they have faced serious obstacles when trying to enter the 'temporal world'. A principal reason is that it is through the medium of the mind that we have sought to relate to them. Another cause is that we have distanced and differentiated God from man, and come to believe that so long as we are nice to God it doesn't matter if we are nasty in our behavior.

We cannot long wander around any serious metaphysical speculation or even materialistic mindset without encountering the age-old questions: Must morality be grounded in God? And can there be religion without God? Has science made religion obsolete? Some say that goodness is good enough, a life well-lived is a good life, and that God is at best an add-on that makes it easier to be virtuous. Some, like Einstein, say that they believe in God not as a person but as an 'illimitable superior spirit'. Dostoyevsky's Ivan Karamazov says, "If God does not exist, then everything is permissible". The implied statement is that 'God must exist, because morality is a must'. Some also draw a distinction between *is* permissible, and *ought to be* permissible. Nietzsche took a different stance, and by pronouncing the death of God he implicitly said morality too need not exist. What all moral philosophers and humanists have grappled with is where and how to draw a line in our conscious behavior in the absence of universal and unchanging moral values. We must also keep in mind that the ultimate purpose of new morality is that in any attempt to create a fabric of human destiny we cannot escape, however elusive and effervescent it might be, the moral dimension. Nor can we take off the table what Armand Nicholi called 'the question of God', independent and irrespective of religion. The point is we will never be short of people who can passionately and persuasively argue in favor of or otherwise about the existence, nature, purpose, and power of the divine. Even if one sees God, another can dismiss it as a visual hallucination. In very simple but profound, even poignant, terms, the sense of God for the vast majority of mankind is nothing else than another name and form of hope, as much a part of their lives as any other living person; and this is so despite all the hardships, misery, inequity, and injustice they might experience in their lives. If God is dead, they too are dead. And it is so too, regardless of who we are individually, sinner or saint, villain or victim, oppressor or oppressed, rich or poor. And their faith in the relevance of God is larger and higher than their allegiance to any religion. They are not interested in issues such as religious atheism or theistic irreligion. Or, in issues like whether God is a person or a force, entity or energy, or about the attributes of God and how to reconcile the relevance of the divine with the reality of the wretchedness of the world. God is beyond religion; in one sense, He is infinite, impersonal, abstract; in another, He is particular and very personal; even if He will not talk, He listens, as opposed to humans. We cannot see Him but He can—and does—see us. Those who know nothing of the substance of any religion or even of their own religion, those who know nothing of any scripture or sacred text, still bow before God, sometimes seek nothing, oftentimes the smallest thing. The important thing is that they feel God's 'presence', and feel equipped to face the world, solaced, comforted, renewed, ready to endure suffering. God may have sworn to protect the righteous but the unrighteous too can seek God's grace or mercy or help. Hindu scriptures are full of stories where the demons pray to God and obtain boons which, so to say, boomerang on Him!

One of the striking paradoxes of contemporary life is the coexistence of a world soaked in materialism, selfishness, avarice, and bigotry, and the growing popularity of places of worship. We can look at it, or rationalize it, in various ways. One, that a sinner needs and turns to God more than a saint. Two, for God, everyone is the same. Three, there is no good man or bad man; only good deed and bad deed. Four, we are all playing different roles in the cosmic drama. Lastly, this is all the mischief of *maya*; it is all appearance, our mistaking the unreal for the real. And so on, so forth. Whichever is the truth, the fact is that those who defy the dictum of God—who are corrupt and unethical, and who commit every conceivable crime or sin—do not find any qualms or contradictions in seeking God's help while violating His word. The weak and the meek, the wretched and the ostracized, the downtrodden and the deprived, they are the ones who have reason to cavil, but they don't. Although being the ones most victimized, they don't ask questions like 'How can we reconcile the apparent ascendancy of evil with the existence, omnipotence or justness of God?' It is not that they have no expectations, frustrations or unfulfilled desires, but none of that shakes their divine disposition. They may not see or speak to God; they might not be able to recite a single verse from any scripture, but He is simply integral to their lives. They forgive Him even if their prayers are not answered in the way they wish. In one sense, God is more a part of the lives of those who negate or mock Him than of those who believe in Him. For, one needs more knowledge to disbelieve than to believe. Belief is a matter of the heart; disbelief is a matter of the mind. In either case, the divine has always been inseparable from human consciousness. As biologist Edward Wilson says (*Consilience*, 1988), "The human mind evolved to believe in the gods. It did not evolve to believe in biology. Acceptance of the supernatural conveyed a great advantage throughout prehistory when the brain was evolving". What Wilson calls 'mind' could also be described in broader terms as 'consciousness'. It is another matter that that very consciousness now calls God dated, defunct, even inefficient, and wants to take His place. And since he does not know exactly how God looks like, man does the next best—make himself into a form of life variously described as supernatural being, supramental being, superman, transhuman, overman, etc. Some say that man is an unfinished product, a transitional being, deliberately left that way by God as a kind of challenge to human ingenuity and sagacity. Underlying all conceptions of the divine is the tendency to look at everything with man as the epicenter and the center of creation, which leads us to look at God also in human terms, to imagine Him in a human form. For example, in Hinduism, God's earliest avatars are other creatures like the fish (*Matsya*), the tortoise (*Kurma*), the boar (*Varaha*), and half-man-half-animal (*Narasimha*). God could have chosen, omnipotent as He is, to do what He had to do, but instead opted to take the form of non-humans to tell us that all creatures are equal to Him and that He has no particular preferential form. This can also be viewed as symbolic of the path of evolution, which envisions that animal life first appeared in the ocean, then turned amphibious at some point in time, and from these developed terrestrial life of lesser orders, eventually leading to more advanced forms of carnivores, to less advanced humanoid forms, and finally to man today. But in general, the message from both scriptural and scientific thought is that man is the God's finest—and highest—creation, and, at the same time, as Thomas Aquinas famously described, God is man's 'beatitude', his highest blessing, and aspiration. They also say, in varying degrees of emphasis and equivocation, that the final aim—indeed the manifest destiny of human life—is to unite with god, not in flesh and blood, but in spirit or as a soul, which we also say is exclusive to the human. No other form of life, however virtuous and noble, can at death dissolve into divinity. From that perspective, god is the logical 'satisfaction of human desire'. We are not striving for the imperative of consciousness-change; we are aiming at erasing bodily imperfection and impermanence, which science in essence equates with 'being god'. In short, while admonishing God as a 'failed god', we are turning ourselves into 'fake gods'. The fact is that our quest for bodily invincibility and existential eternity is directly against the laws of nature and is bound to deeply destabilize the direction of human evolution.

Whatever are the underlying factors, everyone, even the worst of offenders, bemoans the decline of moral values of modern society, that the world is in a bad shape, that man has become more self-centric than ever, that evil is both banal and brazen, that money rules the roost, and so on. The primary reason why everyone, both the virtuous and the wicked, can, as objectively as they could, say such things and still lead guiltless immoral or amoral lives is because we all have different perceptions of what morality is, or could be, in the modern world. Even in the ancient times, not all thought that all wickedness was absolute. For example, the Roman philosopher Anicius Boethius wrote, "Just as you might call a corpse a dead man, but couldn't simply call it a man, so I would agree that the wicked are wicked, but could not agree that they have unqualified existence" (*The Consolation of Philosophy*, 524). He also added, "For just as weakness is a disease of the body, so wickedness is a disease of the mind".

We lead such conditioned lives—conditioned by society, by law, by culture, by time, by religion—that the question comes up: How much moral space does an individual really have in organizing and conducting his or her life and in dealing with other people? Whatever we are witness to in the world—the lawlessness, crime, callousness, cruelty, depravity—, is that all because of or despite the conditioning? Are we like the animal in the zoo, more violent in confinement than in the wilderness? Put differently, are we less human because of what culture, State, and scriptures induce or enforce us to do? Are we, in Rousseau's celebrated phrase, a 'noble savage' or a 'civilized brute', which means in either case we are not our true selves? But then, one could also argue that being different from the original is not necessarily unwelcome; the question is, what has that difference made us out to be? If we, for example, had remained hunter-gatherers or agriculturists, would we—and the world—have been better off? That again raises the question: what is 'better-off'? Few will demur that the physical quality of human life, in terms of what we need to do to stay alive and to ward off disease and debility and hard labor, has incomparably improved.

The Five-Point Formula for Moral Decision-Making

Every crisis the world faces—ecological, economic, ethical, moral, and spiritual—is a result of the poor decision-making capacities of our human brain-based intelligence. We are just unable to get it right, get a grip on what causes them, and what is required of us to resolve them. These are also an extension of the internal crisis, inner struggle for supremacy—the war within—in our consciousness. While we are busy toning our disaster-management skills to face up to natural disasters, which are increasingly man-made than natural, the turmoil in our 'inner world' gets no attention, or even recognition. Firestorms, tornadoes, typhoons, volcanic eruptions, and earthquakes are taking place within our consciousness, more turbulent and tempestuous than the ones we experience in our outer world. The Indian mystic Osho said that to find harmony and happiness in life, one must shift the gaze from the 'objective' to the 'subjective', and try to look deep into our inner world, the world that is absolutely private to us. Just as our physical acts affect the outer world, similarly the play of forces that control our consciousness directly affects the inner world. Our *world within* and our world outside are intertwined and they mutually reinforce and reflect each other.

The outer world is a mirror of our inner world. Trouble is that we have been trying to focus all our attention and ingenuity on the extrinsic world without paying any heed to the endogenous world. At the basic level it is a question of how we look upon ourselves in relation to nature. We abuse and ravage, plunder and pillage the external world because we think it is 'separate' from us and that what happens in the world has nothing to do with us. There are unmistakable hints and portents that we are very near to what Nietzsche called "the hour of the greatest contempt"[247], an hour at which one asks: 'What good is my happiness?' and 'What good is any *good?*' and 'Why is bad *bad*, when it makes me feel so good, and when few, if any in all of humanity, seem worthy of respect, let alone reverence?' Happiness, or human flourishing, what the Greeks called *Eudaimonia*, is the magical word. That is what everyone, all the time, seeks, strives for, pursues, and prays for but never seems to have it, or enough of it for

---

[247] Nietzsche, F. 1891. Thus Spoke Zarathustra: A Book for All and None.

satisfaction. It is because we want to monopolize it and identify it with satiating our desires and dreams. Once someone said to the Buddha, "I want happiness", and the Buddha replied: "First remove 'I', that is Ego; then remove 'want', that is Desire; what you are left with is 'Happiness'. Buddhism says that anytime we identify with a sense of 'I'—as in: "I feel something"; "I have lost something"; "I am lost"; "I have done it"—we are identifying with the wrong person. We are identifying with the ego, with our pain body, not with our pure nature. The famous Buddhist saying, *Sabbe dhamma nalam abhinivesaya* (nothing whatsoever should be clung to as 'I' or 'mine') is considered as a summation of all teachings of the *Tathagata* (the word that Gautama Buddha uses when referring to himself in the Pali Canon). The Buddha says that if you have heard this phrase, then you would have heard everything there is to hear. In moral decision-making, that is a very handy point of reference. In practical life, we cannot confine happiness to a few crisp words but we can experience it, even if ephemerally. Whatever it is and however much it varies and is elusive, the bottom line is this: true happiness is never either or; it doesn't diminish if we spread it. Even our daily experiences tell us that the happiness we can get by making another person happy is immeasurable. And it lies not only in doing good, but also in realizing that there is nothing we gain by being bad, even to those who are, or at least we think are, bad to us. Returning 'good' for 'bad' is smart one-upmanship, the recipe to dissolve 'bad karma'. The attitude of others towards us often causes unhappiness, but seldom do we realize that it could be a reflection of and reaction to our own attitude. If you deny others their happiness, you are wasting your own power of happiness. Sadly, most of us have become incapable of respecting those who can be of no possible service to us, or to treating with consideration those who can do nothing for us, or are so positioned that they cannot return our rudeness. We tend to look down on people who we think are intellectually inferior, socially low-standing, or economically disadvantaged. Looking-down is, at a deep level, another attribute of the mind; the mind instinctively looks up at someone it thinks is stronger, and looks down on those it considers so weak that it can exercise control over them. What we should always remember is the sage advice, "Never look down on anyone unless you are helping them up". Ours is a time when a growing number are coming to feel a deep disgust with our 'wretched contentment', or *à la* Nietzsche, with our life of complacent comfort and languid ease amidst numbing poverty and pervasive filth. And the 'filth' is both within and without, in the content of our consciousness and in our living context.

We can improve the quality of human decision-making through a five-point formula:

(1) In considering what its consequences might entail, go beyond our family and friends, kith and kin, and bear in mind the dictum of Peter Singer that "Any preference for [one's] own interests must be justified in terms of the broader impartial principle". While what is called kin might have developed as a part of survival strategy, we should not let our love for family do injustice to others. But then, injustice itself, according to karma theory, is justice delayed over past lives. Our task must be, as Albert Einstein said, to free ourselves from this prison [of being separate from the rest] by widening our circles of compassion to embrace all living creatures and the whole of nature in its beauty. This is in line with ancient wisdom. The *Maha* Upanishad, while describing the *lakshana* or characteristics of a great man, says that the "discrimination 'this one is a relative, this other one is a stranger' is for the mean-minded. For those who are known as magnanimous, the entire world constitutes but a family". Baha'u'llah, founder of the Baha'i Faith, wrote in his Tablet of Maqsud (1882 CE) that "The earth is but one country, and mankind its citizens".

(2) A very good practical test is Mahatma Gandhi's advice about imagining in your mind's eye the most miserable person you saw

in your life, and then choosing a course of action for yourself that would make his life a little less miserable. In other words, it is not only the larger good but the good of the underdog that must be furthered.

(3) It has been said that the human brain is incapable of factoring a timeframe beyond at most fifty years. That might be a handicap now, but it was a huge advantage, indeed a survival need, in the words of sociobiologist Edward Wilson, "during all but the last few millennia of the two million years of the existence of the genus *Homo*". And, "so today the human mind works comfortably backward and forward for only a few years, spanning a period not exceeding one or two generations". At a time when we face grave threats to our very existence, and the problems are global in nature, which can only be resolved with a long-term perspective, this 'handicap' could be a crippling flaw. That is at the root of, for instance, the crisis of climate change. That being the case, the way to go beyond is perhaps to imagine your great-grandchildren and factor in how this decision, or choice, might impact on the quality of their life: if they will have cleaner air, water, and food to live on, and what kind of earth they will inhabit, and what you can do about it.

(4) Inject the moral dimension. Will our decision-making cause pain and suffering to any living creature? And which choice of ours will alleviate or reduce the global stock of suffering? When spending money, imagine which other use it can be put to that would be socially more appropriate. In today's world, the way in which a man spends money is often one of the surest tests of character. It is good to constantly remind ourselves that each one of us is a trustee—not an 'owner' of anything, not even of the money we 'earn'—of the 'trust' that is entrusted to us by society and nature. We are entitled to our fair share of the earth's bounty, but since

we can never know what that fair share is, it is safe to go on the premise that we are using more. Our 'moral' share from what we possess and enjoy in whatever form—wealth, property, even leisure—is always different from our 'monetary' entitlement. It means that we must make every effort to share and spread as widely as possible, whatever and however much or little of it we might have. One does not have to be rich to do so; even small amounts can make a big impact on someone else who is in greater need. It is not at all a pious pipe-dream; nor does it necessarily entail any sacrifice. A Harvard Business School study found that spending money on others actually makes us happier than spending it on ourselves. These only reinforce what we all in our own mundane and meandering lives experience: helping others by giving money, or by any other means, makes us feel a bit good about ourselves. In other words, we can enjoy and give at the same time. But when making choices, we sideline this factor; we assume that 'giving' is giving away and diminishes what we have. We have to find a way to factor this awareness into our myriad decisions of everyday life.

(5) Last, we must try to complement our brain-incubated intellect with heart-centered 'moral intuitions', which enable us to determine most of our everyday decisions about how to act. Most of our behavior as good or bad people takes place routinely, without reflection; it is only the occasional moral dilemma or very novel circumstance that requires us to stop and reflect. If we can bring to bear in mind the five factors and weigh everything we do, buy, sell, acquire, or dispose of, there is a good chance that we can not only enhance our decision-making capabilities but also enable us to be what man always wanted to be: a moral being. It is not that we are incapable of being moral. We are indeed moral. We do good when the going is good; but to be a 'moral being', 'being moral' has to be natural, normal, effortless and consistent, though not

continuous. Let us be clear what that effort is tantamount to. It is to go beyond biology, against the grain of the ruthless process of natural selection that brought us to where we are. And for that we have to do something that we have never been able to do before: find a way to take sides and tilt the scales in the relentless war within between our better passions and nobler instincts and our darker and meaner ones. We cannot any longer afford to sit on the sidelines, stay neutral or be an observer or a witness to that which defines and frames who we are and how we take decisions in our daily life.

The Age of the Anthropocene?

While scripture and science differ on almost everything under the sun, they were on the same page about one important subject, at least until the other day. It is that, according to Hinduism, out of millions of forms of life on earth, the human is the chosen, the exceptional, the special and the superior. But science, in the past couple of decades, has been methodically chipping away at this assumption. It turns out that for almost everything we have or are capable of, there exists another animal that is even better endowed. It does not mean we are not unique; but then every species is unique too. We do have two exceptional attributes, one negative and one positive: malice and morality. On malice, we truly are *superior* and *sovereign*. Defined loosely as the will to wish ill of another without any self-gain, we alone harbor that emotion in abundance in our mind. Malice, for the record, is not the profound absence of empathy or conscience; it is more toxic because an ill-wisher actively works to cause distress or despair just for that sake, as he knows all along there is nothing in it that could be of any use to him. It is the evil in the 'evil within'. It is not simply a matter of malfunctioning synapses and neurons in some people's minds. It is mainstream, not the monopoly of monsters or of crooked minds. In fact, mind and malice are cut out for each other. Together they form a formidable foe. C. Joybell C. (*The Sun is Showing*, 1864) says that a mind full of malice and hate is able to actually attack another's body and mind and thus prevent good from taking place (or at least delaying and disrupting the good). Why man alone is endowed with this toxic trait when not even a tiger has it, is something to ponder over. Is it too one of those noxious needs of survival which linger long after the need is not there? If so, how is the intent to do harm to another person, knowing in advance it would do no good to you, help survive? On the other hand, experts say that morality itself arose in response to the need to get others' help to survive. Whichever way, the very fact that man alone is capable of harboring malice has persuaded some like Mark Twain (1896) to say that we are the lowest, not the highest animal. Philosopher Arthur Schopenhauer puts it across when he says that 'men are the devils of the earth, and the animals, the tormented souls'.

The more pertinent point is, can a being with natural inclination towards malice even stake a claim to be a moral being? We must understand that it is morality that governs how we are together and rests on how we conceptualize right living. At first sight, malice and morality negate each other. A more measured relook reminds us of one basic bedrock of nature: the doctrine of *dwanda*, or dualism, that everything in creation is a part of a pair of opposites. Malice and morality are another pair. They do co-exist, albeit in a state of constant combat. Still, we can take some heart from recent research by organizations like *The Greater Good Science Centre*, who have uncovered evidence that humans are biologically wired for moral attributes like compassion and generosity, and that they are good for our health and well-being, not simply social virtues and spiritual tools. But, be it as it might, what we do to animals itself calls into question our moral credentials. It is the extreme expression of our selfishness, arrogance, cruelty, and sadism. The other question is, in the narrative of creation, is it exclusive to us? There is mounting evidence that it is not. Some other animals do have the essentials of what we consider is morality, like empathy, selflessness, and sacrifice. Dale Peterson, in his recent book, *The Moral Lives of Animals* (2011) argues that ultimately, human morality is like animal morality, an organ residing in the limbic system of the brain. He identifies the profound connections—the moral continuum—that link humans to many other species, and shows how much animal behavior follows the principles embodied in humanity's ancient moral codes. All said and done, in the words of Robert Wright (*The Moral Animal*, 1994), "Human beings are a species splendid in their array of moral equipment, tragic in their propensity to misuse it, and pathetic in their constitutional ignorance of the misuse". In other words, even if we assume we do have some social moral capability, we are prone to misdirect that power and, what is worse, we cannot make amends because we are incapable of being aware of it. We must understand that both the propensity and the constitutional ignorance stem from our consciousness, and unless we engineer a consciousness-change we cannot overcome them. And then again, right and wrong are not static issues; they are always in flux.

In a society such as ours with a bewildering array of priorities—economic, environmental, social, political—making the right moral choices has proven to be beyond our cognitive capacity, particularly because we do not have any solitary litmus test. And we cannot have any such 'test' because it is often not a choice between right and wrong but between right and right, or rather balancing two or more 'rights', to choose the greater good or lesser evil. What matters most morally are the consequences. How and whom do they affect? Perhaps the best one can come up with is the utilitarian dictum 'the greatest good of the greatest number'. That brings up the question: What is 'good', let alone greater good? How about the evils of majoritarianism? Perhaps we can modify it as consequences that allow us to create all the happiness we can create and remove all the suffering we can remove. And that is not a favor to another. For, in the uplifting words of philosopher Jeremy Bentham,

"... for every grain of enjoyment you sow in the bosom of another, you shall find a harvest in your own bosom; while every sorrow which you pluck out from the thoughts and feelings of a fellow creature shall be replaced by beautiful peace and joy in the sanctuary of your soul".[248] In other words, helping others by enhancing their happiness and diminishing their misery is enlightened morality. It helps us to cleanse our own consciousness, which, in turn, acts as a catalyst for consciousness-change. The fact is, it is much easier for animals to lead more moral lives than we humans. That is because animals cannot but live morally; for us it is huge effort. For them, there is no need to know right and wrong. For us, knowing by itself does not meet the need. Human society is far more complex than animal society, and it is through morality that we try to reconcile the inherent conflict between self and others, a tool for social order, amity, and brotherhood. Society is a conglomerate of autonomous and self-centered individuals, and if they can manage the conflict in a spirit of accommodation and sharing then society will be tranquil and peaceful. For that we have to subordinate *Eudaimonia* or pursuit of personal happiness of an individual to the pursuit of public interest. But that is not easy because we do not possess any moral safety net, and no God, no scientific insight can protect us from the forces of immorality and evil. In fact, these forces have proven much stronger both in the world outside and the world within. They attack our will to live morally from two fronts. First, they do not allow us to choose what is right. Second, they do not let us act on our moral choice. A factor that further muddies the matter is that morality too, like much else, is contextual and sensitive to the passage of time. And the passage of time can change the dynamics and the priorities, or make room for the entry of the new. The moral context influences the moral content, and moral content must serve the common good. For long, the common good was served through individual goodness. If individuals are truthful,

---

[248] Extract from Jeremy Bentham's 1830 letter, to the daughter of a friend, cited in Richard Layard's book *Happiness: Lessons from a New Science*, (Penguin, 2005).

honest, sincere, dutiful, considerate, and conscientious, then *ipso facto* what is common good becomes a logical outcome. That is still true but not sufficient. The center of gravity of modern life has shifted from the personal to the interpersonal, and from private to public, from home to the workplace. How we conduct ourselves away from home, to make a living, is now a matter of serious moral concern. In fact, a good deal of anxiety, stress, and tension is generated in our effort to reconcile our private persona and our public persona in moral terms.

In very elementary terms, the most important public moral issue, perhaps of all time, pertains to our own, as a species: have we by now, by our own conduct, forfeited any moral right to tarry much longer on this planet? The ugly and uncomfortable truth is that, any rational reckoning must conclude that we have not conducted ourselves as a responsible species. We have fallen far short of what is needed to harmonize morality and modernity and have, on balance, failed to use the immense power of science-based technology for the common good and inter-generational justice. We have missed out on a critical tenet: as traditional Tibetan Buddhists repeat over and over, all things have at some time been our mothers, just as we have at some time been theirs, and that the interconnected and interdependent nature of things is the heart of ecology and ethics. And that morality is a mirage if it does injury to any other sentient being. On the other hand, we have been grossly exploitative, rapacious, and predatory. Sharing the earth with other species is an important human responsibility, and we have so grievously betrayed that responsibility that our own moral right is in question. As a result, life on earth, and *Earth* itself as a planet in the solar system, is at risk now. This, in fact, is the lethal fallout of the much-talked-about advent of the *Anthropocene* epoch, the recent age of man, which is believed to have begun around 1950. In such circumstances, what should be our moral duty and existential response? The morally responsible answer can only be that if we cannot bring about a fundamental course correction in our mindset and the whole way of life, then we should hasten our extinction. But that might not be necessary; course correction is possible if we ensure that the forces of good, virtue or righteousness gain and keep an upper hand in the endless war within. If that happens, the very Age of Anthropocene—the *Kali Yuga* of Hinduism and the *Iron Age* in Greek mythology—could become a time akin to the Greek *Golden Age*. We then don't have to take recourse to desperate measures like merger with machines or try to be gods because, it would then be said that mankind lived harmoniously among the gods and interacted with them. And we will be able to live to a very old age, and when our time gets over, death will come during sleep without subjecting us to any pain. And, at last, we may even dare hope that a morally contented man might not then even seek immortality, as a gesture of justice to generations to come and to other sentient life awaiting elevation to become human.

From Death to Immortality

———◆◆◆———

Death, Be Not Proud

Many things in the contemporary world are unsettling. Many tell-tale portents tell us that some truly momentous or monstrous things are impending but none is more pregnant with possibilities than what we are doing with death. We may end up with that 'doing' as the greatest moral issue and the most destabilizing factor in human civilization and the ultimate *casus belli* to the laws of cosmos. The current coronavirus pandemic has brought to center stage what used to hover beyond the margins of our consciousness. The pandemic has highlighted the age-old issue of meaning in our own lives, and has brought up the prospect of our own personal oblivion, our inevitable futurelessness. Mortality as a topic of metaphysical meditation has seen something of a rebirth in recent literature. The riddle of human life—and death—has been this. In the words of EM Cioran, "Deep inside, each man feels—and believes—himself to be immortal, even if he knows he will perish the next moment. We can understand everything, admit everything, realize everything, except our death, even when we ponder it unremittingly and even when we are resigned to it" (*The Trouble With Being Born*, 2012).

295

Much of the discussion centers around the question of its potential harm, whether or not it ought to be considered an evil, and the degree to which it deprives us of a good, if indeed it does. Death baffles us because it is not experienceable because we are not capable of experiencing postmortem. Nothing fascinates us more than death, nothing frightens us more, nothing so certain seems so uncertain as death, and yet, nothing so near is treated as so remote. Death remains abstract, even logical, until it hits home, and then it takes a wholly different meaning or 'meaninglessness'. It then defies our understanding, or explanation or justification: how can a full-grown human being, just like any one of us, and such a vital part of our world for so long, whom we loved and who touched so many lives, good or bad, disappear without any trace so suddenly, leaving such an absolute absence? Or as the poet Victoria Chang puts it, leaving "a hole in the ground the size of violence"? (*Obit*, 2020). We agonize: how can a beautiful body turn putrid, get disposed of in haste, and, in the words of Wolfgang Borchert, be "forgotten without a trace; as if [it] had never even existed"? How could it be, why should it be? But life goes on, and nothing changes; the death of one even dearer than our own life does not teach us any lessons; we go back to where we were interrupted, back to a life of putdowns, pettiness, perfidy, nitpicking, 'one-gunmanship', ill will, etc. No amount of death can dull our desire to escape its clutches. Actually, this very yearning, however far-fetched it might be in reality, for never-ending youth and immortality, for the elixir of life, and to, so to speak, 'out live' one's self, connects us to every civilization and culture that has graced the earth. Almost every religion on earth has celebrated the ideal of immortality. As Ivan Karamazov, in Fyodor Dostoyevsky's novel *Brothers Karamazov* says, "If you were to destroy in mankind the belief in immortality, not only love but every living force maintaining the life of the world would at once be dried up. Moreover, nothing then would be immoral; everything would be lawful, even cannibalism" (Chapter 6, *Why is such a man alive?*).

Our birth is pretty prosaic but our death is infinitely varied. No two deaths are wholly identical. Death can visit in the weirdest way. It is something we so assiduously try not to have any truck with. We even try to avoid uttering the word 'death'. In the words of Lucia Benavides, "As if the word 'death' were—paradoxically—alive and, if I said it out loud or wrote it down, it would see me and chase me down".[249] We have long labored under the resigned belief that, as Francis Bacon said, "What then remains but that we still should cry, For being born, or, being born, to die? (*The World's a Bubble*, 1629). While we bemoan the involuntary end of life, the truth is also that the unavoidability of death is the glue that holds life together. As Yoda of the *Star Wars* franchise tells Luke Skywalker, "Ah, strong am I with the Force, but not that strong. Twilight is upon me, and soon, night must fall. That is the way of things. The way of the Force". One of the enduring enigmas of life is that, much like Tolstoy's *Ivan Ilyich*, "we all know that we will die, so why do we struggle to believe it?"[250] What does nature get out of so much wanton waste, which is what death at first glance seems to be? It is no solace to be told, *à la* Epicurus (*Letter to Menoeceus*), that "Death, therefore, the most awful of evils, is nothing to us, seeing that, when we are, death is not come, and when death is come, we are not". That, Epicurus says, allows us to "enjoy the lethal nature of life". For the modern man, that gives philosophical underpinning to his zeal for immortality. For, if death is 'evil' and if we should fight evil, then logically we should fight death too. Yet for long it was meant to keep us moral. It is well captured in the refrain, "To death we are hastening, let us refrain from sinning". In today's world, death and sin are virtually disconnected, and the scriptural seven deadly sins—anger, envy, gluttony, greed, lust, pride, sloth—are almost integrated into our daily life. To eternal life, and deliverance from the cycle of death to

---

[249] Benavides, L. 2020. What Neapolitans Understand About Death (Better Than Most): Lucia Benavides on Confronting That Deepest of Human Fears. *Literary Hub*, 23 Jan 2020. Retrieved from <https://lithub.com/what-neapolitans-understand-about-death-better-than-most/>.

[250] Tolstoy, L. 1886. The Death of Ivan Ilyich.

death, which scriptures say ought to be the purpose of earthly life, we now say we want immortality here and now, not in spirit but in flesh and blood.

We want immortality partly because we do not know what happens after we die. In the *Katha* Upanishad, the little boy Nachiketa asks the God of Death (*Yama*) himself, what happens after death. In the words of Edwin Arnold: "Some say that after death the soul still lives, personal, conscious; Some say, Nay, it ends! Fain would I know which of these twain be true" (*The Secret of Death*, 1885). Which is true: are we really worse-off, as Achilles said after his death, or are we the envy of angels, when alive? Is death no different from repositioning molecules at the physical level, and liberating consciousness from a walking cage to one of a free nature? Is it death that holds the meaning of the life we seek? Have we got it all wrong? Is death really what we hope life is? Or is death forever an unknowable absolute, nature's last laugh? Can it be codified as part of some basic bedrock, a detail of an unknown whole rather than merely a random and meaningless event? The human death rate is cent percent. Yet, that hasn't stopped us from trying to cheat on death or to find ways to reverse it.

The triad of practical questions that often come to mind are: Why must we die? What happens after we die? And how come the certainty of death is so powerless to influence our daily existence? Shakespeare's Hamlet puts it well: "Thou know'st 'tis common; all that lives must die, Passing through nature to eternity". The circumstance, however, has changed dramatically in the first months of the year 2020, with the global spread of the Covid-19 pandemic. That 'certainty' now looms as both imminent and immediate. Still the bigger question needs reflection. In the Indian epic Mahabharata, this subject was alluded to when the Pandava king Yudhishthira was asked by a *yaksha*, a celestial being, "What is the most surprising, the most wondrous thing in the world?" Yudhishthira answered, "Man sees death all around, but behaves as if he is deathless". Everyone knows that death is the ultimate fate or truth, but everyone behaves as if that truth does not apply to his own life. In short, everyone is mortal, but one thinks and behaves as if he alone is immortal. It is that paradox that frames the human condition. The truth lies in the words of the Spanish philosopher Miguel de Unamuno: "For the present let us remain keenly suspecting that the longing not to die, the hunger for personal immortality, the effort whereby we tend to persist indefinitely in our own being, which is, according to the tragic Jew, our very essence, that this is the affective basis of all knowledge and the personal inward starting-point of all human philosophy, wrought by a man and for all men".[251]

Yudhishthira's answer itself was another riddle, a paradox. But what he did not realize is that that very apparent incongruity—that we will be around when others, particularly our tormentors and enemies bite the dust—was what kept peace and order in human society. What modern science is trying to do is to make immortality not a delusion but an actuality, by technologically empowering man with the means of dodging death. In so doing, it is in fact trying to give effect to what the Bible tells us: "The final enemy to be destroyed is death".[252] So euphoric is science that one is predicting that if we are alive in 30 years, we'll be alive in 1,000 years, which means that at least *de facto*, if not *de jure* man will become immortal. Then, we can mimic John Donne, and crow: "Death be not proud". But it comes loaded with a caveat. It could disrupt human society like nothing else before. Mankind might acquire the technical capacity to radically extend the human life span, but in a world like ours, it will not be within the reach of the vast majority.

We must revisit why mortality is there in the first place in nature. It is through mortality that nature renews itself. Even the natural length of a species life span is a vital part of the overall life-balance that sustains biodiversity on earth. No species has a right to its own life or death. Nature ensures a balance even between predator and prey. One species

---

[251] de Unamuno, M. [Crawford Flitch, J.E. (tr.)]. 1954. The Tragic Sense of Life. New York, USA: Dover.

[252] Corinthians 15:26

seeking to unnaturally disturb it opens a Pandora's box, or a can of worms. Apart from upsetting this delicate symmetry in nature, humanity will get divided into what Yuval Harari calls 'superhuman caste' and the wholly human subcaste, a perfect recipe for a revolution and a dystopian horror. The space entrepreneur Elon Musk offers another horror, and fears that unless artificial intelligence is strictly regulated, we will end up with an 'immortal' digital dictator who could forever trap humanity in its grasp. It could be the most inter-generationally selfish and socially destabilizing and morally troublesome development. For it is death, rather its impartial inevitability and across-the-board ambit, that held a cap on its gross injustice, inequity, inequality, oppression, exploitation. Although death has often been described as an equalizer and a leveler, that is true only in the sense that everyone 'dies' but not *how* one dies. As Étienne Balibar says, the fact is that "Our world is one marked by an explosion as well as the radical inequality of the forms and experiences of death itself" (*Violence and Civility*, 2010). In addition, if we truly come to believe that the ultra-rich, the elite, the plutocracy that runs the world, would live on almost indefinitely, then the world will witness a kind of violence and vengeance the like of which it has not seen so far. That smug belief has now taken a big beating by Covid-19, the virus that swept the world in 2020; it has shown that it spares no one, striking, as it did, a movie star and a prime minister to bring the message home. Then again, immortality is not impregnability; the immortal sentient beings may not die, but they can be killed, just like Tolkien's *Elves*. Although the immortality that science is seeking is of a different genre, most people, regardless of race, religion, or culture, tend to believe they don't dissolve like salt in water with death. They believe that a part of themselves, some indelible core, soul, consciousness, or some sort of essence, will endure—through progeny, name, fame, memory, art, literature—and transcend the body's death and live forever. But that is different from what science is focusing upon: to perpetuate what physicist Alan Lightman calls, "three pounds of neurons".

It is also very different from what most religions envision as immortality. For example, according to the Upanishads, 'the mortal in whose heart desire is dead becomes immortal'. The Katha Upanishad says, 'the mortal in whose heart the knots of ignorance are untied becomes immortal'. These are the highest truths taught in the scriptures. The very two things that we are summoned to overcome—desire and ignorance—are the very two things we are hostage to. Our feverish pursuit of scientific, not spiritual, immortality throws up another huge downside. It is siphoning off vital intellectual and financial resources at the expense of more worthy and socially imperative priorities that can lift the lives of billions of people from subhuman misery.

In any case, immortality, in its literal, strict sense, is impossible, just pie in the sky. Even if one lives for a thousand, or ten thousand, or a million years, he will still not be immortal. One day, he too will 'die'. In the Mahabharata, the great Bhishma was given the boon to choose the *time* of his death (*Ishtartha mruthyu*), not deathlessness. Although his mother was a goddess, River Ganga, he was nevertheless born a human, and could not wriggle out of reach of death. Even if the current limit to human life extends from 120 years to 1,000 years or more, a person could still be killed in an accident, or die from disease. We would tend to think that it is simply a radical reflection of what is already happening: humans have been living longer and longer all the time incrementally, much more in recent times. But it is not that simple. Although some zealots say that there is no biological limit, new research suggests that humans can only live so long, and we are reaching the natural biological limit. For other researchers, "If a human life span was extended beyond 125 years, it would require other scientific interventions beyond improving someone's health".[253] It means that any significant extension, let alone immortality, can only happen through non-biological ways. It would then be nonhuman life, not human.

---

[253] Britton, B. 2016. Humans Have Reached Their Lifespan Limit, Researchers Say. *CNN Health*. 06 Oct 2016.

As we now define it to be. And the children of these 'immortals' will not be born immortal, unlike gods or angels; they will have to start all over again or else we will have the perverse situation of the 'immortals' having to bury their own children and grandchildren.

The other important question is if some humans acquire superhuman abilities—and live like the biblical Methuselah for 969 years, or like *Lazarus Long* of Robert Heinlein's science fiction novels, live up to 2,000 years—how would they behave? How would it affect their mindset and consciousness? Would they be more responsible, kind, and compassionate, or more reckless, predatory, and cruel? Would it lead to, for example, the abatement of the climate crisis, or will it get aggravated? Will inequity, indifference, intolerance, injustice, and selfishness become less or more? If they cannot die but get bored to death, would such humans seek out and check into 'killer clinics' to end their lives? Already, even with our current life span, some apparently healthy people are seeking help to end their lives, out of sheer fatigue or revulsion with what the human condition has come to stand for. A good way to look at it is to see what happened since 1900 to now: average life expectancy has doubled but human behavior is no better; if any, it is far worse. There is no reason to believe it will be any different if some of us live up to a thousand years. The bottom line is this: without consciousness-change that involves a radical reduction in the leverage of our mind, a *de facto* immortal man is likely to be far more mean, malicious, and malevolent. That, in turn, could provoke more violent and vengeful reactions. As a species that prides itself on being the only one capable of reflection, reasoning, and rationality, we should carefully contemplate and cogitate on how we are trying to transit through the human condition.

In the *Brihadaranyaka* Upanishad, there is a famous mantra called the *Pavamana Mantra*: *Om, asato ma sad gamaya; tamaso ma jyotir gamaya; mrtyor ma amritam gamaya*. It is loosely translated as, "Om, from falsehood lead me to truth; from darkness lead me to the light; from death lead me to immortality". Some scholars substitute the word 'through' for 'from', and say that we cannot get away from illusion, darkness, or death. This mantra captures the essence of the human spiritual journey. Although they look different, many interpret that all three portions of the *mantra* have the same meaning, and complement each other. Death here symbolizes not only the end of a life, but also darkness, delusion, untruth, and the unreal. Immortality signifies truth, light, self-realization, and eternal life of the *Atman*, which itself is described as "unmade, immortal, changeless, primal". The mantra is not just talking about physical death, but also about the ones in our minds. Man might yet conquer death, but could still lose his soul; and what earthly good would that do? The fact of the matter is that we cannot comprehend death unless we comprehend life. Death becomes a 'problem' if life is viewed as a problem, and life becomes a problem if it is viewed as inane, or as one might like to call it, an insane interlude from birth to death.

The Mystery of Mortality

We might not know what is worth living or dying for, but death has been so traumatic for so long that we know not if there was a time when, as Thomas Hardy tells in his classic poem *Before Life and After* (1909), "If something ceased, no tongues bewailed; if something winced and waned, no heart was wrung; if brightness dimmed, and dark prevailed, no sense was strung". But the mystery of mortality has always fascinated as well as frustrated the human. Deep within, we know that we too will follow, but we scarcely glance at those who have gone before. Human culture itself is ultimately an orchestrated, symbolic defense mechanism against the awareness of our inevitable mortality, which in turn acts as the emotional and intellectual response to our basic survival mechanism. The level at which human consciousness functions in most people has never allowed us to accept death with a certain measure of equanimity. The Buddha said, "Death is only the temporary end of a temporary phenomenon". For Tagore, "Death is not extinguishing the light; it is only putting out the lamp because the dawn has come". We wish we could all adopt and maintain such an attitude, but when death does strike and snatches a loved one, all our restraint goes up in smoke. Even great people and avatars are not immune. In the *Ramayana*, when Kumbhakarna (brother of the 'evil' Ravana and of the virtuous Vibhishana) dies on the battlefield and Vibhishana is grief-stricken, Rama consoles him and says that death is inescapable for everyone born. But when his own brother Lakshmana is mortally wounded later, Rama becomes inconsolable and even says he will take his own life. In the Mahabharata, Lord Krishna teaches the Bhagavad Gita to Arjuna. One of the main messages he offers is to treat death with equanimity, as it is just another passage. But when Arjuna's son Abhimanyu is killed, Arjuna becomes distraught with grief and vows vengeance. All teachings of Krishna seem to have simply gone out of the window, as though Arjuna never heard them—that death is but another phase of life, no different than discarding of worn-out clothes; that only the body 'dies', not the soul; that we should not grieve over that which is inescapable. However much one gets prepared, we are never prepared enough when the creepy shadow of death comes close. What baffles and beguiles us is not only death's invincible inevitability—that someday we will turn ice-cold—but also the unsettling uncertainty about when and where death will lay its icy hand on our brow. There have always been masters like Swami Vivekananda and Adi Sankara, who just *knew*. Vivekananda had not only said that he would not cross forty years, but also that he 'knew the time and place' of his death. The point is that knowing made a difference to their life, not to their death.

The fact is that there is not much room in death but a lot in life, and that is the difference between life and death. Then again, as Socrates said, after being sentenced to death and minutes before the hemlock took effect, "Which of these two (life and death) is better, God only knows". He also placed life and death contextually and said, "This would imply that life and death do not have a definitive end, but exist in a perpetual cycle". It is interesting that what Socrates said was but an echo of the famous *sloka* of the great Indian Vedantist Adi Sankaracharya: *Punarapi jananam punarapi maranam; Punarapi janani jatare sayanam*—Again and again one is born; And again and again one dies; And again and again one sleeps in the mother's womb. The medieval Christian expression *memento mori* ('remember that you will die') is another variant of the same refrain. Although views vary on what to expect after death, the idea that death is certain, inevitable, and irreversible has been central to human culture and cognition. Socrates characterized the right way to apply oneself to philosophy is to directly and of one's own accord prepare oneself for dying and death. Man is now trying to dethrone, destabilize, disrupt, and destroy death, to treat it like another disease, and to find a cure for it like, say, for the common cold or cancer. And, so goes the premise, if death can be defeated, we hope to be able to bridge the gap between the bodies we live in, and the bodies we desired. Thus transforming *Homo sapiens* into a *Homo deus*, a walking, not floating, god on earth. We want to be at least a Methuselah (the grandfather of Noah), whose life span was said to be 969 years, if not Markandeya, the Indian immortal sage. This is man's audacious, and potentially fateful, agenda for the 21st century. We must also up front recognize and realize that the abundant resources, financial and scientific, that are being funneled by tech-titans for research on immortality and eternal youth carry serious risks on four fronts. First, it gives irreversible momentum, enough to push the forbearance of nature beyond the tipping point. Second, by starving far higher social priorities like the climate crisis, malnutrition, and mass poverty, it could exhaust the patience of the masses. Three, it could fatally wean us away from the spiritual path. Four, the behavior of a man who believes he doesn't have to die, could strengthen the forces of evil in the war within, irrespective of what such a man does. A truly or nearly immortal man can be the ultimate monster. Will science succeed? No one—not at least those who are pursuing such an agenda with a messianic zeal—can foretell what, how, and where this venture is likely to end. Whatever it may be, soon, neither death nor its twin sister, life, will be as we have known it to be since the advent of the first human on this planet.

The thought comes up: everyone, be it human or nonhuman, dies (save a handful), but is everyone equally aware of it? One of the sacred cows of human thought, for which there is no credible evidence, is that animal consciousness cannot comprehend death. Ernest Becker, in *The Denial of Death* (1973), reflects this view: "The animals don't know that death is happening and continue grazing placidly while others drop alongside them. The knowledge of death is reflective and conceptual, and animals are spared it. They live and they disappear with the same thoughtlessness: a few minutes of fear, a few seconds of anguish, and it is over. But to live a whole lifetime with the fate of death haunting one's dreams and even the most sun-filled days—that's something else".[254] The 'animal', we associate with a lower form of life, but it is also said, "What we here feel as 'animal' in quality and nature is the basic element in which the dead live. The kingdom in which the dead live can easily be changed when it enters into us; what is higher life in yonder world can become lower when it is within us on earth".[255]

The Moral Purpose of Mortality

Mortality has failed its practical purpose: to give us a moral meaning to life. Instead of inducing himself to look at the finiteness of life as an incentive to spend quality time on earth, and to make his temporary presence of permanent value, man has turned that perspective to make life itself finite-less, a license for profligacy. Instead of spending the limited time to prepare himself to 'meet his maker', man is doing his best to permanently postpone

---

[254] Becker, E. 1973. The Denial of Death. New York, USA: Simon & Schuster.
[255] Steiner, R. 1918. The Dead Are With Us. A lecture by Rudolf Steiner on 10 February 1918 at Nuremberg, Germany.

such a tryst. Emily Dickinson wrote, "Because I did not stop for death; he kindly stopped for me". Now we do not want any such 'stops'; we want *sops* to live forever. It all comes down to perspective and practice. Perspective, either as a means for harmony in life, or to make life itself everlasting, or so long that death ceases to be a factor in life. Practice, or *abhyasa* in Sanskrit, is needed to achieve anything in life, or even to die with dignity. Plato wrote, "True philosophers are always occupied in the practice of dying". Human response to the inexorability of death has, over the ages, ranged widely, from outright denial to defiance, from 'accept and make merry' to outright combat and conquest. And we tend to look at an other's death from our perspective. Confronted by conflicts and contradictions all around, man's mind has found an ingenious way to outflank them: it is to acknowledge its inevitability, at least in the immediate future, but to indefinitely defer its applicability to his own life. In other words, death cannot be wished away; but he must shut the doors of his mind to his own death. On the other hand, at another level of consciousness, man continues to wonder: 'Is this life all that there is?'; 'What happens to me when I 'die' and where will I be in the hereafter?'; 'Is death the enemy of life and who ordained it that way?'. The state of the mind of man is well captured by William James in his book *The Varieties of Religious Experience* (1901–1902), when he wrote, "The fact that we can die, that we can be ill at all is what perplexes us; the fact that we now for a moment live and are well is irrelevant to that perplexity".

Along with the evolution of the human brain and dramatic changes in the modes of living, human perceptions of death in life have also changed. In his book *The Hour of Our Death*, Philippe Ariès emphasizes "the relationship between man's attitude towards death and his awareness of self, of his degree of existence or simply of his individuality". According to him, the concept of death as a familiar, anonymous event was replaced by suppression of death. In the very early human communities, the motif was 'death-in-life', and death was marked by a simple, public ritual largely controlled by the dying person, which continued till the Middle Ages. With increasing individualism and weakening of traditional communities, an individual life was no longer subsumed in the collective destiny of a group, and that led to a shift in the focus of redemption from group ritual to personal conscience. With the early advent of science, death came to be perceived not as part of a continuum, but as a rupture or a break of life, something very unpleasant, a matter better put out of mind. With industrialization acquiring a firm hold over human culture, the focus of death shifted from the dying individual to the death of one's significant others and death became romanticized, and the graveyard became the focus of somber and mournful dispositions relative to death. With increasing privatization and institutionalization in the twentieth century, death denial became the reigning orientation, which soon gave way to the endeavor of science to conquer death and make man eternal. The irony is that despite all the accumulated wisdom about death, very few actions in life of very few people are influenced by this knowledge. Such a strong disconnect, it is hard to imagine, is a wholly human failing. If there is Divine sanction for this amnesia, what was the purpose? It may be so, because if man truly and wholly believes that he could die any time, he may lose all interest in life and cease to do his *karma* and *dharma*. Without death, life can be an endless entrapment and unbearable burden, no end to misery, no hope of betterment. In fact, it is the definitiveness of death that makes life worth living. There is life because there is death. It is due to death that man understands the value of life; it is its task to make man realize and enhance life. Death really is a gate, not the, the "sluice through which the different elements of this world go as they move from one stage to another in the cosmic evolution of all empirical reality".[256] In Markus Zusak's *The Book Thief* (2005), the story's narrator Death says, "Death

---

[256] Panikkar, R. (ed., tr.). 1977. The Vedic Experience: *Mantramanjari* An Anthology of the Vedas for Modern Man and Contemporary Celebration. London, UK: Darton, Longman & Todd. p.572.

believes that dying represents a humane dynamic in the grand scheme of life. As an immortal, he experiences existence as an unending burden that humans by contrast don't need to carry forever".

Mortality has framed every aspect of human activity and creativity, and has always been a defining element in literature, poetry, theater, drama, art, religion, philosophy, and science. Mortality, which some say is a gift while many consider it a curse, is perceived in multiple ways, as the authentic existential dilemma, a part of the natural cycle of decay and renewal, a stepping stone to spiritual self-discovery, a means to finding immanent meaning in life. In effect, it has come to be the unknowable center around which our thoughts inescapably, even morbidly, swirl. As someone succinctly put it, "The question here is, how do we live? We want to be gods, or at least angels, heroes, or saints. But we are animals. Plus, we don't want to die, or even admit the possibility of death".[257] But we still die, lock, stock, and barrel. There is nothing we can do about death, but everything we do has something to do about it. We cannot escape it, but we cannot also accept it. We feel so impotent, emasculated, embittered, enraged when confronted by it. Dylan Thomas expressed the mood memorably when he wrote, "Do not go gentle into that good night... Rage, rage against the dying of the light". Sacred texts and seers might say that 'dark is right', that is, that death is integral to life, but most men, when that 'night' creeps in, are always aghast and not ready to 'go' at all.

Becoming a Jellyfish, at the Least a Turtle

The central theme of our great epics and enduring works of literature, like the *Epic of Gilgamesh* (Mesopotamia) is the mystery of mortality. King Gilgamesh attempts to learn the secret of eternal life by undertaking a

---

[257] Source: The Denial of Death. Goodreads. Retrieved from <http://www.goodreads.com/book/show/2761.The_Denial_of_Death> on 23 Apr 2014.

long and perilous journey to meet the immortal flood hero, Utnapishtim, who tells Gilgamesh, "The life that you are seeking you will never find. When the gods created man, they allotted to him death, but life they retained in their own keeping".[258] And the epic gives us some wrenching advice, which is music to modern ears: "Fill your belly; day and night make merry; let days be full of joy; love the child who holds your hand; let your wife delight in your embrace; for these alone are the concerns of man". What Gilgamesh was told was *not* possible is what is high on the wish-list of the man of this millennium. We take heart from the fact that it is not *unnatural*. For, that which exists already in nature in a lowly creature cannot be unnatural, or cannot be dismissed as an unreasonable aspiration for the human, the most evolved species. Scientists have, in their search to find the cause of what they call 'inefficiency of ageing', discovered that the tiny immortal jellyfish has found a way to cheat death by actually reversing its ageing process. If the jellyfish is injured or sick, it returns to its polyp stage over a three-day period, transforming its cells into a younger state that will eventually grow into adulthood all over again. Another case is that of the slow and steady turtle, known to live for centuries; research has found that their organs don't seem to break down over time.

It means, literally, that we, as individuals—not as a species—want to be still walking on earth centuries from now, essentially with the extant body and brain. The single most important truth that has so far stood the test of time, the substratum of all scriptures, the common thread of all human thought has been, as Acharya Rajneesh (Osho) puts it, "Death has already happened in birth; there is no way to transcend it. It is going to happen because it has already happened. It is only a question of time unfolding. You are rushing towards it each minute".[259] Rabindranath Tagore, in his classic poem *Gitanjali*, expresses it exquisitely: "Thou hast

---

[258] *Epic of Gilgamesh*. Wikipedia: The Free Encyclopedia. Wikimedia Foundation. Retrieved 28 Aug 2014.

[259] Source: The Speaking Tree. *Times of India*. India. 7 Aug 2011. p.4.

made me endless; such is Thy pleasure. This frail vessel thou emptiest again and again; and fillest ever with fresh life". Scriptures say that the only way to avoid or escape from death is to avoid or escape from birth. But science says 'not necessarily'. Advances in sciences such as microbiology and genetics seem to indicate that the prospect of physical immortality, or at the very least, the prospect of radically increased individual life spans, does not seem such a pie-in-the-sky as it appeared even a couple of decades ago. Some say that well before the end of this century, '90s could be the new 50s'. That will fall far short of the outright immortality that man has been seeking for millenniums. And if immortality means the inability to die, it means the inability to actually be killed by anything. That is not going to happen; no organic body can be indestructible. In fact, beyond a threshold, say half a millennium, living 'forever' has no practical meaning. The aim is, as the immortalists put it, "to live long enough to live forever".

Science is now trying to achieve, besides physical or biological immortality, another kind of immortality—*digital* immortality. That is, making permanent what is being referred to as the 'online presence personality', distinct from the physical, to ensure that our digital 'footprints' outlive our physical forms. It is explained as having the means to store and restore the thousands of trillions of bytes of information represented in the pattern that we call our brain. Ultimately, "software-based humans will be vastly extended beyond the severe limitations of humans as we know them today. They will live out on the Web, projecting bodies, whenever they need or want them, including virtual bodies in diverse regions of virtual reality".[260] It is suggested that it might be possible that our brains and memories could be transferred into a synthetic medium, that is, we will become 'immortal' through a machine. In essence, this would involve the uploading of human consciousness into artificial, robotic bodies. That

[260] Gray, J. 2011. On the Road to Immortality. Review of *Transcend: Nine Steps to Living Well Forever* (Ray Kurzweil and Terry Grossman); and *The Singularity is Near: When Humans Transcend Biology* (Ray Kurzweil). *The New York Review of Book*. USA. 24 Nov – 07 Dec 2011. p 48.

would mean that individuals could carry their "personhood" for decades or centuries into the future. Then again, we are told that hackers are developing a virus to infect human brains; that synthetic biology—deliberate creation of living organisms from elementary materials that are not themselves alive—is accelerating faster than computer technology, which could be used for behavior control and bioterrorism. We also read reports that 'headless human clones can grow organs in ten years'. Elsewhere, one tells us that we could have amidst us 'biological robots' sooner than electronics-based robots.[261] Yet another says that a 'crawling bio-robot runs on rat heart cells', which could 'someday attack human disease'.[262] And maybe soon, mindless 'human' robots can be cloned for manual labor or as sex slaves? Such prophecies are usually paraded to demonstrate what man can do to transcend biology and outsmart nature! There are some who sound a note of caution. In the words of Prof. Andrew Linzey, Director of Animal Ethics at Oxford University, "It is morally regressive to create a mutant form of life… scientific fascism". How are we supposed to put this in perspective? Should we say it is incredulous, impossible, or is it the end of the bridge between animal and *Overman*, with man being the connecting rope, that Nietzsche talked about? Zarathustra says, "Man is something that shall be overcome. What have you done to overcome man? All beings so far have created something beyond themselves; and do you want to be the ebb of this great flood, and even go back to the beasts rather than overcome man? What is the ape to man? A laughing stock or a painful embarrassment. And man shall be just that to the Overman: a laughing stock or a painful embarrassment".[263] Is the human organism that nature fashioned as a part of the living world, his brain and/or body capable of such manipulative, mechanical metamorphosis? Trouble is that human beings are still on the

---

[261] Durrant-Whyte, H. 2013. Robotics Asks a Fundamental Question: What Makes Us Intelligent? *The Times of India*. Hyderabad, India. 10 May 2013. p.16.

[262] Than, K. 2012. Crawling Bio-Robot Runs on Rat Heart Cells. National Geographic Daily News. 19 Nov 2012.

[263] Nietzsche, F. 1891. Thus Spoke Zarathustra. First part. Zarathustra's Prologue.

prehistoric mode—a 10,000-BCE model as it is dubbed—designed for agriculture, with decision-making software adequate for walking, running, digging, and climbing trees. Mechanization has further eroded even that vitality. Perhaps it is useful to pause and ponder over what we think is missing in mortality. "The desire to live forever is the desire never to be ended or closed-off; the desire, in effect, to contain everything, so that there is nothing outside oneself that one will not eventually grasp".[264] Or is it that we are aware of the sea of possibilities for us which are going to be shut off by death? Is it that there are places that we cannot reach or simply that there will be people we know who we will cease to know? There are no certain answers, and we end with the paradox that while there will always be reasons to labor to live longer, even much longer, there will always be reasons to worry why living forever would turn 'death' into what we think life is.

Immortality—Are the Gods Hitting Back At Us?

The irony is that humans want to conquer ageing, disease, and death, but at the same time, every day, they are discovering or inventing new and innovative reasons to kill each other, not reasons to live for or die for. The ultimate power one can acquire is to get other people to die for you. And one always wonders, "What's worth enough for a man to give up his life?" Every human killing falls into two types: authorized and unauthorized. It is only the latter that is deemed as a crime or sin or evil. And whether it is 'authorized' or not depends on who you are, where you are, and how it happens. The same action by the same person at a different time, place, and circumstance can become horrendous or honorable. Leonardo da Vinci said, "We live by the death of others. We are burial places". Byron wrote, "This is the patent age of new inventions for killing bodies, and

---

[264] Barrow, J.D. 2005. The Infinite Book: A Short Guide to the Boundless, Timeless and Endless. London, UK: Vintage Books. p.256.

for saving souls. All propagated with best intentions", words which served as an epigram for Graham Greene's classic *The Quiet American* (1955). Man has always physically eliminated another man since the time he sharpened a stone, and will continue to do so, increasingly for more reasons than he thinks he has to live for. 'Killing' satisfies many diverse urges. In Biblical terms, at least man's revolt against God in the earthly paradise was followed by the deadly combat of man against man, Cain and Abel. Although debatable, by and large human society has tended to view killing as the ultimate crime as well as punishment, and a deterrent against future unlawful killings. Individually, it can be a product of unbridled passion and anger; it can even be unintentional and circumstantial; it could be simply a matter of sheer survival—'it is either he or me'. In *karmic* terms, killing or getting killed is not very different from other forms of death; it is another settling of karmic debt. The killer and the killed are playing their parts. In the Bhagavad Gita, when Arjuna hesitates to kill those he revered, Krishna says that those people are already standing to be killed; that Arjuna is simply playing his part as an instrument. Man will do anything to enjoy perfect health, but he is almost hypnotically poisoning the very infrastructure of life on earth, raising the question if that is the manifest of our collective death-wish. Could this be the way gods are getting back at us for seeking to undermine their monopoly on immortality? Whether it is divine wrath or human folly, the fact is that after over a million years of human evolution on earth, "the global human enterprise is on a collision course with the physical and biological limits of earth".[265]

We may like to defy death, physically, or digitally; but the grind and grandeur of life is a given, something we learn to live with. Also 'given' is our state of ignorance about the fundamentals. Socrates lamented that all his life he had sought knowledge and didn't find it, and it was said that

---

[265] Terborgh, J. 2011. Can Our Species Escape Destruction? Review of Tim Flannery's *Here On Earth: A Natural History of the Planet. The New York Review of Books.* USA. 13–28 Oct 2011. p.29.

he was called the wisest man among his contemporaries because he knew that he knew nothing. We are told that the human alone, among all the creatures on earth, wants to know more than we need to know to be alive. Lest we miss the point: according to the Bible, man was thrown down from the heavens because he ate the fruit of 'The Tree of Knowledge' (called *Etz haDaat tov V'ra*, in Hebrew). It is the lust 'to know' that defines us. Indeed, the very name we have given to ourselves, *Homo sapiens*, means 'wise being' or 'knowing being'. We have known a lot but the essence has been elusive and like Tennyson's *Ulysses* (1842), we too are made weak by time, but still we want to strive to seek, to find, and not to yield, and hope that some work of noble note, may yet be done, while still doing what we need to do to stay alive. But unlike Ulysses we are not strong in will; nor are we 'one equal temper of heroic hearts'. We are wobbly in will and our hearts too are getting weary of us. Still, that weary will is the most powerful force on earth, rivaling the very divine. That is the paradox—and peril. We cannot speak for other species, but as far as the human is concerned, the human consciousness, more precisely the human mind, has demonstrably fallen short in handling power, domestic or societal, personal or public, physical or psychological, economic or political, religious or spiritual. Our darkest desires, deepest flaws seem to come into full play in circumstances when we dispense power over those who have none or not in equal measure. Some say 'will to power' is intrinsic to being alive. Nietzsche wrote (*Beyond Good and Evil*) that "Anything which is a living and not a dying body, will have to be an incarnate will to power, it will strive to grow, spread, seize, become predominant—not from any morality or immorality but because it is living and because life simply is will to power. Exploitation... belongs to the essence of what lives, as a basic organic function; it is a consequence of the will to power, which is after all the will to life". Without some kind or degree of exploitation, at least human life is almost impossible. The poet WH Auden said, "Almost all of our relationships begin and most of them continue as forms of mutual exploitation, a mental or physical barter, to be terminated when one or both parties run out of goods". One of the tragedies of human life is that although a healthy relationship is supposed to be mutually reinforcing, they have become mutually restrictive. No relationship can be exempted from this restriction including the most important, the man–God relationship. Our behavior also substantially changes depending where we are positioned. We are almost different human beings at home, at work, at play. This, in turn, brings out a philosophical question about the innate nature of life. Is it irretrievably, irreversibly unfair, unequal, a 'hell', as Schopenhauer characterized it, to be done away with as soon as possible? Death too is arbitrary and unfair in many ways. Some die before their time; some 'overlive'. As Emily Wilson puts it in her book *Mocked with Death: Tragic Overliving from Sophocles to Milton* (2004): "Sometimes people go on living even after the moment when they or others feel they should have died". That apart, one existential question that crops up is: how should we do our time here on earth? Some say that it is to get away as far as possible and the way is self-sacrifice and self-imposed poverty. Others say enjoy it as much as you can, live for the day, let the senses have their fill…

When Death Strikes Home

Our 'differences' with death essentially are four. One, it is its awesome finality, its utter completeness; its no-holds-barred nothingness; its intrinsic irrevocability. Two, the absolute absence of any rhyme or reason, fairness or justness, in the way it strikes. Three, death may be ordained but not orderly; pre-determined but not predictable; there is not a single universal principle, save its inevitability, that governs death. Four, it is one state of 'existence' about which experience makes no difference. Nor does our preparedness, or who stops from whom, death or us. Emily Dickinson wrote an immortal poem (*Because I Could Not Stop for Death*) about mortality: "Because I could not stop for Death; He kindly stopped for me; The carriage held but just Ourselves; And Immortality". The poem is often portrayed as the 'mortal experience from the standpoint of immortality', of the conflict of mortality and immortality, defining eternity as timelessness. Emily envisions death as a 'kindly', not grim and cruel, carriage driver, who is lauded for his 'civility', and stops for one who could not stop for him; the only other 'passenger' inside is immortality. The drive, Emily describes, was reassuring, 'with no haste', and the passage is through life experiences, which is captured in metaphors like school, setting sun, children, gazing grain, swelling on the ground, each symbolizing a stage in life, until finally, the last is a grave. The carriage is headed to eternity, with Death as the charioteer; the passengers, mortality and immortality. We travel through life with the twins, *mortality* and *immortality*; sometimes they may clash; sometimes they can be cuddly, but never far from each other. As Schopenhauer said, "Each day is a little life; every waking and rising a little birth; every fresh morning a little youth; every going to rest and sleep a little death".

How we perceive death affects how we live. Some say that when whatever we do comes to a screeching halt, what difference does it make to what we do or do not do? If we kill somebody, so what; anyway, that person is going to die sooner or later... Others posit that the very reason to conduct your life is so that it makes some positive difference to other people's lives. Whatever we might say, we do adopt double-standards. To put death in perspective and to erase the morbid fear of death, scriptures like the Bhagavad Gita tell us that death really is no big deal, that life and death are parts of a continuum, that what we deem as death is but another passage, like from youth to old age, and that what passes through or out is the physical body, not the imperishable *Atman*. But in actuality, we mourn death and celebrate life. And when death does come too close for comfort, all wisdom and equanimity evaporates. That is true of great people as well as the garden-types. Two examples illustrate the point, as mentioned earlier. In the Ramayana, when the mighty Kumbhakarna is slain by Rama, and Vibhishana (Kumbhakarna's brother) wails in grief and remorse, Rama consoles Vibhishana saying that his brother died doing his dharma, that death is only for the body. But when Rama's own brother Lakshmana is mortally wounded by Indrajit (son of Ravana, and nephew of Vibhishana), Rama becomes inconsolable, and even says that suicide is preferable to going back to his kingdom Ayodhya without his brother Lakshmana! Similarly, in the Mahabharata, Krishna expounds the great Bhagavad Gita to Arjuna, on the battlefield of Kurukshetra. The essence of the Gita, according to Krishna, is that one must perform *nishkama karma* (action without attachment to the fruits thereof). Arjuna then picks up his mighty bow and kills his own very dear and revered grandfather, Bhishma. But, later, when his own son Abhimanyu gets killed in the battle, Arjuna becomes inconsolable and vows vengeance on Jayadratha, who had simply blocked the attempt of Arjuna's brothers to aid Abhimanyu, but had no hand in his actual killing. Although one could argue that a young boy is different from a centurion, the point is that in death too we discriminate, and that when it actually strikes where it hurts most, we react differently.

But it is noteworthy that no Hindu avatars flinched from killing to fight evil. In fact, it was the preferred mode, the very aim of the avatar. The evil ones that God descended to kill were actually His devotees who were cursed to become demons, and it was a favor that He did to them, to liberate them from the curse. In the epic wars of Ramayana and Mahabharata, no one was taken prisoner or let off mortally wounded or incapacitated to wage war. No villain or evil-doer repented and sought forgiveness or surrendered, or was even allowed to surrender, to bring the war to an end without further killing. In fact, 'killing' is considered 'logical', the only way to achieve the purpose of war. In the Kurukshetra war, after almost every enemy warrior is killed, and Duryodhana is left hiding alone in a pond, Krishna says that killing Duryodhana — not his surrender or capture — is necessary to end the war. Maybe our very premise, that killing is the highest evil, is wrong.

Desirable Death and *Anaayesaena maranam*

The shadow of death is everywhere but we pretend as if it is nowhere. In fact, as the English clergyman Thomas Fuller said, "The first breath is the beginning of death". And Nietzsche said that our very language is a cemetery, and if we scratch any word, we'll find a dead metaphor. Although we tend to think that even thinking about death is inauspicious, scriptures have told us otherwise; in the words of the ancient Therevada Buddhist text *Visudhimagga* (The Path of Purification), our "Constant task will surely be; This recollection about death". Death is everywhere all the time, and yet we fear that even to think or talk about it is inauspicious, and brings our death nearer. It is the ultimate relief from life but we view it as the 'ultimate evil'. That is why we treat it as taboo, and avoid even to utter the dreaded 'D' word. Instead, we use euphemisms and say things like 'he is no more', 'he has gone', or 'passed away'. Someone said that death has replaced sex as the great forbidden subject. As we grow older, we see more and more of 'no mores' till we ourselves become another 'no more'; and the world moves on to other 'no mores'. We want to banish death from life, on the implicit premise perhaps that that which we don't even think about cannot come to pass. The *Taittiriya* Upanishad says: "When the body falls into weakness on account of old age or disease, even as a mango-fruit, or the fruit of the holy fig-tree, is loosened from its stem, so the Spirit of man is loosened from the human body and returns by the same way to Life, wherefrom he came". In the Bhagavad Gita, Lord Krishna says, "As leaving aside his worn-out garments, a man takes other new ones, so leaving aside worn-out bodies the embodied soul goes to other new ones".

Why do we then mourn death, move heaven and earth to put it off, or postpone as long as we could, and long and wish each other to be a *chiranjeevi* (immortal)? If death is like changing an old car for a new one, then why do we go to such extreme lengths to maintain, repair, and rejuvenate this creaking, rickety body? We often lament and ask why the good and the young die early, and why the evil ones linger and live long.

It is hard to fathom the aspects of how and why each mode of death is chosen. We cannot explain why in the same accident, or deadly collision, some walk away unscathed, some are injured, and some die. Or, why one falls in the garden and breaks his neck, while another falls seven floors and is saved, cushioned by the same lawn. Although no one really knows what a good death means, we usually mean it to be *Anaayesaena maranam*— quick and painless. In other words, a 'bad death' is one that is protracted and painful, or violent. The Vedic prayer, *Anaayesaena maranam; Vinaa dhainyaena jeevanam; Daehi mae kripayaa shambho; Thvaya bhakthim achanchalam*, is a prayer to Lord Siva, requesting him to give death without trouble or pain, life without poverty, and to grant out of compassion unwavering devotion in Him. Everyone says that those who die at a ripe age, without any preparation or pain, are blessed people. It does not mean that those who die ailing and in agony are sinners. Maybe they are burning a bulk of the bad *karma* that way. Each dies according to their own *prarabdha karma*. We must also view death in a broader setting. Everyone has a dharma or swadharma, the natural righteous duty to perform, not only to redeem his karmic dues and for the common good, but also to contribute to a cosmic cause. Not only is one obligated to perform it, but also each is given moral leeway that others are denied; but they have their own. God too has His own swadharma with limitless leeway, as it embraces the entire creation. Even death has a dharma to do. That is why in Hinduism the god of death is called *Dharmaraja*, the Lord of Dharma. But the complicating factor is that the concept of swadharma is a casualty of the passage of the *yugas*. No one can say or know what one's swadharma is, since everyone does what anybody else does; it depends on one's capability, and what a certain relationship or work requires. Nothing, no career or job or work is barred because of one's birth or family or lineage or heritage, and that is modernity and equality in law. Without anything we can call 'swadharma', and caught between conflicting obligations and responsibilities stemming from various relationships, it becomes almost impossible to zero in on anything as one's essential, overriding duty, often at the expense of something else apparently equally important. There are no 'entitlements' on life, not even life.

All these are assumptions that stem from the primal perspective that living is good and death is bad. The good or the young die not because they are good and young, but because simply their time is up; they have expended their allotted karma, paid back their karmic debts in various ways, and must move on. The old or the bad live not because the nature and quantum of karma required them to stay on. A good life may guarantee a good after-life; but does not necessarily lead to a good death. 'Good men', like sages Ramakrishna and Ramana, died of cancer while many 'bad' men died in their sleep. A good death might amount to spending away a lot of good karma; and a bad death, the spending of bad karma, which is good. But then again, neither karma enables us to break the cycle of birth and rebirth. While good karma gives you a temporary time in heaven, bad karma takes you to hell, but still temporarily. Good karma binds us with golden chains, while bad karma binds us with iron chains. Depending on what and how we do, and with what intent, we earn both good and bad karma through almost everything we do every day. If we help another person, we earn good karma. If our actions hurt or harm, we attract bad karma. There is no way to either prove or disprove any of it, whether it is a scientific method or spiritual effort. For, "absence of evidence is not evidence of absence", but it also does not establish that anything actually exists. Basically, and logically, it is possible to prove 'existence', and impossible to prove or disprove that something doesn't exist.

We think we die only once, but death occurs all the time inside each of us; every minute, 300 million cells in our body die. According to Dogen Zenji, the founder of Japanese Soto Zen, Shakyamuni Buddha said that in twenty-four hours, "Our life is born and dying, rising and falling, 6,400,099,980 times. So in one second our life is born and dies around

70,000 times".[266] In another sense too, we die inside: our sensitivity, our tenderness, our righteous reactions are smothered to death by our own behavior. Someone once said, "Death is not the greatest loss in life. The greatest loss is what dies inside us while we live". That 'death' we don't see but the one we do see every day does nothing to empower us to be better prepared to face it when our time comes. It is amazing how we never allow death to interfere in our daily decision-making. We never ask ourselves before choosing, 'What if I am dead tomorrow or the day after?' And we never ask questions such as: What did the dead lose by dying? How should we live, what must we do, if we do not fear death and accept it as natural? And what if there is life after death? Whose loss—or whose gain—is it anyway? Our small mindedness, short-sightedness, pettiness, squabbling, bouts of irritation, and accursed anger, pleasure-in-others'-pain mindset, do not get dented by the certainty of death. We erect a firewall between the dynamics of our daily deeds and the fickleness of our life. In practical terms, what bothers us is not someone 'being dead', whatever it might mean; it is the physical aspect that irks us. It is our inability to relate with them through our five senses that bothers us. We can no longer feel their presence; we cannot touch or talk to them; there are no longer there when we need them; they become faint memories. One of man's irrational longings is to be remembered, not to be forgotten even after he is dead. In turn, it stems from our irrational aversion to anything ephemeral, to the fleeting nature of things. It is irrational because we have no clue what happens—what, if any, 'me' or 'mine' lingers after death—and still we want permanence, if not physical, at least as a memory. Today's virtual technology can even arrange a seemingly actual 'tryst' with our dear departed ones. Sometimes, the bereaved go to psychic mediums to talk through them with their loved-dead, and once they do, or believe that they

---

[266] Roshi, M. 2001. Appreciate Your Life. Dharma Talk. *Tricycle Magazine*. Spring 2001. Retrieved from <https://tricycle.org/magazine/appreciate-your-life/>.

have done, they no longer grieve, or even want to talk a second time. We feel okay that they are 'okay', wherever they are.

Immortality of the Soul

Mythical tales of immortals are found everywhere, from Greek myths and alchemists' notebooks to modern movies and futuristic science-fiction books. Ever since humans first saw death, our mortality has been front and center in our long list of woes, the most enduring of the challenges. In every culture, in every age, many people have attempted to cheat death. Qin Shi Huang, Emperor of China in the 3rd century BCE, feared death and desperately sought the fabled elixir of life that would allow him to live forever. The biblical Adam and Eve lost it. Alchemists have long tried to brew magic potions for immortality. To live forever while keeping well and retaining the glow and vigor of youth is one of humanity's oldest and most elusive goals. Science is saying that it can deliver what legendary figures like Gilgamesh had failed to grasp. According to the distinguished Russian scientist and philosopher Igor Vishev, it is likely that there are people alive today who will never die. He calls his line of thought 'practical immortology'. As the science of ageing advances, scientists have made tremendous progress in extending the human life span. From lowering infant mortality rates to creating effective vaccines and reducing deaths related to disease, science has helped increase the average person's life span by nearly three decades over the past century. Genetic engineering, replacement of natural organs with artificial instruments, nanotechnology, and other developing technologies could now extend our lives well beyond today's assumed limits.

But immortality will not mean invincibility, or bodily impregnability. People could still die, accidentally or by their own hand, or by some disease or other. People will still kill; the body can yet be destroyed. Suicides and homicides and fatal road accidents will not vanish. Eventually, techniques of 'practical resurrection'—towards which today's cloning is but a tentative first step—would be able to restore life to those who somehow lose it. Does that mean that a million years from now, man will still be walking on earth with the present body? If that were so, what about mutation and evolution? What about the mind/consciousness? In an immortal society, how do you make room for new generations? Science also dangles before us, through what it calls 'age disrupters or interrupters', a cure for ageing, if not the elixir of eternal youth. One line of thinking is that ageing is plastic, that it is encoded. And that if something is encoded, you can crack the code. The secret to becoming immortal lies, according to scientists like Aubrey de Grey, not in some mysterious elixir of life, but in the power of regenerative medicine. His strategies for engineered negligible senescence (SENS) are based on combating what he identifies as the 'seven deadly assassins' in our bodies, including our immune system. We must remember that what differentiates the immortality of the scriptures and of science is that the scriptural is indirect, implicit, and of the soul or spirit, while the scientific one is direct, explicit, and of the shell, but melded with a machine.[267] In the Bhagavad Gita, Lord Krishna explains: "For the soul there is neither birth nor death at any time. He has not come into being, does not come into being, and will not come into being. He is unborn, eternal, ever-existing and primeval. He is not slain when the body is slain". The body is simply an external covering of the soul. Being material, the body is by nature temporary, and must at some point decay, deteriorate, and die. The soul on the other hand is spiritual in nature. For it, there is no beginning or end. Krishna further clarifies: "One who has taken his birth is sure to die, and after death one is sure to take birth again. Therefore, in the unavoidable discharge of your duty, you should not lament". He describes death thus: "A man casting off worn-out garments taketh new ones, so the dweller in the body casting off worn-out bodies, entereth into others that are new".

---

[267] The theory goes: Man can meld with the machine, and he can survive as a cyborg with robotically enhanced features; survive, that is, until the day when he can eventually upload his consciousness onto a hard drive, enabling him to 'live' forever as bits of information stored indefinitely; immortal, in a sense, as long as he has a copy of himself in case the computer fails.

Swami Vivekananda further amplified it and said, "Even the lowest of the low have the Atman (Soul) inside, which never dies and never is born, immortal, without beginning or end, the all pure, omnipotent and omnipresent Atman!" Not only scriptures and sages but also philosophers have envisioned the 'immortality of the soul'. One of them is Immanuel Kant (*Theory of Ethics*) who wrote, "Pure practical reason postulates the immortality of the soul, for reason in the pure and practical sense aims at the perfect good (*Summum bonum*), and this perfect good is only possible on the supposition of the soul's immortality". Another 18th-century philosopher Marquis de Condorcet wrote, "Would it be absurd now to suppose that the improvement of the human race should be regarded as capable of unlimited progress? That a time will come when death would result only from extraordinary accidents or the more and more gradual wearing out of vitality, and that, finally, the duration of the average interval between birth and wearing out has itself no specific limit whatsoever? No doubt man will not become immortal, but cannot the span constantly increase between the moment he begins to live and the time when naturally, without illness or accident, he finds life a burden?" (*Sketch for a Historical Picture of the Progress of the Human Mind*, 1822). The irony here is that on the one hand, we want to shrink or slice off or slow down ageing and attain bodily permanence, while at the same time deliberately poisoning everything that goes into our body through our sense organs—what we see, eat, drink, hear, and breathe—which ends up making us sick and debilitated. It is only when we can instinctively connect with others' pain that we can attain the kind of immortality that is implied in the words of Norman Cousins: "If something comes to life in others because of you, then you have made an approach to immortality". In fact, man's time-worn longing for immortality belies his claim to be the only rational animal. In life, he wants everything 'new'; discards everything out of boredom, even partners; he constantly wants to experiment; yet, he wants to cling to this body, even when it is terrible to behold, worn-out, when it is no longer able to give the one thing man pursues all life: physical pleasure and sensory satisfaction. Why does he want to carry the boulder of such a body eternally? Is this some kind of cosmic curse on the *Homo sapiens*, his inane or insane desire to evolve into *Homo immortalis*?

While scientists and researchers are trying to curtail, if not cure, old age, and double or triple our life span (if not outright personal eternity on earth), an ever-escalating number of people are unable to absorb or accept what 'being alive' entails, and are prematurely terminating their allotted tenure on earth. For the rest, every minute they are alive is actually a sort of suspended animation, simply living by default, or, as the 112-year-old Japanese supercentenarian, Sakari Momoi put it, "simply have not died yet". Despite the fact that "in less than a century more years were added to life expectancy than all years added across all prior millennia of evolution combined",[268] and despite the wonders of medicine and our bodily obsession, the truth still is that both an individual life span and the timing of death remains a matter of random luck and pure perchance. But every minute also, as Henry Miller[269] noted, "is a golden one for him who has the vision to recognize it as such". Whether it will be 'golden' or 'ghoulish' hinges on the state of our consciousness. The pertinent question about practical immortology is, if freed from the fear of death, how will man behave? What will man do with eternal life? We are completely at a loss about what to do with ourselves in a life span of less than a century. Those who want immortality have no idea either; they just don't want to die, that is all. If the entire complex of our culture, mindset, and perception of life were to move from one based on the certainty of human mortality to one based on the prospect of human immortality, what will happen in the war within? What might happen to man's quest to be a moral, spiritual being?

---

[268] Carstensen, L. 2015. The New Age Of Much Older Age. Time Magazine. USA. 02 Mar 2015. p.57.

[269] Henry Miller, author of *Tropic of Cancer* (1934) and *Tropic of Capricorn* (1939).

The practical possibility of death becoming a human choice, not an implacable inevitability, has affected the human psyche profoundly. It raises some very fundamental issues and turns everything upside down. Our evolution has not prepared us for this, nor our consciousness. How to prepare for and cope with the certainty of death at an uncertain time is the central theme of all religions. We cannot pinpoint when man first became aware of the fact that life ends in the endless darkness of death, but nothing has been the same since. In fact, it was that 'awareness' that was the beginning of religion, philosophy, and human inquisitiveness about the meaning of his being and his manifest mission on earth. The two things that make life so difficult for man are the certainty of death, and the uncertainty of the hour of death. Although all living beings die, death is, in its effect and impact, a quintessentially human grief; other animals are not tormented by it as we are. When the time is up, most animals often end up as a prey of another animal, they just die and are done with it. But after billions of words spoken about it, and despite John Donne's *'no man is an island'* and *'every death diminishes me'*, the fact remains that each of us wants to be a 'walled island'. What we truly detest is not death but *our* death. Some deaths we might mourn, because a bit of us too dies when someone we love dies; other deaths we do not mind at all; inwardly we might even be relieved.

The social dimension of mortality must be given far more importance than we do now. On a planet so crowded and with so many deprived of dignity and decent living space, the question crops up: Is immortality itself immoral? And could it be that hastening a mortality is the height of morality? Is death dissolution or deliverance, simply shedding of worn-out clothes for new ones, as the Bhagavad Gita says, or is it turning totally 'naked'? Is mortality the only route to reach God? If human birth, being the highest form of life on earth (so we self-proclaim), is required for all creatures to end the cycle of birth and death, then does the deathlessness of a few deprive the rights of millions? Do we have other bodies besides the physical one we live in, and is there such a thing as soul, and are we the only privileged ones? And the most troubling question: Is there any cosmic cause and divine design in the suicides and homicides in the world that are fast approaching pandemic proportions? In other words, could this be nature's response to man's pursuit of bodily permanence?

Four Paths to Immortality

To arrest the 'drift', to recover lost ground, we must get down to the basics; get to know what happens inside each of us as we get on with the myriad choices of our mundane lives. It is a telling paradox—how much knowledge we have of the world outside and how little of the one within. Billions of people go about their lives without any awareness of anything about their essence and inside. And it also tells a lot about the human condition, about human travails and frustrations, and about why we behave the way we do, so completely beyond our own control. We do not know why we behave the way we do, simply because we do not know what makes us do what we do. It is like wondering why our car is breaking down, without opening, or being unable to open, the bonnet and peering in. Our behavior, our very way of thinking, our priorities are all baffling paradoxes. Had they been exhibited in any other species, we would have called that species either daft or deranged or perverse. On the one hand, we are doing everything we can to hasten our collective mortality and, on the other hand, we are sedulously seeking individual immortality. The belief is that immortality might be possible if we stop programming our consciousness about mortality, and reject all our preconceived notions about death. We are also not sure what we really mean by 'immortal life', and what we want from it. Does human immortality offer immunity from suicides or homicides or fatal accidents? In fact, in all probability such deaths could well be the major and infectious diseases of the future. Among the three—suicides, murders, and accidents—the less noticed but increasingly more lethal is accidents. And within the rubric of 'accidents'—which include industrial accidents like Bhopal and Chernobyl and Fukushima—airplane crashes, crippling injuries, and fatalities on the road are mounting. In fact, our roads and highways have become the new killing fields of the world, outranking the toll in wars and natural calamities like typhoons, volcanic eruptions, and earthquakes. It is sometimes said that war is 'death's best friend'; now we can say our homes and highways outdo wars. Man kills himself on the roads with the aid of the very machines he has developed to 'kill' distance. Our insane fascination with speed also contributes. An estimated 1.2 million people are killed in road crashes each year, and as many as 50 million are injured, occupying 30% to 70% of orthopedic hospital beds in developing countries. And if the present trends continue, road traffic injuries are predicted to be the third-leading contributor to the global burden of disease and injury by 2020.[270] According to the Commission for Road Safety, fatalities on the road are estimated to go up to 19 million from the current level.

The core of the problem is that man chases the mirages of permanence and perfection, which are the province of Providence. Death is the most frequently happening *happening* in the world. In the year 2012, an estimated 56 million such happenings happened, but we behave as if it is someone else's happening, another person's sorrow. It has been said that "The classical man's worst fear was inglorious death; the modern man's worst fear is just death".[271] The paths towards achieving 'permanent life' are four-fold. One is to freeze the status quo: to simply go on living in this body and on this earth. Two, to rise again and/or live in different bodies with some sort of continuity, like a soul, Atman, spirit, etc., which is the essence of religious 'immortality'. Three, to live forever through some sort of 'legacy': biological, through children and blood-ties, cultural, like art,

---

[270] Worley, H. 2006. Road Traffic Accidents Increase Dramatically Worldwide. Population Reference Bureau. Retrieved from <https://www.prb.org/roadtrafficaccidentsincrease dramaticallyworldwide/>.

[271] Taleb, N.N. 2010. The Bed of Procrustes: Philosophical and Practical Aphorisms.

literature, and so on. The fourth is a modification or improvement over the first, in fact of all the above, which is what science is trying to do. It has convinced itself that bridging the gap between life and death is the only true measure of success; everything else is a detail. It is to make death not final but temporary, restore the dead to life after a period of deep slumber through technologies like cryonics.[272] It is a process that is summarized as "freeze–wait–reanimate". The curious question is: If someone who has been dead for a century or two comes back to life, what kind of person will he be? Will he carry and retain all his characteristics, say stammering or alcoholism, or say spouse-bashing? Or will he be a different personality? If he is 'different', how can he be the same person? And if he is the 'same', mentally, psychologically, and habitually, then what is the point? For the whole idea of immortality is to overcome the state "in which they strive to devour each other", to borrow the words of the 19th-century thinker Nikolai Fyodorov, or overcome their 'state of cannibalism'. If human consciousness remains frozen along with the body, then any such immortality would be the grossest monstrosity. We want to give death to death and substantially shrink old age. Woody Allen simplified how we want to deal with death: "I don't want to achieve immortality through my work; I want to achieve immortality through not dying. I don't want to live in the hearts of my countrymen; I want to live in my apartment". As of now, people do die in abodes and apartments, and dying still means a physical process. We live and die in the world of mortality; we live in a world of physical reality to which the laws of 'increasing entropy' apply, and a world which ends at the moment of death. When that moment arrives, only the good we do helps. Humans have long struggled to make life's fragility salient as a way to better appreciate opportunities in the time they have. Medieval monks kept a human skull on their desk to help them reflect on their impermanence. In *Engaging in Bodhisattva Behavior*, a Tibetan Buddhist

---

[272] Already, there are over 900 cryogenically stored bodies, including that of baseball player Ted Williams, in Scottsdale, Arizona, USA.

scholar writes, "So, for the sake of this impermanent life, I've caused so much negative karmic force to build up… When seized by the messengers of the Lord of Death, What help are relatives? What help are friends? Only my positive karmic force will provide me a safe direction then".[273] Danish philosopher Søren Kierkegaard advocated embedding death in our consciousness to spur us towards a deeper appreciation of life and a greater motivation to help fellow humans. It helps many people to get unplugged from routines, and work hard on making their best contributions. It also makes some people more prosocial—that is, more willing to give to others. But it can also go the other way; make people more biased, selfish, and narrow-minded. It depends on the state of our consciousness and the state of the war within.

While seeking and searching for immortality to the species, what modern man has done is to turn death itself into the ultimate weapon against another man. Killing, in essence, induced or enforced deliberate death, is fast becoming a preferred choice for dispute settlement, a fevered finale to personal frustrations and inadequacies in the human world. What we forget is that, as Bernard Rieux says, "The order of the world is shaped by death". For some kind of killing takes place all the time, in nature, inside our own bodies. Doctors kill pathogens, bacteria, and viruses to cure a disease. We terminate and exterminate 'life' in our life every day in the guise of self-preservation, but actually for supremacy. We can kill without actually killing; and it does not have to be one lethal blow. We can kill with a withering glance, a curt dismissal, a cutting word, even brusque body-language. Each time anything makes us feel small, each time anything makes us say 'I wish I were dead', something *does* die inside us. We can kill, not necessarily by taking a life, but by taking away one's dignity and self-respect. And we can die drip by drip, until actual killing,

---

[273] Berzin, A. (Tr.). 2005. Engaging in Bodhisattva Behavior. By Shantideva. [Translated from the Tibetan, as clarified by the Sanskrit]. Retrieved from <http://www.buddhistische-gesellschaft-berlin.de/downloads/bca.pdf>.

or death in any other way, becomes a breather. All killing is of course not the same. Killing a mosquito is not the same as killing a man, although the mosquito might think otherwise. It might think, 'I am just acting according to my nature and I will die if I don't'. Man has no such alibi. The human is the only one responsible for unnecessary, unwarranted, and unnatural killing in nature, particularly in relation to other species. But man alone is capable of turning killing into an act of mercy, like in euthanasia. The word euthanasia itself, in Greek, is translated as 'good death', ending a life without pain and suffering. Our rational mind argues that if good death is good as a solution to suffering, what is bad about using death itself as a way to navigate through the rough seas of life?! Man alone also kills for food, for profit, pleasure, and for fun and for control. It is estimated that we breed and kill at least 100 billion animals per year for food and at least 115 million per year for research. Other animals more routinely kill, but often no more than needed for filling their stomachs. After his famous 'anaconda and earl' experiment, Mark Twain said, "The fact stood proven that the difference between an earl and an anaconda is that the earl is cruel and the anaconda isn't; and that the earl wantonly destroys what he has no use for, but the anaconda doesn't. This seemed to suggest that the anaconda was not descended from the earl. It also seemed to suggest that the earl was descended from the anaconda, and had lost a good deal in the transition". Indeed, there are few, if any, causes or reasons, for which man does not kill anyone who is deemed an obstacle or inconvenient, not even his own children or parents. It is the 'circumstance', the context, which determines, to a large extent, any act's moral standing. But circumstance is so circumscribed, so elastic that, without right intent, it can become a cover. And in the English language, at least, ironically, as a kind of Freudian slip, 'killing' also means a great success; we say 'we made a killing' when we hit the jackpot.

Mrityor ma amritam gamaya: From Death to Immortality

All religions and scriptures accord centrality to matters of death. Indeed, it is death that makes them deathless. The famous *Shanti Mantra* in the Brihadaranyaka Upanishad says, *inter alia*, *Mrityor ma amritam gamaya*—lead me from 'death to immortality'. The Isha Upanishad says: "May my life merge in the Immortal, when my body is reduced to ashes. O Mind, meditate on the eternal Brahman. Remember the deeds of the past. Remember, O Mind, remember". The Old Testament says: "The dust returns to the earth as it was, and the spirit returns to God who gave it".[274] The Bible says that God alone possesses immortality, and in Islam, Allah alone can bestow immortality. An Anglican funeral liturgy which is recited at the gravesite says "In the midst of life we are in death: of whom may we seek for succor, but of thee, O Lord, who for our sins art justly displeased? ... Earth to earth, ashes to ashes, dust to dust".[275] We must not forget that gods always punished man for trying to 'become like one of them', and man was banished from Eden perhaps not for his divine disobedience, but to preempt him from seeking immortality.[276]

Death has been the final frontier, the ultimate conquest, the true challenge to human intelligence. Ever since man came face to face with 'mortality salience', that is, awareness of his eventual death, man's attitude towards, and relationship with death has radically changed, including his fellow-men and nature and God. It has also affected man's moral sense. It has, on the one hand, strengthened people's connection with their in-groups and, on the other hand, led people to feel more inclined to punish minor moral transgressions.[277] The means have changed, as also the

---

[274] Ecclesiastes 12.7.

[275] Book of Common Prayer. The Burial of the Dead. First Anthem.

[276] Genesis 3.22.

[277] *Mortality salience*. Wikipedia: The Free Encyclopedia. Wikimedia Foundation. Retrieved 15 Sept 2014.

destination but the almost visceral revulsion of death and quest to conquer it remain. All that the scriptures have told us and science tells us have made little impact. Why death is 'bad' and why we fear, dread, and loathe death is inexplicable. We do not dread similar, albeit less draconian, situations. We do not fear, indeed long for, sleep, which in many ways is similar to death. We do not resist, even if we do not welcome, other passages and transitions such as youth to old age. We hate pain but we detest death, although it relieves us of a lot of pain, physical or mental or psychological.

The very meaning and aim of immortality has changed; from going 'beyond the body' to retaining and augmenting the body. The means have changed from spiritual to scientific. We are now told that, in another decade and a half, we might have the option to 'keep repairing our current body or move into a new one'. As the article predicts, "[In the year 2032]… the growing of 'blank' bodies has become all the rage, and by using your own genetic material, body farmers can even recreate your own face at age 20".[278, 279] In the process, the very 'logic and language' of death have profoundly changed. In death, the apparent end of what we know as life, nature confronts man with the most daunting dilemma. Despite its unpredictable imminence, few are prepared and most would say, like the hero in Philip Roth's novel *Everyman*, "O Death; thou comest when I least had thee in mind". Death might become optional, but it will still be the cessation of life. But the causes that culminate in death have changed, encompassing all the way from involuntary bodily decay and dissolution, to voluntary embrace of death. New phrases have come into play like suicide bomber, human bomb, ethnic cleansing, collateral damage, drone deaths, and new and sinister associations have sprouted. Mass murder is now called a 'just war', and the killing of innocents from half way around

---

[278] Frey, T. 2012. When Death Becomes Optional. Future Speaker. Retrieved from <http://www.futuristspeaker.com/2012/03/when-death-becomes-optional/>.

[279] Frey, T.J. 2011. Communicating With the Future: How Re-engineering Intentions Will Alter the Master Code of Our Future. Colorado, USA: DaVinci Institute Press.

the globe is 'target killing'. There is a growing convergence of suicide and homicide, some in the name of love and some in the name of religion, and some just for the thrill of it. Killing has come to be viewed as the ultimate test of faith and a revered rite of passage into martyrdom, and a hallowed highway to heaven. Birth, for some time has been optional, but now even death looms as a choice. While scriptures profess that death is no different from being a phase and part of life, science posits that death is the opposite and antithesis to life. We are living at a time when human power can fix anything, even a broken heart, and regain anything we might lose, even youth and vaginal virginity. Now we are being reassured that even 'lost life' can be restored. While scriptures say that the way to be deathless is by overcoming desire, science says deathlessness is just another desire to be satiated, just another disease to be cured. As man has entrenched himself on earth and assumed ascendancy over all other forms of life, a profound change in the place and perception of death in the context of life has taken hold. In no other aspect of life is the gap between scripture and science as wide as it is in regard to death. A centrality in human thought has long been that the cycle of birth and death are inseparable in the continuum of life, of cause and effect. Man has always recognized, but not accepted, that 'centrality', and has turned either to the divine, and when it seemed impervious to his pleas, to science. If science prevails, man will then be able to make life at will and keep death at bay, as if it were on call, another toy or ploy to play with. The idea is that if eternal life becomes banal tedium, then we can summon death to deliver us. Man has always entertained two dreams: to live as the gods do—eternally and in bliss; and, even if he does not know what to do with a single dreary day, to 'go on living', forever and ever; to live for life's own sake, not to achieve something. What used to be the stuff of mythology, legends, epics, and fantasy fiction, we are being told, could be a reality soon, that man could well conquer, or cure, the 'disease of death', that mortality (even that was the lot fated by the gods) need not be our destiny.

The ultimate test of morality is how man handles mortality. It has long been a subject of much comment and commentary. Most humans are too busy to have any time to think about such irksome matters. They live, as has been said, as if they will never die, and die as if they never lived. Some are so terrified that, as Henry Van Dyke said, 'they never begin to live'. Goethe said, "As long as you are not aware of the continual law of Die and Be Again, you are merely a vague guest on a dark Earth". An Italian proverb perhaps best sums up how to expend the interlude between birth and death: "When you were born, you cried and the world rejoiced. Live your life so that when you die, the world cries and you rejoice". We now have money as a new factor. With enough money, we might soon be able to 'buy immortality'. The truly rich can even 'design' their own death, and plan and pay for 'grand farewell parties' while the poor continue to die painful and unchosen deaths. The question, according to science, is not, *if* but *when* man will achieve technological singularity, and be able to cheat death by merging with the machine. We read predictions like, 'If you draw the timelines, realistically by 2050 we would expect to be able to download your mind into a machine, so when you die it is not a major career problem.'[280] Another says, "The human race will achieve immortality within 25 years as a result of minds being transferred into computers", and that "robot bodies capable of housing human brains could even be available by 2025". By that year, "Dying bodies could be replaced by robot vassals housing human brains. By 2035, human minds will be transferred into computers, eliminating the need for a body altogether. By 2045, artificial brains will control hologram entities".[281] Another probability, we are told is that in 30 or 40 years, we'll have microscopic machines traveling through our bodies, repairing damaged cells and organs, effectively wiping out diseases. But we are also warned that, "In a mature form, molecular nanotechnology will enable

---

[280] Prediction of Ian Pearson, futurologist and mathematician, former head of the Futurology Unit at British Telecom.

[281] Russian multimillionaire, Dmitry Itskov.

the construction of bacterium-scale self-replicating mechanical robots that can feed on dirt or other organic matter. Such replicators could eat up the biosphere or destroy it by other means such as by poisoning it, burning it, or blocking out sunlight. A person of malicious intent in possession of this technology might cause the extinction of intelligent life on Earth by releasing such nanobots into the environment".[282] The nanotechnology will also be used to back up our memories and personalities. Craig Venter says, "We now have the ability to transmit life at the speed of light, just sending it through the computer. When we colonize Mars, we could [transmit] a new organism to the colony in Mars".[283] We read about other real probabilities, such as 'teleporting',[284] the capability to design and create life from scratch.

These are all exciting, or, for some, paralyzing predictions. The lay public is left wondering what to make of them, whether the awesome risks are warranted and what kind of 'humans' their grandchildren are likely to be, and what kind of life they are likely to live. But we must get some clarity on what 'biological immortality' means. For example, would man survive and live on despite a direct hit by a rocket or collision with a truck? Does immortality mean an impregnable and indestructible body? And suppose we get bored with the tedium of immortality, can we give it up and become mortal again? In other words, can immortality be temporary but reversible, a kind of default condition? Would it assure us of perpetual physical health and unimpaired mental agility? But then we cannot, at the most basic level, address any such issues without knowing what it means to be dead. How can we choose life itself, let alone endless life, without any inkling of what the alternative is tantamount to? Since that knowledge is

---

[282] Bostrom, N. 2002. Existential Risks: Analyzing Human Extinction Scenarios and Related Hazards. *Journal of Evolution and Technology*, Vol. 9, No. 1. Retrieved from <http://www.nickbostrom.com/existential/risks.html>.

[283] Venter, J.C. 2013. Life at the Speed of Light: From the Double Helix to the Dawn of Digital Life. New York, USA: Penguin.

[284] Transfer of matter from one point to another without traversing the physical space between them.

denied, at least, while being alive, we have no logical reason to change the *status quo* of life coming to close at a certain but unknowable time. For a species that takes pride in its ability to make informed and intelligent choices, our timeless desire to transit from a time-bound life to endless life is perhaps the most irrational of all our choices.

Assuming that death is bad, undesirable, to be evaded in every way, the big question then is this: would physical immortality or unending existence make man a better being, at peace with himself and with the world, and help him to evolve in the right direction? Or would it, in the words of Bernard Williams, mean 'endless life [that] would eventually collapse into infinite boredom'[285]—and possibly unhinge the psychic balance that makes us human? Put differently, would endless existence, or a life span so long that 'forever' is pointless, transfer the human into a humane being or, freed from the fear of being killed, turn him into a demon? Can man be both moral and immortal? The implied assumption about immortality is that we will live as the same person with the same body. We will not be wasted by the daily dribble of death nor do we have to ruminate, in Philip Larkin's words, "Unresting death, a whole day nearer now, Making all thought impossible but how, And where and when I shall myself die".[286] We are not interested in 'anonymous' or 'indirect' immortality, which is inherent in nature. All of us are immortal through remembrance, memory, progeny, writing, art, music, anything creative. Modern man is not interested in that kind of immortality. He wants permanence of the physical *status quo*. He wants to be immortal by just being 'alive' without an end, and even if he has no idea what to do with the present life, let alone eternal life. He is not interested in ideals or artistic excellence or questions of morality, or even of the Fate of the Earth.[287]

---

[285] Williams, B. 1973. The Makropulos Case: Reflections On the Tedium of Immortality. London, UK: Cambridge University Press.

[286] Philip Larkin. *Aubade*.

[287] Title of Jonathan Schell's book.

We have long convinced ourselves that, whatever death might or might not mean, however dreary and distasteful life might be, the ultimate test of our creativity is to destroy death. Tagore says, "We have come to look upon life as a conflict with death—the intruding enemy, not the neutral ending—in impotent quarrel with which we spend every stage of it".[288] Someone said, "We do not believe in immortality because we can prove it, but we try to prove it because we cannot help believing it". Whichever way, the idea of immortality, which the serpent in the Garden of Eden claimed was the word invented by it for eternal life, has long been the stuff of epics, mythology, science fiction, and science. Some argue that the continued existence of humanity far into the future is important not only for the future but also for the present, and that "we are not individualists; we are dependent for much of what we value in our lives on the survival of humanity into the future".[289] And that, "even the present value of much that makes up our lives depends on its continuation and development long after we are gone".[290] It means that if we seriously entertain any thought about 'early extinction' of the human species, that by itself has a direct and immediate bearing on our lives.

No one really knows who the first human was, who, on seeing someone dead, wondered what happens hereafter, but that question has haunted mankind down the ages. The mystic and mystery of death has always transfixed the human mind, and although there has been remarkable unity about the nature of death at the esoteric core of religious faiths, there has been an equally striking diversity of cultural beliefs at the exoteric level. At the behavior level, dying or killing have always had something to do with human aggression, cruelty, and barbarism, and even honor and heroism. Death, for the classical hero, was a 'masked figure, willing to struggle, face

---

[288] Tagore, R. 2012. Religion of Life. India: Niyogi Books. p.199.

[289] Nagel, T. 2014. After You've Gone. Review of the book *Death and Afterlife* by Samuel Scheffler. *The New York Review of Books*. USA. 09 Jan – 09 Feb 2013. p.26.

[290] Nagel, T. 2014. After You've Gone. Review of the book *Death and Afterlife* by Samuel Scheffler. *The New York Review of Books*. USA. 09 Jan – 09 Feb 2013. p.26.

to face, one to one, for trophy or dust'.[291] In the Katha Upanishad, the young Nachiketa asked none other than the god of death, Yama, himself, "There is this doubt about a man when he is dead. Some say that he exists; others say that he doesn't. What is it?"

Put more personally, the question is, "Will I be there, and where will I be, and what might happen to me, when it all ends down here?" There has been no direct satisfactory answer to that simple question since then, not even from the god of death. We are left hanging in doubt. The result is that we meander and muddle through life, not knowing what to do, or not do, to insure ourselves for an uncertain and unknown future. 'Surviving death' has been viewed by men of all times and cultures and civilizations as the final frontier, the ultimate challenge to 'being human'. What has maddened man is his realization that life really is not 'living' but, in the words of Schopenhauer, at best 'delayed dying'. But what is profoundly problematic is the pace of dying which varies from person to person. Or, in the words of Tolstoy, the 'dragon of death' waiting to tear us apart. Whatever the scriptures and sages might tell us, our practical experience tells us that every breath we take delays that sinister shadow hovering over us. It plays with us and ultimately triumphs, for, by being born, we already became its prey. We do not mind being played with so long as we can prolong it, in the words of Schopenhauer, "just as we blow out a soap-bubble as long and as large as possible, although with the perfect certainty that it will burst". Unlike other experiences, our awareness of death is by analogy and observation of people dying. Other animals, we are told, 'know' death only when they die, and that in fact enables them to lead fuller lives, freed from the fear that the very next minute they might be dead.

The fact is that no other aspect of earthly existence is as impenetrable and impervious to human insight and imagination as the mortal triad of

---

[291] Parabola. 2001. (Eleventh Printing). Volume 2. Issue 1. Tamarack Press. Publisher D.M. Dooling. Review by Robert Meagher of the book *The Survivor: An Anatomy of Life in the Death Camps*. Terrence Des Pres. 121

why, when, and how life ends, and what happens thence. The question is one of 'absoluteness'. Is birth an absolute beginning, and death an absolute end? Are we born or 'reborn'? And, if it is the latter, what remains after death, and what is the continuum between birth and birth, and what moves on into the new body? If the body is mortal, and the soul, as the Gita says, is birth-less, death-less, immortal, eternal, and pure, then who is the 'dweller in the body' that sheds off one body and assumes another? Is that the *Jivatma*? But the jivatma is a part of the *Paramatma*... how can it be subject to birth, death, and rebirth? Then again, how does one put it all in the context of the Upanishadic mahavakya *Aham brahmasmi* (I am God)? If the body disintegrates and gets absorbed into the *panchabhutas* (earth, water, fire, air, and space), if the Atman or soul is eternal and cannot be corrupted and sinless, if we are inherently divine, the question is who or what is 'reborn', and who pays for past sins and pays back? In other words, when we say we want to be 'immortal', whose immortality is it anyway? All this spiritualism and sophistry apart, whatever the Gita or some scripture might have meant, when modern man talks of immortality he means—as brutally laid bare by the student Thrasymachos to the philosopher Philalethes—"Don't you see that my individuality, be it what it may, is my very self? To me it is the most important thing in the world. 'For God is God, and I am I'. I want to exist, I, *I*. That's the main thing. I don't care about existence which has to be proved to be mine before I can believe it".[292] To which Philalethes replies: "It is the cry [for immortality], not of the individual, but of existence itself. It's the intrinsic element in everything that exists". Schopenhauer adds, "The effect of this is to make the individual careful to maintain his own existence; and if this were not so, there would be no guarantee for the preservation of the species". So, it could be that our love of our body, love of life, craving for sheer existence isn't all that selfish and could be turned around for common good.

---

[292] Schopenhauer, A. 1851. Immortality, A Dialogue. (Translated by Saunders and Kline).

When we look around nature, we are also befuddled about the normal length of life spans. No one can tell why different species have different normal life spans. For example, why do turtles and parrots live so much longer, ten times longer than dogs? And why, even within a species, is the length of life so indeterminate and whimsical? We are not even sure if without 'prolonged or perpetual youth' we want eternal life. Do we want to live long or forever, as it were, as is where is, subject to decay, old age, disease? Can our body become indestructible and can we 'live' if we fall from the Eiffel Tower? Does it mean that no one or nothing can kill any human being? William James pictures what we want, "The fact that we *can* die, that we *can* be ill at all, is what perplexes us; the fact that we now for a moment live and are well is irrelevant to that perplexity. We need a life not correlated with death, a health not liable to illness, a kind of good that will not perish, a good in fact that flies beyond the Goods of nature".[293]

Factually, it all comes down to the 'body'. Our attitude to our physical frame is riddled with paradoxes. Even scriptures are ambivalent. On the one hand, they say get rid of body-identification, and that that is the chief obstacle to spiritual growth. The great Adi Sankara wrote, "You never identify your self with the shadow cast by your body, or with its reflection, or with the body you see in a dream or in your imagination. Therefore, you should not identify yourself with this living body either".[294] On the other hand, scriptures also say it is the abode, a temple, of God, and that we must tend and take care of it. How we came upon earth and how we depart has little to do with what we do. Not to be born is, beyond all estimation, best; but when a man has seen the light of day, it is next best by far, that, with utmost speed, he should go back from where he came. For when he has seen youth go by, with its easy merry-making, what hard affliction is foreign to him, what suffering does he not know? Envy, factiousness, strife, battles,

---

James, W. 1902. The Varieties of Religious Experience: A Study in Human Nature. Lectures VI and VII.

Adi Sankara. *Vivekachudamani.*

Bhimeswara Challa

and murders. Last of all falls to his lot old age, blamed, weak, unsociable, friendless, wherein dwells every misery among miseries.[295] Put differently: "Naked came I upon the earth, naked I go below the ground—why then do I vainly toil when I see the end naked before me?" We feed it and starve it too; we put in 'supplements', but poison it too. We are not really happy with it but we want to keep it forever. We worship it, but we abuse it perhaps more than any other material thing. We don't mind, in fact, welcome, a better body, but so long as it is 'alive' in this body. We are not happy with any back-door, indirect or implicit immortality through things like procreation, pencil or pen or paint. Plato's prescription, in *Symposium*, that mental procreation is the sublime way to immortality has never quenched the human thirst to live forever. Nor has the Hindu belief—that it is only the body that perishes but not the soul, which is deathless, immortal, and eternal—dimmed our dream of immortality. We want to freeze the physical frame, here and now, nothing else, nothing less. We don't want to live in or through others; we want to be ourselves and yet become immortal. We want life, even if it hurts a lot. We are prepared to tolerate any kind and amount of suffering, if only we can survive. Philosophers like Socrates might say that death is not a bad thing; indeed, it is even a good thing, but most people will skip 'good' death and choose 'bad' life. We are not too interested, in the words of Mark Johnston, to live in the 'onward march of humanity';[296] we want a continuum of this very life. We do not want to live either as an invisible but eternal soul, or as a corpse in a freezer. We want this body, worn out and wrinkled, feeble and frail it might be, to experience life. Our obsession with immortality is but a reflection and extension of our obsession with our body. For some, man becomes a soul, *à la* Henry Wood, "after a certain event called death", but that he is the same here and now does not occur to them... man is not a body having a soul, but a 'soul having a body'.[297]

---

[295] Sophocles. Oedipus at Colonus.

[296] Johnston, M. 2011. Surviving Death. USA: Princeton University Press.

[297] Wood, H. 1923. Studies in the Thought World, or Practical Mind Art.

Climbing Heaven's Hill With Mortal Skin

Contemplation on death and impermanence of life are regarded as very important in Buddhism for two reasons: it is only by recognizing how precious and how short life is that we are most likely to make it meaningful and to live it fully; and by understanding the death process and familiarizing ourselves with it, we can mitigate our fear at the time of death and ensure a good rebirth. Paramahansa Yogananda, in his essay *Where There Is Light*, described death in these words: "The consciousness of the dying person finds itself suddenly relieved of the weight of the body, of the necessity to breathe, and of any physical pain. A sense of soaring through a tunnel of very peaceful, hazy, dim light is experienced in the physical body".[298] However irrational it might appear to be, what unites most people is the wrenching terror of death, which cuts across all cultures irrespective of which religion one swears adherence to. A Hindu fears death as much as a Christian. Whether it is the Law of Karma or the accounting on the Day of Judgment, it makes little difference to the dread of death. The favorite blessing in all cultures, despite what their scriptures say about the 'naturalness' of death, is 'may you live long!' Despite the belief in multiple rebirths, some possibly better than the misery of the current one, prolonging the present life is the most longed-for desire even for Hindus. Despite the angels, damsels, and allures of Heaven, few Christians or Muslims want to die. As someone quipped, many want to go to heaven but none want to die. Or, like Yudhishthira, in the Mahabharata, all of us want to climb up heaven's hill with a mortal skin. There are still exceptions. For instance, Niccolo Machiavelli (*The Prince*, 1513), supposedly said, "I desire to go to Hell and not to Heaven. In the former I shall enjoy the company of popes, kings and princes, while in the latter are only beggars, monks and apostles".[299]

---

[298] Source: Understanding Death, Selections from the Writings of Paramahansa Yogananda. Retrieved from <http://www. yogananda-srf.org/writings/death.html>.

[299] Source: English Club quotes. Retrieved from <http://www. englishclub. com/ref/esl/Quotes/ Last_Words/I_desire_to_go_to_Hell_and_not_to_Heaven._2722.htm>, on 22 July 2014.

While Hinduism and Buddhism, for instance, advocate a 'desireless' state as the transparent path to *moksha* or *nirvana*, neither religion tries to curb the strongest of all desires: the desire for eternal life. They castigate attachment as the source of sorrow, but not the most addictive attachment: to life itself. Perhaps it is in the very nature of life itself to hold all living beings in its hypnotic thrall. Not only humans but also the lowliest of creatures, even a worm in a dung heap, cling to life, and want to prolong their miserable existence even if a better life after death is dangled before them. The human mind clings to the seeming certainty of the present package to the apparent uncertainty of the future. Such reassuring statements as "Nothing changes with death, it is only a change of the state of consciousness", and, *à la* Oscar Wilde, "To have no yesterday, and no tomorrow. To forget time, to forgive life, to be at peace", make no difference to our state of consciousness. What we fear most in life is 'definitiveness', because it robs us of hope; and death is nothing but definitiveness. Death has been, since time immemorial, the primary obsession and the biggest business in the world. Someone estimated that every day about 150,000 humans die, but when the day begins no one knows who they will be and who will see the next sunrise. Anyone could be, anyone need not be, no one can tell.

We do not how the dead feel, but the living mourn the dead and presume to be sorry for them. Even for those whom we hardly know, when death strikes, we feel sad and sorry, though for what and for whom is not quite clear. Maybe the dead, if they could compare their 'dead lives' to ours, feel sorry for the 'living dead', which most people are. Death and dying are deemed so horrendous that even a dying person is left in a cloud of deception, in a you-are-going-to-be-okay syndrome, rather than being told that he or she is dying, which we say is all-natural and inevitable in any case. Even the talk of death is called inauspicious, harmful, and impolite. We shun death; even the thought of it is considered morbid. The body that we hugged just the other day, we fear even to touch. The loved one becomes the feared one. The warm body becomes ice cold and decays before our very eyes. If one touches a 'dead body', the very one we hugged and loved before, we are told to take a cleansing bath. No one understands a dying person's state of mind. No one helps him to face the fact of death or to prepare for what inevitably follows. Even doctors are afraid to tell the truth, and those that do are often called insensitive. Since we don't know what happens after death, all this doom and gloom seems downright silly. Those who know they are going to die within a certain time are the luckier ones. In the Srimad Bhagavatam, when King Parikshit is cursed to die on the seventh day of a snake bite, and is paralyzed with fear, the Sage Suka tells him what a lucky man he has been, to know how much time—seven full days—he has unlike others who could die any minute. It is widely believed in many cultures that the dying moments are precious and that the state of mind at that time has a bearing on the nature of after-life. Vedanta advocates limiting or restraining passions, obligations, relationships, and transactions. Such a state of mind, it says, leads one to obtain *Nitya mukti*— liberation as you are, where you are, right now, without waiting for any future event, or for death, or going to heaven, etc. According to medieval Christian belief, the last moments of life were the most critical, for demons lurked around the deathbed ready to seize the unprepared soul as it emerged with the last breath. 'The last moments of life' also, according to Hindu scriptures, determine the nature of the next life. In the Bhagavad Gita, it is said that whatever state of being one remembers during the dying process, he will attain that state, being absorbed in its thought. In India, even today, people go to *Kasi* (Varanasi) to die, because it is a holy place. It may sound simple and a bit unfair that one last moment of thought or remembrance or utterance can outweigh a lifetime of work, good or bad. The fact is that when the moment of death comes, it takes something to be aware enough to say what you want to say. Most people die in unawareness but we really do not know their state of consciousness. But to come to a certain kind of awareness in that moment, you must practice such awareness for a lifetime.

Conclusion

So, then, what do we do with death? It has been like a bone in the throat. We can't spit it out, nor can we swallow it. Why do we despise death? Do we really know what we want from immortality? Is it glory or greed, a trophy in the showcase, very little to do with death itself? Heaven forbid, have we got it all wrong? Is our unquenchable longing for immortality the ignorance of life's meaning, of death's purpose, and of the state of after-death? As Milan Kundera (*Immortality*, 1990) says, "Man doesn't know how to be mortal. And when he dies, he doesn't even know how to be dead". In this light, which Achilles should we trust: what he said to Briseis when alive ('gods envy our mortality'), or what he said to Odysseus after his death ('I would rather be a paid servant on earth than the king of kings in the land of the dead')? Is our almost obsessive desire to be walking (not floating), blinking gods, completely self-defeating? Is immortality the ultimate *immorality*, or is it delayed justice for denial of deathlessness by the divine? If we have to measure up to our claim to be a moral being, let alone a spiritual being, what must we do about our mortal fate?

First, let us have some clarity on what our mind conjures as immortality, and what science is trying to achieve, what is possible and probable, and what the likely implications and consequences are. Immortality means a state of absolute, total deathlessness; we continue to live indefinitely for millions of years, whatever happens to earth. That is simply impossible, and we should eliminate such an expectation from any serious consideration. For, even if we do achieve biological immortality, we can still die by other means like injury and disease, and we can get killed. We must understand that our quest for life forever makes sense only as a quest for eternal youth. Who wants to live forever as a frail, debilitated, disease-prone animal walking on three legs? This too is practically impossible. We cannot freeze our age at a certain point (whatever that might be, twenty or forty) and live ever after at that age. It means that the three things that appalled Prince Siddhartha and transformed him into the Buddha—sickness, old age, and death—will continue in some form or degree or the other. Even if we merge with a machine, that will be inescapable. Machines also age, break down and finally 'die' or get discarded. The human body, through techniques like organ-augmentation and periodic repair and renewal, can go on only up to a 'point'. The irony is that we replace a machine at the first sign of trouble, but we want the human machine to last forever. We replace models almost every year, but we want this particular 'model' of earthly existence to be permanent. For science, the bottom line is the body. It wants to keep the shell of the body as much as possible intact, and mechanize every organ therein to not only overcome a disability or disease but to enhance or improve its power and performance. As for the brain, the tactic here is to do what is called 'mind' uploading, uploading mental contents to computers or to the 'Cloud', as a way of preserving the 'software' even as the hardware 'dies'. For, the Cloud too is not a metaphysical structure, but rather a complex network of servers, and is therefore not itself indestructible or infallible.

What will probably happen, even if science finds the elixir of eternal life, is that we will still fall sick and get old and die, albeit some of us will live much longer and be more fit, and be more of a machine than a human or a god. The only question is how much longer. It is generally believed (even the Bible is supposed to have said it) that the age limit for the human is 125 years. It is unlikely that the maximum will rise much higher, but more of us might cross the century mark. It also depends on who we are referring to: a wholly human superhuman or humanoid or cyborg. Indeed, the future world might well be inhabited by a conglomerate. Humanity will probably be divided into a few who will be *de facto* 'superhumans', and the rest pretty much as we are now, and that could very well turn out to be the last straw on the broken backs of the non-rich. The all-important question is what kind of consciousness such a being will have. The more powerful *it* or *he* is, the more the need for a compassionate consciousness. We have to ask ourselves: Will physical immortality or inexorable death be a better catalyst for human beings to move to a higher plateau of consciousness? The answer is that immortality, which is just to keep this body going on and on, is stagnation and regression. Only through new lives and new experiences and adaptation to new environments could man develop his consciousness, which will ultimately cause him to live in such a manner that it raises the awareness of other people around him and transform the world into a better place for everyone.

What we have to do is to take full cognizance of what it entails and implies, if we acquire the technical means of exponentially longer lives, more intelligence, improved physical and mental health, and elimination of limits to personal development. It is, in short, the vision of thinkers indeed, with such colorful *noms de plume* as *TO Tomorrow* (Tom Bell), *Max More* (Max T O'Connor), and *Natasha Vita-More* (Nancie Clark) It is a tall order. Without consciousness-change, immortality will not resolve any of the problems that afflict human society. Poverty, prejudice, discrimination, inequity, bigotry, will not only continue to exist but also get further exacerbated. The climate crisis will not get resolved; it may make the 'One Percent' more brazen with the knowledge that they could be less affected, as they already are. We will still have wars, when the dead, in Homer's (*Iliad*) ghastly image, lie "sprawled across the field, craved far more by the vultures than by wives". In short, if you do not die in any other way, you could expect you won't die of death. Most deaths then will be violent deaths and escaping such a death will have a high premium; because then you can live virtually forever. But, make no mistake, death will still get you: or, for example, a smartphone might explode in your face; the roof might collapse on your head, or a drone could hit you by mistake.

Whatever science can do to prolong life or make us deathless, it cannot shield our body from harm's way, even if we become all-metal; in which case, it makes no difference anyway. What is called 'digital immortality', or mind-uploading, does not also sound so endearing. Who wants to 'live' in a machine without the pleasures of the flesh? In any case, we will still die and be reborn as our digital copy. And, on top of it, what we might end up with in our quest for immortality will add one more dangerous divide, and as good a reason as we can ever get to kill each other. The immortals will still live in dread of death, as they will not be impregnable to either disease or accident or the wrath of the left-behind and locked-out humans. We will have two more sedative triggers for suicide: extended boredom for some, and deep disaffection of much of the rest. The massive diversion of scarce resources, creative and economic, to this line of research, at the expense of far more worthy and critical priorities, will be tantamount to adding fuel to the fire. Really, there will be no winners but a lot of losers in such a wounded world. What science needs to focus upon is not technologies that cure the disease of death, but on technologies that improve the infrastructure for a healthy and fulfilling life of the masses and, which, in turn, will automatically improve the average life span. It is important that the global community, not individual nations or corporations, take a fresh look at what science is trying to do by dangling before us the irresistible lure of never having to die, bearing in mind that, without a new mindset or a new consciousness, whatever emerges from the current effort could only make the world a more destructive and dangerous place. Along with the other two 'M's—morality and money—, the way we are thinking and dealing with this 'M' (mortality) has become a serious impediment to influence the flow of the war within in the right direction. And if that doesn't happen, nothing will happen for the good in the world.

The Summing Up

Are Humans 'Worthy' of Survival?

However much we might ruminate, brood or ponder over our essential identity as earth-bound creatures, we surely are one of a kind, quite a formidable mélange of powers, passions, prejudices, and fragilities that Mother Nature fashioned, or God wrought from His own breast, or perhaps magically grew from a blundering baboon. In the grand game plan of the cosmos, the human has been described in a multitudinous ways—'made in the image of God' (*Imago Dei*, the Bible), the measure of all things[300] (Protagoras), the only creature who refuses to be what he is (Camus), nature's serious mistake[301] (Alan Watts), rational animal (Aristotle), molded mud (the Upanishads), a modified monkey (Thomas Huxley), the sexiest primate alive (Desmond Morris), a thinking thing (Descartes), a wretched thing (Homer, *Iliad*), an ungrateful biped (Dostoyevsky), a blank slate, noble savage, civilized brute, unfinished work, etc. A standout

---

[300] *"Man is the measure of all things"*. Statement of Greek philosopher, Protagoras, of the 5th century BCE.

[301] *"…has not nature, in bringing forth man, made a serious mistake?"* Quote of Alan Watts [1951. The Wisdom of Insecurity: A Message for An Age of Anxiety. New York, USA: Pantheon Books].

is how Thomas Browne described, "Man is a noble animal, splendid in ashes and pompous in the grave". Are we a biological muddle, a mental scamp, an ethical abomination, a rational absurdity, an awful exaggeration of all that is disastrous in nature? Are we the noblest and best that can be in nature, or are we all modelled from *trash*?[302] Has our might become too heavy for the 'secret wellsprings' of our soul? Have we forfeited our 'right of residence' in the universe by the way we have abused nature's hospitality? It is hard to say if human nature is sold short or fallen short. Is human nature the opposite of any utopia we can imagine, and have we come to such a pass that one is not quite sure anymore if we are someone to laugh at or feel sorry for? Side by side with our soaring aspirations, we are beset with mistrust even about our authentic essence. We still cannot figure out what is the manifest destiny of mankind. What is perfectly clear is that we have proven unequal to the Biblical mandate of earthly stewardship. As it has turned out, the human is an amply endowed but deeply deficient form of life on earth. It is this paradox that has plagued the human condition. Our unappeasable lust for ease, comfort, and control has become a planetary peril. We are smitten by the eclectic idea of 'progress', but in the face of naked technological power, cultural *progress* has turned into social *regress*. It evokes a hubris that, as O'Brien tells Winston in George Orwell's *1984*, "we make the laws of Nature", and the world is there for our picking and pleasure. Despite such pompous pretension, we have always been haggled by doubt, depression, and defeatism. And despite our delusions of invulnerability, some have seen chinks in our armor and threats to our survival from unexpected quarters. For example, in his book *Men Versus Insects* (1933), Bertrand Russell foresaw that the threat to the human race may be as much from insects and micro-organisms as from wars. The current condition of man is now being characterized (*à la* Timothy Morton) as 'subscendence', an antonym of transcendence, a state of humanness where the wholes are smaller and more fragile than the sum

---

[302] Ishiguro, K. 2005. Never Let Me Go. Faber and Faber.

of their parts. The whole is fragile because the parts are fundamentally flawed, and 'the center cannot hold'.

What this Covid-19 pandemic has brought to the limelight is one of our endemic handicaps, our almost pathological paralysis, the *kanashibari* (sleep paralysis) of not being able to do what we *know* is what we have to do, which in itself is another manifest of our almost pathological twin 'inabilities' that are the focus of this book. While we have long wondered what could be the actual breaking-point for a civilizational meltdown, something totally unexpected has emerged: what is being called the infertility crisis, or 'endocrine disruption' or a global baby bust of unprecedented proportions. Whether it is purely human or divine retaliation, procreation, the principal source of human continuity, is being seen as unaffordable, irresponsible, and a moral error, even '*de facto* child abuse'.[303] The environmental group Voluntary Human Extinction Movement (VHEMT) advocates voluntary childlessness as a way to live long and die out as a species. According to their ideology, "we are the only species evolved enough to consciously go extinct for the good of all life". A recent study has revealed that what is being categorized as 'spermageddon'—humans becoming extinct by the continuing fall of sperm counts in men—is a possibility in the next fifty years.[304] What is making matters worse is the advent of the economic dimension. In some economically affluent nations, many are coming to believe that they cannot make enough money to have kids, or put differently, it is a choice they have to make to have the kind of good life they want to live. Such a perception is likely to spread everywhere, what with every country wanting to gain entry into the 'affluent club'. Tellingly, if nothing else it is a message to mankind to stem the poisonous power of money in human affairs. The message behind this message is this: unless we configure and conjure an alternative way of life—less individualistic

---

[303] Les U. Knight, founder of the *Voluntary Human Extinction Movement* (VHEMT).

[304] Cited in: *Spermageddon: Why the Human Race Could Be Infertile in 50 Years*. Interview with Stefan Chmelik. *The Telegraph*. 27 January 2018.

and more communitarian, less 'want-oriented' and more 'need-based', and, most of all, more in harmony with nature—we are in deep trouble. Some, like Norwegian philosopher Peter Zapffe, think (contrary to the popular belief that we are an 'unfinished' and 'unfulfilled' species) that the human condition is tragically overdeveloped, a biological hotchpotch. In Zapffe's opinion, "As long as humankind recklessly proceeds in the fateful delusion of being biologically fated for triumph, nothing essential will change".[305] Whatever, what we are endeavoring to accomplish is to technologically triumph over our biology and nature, meddle with the bedrock processes of life and death, which are so intertwined that unless we feel what it is to die, we cannot enjoy what it is to live. We want to extract order and purpose from earthly life, whereas disorder and diversity are the unwritten natural laws that govern life on earth and act as insurance against the uncertainties of a changing climate. But that should not be allowed to come in the way of equity. For the process of life is designed to be oblivious to the beings it makes and breaks in the course of its perpetuation. If human will wishes to impose itself into this 'perpetuation' of life, how nature might retaliate is something we are not even enabled to imagine.

All these problems and possibilities might seem disjointed, chaotic, and haphazard, but they all stem from a central fountain: our inexorable inability to put personal moral responsibility at the center of all public choices, and everyone's assumption that someone else will take a stand for morality—and then no one does. If nothing else, the present coronavirus crisis has highlighted, on the one hand, how unequal and unjust human society is, and, on the other hand, the puerile and pyrrhic nature of our evangelical zeal to transform ourselves into impregnable, interplanetary, immortal beings. While science is promising radical life extension in our own lifetime, what most people see is death in every presence and possibility. The present pandemic has actually shrunk the life span by

---

[305] *The Last Messiah* (1933 essay by the Norwegian philosopher Peter Wessel Zapffe). Wikipedia: The Free Encyclopedia. Wikimedia Foundation. Retrieved 20 February 2021.

a year. In the tussle between the 'cult of the capitalist individualism' and a 'sense of shared collectivism', this pestilence has exacerbated our mind's default aversion to anything that threatens the *status quo* or to take incremental half-measures to sanitize our guilt. We have long despaired why we are so divisive, disparate, cantankerous, and brutal in our behavior, despite having, as Erich Fromm says, "an innate impulse for cooperation and sharing, rather than for killing and cruelty" (*The Anatomy of Human Destructiveness*, 1973). We have also long despaired why we are so egocentric and pharisaical despite having an 'impulse' for altruism and empathy, and why we view difference and diversity as difficulties and roadblocks, not as sinews of synergy. The answer to all such questions is simply that we seek answers where they don't exist—in our worldly life—and overlook where they are—in our inner life.

It may be that a 21st-century pandemic offers us a chance to prove that all is still not lost. The way the world transits from the 'old normal' to a 'new normal' would be a once-in-a-lifetime chance to make the sort of transformative changes the world and we so desperately need. But the essential problem remains: the gap between what we need and what we *think* we need. If it is the latter, any change will only reinforce the failed *status quo ante*. But it offers an opportunity to show that we are capable of overcoming what drags us down, and of realizing what the ancient Upanishads had highlighted so long ago, i.e., the elemental connectivity of all life on earth. The American Indian Lakota people offer an eloquent message, a prayer of oneness and harmony with all forms of life: *Mitakuye oyasin*—meaning 'we are all related'. Maybe we need to stretch it to include the Maori concept of *Whakapapa*—the idea that we are all bound in a great chain of life that connects the present back to the generations of the past, and forward to all the generations going on into the future. And, as Alexandre Dumas says, "until the day God will deign to reveal the future to man, all human wisdom is contained in these two words: Wait and Hope".[306]

---

[306] Alexandre Dumas. 1844. *The Count of Monte Cristo*.

Whatever triumphs and tragedies lie in store for us—some say it is the end of the dark age; some, that the nightmare has barely begun—but it does seem that our chickens are coming home to roost, and that our sins of the past and present, of commission and omission, have run out of road. Our long-anticipated moment of truth in an 'age of non-truth' is close at hand, and, truth be told, we are both the accused and the cursed, predator and prey, villain and victim. Like in every traumatic time, our mind turns to God. Surely, all this cannot be without His implicit acquiescence! Have we become like the cursed citizens of Biblical Sodom, who reveled, like us, in the "fullness of food, and abundance of idleness".[307] Like them, we too are afflicted by what Jewish ethicist Meir Tamari epitomizes as 'economic egoism'. Around us too, chutzpah abounds, and we too are dazzled by wealth and proud of might, and are cruel towards the impoverished and impious towards God. Yet another parallel that springs to mind is the tragic fate of the citizens of Atlantis, about whom it was said: "The immense growth of wealth and of luxury gradually undermined the most splendid civilization that the world has yet seen. Knowledge was prostituted to individual gain, and control over the powers of nature was turned from service to oppression".[308] We must also understand that for all the ills that befall humanity, we are all capable and culpable, each and every one of us, and must partake in what is called 'ontological guilt'. The hard truth is that every crisis we have had to face, we have helped create ourselves. We have consistently failed to heed the warnings before, and we will do no different in the future. Our mindset is such that, as Elisa Gabbert says, "We believe it won't happen to us" (*The Unreality of Memory*, 2020). And that is perhaps why, in the words of Debora MacKenzie, "a pandemic that should not have happened" has happened. Although there are some who see it as divine dispensation and ask, 'So why resist it if it

---

[307] Ezekiel, 16:49-50.

[308] *Man: Whence, How and Whither, A Record of Clairvoyant Investigation.* Compiled by Annie Besant and Charles W. Leadbeater, published in 1913.

is God's will?', many simply cannot feel any crisis coming in their brains or bones. Our mind makes it abstract, a problem for another day. Some seek solace in the idea of eternal or cyclical time, *kalachakra* in Buddhism. According to Hinduism, the current dark era, Kali Yuga, will give way to a virtuous era, the *Satya Yuga*—a time when 'the universal soul is white' and there is no hatred, or vanity, or evil thought whatsoever, no sorrow, no fear. So then, when can we put the current dismal and depraved age behind our back? Opinions and estimates widely vary but, according to one prediction, which should be of some immediate interest to us, it could arrive as soon as the year 2025.[309] It may not be a mere coincidence that some climate experts warn that global warming might reach boiling point in the next five years. By any reckoning or reflection, all the auguries and portents indicate that the next five years are destined to be a fateful time, a time like which comes every once in a while in history.

How we respond to the challenges that we will surely encounter will hinge principally on how the prevailing power differential between good and evil in the *war within*—within each and every one of us—will play out. Without waging and winning this war, we cannot have the kind of change we need in our consciousness, and we will not be able to overcome our twin inabilities—why we can't be good when we want; and not do bad even if we don't want. And without that, we will never be able to avert any existential threats like the ones we now face, the coronavirus pandemic and the climate chaos. Another change we need is to give up the idea that the evil out there is an abnormality or an alien enemy. Evil is an inseparable part of who we were, who we are, and who we will be. Finally, we must save the good in us even more than fight the evil within. And the only way to save the good inside is to do 'good' outside. That is the vicious cycle we are now required to turn into a virtuous circle. What is now a lose–lose situation—evil is winning both inside and outside—must

---

[309] Misra, B.D. 2015. The End of the Kali Yuga in 2025: Unraveling the Mysteries of the Yuga Cycle. Graham Hancock. 15 July 2015.

be reversed. Good must be helped to prevail over evil in our behavior and in our consciousness.

But how and where do we begin? As Lao Tzu said, a journey of a thousand miles begins with a single step. That single step is to step outside of our physicality and look down and see what Mary Oliver called our 'wild and precious life' (*A Thousand Mornings*, 2013) in the raw. What we will see is a being who has no control over how he lives and what he thinks and feels, and, more worryingly, no control over his wants. Our predispositions, perceptions, preoccupations, passions, and prejudices seem so petty, it would have been laughable if only not so pernicious. The way forward is to put into practice the American philosopher Thomas Scanlon's memorable message: 'Goodness consists in what we owe to others'. And in what George Eliot wrote a while ago: "The growing good of the world is partly dependent on unhistoric acts" (*Middlemarch*, 1871). It doesn't need to be confined to dramatic examples of unerring perfection. We can be mere middling, even deeply flawed and compromised, and still do some good, little by little, day by day. We have the wherewithal with which good can be amplified on a different scale now than ever before. We must also never fail to forget that the complicit often are *more* guilty than the real guilty. Evil, as they say, thrives in silence. Through our silent approval, we indirectly participate in all the shameful injustices, including 'animal injustice', and in the social, racial, and climate inequities that smudge our diurnal lives. And, as Jean Tarrou, the character in Albert Camus' novel *The Plague* says, "We can't stir a finger in this world without the risk of bringing death to somebody". And Tarrou adds, "Each of us has the plague within him; no one, no one on earth is free from it". Or, as Rabbi Yonatan Neril of the Interfaith Centre for Sustainable Development says: "There's a Pharaoh within us that wants to continue to do something that's not right". We can suppress or eclipse the 'plague or the Pharaoh' for a while, but it may break through in all our actions, even in those that seem insignificant to us. We must also understand that injustice can be both personal and intrapersonal and impersonal, and manifest in multiple ways like, for example, environmental and intergenerational.

We pride ourselves as the lone moral species, but still, we have much to learn from other species, even from insects. For instance, lessons of altruism from a species of moth in Madagascar that drinks the tears of sleeping birds. In whatever we do, we should keep at the back of our mind the idea of the 'butterfly effect' (Edward Lorenz), to wit: the flapping of a butterfly's wing in one part of the world could cause a hurricane in the opposite part of the world. Every inconsequential action carries consequential consequences, and possibly, even on ones to come, (to draw on the analogy of Ray Bradbury's 1952 short story *A Sound of Thunder* which illustrated the concept of how the death of a butterfly in the past could induce drastic changes in the future). We must also remember what the dying Bhishma told King Yudhishthira in the *Mahabharata* (*Anushasana Parva*): "Compassion applies not merely to one's actions, but to one's words as well as one's thoughts". The Dalai Lama says that at a time when radicalism is equated with terrorism, what the world needs now is radicalism of compassion, or Olga Tokarczuk's 'radical tenderness'. As some kind of 'booster' shot, new research reveals that "Conscientiousness—a tendency to be responsible, organized, and capable of self-control—is one personality trait linked to a lower risk of mortality.[310] It means that being good is not only good for being good, but also good for the health and length of our life. Let us also remember that by compassion, as Thomas Browne writes, "We make others' misery our own, and so, by relieving them, we relieve ourselves also" (*Religio Medici*, 1643).

What modern man—who is degenerate in spirituality and perfected in materiality—chooses to forget is that, configured and conditioned as he is, he cannot transform or transcend himself by artificially mollifying his behavior or through commandments and codes of conduct. When we

---

[310] Drake, K. 2021. Research Suggests Conscientious People May Live Longer. *Medical News Today*. 24 February 2021.

decode or choose, our conscious decision just takes note of what is already going on inside, offering its proforma authorization to a *fait accompli*. For both singular and species-wide awakening, we must venture *within*, by shifting our gaze from the cosmos to consciousness, from the stars to the soul. And we must train ourselves to do things 'consciously'. We must remember that whatever we do unconsciously can also be done consciously. That can make a huge difference. For example, if we are constantly conscious that whatever we must do should be with what historian Tony Judt calls 'simple decency', and ceaselessly strive our utmost to do the least harm to any sentient being, then that would ensure that the forces of goodness gain and retain a whip hand in the war within. And not to do harm is not to hurt. Hurting and getting hurt are both commonplace and contemporary; one feasts on the other. The way to break free is to learn to forgive. It is by cultivating forgiveness, both on one's own self and on others, that we can heal the wounds of the world. It becomes easy if we recognize that those that hurt you are playing their prescribed parts in your life. Nothing can hurt you anymore, and, in turn, you stop hurting others. No bitterness; no betrayal. It, so to say, drains the swamp and makes empathy easy.

The crux of the matter is that we are utterly blind to the central fulcrum of our life: that even as we think, we robotically go about our comforting choices, chores, and rituals of everyday life, the truth is that whatever we do in the world is, in reality, a mirror image of what has already occurred elsewhere in a parallel, deeper dimension of our consciousness. We bemoan and berate many things in the world: wars, violence, selfishness, cruelty, venality, dishonesty, bigotry, meanness, etc., but we turn a blind eye to their root. We talk about the likelihood of what the *Russell–Einstein Manifesto* (1955) called 'universal death' and 'sixth mass extinction' and so on, but amazingly, we feel we have nothing to do with it. If, by our actions or inaction, we hasten human extinction, it will be tantamount to what Jonathan Schell called "a death in the cradle—a case of infant mortality"

(*The Fate of the Earth*, 1982). But all is never all lost. As David Graeber said, "The ultimate, hidden truth of the world, is that it is something that we make, and could just as easily make differently".[311] In ancient Greece, gods were blamed when a tragedy struck or something inexplicable took place. Then, the great Greek tragedian Aeschylus changed that perception and said, "The gods do not direct human actions; the direction comes from within". As Hermann Hesse's Harry Haller says, "There is no reality except the one contained within us" (*Steppenwolf*, 1927). What we do in life resonates in the infinite world within, and what transpires there translates as circumstances and events of the finite outside world. In her magnum opus *The Secret Doctrine* (1888), the 19th-century mystic and medium Madame Blavatsky aptly says, "The Universe is worked and guided from within outwards". She also says, "Our attention and energy are drained in exploring distant stars whereas we should be exploring the subterranean caves of the consciousness". Another Hermann Hesse character in the novel *The Glass Bead Game* (1943) says, "Let us turn our gaze inward then we will have discovered the universe incarnate".

One of the cardinal tenets of the ancient Indian philosophy of *Advaita-vedanta* (non-duality) is *atma-vichara*, or Self-inquiry, our faculty of reflection, contemplation, and discrimination directed inwards. This 'inquiry' is about the sort and scope of the nexus that connects and, at the same time, separates the Self as an autonomous individualized, unique, free, self-determining unit, and the Self as a part of or the reflection of the Supreme Self. The prevailing paradigm is the idea that we are discrete individual entities opposed to an objective, neutral world that exists independently of us. To mend anything for the better, we must mend our consumption–extraction mindset, which is addicted to the thought that anything we want we must get. Maybe the time has come to pray, as a Jenny Holzer truism says, "Protect me from what I want". We must nurture

---

[311] Graeber, D. 2015. The Utopia of Rules: On Technology, Stupidity, and the Secret Joys of Bureaucracy. New York, USA: Melville House.

a mindset that is not dominated by the mind. We must understand that the temper of our mind is to seek understanding and safety. And to that end, the mind finds it necessary to see some things as good and some things as bad. We have to step outside the positions and prejudices we have grown up with, abandon the perks we believe are our entitlements. It is to move past from the mind-centrality of human life. The mind is monopolistic and does not let us see the full picture. It does not let us, in the words of an ancient Chinese philosopher, 'cease to cherish our opinions'. At the same time, as the *Katha* Upanishad says, "The senses can [only] be controlled by the control of the mind". All remedies to all our ailments are within. The path to harmony of science and spirituality has to be headed within. The route to a better world and a more moral man is within. The will and strength to end the 'vampiric cruelty' of man, especially towards other animals, can only be lasting if it emanates from our within. Our perceptual predilection not to be cognizant, even be conscious, of this *within* has ruined our best laid plans, and has cost us dearly. We tend to treat the future as some sort of *Terra nullius*, a no-man's land, an unclaimed territory that is devoid of inhabitants and therefore ours by default. We do not associate our own posterity, which is real but temporally remote, with the future of the world. While we want to bend destiny to our demands, we are actually freefalling into our future. We are freefalling because we fail to bear the truth that we are fast becoming a 'failed species'. Failing because we cannot get our act together. Although we cannot put a finger on the pulse, we know that well-ordered, human-centered narratives do not wholly govern our lives. But what we have consistently *failed* to know is the fundamental *narrative* unfolding constantly inside each of us. Sacred texts, prophets, mystics, saints, and rishis have had their say, but have made no discernible dent on this causal ignorance. We are rooted, absorbed, and obsessed with the visible, outward world and spill blood over its spoils. But what we are ignoring is that, in the words of GK Chesterton, "The human house is a paradox, for it is larger inside than out" (*The Common Man*,

1950). And what is happening inside is actually that which brings out the worst in us, what we call a war. And it is no ordinary war; it is the mother of all wars, the most fateful and consequential of them all. And yet it is what we do ordinarily that charts the course of this war, not occasional efforts, heavenly or hellish.

The struggle between good and evil is one of the oldest themes of religious and philosophical thought. It occupies a central place in nearly all major world religions. This theme is pivotal in one of the world's oldest continuously practiced religions: Zoroastrianism. The difficulty is that although millions of words have been spoken and chronicled, the dynamics of the dichotomy of good and bad still defies delineation. If we really do not know what is 'good' and what is 'evil', how then can we do 'good' and avoid doing 'evil'? The relationship between the two is deeper than that of a formal homology; the two are fragments of the same totality, As Nietzsche's *Zarathustra*, named after Zoroaster, says, "Every people speaks its own tongue of good and evil—which the neighbor does not understand". The closest way we can characterize it is what the poem *Zebra Question* of Shel Silverstein alludes to: "I asked the zebra, Are you black with white stripes? Or white with black stripes? And the zebra asked me, Are you good with bad habits? Or are you bad with good habits?" (*A Light in the Attic*, 1981). Some say that good is the only good in the world, and all evil must be rooted out. While others like Arthur Schopenhauer say that "Evil is just what is positive; it makes its own existence felt" (*On the Sufferings of the World*, 1859). Some suggest that we are all 'sinners in the hands of an angry God' (Jonathan Edwards), and therefore even if all the bad guys in the world are dead, the world will retain the same blend. Some others say, 'All the evil that exists is of man; All that God has done is only good'. The opposite argument has been that 'man is as he is by the ordained design of God, and, therefore, God is responsible for all the suffering, shame, and error, spread by human agency'. Yet, others chip in and interject: 'If God is to be blamed for our badness, why are we so shy of thanking Him for the good in us? Such a dialectic discourse is always interesting, but in our torrid times, when the winds of the world carry the stench of evil and we are so overwhelmed, it is instantly empirical.

What is practically problematic is that it is difficult to classify who qualifies as a 'good person'. Bad is more easy to segregate. The nagging headache is that time and again we find that the one who goes by as a good man has feet of clay, and that often that which we call greatness—in the potential sense of altering history—comes at the cost of goodness, in the sense of bettering other's lives. Many great writers have failed to practice in their lives what they so movingly wrote about in their works. They are as mean and petty, callous and cussed as any of us; even worse, they believe they are entitled by their sense of self-superiority. It is because "doing good is hard—even beginning to do good is hard", as proclaimed by an inscription left by the Indian emperor Ashoka (304–232 BCE), who was horrified by the barbarity of war. Ashoka also realized that injunctions and inscriptions are good but not good enough, and instituted an 'infrastructure for goodness'. And we too need to do the same: establish an infrastructure or architecture, a set of systems that are germane to our own morally foggy times.

Functionally, it means that we have to include another dimension to what we routinely and reflexively do: decode which of the two fighting forces—under the broad rubrics of good and evil—in the war within, is the intended action likely to help or hinder. For neither of them can exist or endure except through what we ingest, which is more than what we put into our mouth; it includes what we let in through our eyes, ears, and even skin. So, it is in our power to influence who prevails in the war. One of the central tenets of Zoroastrianism is that the world is primarily made up of good and evil, and the duty of a Zoroastrian is to ask himself or herself every day, "Which side am I on?" According to the philosophy of Manichaeism, life can be divided neatly as good or evil, light or dark, or love and hate. The 'alchemical trick' to turn our life around is to wage and win this war the right way. However much we may manipulate or stimulate our brain (which is in a state of burnout or meltdown), or be able to link it directly with a digital machine (Neuralink), or read each other's unfiltered thoughts, or augment our body parts, nothing in the world is likely to change for any better. What is most alarming is not that machines are coming closer and closer to resemble human beings; it is that human beings are creeping more and more to resemble machines. That is primarily due to the fact that we are *augmenting* that which is the source of so much of what went wrong: *brain-based intelligence*, at the expense of the heart. That brings in what we may call 'imbalance in intelligence', or in the words of Jane Goodall, the world's foremost expert on chimpanzees, "a disconnect between that clever, clever brain and human heart, love and compassion". Goodall adds, "Only when head and heart work in harmony can we attain our true human potential".[312] And, as Milan Kundera points out, "When the heart speaks, the mind finds it indecent to object".[313]

The key is the ability to attune ourselves to lead a normally moral life, without having to battle every time we do a chore. For long, we have relied on religion to navigate through troubled times, and moral philosophy to distinguish right and wrong, or to know, as Stoics say, what is 'up to us' and what isn't. We have, in practical terms, consistently fallen short of finding what the ancient Greek philosophy *Pyrrhonism* describes as the 'criterion of truth providing any stable basis for judgment'. We have a predisposition to irresistible misfeasance, seemingly propelled by what Edgar Allan Poe paints as 'the one unconquerable force' (*The Imp of the Perverse*, 1845). Actually, the focus should be on homogenizing, not segregating, the two. Like good and evil, wrong too cannot be eliminated. Despite all theological explanations, we still rack our brains as to why our good God was so resolute that the human should not get to 'know good and evil'. How can that be considered as the ultimate defiance and the

---

[312] Tippett, K. 2020. Jane Goodall: What It Means to Be Human. *On Being with Krista Tippett*. 6 August 2020.

[313] Kundera, M. 1984. The Unbearable Lightness of Being.

Original Sin that cursed mankind ever since? Was it that God wanted man to be no different from other animals who do not 'know good and evil' and therefore cannot sin? If so, why was man alone (at least so we assume) endowed with rational and discriminating powers if he is supposed to simply obey? Is the possibility of man 'living forever' the real reason for His alarm and wrath? Yet, in real life, each one of us must try to know good and evil and try to strike a balance. And balance implies acceptance— acceptance that not everything is wrong with 'wrong'.

As Kathryn Schulz says, "The capacity to err is crucial to human cognition. Far from being a moral flaw, it is inextricable from some of our most humane and honorable qualities" (*Being Wrong: Adventures in the Margin of Error*, 2011). Without error, there can be no improvement. Many believe that to correct or counter one 'wrong' with another 'wrong' is permissible, or even necessary, as Lord Krishna Himself implied in the Bhagavad Gita. He said that those who side with evil, even if they are virtuous, have to be dealt with by any means. But some like Socrates thought otherwise. He told his friend Crito, on the very eve of his tryst with hemlock, that "one must never, when wronged, inflict wrong in return, as the majority believe, since one must never do wrong". Gandhi, who revered the Gita as his daily guide as well as an anchor in difficult situations, used to emphasize that "wrong ends do not justify the right end". It was a model that Martin Luther King Jr adopted in the American Civil Rights movement in the 1960s. It all, like everything else in life, hinges on the character of the context. For instance, even though it is hard to accept, we have always considered the moral *context* of a war differently from the ethical context of daily life. Matters that used to agitate the minds of men like Krishna or Socrates or Gandhi, lesser mortals like us now face, what we may call Sophie's Choices (William Styron, 1979). We cannot anymore have it both ways, and not making a moral choice itself is now tantamount to making a sinful choice. Unhelpfully, our sheer threat-oriented evolution has not endowed us with what it takes to judge such issues. In the end, we are left with our own wits, and fall back on what Nietzsche says in his much-quoted work, *Beyond Good and Evil* (1886): "You have your way. I have my way. As for the right way, the correct way, it does not exist". We want to change, but we don't know into what, and what the moral way is. Our rational mind reasons that since we are already God's viceroy on earth, the next step ahead can only be *de facto* divinity. And again, rationally, since we are actually *de facto* machines, the short-cut to celestial status cannot but be, so it is suggested, an actual 'animatronic' machine powered by AGI. The machine has long served another opposite purpose: a metaphor for what we shouldn't be. Thoreau, for example, wrote, against the backdrop of the ills of industrial society, of men having "no time to be anything but a machine".

Essentially, our proneness to self-righteousness and self-destruction removes all restraints from a life of 'luxurious hedonism' and an attitude of *après moi, le déluge*. It hasn't been easy, but we have just about finished the heavy lifting of destroying ourselves. Whether the actual trigger is what is described as 'apocalyptic twins of nuclear and climate threat'[314] or runaway automation, or a malicious mass leader gone mad, is a matter of detail, albeit deadly. At another level, they all signal our reluctance to give up our goodies like gadgets and fossil fuels. To paraphrase the theologian Richard Niebuhr, man is a sinner not because he is limited but because he is betrayed "by his very ability to survey the whole to imagine himself the whole" (*The Nature and Destiny of Man*, 1941). Modern man abhors the 'L' word: *limits*. He thinks it is an affront to his dignity. In trying to upgrade himself through technology, man is endearing to become 'limitless'. What he fails to remember is that so much that is so good in us is *because* of our limits, the designated bounds of who we were intended to be.

We must once and for all acknowledge that the human 'package', in the tapestry of terrestrial life that nature has put together, can never make

---

[314] Lifton, R.J. and Strozier, C.B. 2021. The Psychological Pandemic: Can We Confront Our Death Anxiety? *Bulletin of the Atomic Scientists*. 1 March 2021.

human society truly egalitarian, even-handed, and just. Human society cannot be better or worse than who we are, and how we connect with each other. And 'who we are' is an extension of what we are inward. Long paralyzed inside with the two questions—*Why can't we be good when we want to?* and *Why we do bad when we don't want to?*—we have become nihilistic, and might well end up committing what Vladimir Odoyevsky's *Last Messiah* suggested to a jaded mankind: 'omnicide by blowing up the planet' (*Russian Nights: The Last Suicide*, 1844). That was then a cautionary metaphor; now, we *do* have the physical power to blow up, or make the planet uninhabitable. What we should worry is how long our mind can restrain itself from exercising such apocalyptic power. Surely, the stakes are too seismic to be left to the feeble mind of a failing species. This throws up another dismal thought. Is this the moment when the *Messiah* that the Bible envisioned, or the *Avatar* that the Bhagavad Gita prophesied, will make his divine advent? But things have changed radically since then. Evil is all over with a smirk on its face, not confined to a few Mephistophelian men. How then can He intervene to help the good and righteous? Therefore, any divine corrective has to be in the form of what the Upanishads call *chitta suddhi*, pure consciousness, or a transcendental 'outpouring of human spirit' in a critical mass of mankind. We have to choreograph what is called 'the hundredth-monkey effect', a metaphor for the idea that once a critical number of members copy a behavior or follow an idea, it will be spread by all *en masse*, like a contagion. The problem though is, as the English poet William Blake observed, "You never know what is enough unless you know what is more than enough" (*The Marriage of Heaven and Hell*, 1790–93). What any of us can then do is to assume that each of us might well be the hundredth monkey, and follow the dictum of the Roman poet Horace: *Carpe diem quam minimum credula postero*—seize the day and don't trust tomorrow (*Odes*, 23 BCE).

When seized with such troubling thoughts, and when we sense we are staring at a dead end, the wisest thing is to go back to the drawing board, back to the basics. In life, nothing is original. The first thing to do is to de-aggrandize—not de-human—the human. To discard the idea of what Joanna Zielinska calls "the grandiosity of the human and this belief in our amazing might" (*Minimal Ethics for the Anthropocene*, 2014). With the advent of the Anthropocene era, that belief is now a fact; our might is geomorphic and geologic. And human activity has an effect beyond the passing of generations, or even civilizations on the planet. That puts additional moral responsibility on our shoulders and raises another riddle: What is a minimally good life? And 'minimally', what does one owe to one another? The answer to that question hinges on from whose standpoint it is—mine, yours or of the rest. And minimally, we should shed *speciesism*—the condescending conceit that one species of animal can be morally superior to another, and so dominate another. It means that we have to nurture and cultivate the spirit of 'oneness'—the feeling of being 'one' with everything in existence. And, most important, what it amounts to is that every one of us is a small but singular 'self', and every one of us can be an alchemist or a terminator on a species scale. It also means that each of us is complicit, even in silence, in whatever any of us might do, holy or heinous, pious or profane.

The quintessential question that won't go away is this: Is it safer to, once and for all, resign to live with whoever we are, a composite of, wacky, weird, and wounded, or take the risk of provoking the objectively tragic sequences by selectively enhancing our capabilities and faculties artificially? Putting it more pointedly, should we put all the bets of our future in the melting pot of science and technology? Should we forever turn our back on the spiritual to better our behavior and finish the unfinished work? Lest we clean forget, the heroic history of science includes not only dizzying discoveries but also what Mario Livio[315] calls 'brilliant blunders'. On a less gloomy note, some blunders can open unknown doors and new opportunities. At the same

---

[315] Livio, M. 2013. Brilliant Blunders: From Darwin to Einstein—Colossal Mistakes by Great Scientists That Changed Our Understanding of Life and the Universe. USA: Simon and Schuster.

time, what we must unflinchingly understand is that, next only to what Greek philosopher Aeschylus called 'the awful grace of God' and the laws of *karma*, it is the Law of Unintended Consequences that could decisively influence human destiny. One of our common pitfalls is to become obsessed with a pet project and abandon our life for the sake of it; and in so doing, come face to face with problems distinct and disparate than the project.

The test of our behavior really boils down to how we instinctively perceive another human being. It brings to mind what Percy Shelley wrote in the review of his wife Mary's 1823 masterpiece *Frankenstein*, "Treat a person ill, and he will become wicked". That, in fact, is the tip-off we should draw from Mary's story. Frankenstein's 'creature' was a monstrous-*looking* hulk; the real *monster* was Frankenstein himself, for fathering and then abandoning the creature. In fact, the ugly creature tells his creator, "I am malicious because I am miserable". Those who are trying to make the human body permanent and perfect should remember that what Frankenstein was doing eerily was not much different, and he thought that a new species would bless him as its creator. As it went for that promethean professor, we too might face our end wishing we could destroy the monster we made.

Yet, we are deaf to all such dire possibilities. What, however, gives us a bit of cheer is that while we focus on the 'problem of evil', there are also a plethora of good possibilities. As William Saroyan reminds us, "Nothing good ever ends. If it did, there would be no people in the world—no life at all, anywhere" (*The Human Comedy*, 1943). The upshot of all this is that as humans, as JRR Tolkien puts it in *Lord of the Rings* (1954), "We have no way of judging what the ultimate effects of our deeds might be, good or bad". To which we may add, we have no way of differentiating fact from fantasy, realism from 'mythorealism'.[316] Worse, we tell ourselves, "It can't be that wrong, if it feels this right". It is important to fully take

---

[316] The Chinese writer Yan Lianke is credited with coining the term 'mythorealism' to designate a new genre of fiction writing in Chinese literature. Lianke is the author of *Lenin's Kisses* (2004) and *Serve the People* (2005).

note of the fact that a good person and a moral life has to be reckoned circumstantially, and that the valence of anything is never unitary, nor universal. Just as there many paths to one truth, there are many factors that have to be weighed in judging the same action by different persons and at different times. It is possible that we are now so masterful that we even, as Lord Acton once said, "make good the evil they did". Too many moral choices these days leave us insecure and groping, and expose us to what Spanish philosopher José Ortega y Gasset called 'moral hemiplegia', the tendency to condemn moral transgressions of other people, but staying close-eyed to the same transgressions of our own. The irksome choice-making we are desperately trying to desist from is either living in a lie or accepting the terrible truth of death. That 'living lie' itself is denial of death. And, as Ernest Becker puts it, much of that human activity is largely driven by unconscious efforts to deny the inevitability of death (*The Denial of Death*, 1973). Any fundamental change in the human mindset can only incubate and emerge from an internal transcendental transformation.

The transformation of man has for centuries engaged the attention of many theologians, religious leaders, spiritualists, mystics, and philosophers, and of late, scientists and transhumanists. Yet, it is as hazy and distant as ever. To put it simply, we want to be 'transformed' without transformation. We want to evolve into a butterfly with wings, but we want to still retain the stumpy prolegs of a caterpillar. We want to give up nothing and get everything. For, human behavior cannot change unless the human mindset changes, and for that, we need *consciousness-change*. Such a change is necessary to bring about a long-overdue change in our equation with mortality. It has now become more urgent as much of the death-dominated world is now in the grip of what psychologists are calling 'collective death anxiety'. Right or wrong, we don't know—because we can't speak for another species—but it is often said that our understanding and knowledge of death separates us humans from all other animals. The problem is that for a man of reason, 'being mortal' defies any sense; what metaphysical purpose can it possibly serve to anyone? Many feel that death's inevitability seems such a terrible tragedy and so utterly needless. Whether one dies at nineteen or ninety or later, it is still abrupt and artificial. Nothing makes this more clear and crystalline than a deadly pandemic. With all the might of medicine, what we are left with is what Peter Zapffe fell back upon: "All I have for facing death myself, is a foolish smile". The scenario resembles what Blaise Pascal described: "Men are slaughtered daily within view of the others, so that those who are left see their own condition in that of their fellows, and, regarding one another with sorrow and without hope, wait their turn".[317] The paradox has always been that life is full of pain, hardship, and sweat and toil, yet we don't want it to end. We are, to borrow the words of Edwin Arnold, "glad to live a little longer span, for so much longer anguish" (*The Secret of Death*, 1885). Science is saying that longer span need not be 'a little', and it is now well within our power to prolong it almost indefinitely. Death, it says, need not any more be nevermore. Whatever the final fate of death in the human hand, it throws a spanner in the works, muddies the waters even more, and makes life more challenging and tangled.

The fine line we have to draw is between immortality as a belief in some kind of continuity after death, and trying to extend earthly life infinitely. In spirit, immortality has always been on the human agenda, but it was of a different genre, close to what in ancient Chinese Taoist philosophy was called *Xian*, a spiritually immortal or celestial being. Bereft of the 'immortality' of the continuity kind, as Dostoyevsky says, "nothing then would be immoral, everything would be permissible, even cannibalism". In the broader ambience, as Simon Critchley puts it, "the question of the meaning of life becomes a matter of finding a meaning to human finitude" (*Very Little... Almost Nothing: Death, Philosophy, Literature*, 1997). We have been hopeful that at last we can answer the

---

[317] Kegan Paul, C (trans.). 1901. The Thoughts of Blaise Pascal (Translated from the text of M. Auguste Molinier). George Bell.

eternal question of the meaning of life by overcoming the finiteness of life. What was once a symbolic or spiritual grail, became physical and corporeal. While once death was viewed, as Thomas Browne said, "the cure for all diseases" (*Religio Medici*, 1643), science now says it is '*the* disease'. Only a few years ago, an immortalist Aubrey de Grey predicted that "people in middle age now have a fair chance" of never dying. The seductive promises of transhumanism, such as indefinite extension of human life span, suddenly seem so brash and hollow. From a different angle, some are saying that "humanity is the 'illness' and Covid-19 is the 'vaccine'". Regardless of the ultimate outcome, what is highly probable is that the very attempt is fraught with grave possibilities. Already many are living a life of 'deadness' without dying. What we dread about death is not its certainty, but even more its *uncertainty*. Not only death, but even in life man has struggled with the certainty of uncertainty. A life with absolute certainties would be an absolute bore. Actually, we need both eternal and temporal, and the limbo in-between, in our life for creativity. Mankind has used its immense creativity not only to build intricate civilizations, but also simultaneously to perfect new and more efficient means of killing one another. In giving birth, we also 'give birth' to death. As French philosopher Paul Virilio[318] famously said, "When you invent the ship, you also invent the shipwreck". It is our disregard and disruption of this law of probable probability that has given us so many surprises and shocks. Reeling from the resultant whiplash, we agonize: Are the gods getting back at us for trying to become one of them? Has God concluded that the time has come, as the Bible says, for 'the seed of mankind to be destroyed' because of repetitive disobedience? What then should we do? Should we go down on our knees and pray for His grace (for giving us good things we don't deserve) and mercy (for sparing us from bad things we deserve), and the wisdom to know the difference? Or, should we try and build a new Ark

---

[318] Virilio, P. 1999. Politics of the Very Worst: An Interview with Philippe Petit. New York, USA: Semiotext(e).

and scramble to get on to the Great Boat? What is more ominous is how close we are to what God found out about man before He unleashed the Flood—that man's thoughts were "evil continuously". When our thoughts are continuously evil, our behavior cannot be far behind.

The pivotal point of departure for any honest heuristic has to be this: that our conscious awareness of everything about us is external and empirical; our vision, our goals, our episteme, our tools, our values, our vision of our civilization, are outwards. What we need for sustainable change is a movement and metamorphosis *inward*. The source of the existential crisis we face is not technology or economy, or cultural or even 'way of thinking'. Transformative changes in these are necessary but not sufficient. The source of the problem is our beliefs and values that define their purpose, which come from within. Unless we make a 180-degree turn, crisis after crisis will fall on us, emaciating us so much that, a century from now or sooner, the living might envy the dead. We all are afflicted by an epidemic of what the ancient Greeks called *akrasia*— lacking command (over one's own self) or weakness of will; acting in a way contrary to one's sincerely held moral values; knowing the right thing to do but induced to do the opposite. In fact, unconscionable suffering had been inflicted throughout history by those thinking that they were doing the right thing, and doing it for the greater good. This was the spirit of what Saint Paul lamented about when he said, "For the good that I would I do not: but the evil which I would not, that I do".[319] Why anyone will do anything that he *knows* is wrong has long been the question that has baffled many, from Greek philosophers to modern-day psychologists. This was what Sage Vyasa (Mahabharata) had in mind when he rued why men choose the path of evil, when 'being good' gives all the goodness of life. Unfortunately, as the Irish bard WB Yeats said, "The best lack all conviction, while the worst are full of passionate intensity" (*The Second Coming*, 1920). And the best are not always at their best, and the worst are

---

[319] Romans, 7:19.

not always at their very worst. Terrible people can be dazzlingly creative. That is at the core of what is wrong with human behavior, which is both particular and peculiar. And what is astounding is that we continue to be astonished by what we ourselves do routinely and reflexively, and by how decrepit our decision-making has been. It has never been free from any 'inordinate attachment'. The frustrating fact is that, with all its marvelous cognitive capabilities, the human form of life is a wobbly choice maker, and a horrible 'equalizer'. Pandemics come and go; wars are waged; famines and hurricanes strike; repression, inequality, inequity, and injustice, remain endemic. We will always discover one way or the other to exercise power and control over someone or the other, a person whom Erich Fromm models as a "necrophilic character type," whose aim it is to "avoid the inconvenience of life by transforming others into obedient automatons, robbing them of their humanity" (*The Anatomy of Human Destructiveness*, 1973). We will always find ways to insulate ourselves from the injustices we perpetuate, and profit by the wreckage of our worst impulses. That is because, as Blaise Pascal once said, "Manifestly then injustice is innate in us, from which we cannot free ourselves, yet from which we ought to free ourselves".[320] Or else, to paraphrase Seamus Heaney, "The longed-for tidal wave of justice can rise up" (*The Cure at Troy*, 1990). What truly afflicts the world is not Covid-19 or climate change, materialism or militarism, capitalism, consumerism, or, for that matter, even jingoism, sectarianism, or fanaticism. These are but sparks; the flame itself is the spite-soaked mind. It is only such a mind that can sustain a global order whose oxygen is unfair access to power and resources. It is only such a mind that makes economic growth a higher priority than the health of humans and the well-being of the natural world. A Persian mystic once said, "If you pull out the chair from underneath the mind, you will fall into God". The Indian sage Ramana Maharshi said it simply: "Man minus mind is God". But what

---

[320] Kegan Paul, C (trans.). 1901. The Thoughts of Blaise Pascal (Translated from the text of M. Auguste Molinier). George Bell.

science is striving to put together is the equation: *'Man plus machine = god'*. What is certain is that the line between man and machine will be blurred; what is completely unknown is what or *who* he will resemble. What is probable is that successor generations down the line might agonize, like Pinocchio:[321] "What's a human being? What is a human being? Why can't I be a human being? Am I still a human being now?" The take away point is that whatever the hybrid form of the 'future human' that unfettered human ego might make—whether it is a humanoid or David Cronenberg's human-fly (*The Fly*, 1986)—a measure of humanity could linger, torment, and finally self-destruct. It is consciousness that finds its way to continue whatever is the exterior.

Behind our bravado and bluster, the unacknowledged message is that we have implicitly adjudged that we don't like who we are, that we are not good enough to do any true good. Every 'advance', every 'progress' has made us feel, soon after, that something else is missing in our lives. The frightful fact is that, much as we have always wanted to remake ourselves, we are equally petrified of what that would crystallize as. This fear is impacting on the present. And every time some life-threatening crisis hits us, we agonize why we didn't heed the warnings and preempted it. We live by hope, but unfounded and squishy hope can be disastrous. We will do no better, or be any less of a menace, until we come to grips with the central storyline of human life: that an endless war wages within our consciousness between two clusters of forces we call good and evil, and that everything that happens in our lives, severally and synchronically, save perhaps a comet strike, is but a reflection and extension of the flux and reflux, the ebb and flow of this protean but perennial war. In the words of Robert Louis Stevenson,[322] "In each of us, two natures are at war—the good and the evil. All our lives the fight goes on between them, and one

---

[321] Carlo Collodi. 1883. The Adventures of Pinocchio.

[322] The beginning quote from the silent-film version (1920) of RL Stevenson's 1886 tale: *The Strange Case of Dr Jekyll and Mr Hyde*.

of them must conquer. In our own hands lies the power to choose—what we want most to be, we are". That 'power to choose' often translates into abuse of power, of which most of us are guilty, not only rulers and tyrants. The tragedy is that acceptance of such 'abuse' is equally insidious, of which also we are not innocent.

We exist and live in a world of duality, a world ruled by duality— as I/thou, up/down, inside/out, black/white, yes/no, male/female, angst and ecstasy, and good and evil. The challenge is to embrace both sides of something and manage the tension of opposites, the war within. In his *Notebooks*, Albert Camus scribbled, "We used to wonder where war lived, what it was that made it so vile. And now we realize that we know where it lives... inside ourselves". We have unfailingly failed to recognize that every visible challenge can be reframed as an invisible one, and that the circumstances that lead to our anger, avarice, stress, envy, hurt, and hardship are only the 'visible' façade; our ingrained impulses and febrile passions arise from our frazzled mind. From childhood, we are hardwired to be captivated by danger, and the notion of fight-or-flight is in our bones. We are also haunted by hurt—our own or those done to us. It is 'feelings' that finally matter, and one of the reasons why we are so unmoved by abundantly transparent threats is that even though "we know something is true; we don't feel that it's true... we don't live as if it's true."[323] We cannot differentiate between what is trite and what is true, between the immediate and the important.

To our troubled mind, nothing that is happening makes any sense; everything looks out of joint and there is 'nothing beneficent in the details' of any of our lives. But then, our mind itself is our main impediment to the birth of a better man and to a stable world. It is the unquestioned domination of our mind over our consciousness that is the cradle of all that

---

[323] Rowson, J. 2019. Integrating Our Souls, Systems, and Society. Podcast *On Being With Krista Tippett* with host Krista Tippett.18 July 2019. Retrieved from < https://onbeing.org/ programs/jonathan-rowson-integrating-our-souls-systems-and-society/>.

is so wrong in the world—moral meltdown, medicalization, mechanization, and the militarization of human life. Historian Mike Davis predicted this more than a decade ago in a 2010 essay, '*Who Will Build the Ark?*', warning that a warm and unstable climate would aggravate and accelerate the already existing divide between the rich and the poor. We must also recognize another reality, that it is always the poor, the castaways, and the left-behinds who are most affected, be it the coronavirus or climate change, for they lack the basic infrastructure to protect themselves. As Friedrich Engels said, "All conceivable evils are heaped upon the heads of the poor" (*The Condition of the Working Class in England*, 1845). Worse, many among the poor are not only bribed into passivity, as the Slovenian philosopher Slavoj Žižek puts it, by being thrown some crumbs of 'good life', but they are also tutored to believe that the way to get rich is to let the rich get richer, not through a fair society and shared prosperity. That is the sneakiest way to rig the system to get rich. Everything seems loaded against those of us whom the Lord calls "the least of these brothers and sisters of mine".[324] Even pandemics seem to love the leisure class and hit more the homeless and those living on the edge of subsistence. Such are the laws of probability, that any impact of any calamitous carnage will not be proportionate. While science is trying to turn the species *Homo sapiens* into *Homo deus*, the outcome might again be a travesty: a minuscule among us few could become super-intelligent, near-immortals, while the rest turn into what Varghese Mani personifies as '*Homo stupids*' (*Homo sapiens Divine*, 2016). And there is a grave risk that these *de facto* 'gods', with a consciousness captive to their mind, might behave diabolically, not divinely. What we need is 'double-acceptance'. As being human and of what your own life is fated to be. The Stoics used a striking metaphor to illustrate this: a dog leashed to a moving cart. If we run alongside and keep pace, we will have a fruitful life; if we grumble and resist, we would be dragged anyway, and we would have a miserable life. It is the same doctrine

---

[324] Matthew, 25:37–40.

that Nietzsche called *amor fati*, translated from Latin as 'a love of one's fate' (*Ecce Homo; How One Becomes What One Is*, 1908). If you love your fate regardless of what its character is, there is no expectation and therefore no disappointment or despair.

It all comes down to the basics of the body and brain. What we fail to see is that a better body or a brighter brain does not make a better man. Roman philosopher Seneca once said, *"Nemo liber est qui servit corpori* (no one is free who is slave to his body). In Buddhism, one of the ways prescribed in death meditation is to get rid of 'body-attachment' by vicariously imagining that even great people eventually die, and that it is the body that is the 'abode of many, many worms'. Such meditation was not much of a help even in Buddha's time. Now, it is the body all the way: body augmentation (even part by part), body-beautification, body-preservation, body-perpetuity. As for the brain, we want to boost it selectively to enhance our performance, and to become mentally immortal we don't mind parking it in a computer-cloud. And it all raises a troubling thought: what precisely is an individual and who are we trying to save? Are we sacrificing the human for the sake of humanity, or is it the other way around? Have we forfeited our 'right of residence' in the universe? Life is replete with questions but then, as Martin Heidegger asked, "Who or what is doing all this questioning?" (*Being and Time*, 1927). That itself is a rephrasing of the basic Advaita Vedantic aphorism: *Who am I?* But if science has its way, we will be asking, '*Where am I?*', as philosopher Daniel Dennett puts it. It is our cognitive and emotive inadequacy to interiorize what we do know that triggers trouble. Much as we yearn for peace, order, and tranquility in our life, our interior life is dominated by conflict, struggle, and war. Living through rolling times of angst and anguish, pain and panic, people's psyches have become pathologically ruptured, disrupted, and detached from what Fritjof Capra called the 'entire web of life',[325] and alienated from one another. There is growing evidence that

---

[325] Capra F. 1996. The Web of Life: A New Scientific Understanding of Living Systems.

the next decade will unleash the deepest, fastest, and most consequential scientific and technological disruption in history.

The message from the checkered annals of science, however, conveys a mixed message. On one hand, it is the single most important instrument that bettered the material condition of mankind. It has also shown that almost all scientific theories, when first propounded, have something deficient, which gets identified with the aid of new methods and scientific instruments. We must also bear in mind that we are living at a time when, as Frank Furedi[326] reminds us, science has replaced God as the archetypal authority at the societal level, and medicine is replacing morals and physicians and priests as the source of authority. Eroded from the anchor of traditional theology, we live in fear of our own power, a fear next only to the fear of finitude. Few of us make a life; all we do is make a living, much less a life worth living. Perhaps, more than hunting for bodily pleasure—which Samuel Johnson said "is of itself a good"[327]—man longs to be free from bodily pain. In fact, the ancient Stoics didn't see pain as an evil or as something to be shunned, but as a necessary source of learning and comprehension.

One event that we have instinctively associated with pain is the end of life. The pain is actually not *in* the end *of* life but of a life that is not lived. And it is painful because, as Graham Greene's Major Scobie rues in *The Heart of The Matter* (1948), "We are all of us resigned to death: it's life we aren't resigned to". That is because, in a strange way, we know more about death than about life. We have consistently failed to give any time of the day to the fountainhead of both pleasure and happiness—our mind-dominated consciousness. Life is not a choice between polar opposites like god and bad, black and white, or pain and pleasure. They are inseparable. Indeed, as Carl Jung says, life itself is the result of the tension between the

[326] Furedi, F. 2018. How Fear Works: Culture of Fear in the 21st Century. London, UK: Bloomsbury.

[327] Boswell, J. 1791. The Life of Samuel Johnson.

opposites in life experiences. All dualities and opposites are actually, in the words of the renegade economist Kate Raworth,[328] a "continual dynamic dance between complementary forces". In Hermann Hesse's novel *Demian*, (1919), the protagonist argues that Jehovah, the Jewish God, is only one face of God; it rules over all that is wholesome. But there is another half of the world, and an infinite god must encompass both sides of this world. It is our mind that allows us to live with blatant absurdities: we want to extend life almost indefinitely and yet kill each other almost routinely. We want good health but still cultivate habits that are ruinous to health. We want clean air and yet "poison is the wind that blows",[329] we want peace and yet constantly look for causes for profligate war making. We yearn to be good despite doing bad. In truth, these are not contradictions; they are different conditions. And all conditions are contextual. And context is king; it rules over content and consorts with circumstance. Similarly, human habits and the habitats we inhabit are connected. Above all, as Vedanta says, our mind makes us mistake appearance for the actual, mistake the 'rope' for the 'snake'. It is this delusion, Vedanta also says, that is at the root of divisiveness, sorrow, and misery in the world. We are poised at a pivotal portal (what the Greeks called *kairos*), a supreme moment, an uncommon opening and a generative opportunity that must be seized by any means. The other word that is apt for our times is the Latin *agere contra,* which roughly translates as 'to act against', a term used in ascetical literature to describe the deliberate effort one must make to strive to overcome one's evil tendencies, what St. Ignatius of Loyola called 'evil spirit' (*Spiritual Exercises*, 1548).

We arrogantly assume that the world is nothing but the human world, and that our disposition is a cause for cosmic concern. Is that so? Or, after

---

[328] Raworth, K. 2017. Doughnut Economics: Seven Ways to Think Like a 21st-Century Economist. UK: Random House.

[329] Lyrics from the 1971 song *Mercy, Mercy Me (The Ecology)* by the American singer Marwin Gaye.

all our dastardly doing, is our story as a species almost done, save collecting the ashes and embers? Are we a doomed species in a spiral of decline, or a divine species in eclipse? In either case, what Simon Critchley illustrates as the 'tinnitus of our existence' (*Very Little... Almost Nothing*, 1997) is modifying the environment on a planetary scale, and many are asking themselves what they should do so that their existence doesn't mean the end for others. At this juncture, it is wise to recall the reflective words of Admiral Adama (in the American television series *Battlestar Galactica*): "It is not enough to survive. One has to be worthy of survival".[330] Indeed, at this crossroads in human history, this seminal issue is worthy of introspective inquiry. But then, the collateral question is, 'Whose survival and for whose sake and by what metric?' It all hangs on who we believe who we are. For example, if, as philosopher John Gray[331] said "humankind's presence on Earth is nothing but a cancer", then the answer can only be negative. Sheer survival is now the all-embracing preoccupation, and it has dramatically demonstrated that for simply to stay afloat we will bear any burden, undergo any hardship, and endure what was once considered as a punishment, solitary confinement, perhaps even life imprisonment. Still, what allowed us to survive the dark potential of our human creativity is not in the main what we are capable of, but sheer chance. In other words, it is not pluck but luck that has saved us.

But every chance is chancy, all luck runs out, any dare can go wrong, and although the chances of being struck by lightning are low, it does strike, more so when we feel safe or scared. Nonetheless, the subject in question is too critical to be left to random discourse or a structural circumstance. It deserves broader and deeper reflection, particularly at a time when science has set its sights not on survival but on 'infinite survival',

---

[330] *William "Bill" Adama* is a fictional character portrayed by Edward James Olmos in the re-imagined *Battlestar Galactica* television series (2004) produced and aired by the SyFy cable network. Source: Wikipedia: The Free Encyclopedia. Wikimedia Foundation.

[331] Gray, J. 2002. Straw Dogs: Thoughts on Humans and Other Animals. UK: Granta Books.

here or anywhere. Our voyages, ventures, and aspirations in outer space, like space colonization, space settlement and space humanization, and manned-missions to Moon and Mars are primarily intended for human survival. The ethical question is, "Are we, the humans who presently inhabit this hapless earth, worthy of living the way we live *ad infinitum* and in perpetuity?" Put another way, does the human form of life as it is currently constituted, and what it brings on the table, constitute a poisonous package or a palliative package, from the standpoint of life in general and of the needs of nature. Or, as David Benatar asks, "Is human existence worth its consequent harm?" (*Better Never to Have Been: the Harm of Coming Into Existence*, 2006). Although Benatar's conclusion is debatable, one of his arguments is broadly on target: that taking into account both the good and the bad aspects of a person's life, most lives are overall very bad and not worth having. Then again, an additional question is: Whose 'survival' must we ensure when the very meaning of 'human' might be in question? Re-making humans is another priority for science, and we have to factor in how those 'humans' are likely to behave and what would be their effect on the planet and in space. The point of departure for any honest fact-checking is to frontally acknowledge that we have long struggled without much success, in the words of Greek philosopher Aeschylus, to "tame the savageness of man and make gentle the life of this world". We have fallen short, because we did not try to tame that which we should have tamed—our mind—, and change that which we should have changed—our consciousness. Without that, we have, to quote EO Wilson again, a "Star Wars civilization, with Stone Age emotions, medieval institutions, and godlike technology" (*The Social Conquest of Earth*, 2012). Sans consciousness-change, it doesn't matter who the human in question is: present or future or post-human or human-like machine or multi-planetary species or whatever concoction science might put together in the cause or guise of human advancement or 'ascension'. Nothing changes: *Homo homini lupus*—man will continue to be a 'wolf' to another man.

If that were so, is this beautiful planet none the worse if we get abolished or eliminated? Some, like EO Wilson, commonly considered as the world's leading living biologist say, "If all mankind were to disappear, the world would regenerate back to the rich state of equilibrium that existed ten thousand years ago. If insects were to vanish, the environment would collapse into chaos".[332] John Gray puts it succinctly: "The earth will forget mankind. The play of life will go on". Yet we, with almost religious fervor, believe we are what stars are to the sky and that the earth gets its meaning by our presence. In Franz Kafka's iconic *The Trial* (1925), the protagonist, Josef K claims he cannot be guilty as he too is human like the other, to which the priest answers, "But that is how the guilty speak". We are all 'guilty' but, being human, we tend to take credit for the good that we do, but duck from accepting responsibility when things go bad. Does that mean that nature and life in general will be better off from our early departure? Some outcomes, even the most noble ones, should not be brought about if we have to give up everything to achieve them. But then, some skeptic with a sneer might say, 'What is there to become? We already *are!*' What Kafka called 'monstrous vermin'. And an ancient theory (of the Greek philosopher Empedocles) even says that we came from monstrous creatures. Be that as it may, what we now have to ponder over is *what* there is to 'save' in saving the human species, and *why* should we be 'saved' if we 'deserve' destruction. The point is that, as Dostoyevsky's protagonist in *Notes from the Underground* reminds us, man is inevitably so self-destructive, that even if we were to finally reduce human will to a scientific formula that would fix our penchant for death and destruction, we would deliberately go mad, if that is the only way to act against our self-interest. In any case, 'saving life' itself has lost its sheen; it is 'saving one's own life' that, in these Covid-times, is the new name of the game. The French existential philosopher Simone de Beauvoir (*The Ethics of Ambiguity*, 1947) pertinently posited that man, "conscious of being unable to be anything…

---

[332] Wilson, E.O. 1992. The Diversity of Life. New York, USA: The Belknap Press.

then decides to be nothing". And from 'nothing' to moral nihilism is a small step. Let us not turn the Nelson's eye to what stares us in the face: the sole serious threat to our continued existence comes from our own agency, from our own mind. Perhaps the saddest story of our day is that so many of our most creative minds are devoted to doing the wrong things in state-run defense research labs or in the Silicon Valley, or their replicas elsewhere, for professional glory or national duty, or simply for money. As Beatrice Severn of Graham Greene's novel *Our Man in Havana* (1958) puts it, would the 'world be in the mess it is if we were loyal to love and not to countries', or to corporations and to 'people who pay us'? The basic difficulty we face in daily life is that even the most benign of choices can be turned malignant by the human mind mired in malice. While we are capable of cascading empathy, and yet despite its prevalence and importance, empathy is not the only way we respond to others' pain. We are capable of an antipodal ability—to feast on other people's misfortune and misery just for the heck of it; what we might call motiveless malignancy. Indeed, it even harms us more than the one our malice is meant for. It is malice, not violence, that has perverted natural selection, and transformed what should have been a more brainy and benign but 'mischievous monkey', into, in EO Wilson's words, a 'danger to himself and to the rest of life'. With malice firmly in command, as Mephistopheles tells the Lord (Goethe's *Faust*) "man is more bestial than the beast".

Whether it is man or beast, at the end of the day, behavior is what matters. And, as Goethe also reminded, behavior is a mirror in which everyone displays his own image. That 'mirror' is the state of our consciousness. If we are able to change *that* state for the better, then our behavior will become better and we will not be a threat to anyone, much less to ourselves. Viewed from that angle, many other animals rank loftier than the human. What is striking is that, even as an animal, we are actually the microcosm in the matrix of the macrocosm of the entire animal kingdom. That is because all human traits exist—to some degree—in other animals and vice versa, and that is probably because our pasts are interweaved, as Darwin said in his *Descent of Man* (1871). We subsume in us almost all the defining features of other animals—the sociability of a lion, the ferocity of a tiger, the aggressiveness of a wolf, the intelligence of an elephant, the meekness of a lamb, the cunning of a jackal, the nobility of a dog, the venom of a serpent, and the free spirit of a bird. In fact, our gold standard for excellence is what other creatures can do normally. Our ego says if they can do, why not we? If a lowly jellyfish can be literally immortal, why not we? If Blanding's turtles defy ageing and remain capable of reproduction into eight or nine decades of life, why not we? If a certain marine worm can literally sprout new heads (including brains), why not we?

The basic quandary is that our ancestry is animal and our aspiration is divinity; we haven't found a way to build a bridge between the two. That is why, we are, as Marilynne Robinson says, "In every important way, we are such secrets from each other". Most important, we have yet to realize what Hermann Hesse defined as the "greater profundity through internalization" (*Romantic: a Conversation*, 1900). Instead, we are seeking not profundity but perpetuation and perfection of physiology. That, we expect, will give us, to reword Anthony Levandowski, Google's robotics wunderkind, not a god in the sense that it makes lightning or causes hurricanes; but something a billion times smarter than the smartest human. While we now associate smartness with success, some fear that we are raising a generation of youngsters who may be smart but who may also be stupid, or even worse, a threat to themselves and others. A grave risk of developing smart, 'self-aware' machines and partnering with computers is that such a 'being' might not be a benevolent human *deus* but a 'Neuromancer'-type malicious fiend. Still, even with all the attendant risks, we cannot turn our back on our symbiosis with automata, the self-moving machines. The human urge to create androids and artificial life has been expressed across cultures throughout much of human history.

Robots have aided humans in their quests to connect to the divine. We have reached a stage when the tables are turned and the human is coming to be seen as an appendage and add-on to automata, robbed of his identity and integrity. We have to move on two fronts: curb our techno-lust on the one hand, and, on the other hand, develop a *mentalité* or way of thinking *not* dominated by the mind.

Part of being caught up, in Marilynne Robinson's phrase, in the 'blind creep of material culture' is the burning urge to be liberated from all limits, social and sexual, and of life and longevity. There are so many limits we live with but we are not sure 'what limits what'. The only limits we grudgingly acquiesce for fear of punishment are, at best, legal, not moral. But we must remember this passage from the Bible: "All things are lawful for me, but all things are not helpful. All things are lawful for me, but I will not be brought under the power of any".[333] It is our aversion to limits, particularly economic and erotic, that has brought humanity to the present pass. As Alan AtKisson argues, the time has come to deal differently with what he calls the Siamese twins of growth and development. As he puts it, "they must now be separated, or human civilization inevitably will come to a screeching halt".[334] But growth like change is inherent in nature, and even *economic* growth can be virtuous in one place, say in Sub-Saharan Africa, and sinful in North America. This is the downside of globalized cures to local needs. But the basic driving force that underlies is the same: get rich. In that sense, what dominates contemporary life is not economics but 'chrematistics'—relating to, or occupied in the gaining of wealth, which according to Aristotle, is "an unnatural activity that dehumanizes those who practice it". Yet, this unnatural activity is the most sought-after activity. But the fact is, "Wealth is like manure: spread it,

---

[333] Corinthians, 6:12.

[334] AtKisson, A. 1999. *Believing Cassandra: How to Be an Optimist in a Pessimist's World*. USA: Chelsea Green.

and it makes everything grow; pile it up, and it stinks".[335] Fearing that the world is heading towards an impending dystopia or a French-revolution-style uprising against the One Percent, or towards climate collapse or the 'sixth mass extinction', the very rich, being very different (as Scott Fitzgerald famously quipped), are virtually creating an independent 'living infrastructure', complete with things like doomsday bunkers and private firefighters as a part of their Plan B.

In his 1873 novel *Demons*, Dostoyevsky wrote, "In sinning, each man sins against all, and each man is at least partly guilty for another's sin". There is no isolated sin. Bearing in mind the fact that the way a person perceives things depends on their perspective, we need a comprehensive change of our vantage point on the world around, particularly in the way we make choices germane to the three dimensions that dominate our mind and mood: *morality*, *money*, and *mortality*. Almost everything we do or happens in every human life is relatable to at least one of these three. They offer the basis to do what is necessary to ensure that the forces of goodness prevail over the forces of evil in the war within. It is hard to tell if today's incarnation of evil is a symbol of our civilization gone astray or of bare brokenness and brazenness. Whatever or whichever, at the most basic layer, evil itself "is the refusal to see one's self in others."[336] And yet, it is 'others' who make, or wreck, our life. Without others, there is no 'I'. In fact, we cannot see or perceive who we are; others can do a better job. The much-celebrated maxim 'know thyself' or the angst-full question 'how can I be myself' is a chimera because we can see 'out', not 'in', and before we can inquire *how*, we must know *what*. The truth is that, conditioned as we are, we, despite prejudices and biases, are more capable of being less prejudiced and less biased about others than about our own selves. Therefore, let us

---

[335] Giridharadas, A. 2021. The American Dream Is Now In Denmark; a conversation with Danish businessman Djaffar Shalchi about why he wants to make rich people like himself pay more in taxes. *The.Ink.* 23 February 2021.

[336] Powers, R. 2018. The Overstory. New York, USA: W.W. Norton.

not take too lightly what others say about us. Take it, if you will, with a grin and a grain of salt; but dismiss not off hand.

We have long struggled with the question of what permissible violence is, and what purpose it serves. Is revolutionary violence justified? Why do we, good, decent, god-fearing people, have such a good time watching onscreen horrors? More to the point, which aspect of our behavior can be called violent, and what is its opposite—nonviolence, or what Étienne Balibar calls 'antiviolence'? (*Violence and Civility*, 2010). The most pervasive violence is not 'violent'; it is more subtle and insidious. Our ability to get a good night's sleep in the face of the ills of our society is the more dangerous violence. And then, we have what Walter Benjamin called 'divine violence', an attempt at the dissolution of the law in favor of justice, a decision that reaffirms the sovereignty of the self against the coercive violence of the law. In its most elementary sense, as Jainism preaches, even to say '*mine* is the only correct way' is to commit what it describes as an act of epistemic violence (*himsa*). In its most sublime sense, nonviolence means accepting others as a part of who we are. The debate about violence is entirely human in its origin and ambit. Fact is that we are the only animal that is violent, because we *alone* know that we are violent.

Systemic violence—which Slavoj Žižek compares to dark matter in physics (or What Rob Nixon[337] calls 'slow violence', violence that occurs gradually and out of sight)—like evil, is invisible, embedded, stealthy, and seemingly so harmless that it evades any attention. It is irresistible and irreversible. For example, even the most egalitarian among us and those who contend most strongly for draconian actions to combat the evil of climate change, live their entire lives steeped in values and ways of life that are hostile to a sustainable world, and we see no big deal in that. We all think, while leading prosaic and pedestrian lives, that we play no part in making such violence and evil possible, but the truth is

---

[337] Nixon, R. 2011. Slow Violence and the Environmentalism of the Poor. Harvard University Press.

that it is this that makes such a life possible. Climate change, which Rob Nixon describes as the "ultimate form of incremental violence as it is shredding our planet's life-sustaining envelope," is striking evidence. The comforts and conveniences that we take for granted draw their sustenance from such 'subjective evil'. And yet, evil has no independent existence; it piggybacks on our implicit biases, self-centeredness, prejudices, desires, ill will, aspirations, and ambitions. And yet, as Stevenson's *Dr Jekyll* reminds us, "All human beings... are commingled out of good and evil". It therefore means that, as Steinbeck says in *Grapes of Wrath* (1939), "There ain't no sin and there ain't no virtue. There's just stuff people do". They are, as Tolstoy said, interchangeable, and have no status in isolation; they are always relative to each other. But Tolstoy also said that evil cannot be vanquished by evil (*The Kingdom of God Is Within You*, 1893). It can only be subdued and kept under check by good. Each acts as a check against excess, bringing to mind an Italian proverb: *tanto buon che val niente*, which translates as, 'so good, that he is good for nothing'. Our biology does not make us innately good or evil. It is not circumstance but *consciousness* that is the key. As Andrew Kimbrell says, our consciousness has become both dysfunctional and destructive, and we need to change the habits of perception and thinking. And as Owen Barfield[338] aptly reminds us, it is not only what we perceive, but also what we *fail* to perceive, that determines the quality of the world we live in. The Greek philosopher Epicurus once said, "You are but an appearance, and not absolutely the thing you appear to be". Deluded by what Advaita Vedanta calls '*maya*', we see what we expect to see and we have no firm basis for knowing that the attributes we agree that objects have are *really* there. Drawing on the famous *rajju–sarpa–nyaya* ('rope appearing as a serpent') analogy in the Upanishads, a state of mind in which we can get discombobulated by

---

[338] Owen Barfield, British philosopher, poet, and author, among others, of *Saving the Appearances: A Study in Idolatry* (1957).

mistaking a rope for a snake in dim light, we spend all our lives in pursuit of ephemeral appearances.

Another entry point for Andrew Kimbrell's 'cold evil'[339] and what Erika Engelhaupt calls 'cold type of aggression' or proactive aggression[340] into human life are through pursuit of power. Quite apart from Lord Acton's lesser noted axiom that 'great men are almost always bad men, even when they exercise influence and not authority', evil occurs, as JRR Tolkien says, 'when individuals fall to the temptation of wielding power for personal gain'. And when we boast about man's power over nature, it is actually, as CS Lewis reminds us, "A power exercised by some men over other men with nature as its instrument" (*The Abolition of Man*, 1947). In effect, we are violating both nature and man. We must clearly realize that confronting this kind of insidious evil is not possible unless we proactively alter many things that we have taken for granted as trappings of our technological civilization, and make our daily decision-making more moral than now. The ugly truth is that our momentary discords and our abiding individual differences have always prevailed over our shared humanity.

We cannot any more be sanguine that the moral arc of the universe will inevitably bend towards goodness. Our moral arc is so badly bent that it doesn't disturb our sensitivity when our leaders scandalously claim that something so emblematic of evil, the killer drone, is a 'moral weapon', ostensibly because it minimizes or even eliminates collateral casualties, and that making and deploying autonomous weapons is a moral imperative as such weapons 'are less likely to make mistakes than humans in battle'. Clearly, we can never measure up to the billing of a 'moral species' unless we find a way to overcome the twin inabilities that we put on record at the very beginning of this book: why can't *we* be good when we want to; and, why do we do bad when *we* don't want to. Behavior that lets us have it both

---

[339] Kimbrell, A. 2003. Cold Evil: Technology and Modern Ethics. E.F. Schumacher Society.
[340] Engelhaupt, E. 2021. Gory Details: Adventures from the Dark Side of Science. National Geographic.

ways, that allows us to rile against the system but savor its spoils, must be weighed in as unethical. In today's world, we have to rethink 'virtue' as an enabling input to reforming society; we have to bring it closer to social, ecological, and intergenerational symbiosis. And there is no longer any moral excuse not to extend the golden rule of virtue—'do unto others as you would have them do unto you'—to unborn generations (the estimated 6.75 trillion people over 50,000 years,) who vastly outnumber those who have so far lived and now live (100 billion). At the societal level, we must endeavor to expand the rule to include what Jacqueline Novogratz says: "Give more to the world than you take from it" (*Manifesto for a Moral Revolution: Practices to Build a Better World*, 2020). It is so simple: in every situation and in every relationship, if we try 'consciously' to give more than we take, we can deprive evil the legs to stand upon. Nothing good will happen unless we put a full stop to our senseless and suicidal war on nature, to borrow the words of the United Nations Secretary General, António Guterres,[341] and unless we revaluate and reset our relationship with nature. We have to go back to the drawing board and, drawing on nature's own design principles, make sense of the world, and set in motion a total transformation in our values, goals, and collective behavior. In short, we need to change the basis of our global civilization. We must move from a civilization based on wealth accumulation to one that is life-affirming: an ecological civilization.[342]

Fact is that far above and beyond the day-to-day fears and flash points capturing our attention, humanity is seamlessly slipping into the throes of what Saint John of the Cross (16th century) called "the dark night (of the soul)". Eckhart Tolle portrays it as the "Collapse of a perceived meaning in life… an eruption into your life of a deep sense of meaninglessness". We

---

[341] United Nations Environment Programme. 2021. Making Peace with Nature: a Scientific Blueprint To Tackle the Climate, Biodiversity and Pollution Emergencies. Nairobi, Kenya. <https://www.unep.org/resources/making-peace-nature>.

[342] Lent, J. 2021. Transforming to an Ecological Civilization: The Alternative Is Unthinkable. Common Dreams. *YES! Magazine*. 19 February 2021.

have sacrificed ourselves to our own fantasies. We have 'dehumanized' so much of human life that it has turned into paralyzing despair. Everyone is suffering but does nothing to end it. We truly think we can survive even if the species is crippled. What it is all a prelude to remains to be experienced. Tolstoy wrote in the introduction to his book *My Religion* (1885) that after he went through a sudden transformation, he realized that he was 'nailed to a life of suffering and evil by an incomprehensible power'. What is paradoxical is that, as the Buddhist scholar Shantideva once said, we want to shrink suffering but love its causes (*The Way of the Bodhisattva*). Oscar Wilde, who surely 'suffered' suffering more than most, just out of prison and in exile, wrote, "To me, suffering seems now a sacramental thing, that makes those whom it touches holy" (*The Complete Letters of Oscar Wilde*, 1962). As it has often been said, 'there are some who have never sinned, but there is no one who has never suffered. In that sense, we are all united by what Peter Zapffe's *The Last Messiah* (1933) called "the brotherhood of suffering between everything alive". That is why Arthur Schopenhauer said it is more appropriate to call ourselves 'fellow-sufferers' than fellow men. And Dostoyevsky, who dived deep into the depths of human nature, once wrote that the only thing we need to dread is not to be worthy of suffering. In a similar vein, we should dread being 'weak enough to pride ourselves upon our sufferings', to echo the words of the Count of Monte Cristo, in Alexandre Dumas' 1846 novel by the same name. This implies that a state of suffering can be cathartic. In a world totally free of trouble, toil, and suffering, Schopenhauer predicted that "Some men would die of boredom or hang themselves, some would fight and kill one another, or there would be wars, massacres, and murders" (*On the Suffering of the World*, 1850). Such a characterization fits like a glove for humanity at the present juncture. So much in the world feels dead now, or dying, and we don't know how to respond to that—with grief, or glee and relief, or with rage.

What it all means is that if we want to change our self-destructive way of thinking, and arrest, in HG Well's words, the "headlong swoop to death", we need to spawn and spark consciousness-cleansing at its deepest depth. The takeaway message is that, as Einstein said, "No problem can be solved from the same consciousness that created it". Perhaps the biggest task and challenge man faces is to make our living heart-based and our consciousness heart-centric. For, as Saint-Exupéry once said, "One sees clearly only with the heart. Anything essential is invisible to the eye". The good news is that the weapons to win this war are made by us by how we live; what can be simpler than that? The war within is the only path to incubate and imbibe a *new image of humanity*, and bring to pass a more humane, more holistic sense of our self, in all its frailty and vulnerability. It is the only formula for what psychologists call self-actualization, and what the Upanishads call 'Self-realization'. But what we are striving to achieve is technological singularity, not spiritual self-realization. Unless and until we acknowledge this and act accordingly, the world will continue to dawdle towards disaster by some name or the other. The point to remember is that human personality is not static; it is changing constantly but in the wrong way, because the forces of evil are increasingly assertive in the war within. That is because evil in the world outside is becoming more aggressive day by day and abomination is at its height.

Can We Win This War?

When we routinely talk about the world, it is both an abstraction and a red herring. No one cares for or speaks for the world. At best, beyond our own selves, we care for our family, community, or corporation or country—not for the world. Given a chance, we will perhaps do to other worlds what we are doing down here: make them uninhabitable to any life. Yet, in our mind there is nothing wrong: *What else is earth for?* Hasn't God given us the unfettered hegemony over earth and over what it contains? We have to change such a state of mind and come to accept that sharing the earth with other species is a part of that divine mandate. Indeed, we cannot set right our moral apathy, and earn any reparation or redemption, unless we learn to treat all biotic life as one of us, worthy of the same concern and consideration. The ugly fact is that humankind is testing the limits of the very space in which we live. There is now mounting awareness, articulated by philosophers like Timothy Morton, that becoming humane actually calls for creating a network of kindness and solidarity with nonhuman beings, in the name of a broader understanding of reality (*Humankind: Solidarity with Nonhuman People*, 2017). For peace of mind, we need the mind to be in its proper place. And for peace on earth, we need our behavior to be benign. For that we have to change our 'self-perception'. The truth is that much of our angst, anxiety, and agony, and the emergent emergency situation we are in, all stem from a simple fact: the *wrong* intelligence (mind) is in command of our consciousness. We are looking in the *wrong* place (outer space and cyberspace), and we are not even conscious of the odyssey that matters most: the boundless immensity of inner space. The Upanishads say that whatever we know in this world, or not know, is contained in this infinite space inside each of us. Billionaires are busy developing technologies for an emergency escape to an outpost in outer space as yet unspoiled by their own parasitic practices, some sort of a hedger against an earthly apocalypse. It is being predicted that soon, say, by the year 2047, 'human intelligence will be expanding into the universe at the speed of light'. That is, we will then be effectively infecting the cosmos with the contagion of the already failed human intelligence. That will be a greater catastrophe than the end of this world. What is worse is that modernity has converted our living space into what Rem Koolhaas calls 'junkspace'. In his words, "If space-junk is the human debris that litters the universe, *junk-space* is the residue mankind leaves on the planet. Junkspace is what remains after modernization has run its course or, more precisely, what coagulates while modernization is in progress, its fallout".[343] We have long viewed human progress as synonymous with being better, but 'better' itself got contaminated as material movement.

---

[343] Koolhaas, R. 2001. Junkspace. The Harvard Design School Guide to Shopping.

What we are face to face with is a fork on the road before us: the path of goodness, struggle, service, and sacrifice—or the path of vice, ease, pleasure, and comfort. For, rephrasing the Greek poet Hesiod, "Evil can be easily found, and freely; what the gods have set upon the way to goodness". There are clear clues that we have perhaps already gone too far on the wrong road. One of them is the very way we perceive each other, that with ill will, crumbling trust, envy, and animosity. We think that if we give, we give away. We must learn to live the way the Buddha outlined when he said, "If you light a lamp for somebody, it will also brighten your path. Thousands of candles can be lit from a single candle, and the life of the candle will not be shortened". The place to begin is where we are, and with the people in the proximate 'acting one at a time, upon those beside them'. For, to steal a line from Dostoyevsky, it is easier to sacrifice in the cause of humanity than not be nasty to the next man. What we don't realize is that the one we view as an 'enemy' also views us the same way, and the truth is, as poet HW Longfellow reminded us, "If we could read the secret history of our enemies, we should find in each man's life sorrow and suffering enough to disarm all hostility" (*Drift-wood*, 1857). Put differently, as the American comic strip *Pogo* famously declared, "*We have Met the Enemy and He is Us!*" (1913 poster for Earth Day). Perhaps the last word about the state of sublime suffering is what Martin Luther King Jr so eloquently spoke of in reference to his opponents: "Be assured that we will wear you down by our capacity to suffer". Such a sublime state of coexistence is impossible without an entirely different mindset than the blinkered one we have. In our own times, the thinker and writer Charles Haanel[344] wrote, "There is a world within—a world of thought and feeling and power; of light and beauty, and although invisible, its forces are mighty". And the American poet Wallace Stevens reminded us that 'the world about us would be desolate except for the world within'.

---

[344] Charles Haanel, American philosopher and author of *The Master Key System* (1916).

But then, not only is there a world within, but also, as Thomas Browne (*Religio Medici*, 1643) says, "There is another man within that's angry".

Whatever happens in the outer world is but a reflection and projection of what happens in the world within. What is happening in there is a process that we call war in the outside world; it is a war between our own innate instincts, emotions, and impulses. According to biologist Jeremy Griffith, our good and evil conflicted, psychologically upset lives are the result of the underlying battle between our original instinctive self and our newer conscious self (*Freedom*, 2016). But he also says that humans are "not just good but the heroes of the story of life on Earth!" Joseph Murphy expresses the same idea in terms of psychology, and says, "Life events are actually the result of the workings of your conscious and subconscious minds" (*The Power of Your Subconscious Mind*, 2015). We have always struggled to cross boundaries and go beyond, and that has given us a pyrrhic-victory. What we should aim at is, in the words of the Jedi master Yoda, to '*grow* beyond' (*Star Wars: the Last Jedi*, 2017). Going beyond is physical and external; growing beyond is spiritual and internal.

Essentially, the warring forces are of two kinds: on the one side, what the Bible calls 'Fruit of the Holy Spirit'—love, joy, peace, patience, kindness, goodness, faithfulness, gentleness, self-abnegation. And on the other side, the opposites—hatred, misery, insouciance, intolerance, cruelty, evil, treachery, insensitivity, and intemperance. Put in Jungian terms, it is a war between the *persona* (what we would like to be, and how we wish to be seen by the world), and the *shadow* (the unconscious mind, which is composed of repressed ideas, instincts, impulses, weaknesses, longings, perversions, and embarrassing fears). It is interesting to note that the word *persona* itself is derived from a Latin word that literally means 'mask', implying that the personality we project is nothing but a collection of masks. And it is hilarious that we now live at a time when wearing a mask is not only socially chic but also a life-saving. Then again, we never show our 'real face' sans an invisible mask; we always put on a face to suit the need.

The fact that the wrong side is winning in this war accounts for why we are so easily succumbing to polarization, tribalism, xenophobia, and sectarianism, and why we are unable to strike a common storyline to tackle complex topics. It explains the apathy of the good and the allure of the evil, bringing to mind what WB Yeats wrote a century ago: "The best lack all conviction, while the worst are full of passionate intensity" (*The Second Coming*, 1919). Whether we are able to manage our mental and emotional fragility at a time of transformative turbulence and convulsive chaos—and whether enough of us can see ourselves as part of a larger '*Us*' instead of an atomized '*I*'—hinges on what happens in this war. In fact, much of our greed and sorrow comes from the nagging feeling of not having enough of anything we want—mostly money. But that 'more money' is not made out of thin air. Long ago, Victor Hugo wrote that "The paradise of the rich is made out of the hell of the poor".[345] The way to redress the situation is to address our mindset about rich and poor. We must move towards an ideal that Epicurus described: "The rich man is not the man who has the most, but rather the man who needs the least. Do not spoil what you have by desiring what you have not; remember that what you have now was once among the things you only hoped for". We must also move away from a way of life that is often described as a ruthless rat race, a no-holds-barred and take-no-prisoners, pointless, self-defeating pursuit. Firstly, rats don't run the rat race; humans are the ones always in a rush and in every race. Secondly, as someone quipped, "The trouble with being in the rat race is that even if you win, you're still a rat"—and as science tells us, always will be.

Part of the difficulty of winning this war is that the ideas, instruments, and strategies we adopt to wage and win the wars of the world are inappropriate for this war. This war is a strange war which we have no choice but to wage, but which, for our own good, we should not aim to 'win'. Worse, we don't even know how to acquire the tools and the skills to

---

[345] Victor Hugo. 1869. The Man Who Laughs.

do the job. Its very complexity is rivalled by its criticality. If we want to be in the main a moral being and not remain, in the phrase of Oscar Wilde, a 'simple beast', if we want to mend and better our behavior, then we need to ensure that the forces of light and goodness (i.e., of the persona) dominate over the forces of evil and venality—of our shadow self. But paradoxically, we also have to ensure that not only the evil side, *but also the 'good' side*, does not totally triumph. For, as Oscar Wilde reminded us, "Darkness and light are not opposing forces. Rather they are a complementary couple, that only together form a whole... Nothing is purely dark or light, good or bad".

In the hectic humdrum of what it takes to live through a day, we are waylaid at every turn. And riled and weary, as Steinbeck says, "Ever'body in the whole damn world is scared of each other" (*Of Mice and Men*, 1937). While the wound is hemorrhaging inside, we are busy trying to break away from our terrestrial roots aiming to become a multiplanetary 'godly' species. We must be clear what godly really amounts to. It means that man plans to unite with god by way of making himself god-like, that is, by acquiring for himself the qualities and capacities which we (till now) experienced as 'divine'. Biblically put, we are trying to, so to speak, 'cancel' the Fall, by way of somehow getting rid of the obstacle of our finite bodily existence. For God Himself said, "Behold, Adam has become like one of us".[346] Our delusionary dream of divinity—which in itself is part of our dysfunctional cognitive reasoning—runs counter to the reconstructive vision of Emerson: every man is a divinity in disguise, a god playing the fool. While exploring so many ways to survive any nasty life-threatening risks, what we are ignoring is the root cause, our self-righteous and self-destructive mindset.

The sorry state of the world raises a sneaking suspicion in our ever-scheming mind. What is the divine intent in making the human alone so venal and vulnerable, and allowing him to lead such a shallow and sinful life? There are a growing number of angst-filled people who are under

---

[346] Genesis, 3:22.

the sway of relentless panic. They fear that *Homo sapiens* have caused so much damage to the planet already that the only thing that can restore the balance is for humanity to go extinct, and the only 'orderly' way to do that is by refusing to procreate. As if prompted by an 'inner voice'— divine or devilish we don't know—some of them are asking themselves the discomfiting question: are kids bad for the planet? Or, is it the other way around? Who is better off without whom? Either way, it is being suggested that this might be the most ethical choice when it comes to our desire to be a responsible parent in the Anthropocene Age, a time when the sum of individual human choices has an effect beyond the passing of generations, or even civilizations. Interestingly, Arthur Schopenhauer anticipated it in a different dimension (*On the Sufferings of the World*, 1850). He said, "If children were brought into the world by an act of pure reason alone, would the human race continue to exist? Would not a man rather have so much sympathy with the coming generation as to spare it the burden of existence? Or at any rate not take it upon himself to impose that burden upon it in cold blood?" This debate is also a portend of a coming inverted intergenerational divide, a time when kids might well admit that, as Lydia Millet's novel puts it, "Hiding our parentage was a leisure pursuit, but one we took seriously" (*A Children's Bible*, 2020). And homes might have a 'parents-free zone'. Through the prism of our posterity, perhaps the egregious terror of all that we face is the dystrophic alienation of the young, many of whom feel like 'troubled guests on the dark earth'.

We don't know which doomsday scenario will eventually unfold when our time is done, and maybe we wouldn't even know if we are already in one; we are incapable of knowing. But a high probability is that it is not human numbers, but reckless and rapacious human behavior, and wanton waste and egregious inequalities of wealth and opportunity, or, as Nobel Laureate Kazuo Ishiguro[347] hints, 'savage meritocracies that

---

[347] Kazuo Ishiguro, Nobel Prize in Literature (2017), and author of *Never Let Me Go* (2005) and *The Remains of the Day* (1989).

resemble apartheid' triggered by runaway technological change. Basically, we just do not know what we should do with ourselves and with our time on the planet. What we have done, nonetheless, in tune with our material mindset, is to marshal our brains and bodies as, in the words of philosopher Susan Schneider, "an arena for future profit".[348] What is even more baneful is that we culturally equate efficiency with money and profit. But, as Barry Schwartz says, one lesson from the corona crisis "is that to be better prepared next time, we need to learn to live less efficiently in the here and now" (*Why We Work*, 2015). The focus has to be not doing better but doing better things.

Modern man looks strikingly similar to Nietzsche's *Last Man*—"An apathetic creature with no great passion or commitment. Unable to dream, tired of life, he takes no risks, seeking only comfort and security, an expression of tolerance with one another". Assuming that we have reached some sort of a dead end, what should we do? Ironically, we take pride in our 'unique' ability to make choices, but 'chosen' death is still a taboo. But then, 'chosen' itself is not that chosen; most are forced, forced by circumstance to feel that their death would solve everything for everyone. Such a feeling can be shared by all and sundry, the low and mighty, a divine Avatar, an American prima donna, a member of the British royalty, a famous author, or a faceless riffraff. Perhaps one of man's greatest weaknesses is his mind's overpowering obsession to convince, convert, and control everyone and everything, be it another human or another species or even god, with one solitary exception: his own self. In fact, since the archaic times, man has chafed under the feeling that he has suffered under the control of gods and, in spirit, our scientific zeal to become a 'god' is a way of vengeance. In so doing, man is trying to erase the ontological distinction between God and his creation. But yet, we are not that stupid. A *de facto*, let alone *de*

---

[348] Cited in: Horgan, J. 2020. Who Wants to Be a Cyborg? Philosopher Susan Schneider Weighs the Pros and Cons of Radical Technological Enhancement. Scientific American. 21 July 2020.

jure, god is not really our goal; it is the model and means to leapfrog the evolutionary ladder. We don't want to appear and disappear, nor, like gods, bestow boons. The godhood we aspire to acquire is also anthropocentric; even as a flight of fancy we visualize God as someone who has qualities and abilities we lack. But it is not that anodyne. There is an unsaid, maybe even unconscious, intent: we want to take what we envy but discard what is irksome even from gods and angels, and not give up what we like about human life. We want to reverse ageing and defang death, but we want to walk on our feet, not float. We want to carry our gadgets, play sports and see movies, have sex, but maybe no kids. We want to 'look good', not *be* good, or eat or breathe good. What we are aiming at is very different from what the ancient *rishis* of India strived towards, through intense *tapas* or deep meditation, and spiritual *sadhana*, or practice. Their goal then was not to *become* a Greek god or a Hindu *deva* but to attain a state of God-consciousness. It was said that in the ashrams of such rishis there was perfect concord in the animal kingdom, such as the one envisioned in the Hebrew Bible when the "wolf will dwell with the lamb" and "the lion will eat straw like the ox".[349] Our consciousness is ego-driven, and by trying to become gods, we are not trying to overcome our ego or vanity, or our frailties and our propensity for evil.

Even if we are not yet gods, we have erected many 'gods' whom we worship, like technology, the marketplace, money, and the algorithm. Experts tell us that 'in the future, warfare will pit algorithm against algorithm'. But we also know that no algorithm can fix a broken system; it only inherits the flaws of the system it is placed in. Many great masters of thought and philosophers have speculated about what the theosophist-cum-atheist Annie Besant framed as *"What is that which men call God?"* Some drew a distinction between 'possibility of the existence of God' and the 'possibility of the existence of that God in whom the orthodox exhorted us to trust'. Nietzsche's answer was, "It doesn't any more matter: because

---

[349] Isaiah, 11:6–7.

God is dead! God remains dead! And we have killed him! How shall we console ourselves, the most murderous of all murderers?" In effect, what Nietzsche is saying is that our idea of God is no longer strong enough to serve as the foundation for truth and morality. That, in fact, is truer now than then. In our post-truth world, with the advent of vocabulary like the 'new normal' and 'alternative facts', morality is pushed into the company of weaklings and wimps.

We are very close to creating, like in Aldous Huxley's *Brave New World*, a society that pops pills to eradicate any vestige of negative feelings and to take flight from the drudgery and doldrums of dreary living. We also need to get a grip on technological change and inject into it what Kevin Kelly calls the 'spiritual dimension and direction'—those intangible forces whose existence we become aware of only through the effects they produce. We need to upgrade our consciousness, and the war within is the conduit for that purpose. Upgrading one's consciousness is also, in the words of Hermann Hesse, to 'find a way to himself' or, as Rumi puts it, a 'long journey into yourself'. As Hesse elaborates, "Down in the weird waters of consciousness, it is only ourselves who can go wading through our selves".

Truth is that, with the genre of consciousness we have, as Robert Burton wrote, "We love the world too much; God too little; our neighbor not at all, or for own ends" (*Anatomy of Melancholy*, 1621). At the most elemental level, we must shift our gaze inwards, and focus on the world within. It is this *truth* that will set us free. And we must focus on the *war* within, which scriptures like the Quran and saints like Saint Paul have spoken about. We now have an urgent duty cut out for us. Invade our own world within to initiate corrective action, which will set right what ails the world outside. The voyage within, it has long been said, is a most important and difficult journey. Scientists envision that space travel, even time travel, are not impossible. But we find it impossible to take the first step towards the travel within.

When his disciples were weeping at his impending death, the Buddha admonished them and said, "Be a light unto yourself; be a refuge to yourself". We seldom realize that any radical realignment is made up, not of peak experiences, but of many imperfect and fleeting, boilerplate circumstances. Part of the reason why we fall and fail in our own esteem is our niggling feeling that the problem is deeper: that what we are trying to do or achieve is what we shouldn't be doing, much of which is unnecessary or downright dangerous. But as Kathryn Schulz tells us, "We need to learn to love the flawed, imperfect things that we create, and to forgive ourselves for creating them" (*Being Wrong: Adventures in the Margin of Error*, 2011). The future of our species depends on how we learn to live with everything we 'give life to' with our inventive ability. The Stoic philosopher Panaetius (c185–109 BCE) suggested that it is the middlebrow man, trying and failing to be good, who deserves to be taken up as the moral benchmark. As the Tibetan Buddhist dharma teacher Lama Elizabeth Monson puts it across, "Encountering the sacred in our lives and learning how to view every aspect of our lives as sacred can shift the very ground on which we stand" (*Pilgrimage Unbound*, 2019). Homer says, "There is nothing alive more agonized than man, of all that breathe and crawl across the earth".[350] Much of that agony stems from man's frustration with the cultural need to choose one of the two, good or evil. That puts tremendous pressure on many who are not moral mahatmas, and raises questions like 'Just how bad are good people allowed to be?' Barred from all 'badness', they will, at some time in their lives, succumb to their evil inclinations. The Book of Ecclesiastes, said to have been written by King Solomon, clearly tells us, "Indeed, there is no one on earth who is righteous, no one who does what is right and never sins".[351] Some argue that evil, like everything else, has no legs to stand on except as a part of divine design. Others posit that evil is nothing but the absence of good, or that it is independent. We

---

[350] Homer, *The Iliad*, Book 17.

[351] Book of Ecclesiastes, 7:20.

often wonder how to choose among conflicting choices. In the Indian epic Mahabharata, the wise minister Vidura gave us the proper perspective: "To save a family, abandon a man; to save the village, abandon a family; to save the country, abandon a village; to save the soul, abandon the earth".

Robert Wright elaborates: "Human beings are a species splendid in their array of moral equipment, tragic in their propensity to misuse it, and pathetic in their constitutional ignorance of the misuse" (*The Moral Animal*, 1994). It means that, as we all know well, it is easy to do bad, but difficult to do good. As Anton Chekhov said, "Happiness does not exist, nor should it, and if there is any meaning or purpose in life, they are not in our peddling little happiness, but in something reasonable and grand. Do good!" (*Gooseberries*, 1898). Evil thrives because we choose not to know; that enables us not to bear the burden of consequences of this knowledge, so that we can continue acting as if we don't know it. As Slavoj Žižek phrases it so succinctly, "I know it, but I don't want to know that I know, so I don't know (*Violence: Six Sideways Reflections*, 2007). Even then the reality is that, as Aleksandr Solzhenitsyn said, "The line dividing good and evil cuts through the heart of every human being. And who is willing to destroy a piece of his own heart?" Kahlil Gibran said, "For what is evil but good tortured by its own hunger and thirst? Verily when good is hungry it seeks food even in dark caves, and when it thirsts it drinks even of dead waters". And, as a kind of a faint flicker of hope to those of us who often fail to do good and feel awful about it, Gibran's *Prophet* reassures, "You are good in countless ways, and you are not evil when you are not good". So, if evil is but a 'hungry' good, and we are not evil if we are not good, then why all this angst and remorse about not being good? Just the same, many scriptures and wise men have told us that good and evil actually need each other, but like siblings they are constantly at war with each other. Echoing scriptures like the Quran, the Bible, and the Bhagavad Gita, Eric Burdon tells us, "Inside each of us, there is the seed of both good and evil. It's a constant struggle as to which one will win. And one cannot exist without the other". It really means that statements and questions like 'why we seem drawn to evil more than to goodness' and 'why goodness everywhere appears to be in terminal retreat' can be answered only in the light of the war within.

Perhaps what we should do is to take a leaf from God's book from the way God Himself copes with and handles evil. He treads a fine line, doing a kind of balancing act. He accepts evil in the world but vows to protect the righteous. But when evil becomes suffocating, He intervenes in favor of the virtuous. He slew many *rakshasas* not because they denied and defied Him, but because they threatened and made life difficult for the virtuous who are also His devotees. To establish or restore dharma or righteousness does not mean that evil or wickedness should not exist on earth; it means it cannot be allowed to overwhelm righteousness and goodness. In the present scenario, some believe that the coronavirus is a kind of 'an epidemiological housecleaning of sorts'. Or an angry avatar, a divine signal that He is increasingly getting annoyed, if not enraged, with evil becoming almost the unbidden mode of human life on earth. It is also essential to note that the ambit of dharma, like Brahman in the Upanishads, is beyond narrow or rigid codification, and it is central not only to Hinduism but also to Buddhism, Jainism, and Sikhism. A celebrated aphorism in Hindu scriptures says, *Dharmo rakshati rakshitaha*—'dharma protects those who uphold dharma'. If we act in accordance with dharma in daily life, then dharma will ensure that good will remain dominant over evil in the war within. Restoration of the dharmic equilibrium is the spirit of the famous and solemn declaration of Lord Krishna in the Bhagavad Gita that He will incarnate from age to age on earth. We must note that He is not saying he will eradicate or exorcize evil from earth; what he incarnates for is to restore the dharmic balance on earth, which is also, in spirit, the purpose of the Second Coming of Jesus Christ.

But then, why and when, and under what conditions, does evil become so overwhelming on earth that God is left no choice but to personally and directly descend? It is said in the Bible that God might have not destroyed Sodom and Gomorrah had there been even ten virtuous men on earth at that time. One wonders what that number could be in our age. The question is, what would have been the divine primary motive: saving the good humans or destroying the insidious evil? Or, establishing the right balance between good and evil on earth, the numbers known only to God? In fact, balance is, in Hindu *dharma shastras*, a critical dimension to what is good and what is evil or bad. Good is represented, among other things, by balance, and evil is represented by imbalance. At least, we can feel a little lighter about one thing. After the devastation of Sodom and Gomorrah, God vowed, "I will never again curse the ground on account of man, for the intent of man's heart is evil from his youth; and I will never again destroy every living thing, as I have done".[352] That means that even if God does destroy much of, if not all of, mankind, the earth and other living beings would endure. That facile and false premise robs us of the guilt that on account of us the rest of life on earth will get destroyed. That is God's choice and Man's Fate.[353] However much we augment or reinforce ourselves and our sense organs, we cannot be foolproof or flawless, impregnable or immaculate. The main reason we have failed in our efforts towards human betterment is because we think the appropriate instrument to that end is our intellectual or 'reasoning capacity', which we are now told can soon be enhanced through 'gene-editing technology'. But as John Gray points out, "If Euripides is the most tragic of the Greek playwrights, it is not because he deals with moral conflicts but because he understood that reason cannot be the guide of life" (*Straw Dogs*, 2002).

---

[352] Genesis 8:21.

[353] Bhimeswara Challa. 2011. Man's Fate and God's Choice: An Agenda for Human Transformation. UK: Trafford.

From Akrasia to Enkrateia

The way to achieve such a goal is the *way within*. Every other way we have tried, but have found ourselves stymied, stranded at the skin level. On the battlefields of this war are two key players: *consciousness-change* within, and *contextual-change* without. A big part of both is to pivot our lives away from mind-mindedness. We cannot fix the world outside without fixing the world inside. If we allow evil to overwhelm the good inside our consciousness, how can the good overwhelm the bad outside? Many of our ills, and much of the evil, have now gone beyond 'singular-centric'; they are embedded, entrenched, institutional, and systemic. We live in a world where horrific crimes are committed every day with our sanction, in our name and allegedly for our good by those whom we elect or allow to rule over us for our good, and yet we feign innocence, ignorance, and moral revulsion.

Albeit still shaky and scant, the relief we expect rests on two counts. One, there are, in the midst of the current disarray and desperation in, to copy the words of Polish Nobel laureate Olga Tokarczuk,[354] "a world that has become a broken heap of people, things, and events", signs of a subtle shift towards a resurrection of faith and spiritual rebirth. As WB Yeats says, "Surely some revelation is at hand" (*The Second Coming*, 1920). These are prescient signs of what the Greeks called 'cosmopolitanism', a sense of global citizenship, and of cosmic consciousness with or without religious affiliation. Across the world, there is a growing, albeit still muted, recognition that we are responsible for each other and accountable to future generations. As an antique Irish proverb says, 'It is in the shelter of each other that the people live'. Second, we now have the technical means to connect and to synergize disparate and isolated efforts. Fact is that the very technology that has brought us to the edge of the precipice can, if we have the needed wisdom, now serve as the infrastructure for

---

[354] Olga Tokarczuk, Nobel Prize in Literature (2018), and author of *The Books of Jacob* (2014) and *Flights* (2017).

consciousness-change and contextual-change. But such wisdom cannot come through intelligence or intellect, however much we may boost it. We must tap a deeper dimension of our being. Much will hinge on how the most potent force in the world—technology—will impact and affect the human way of life. What we have to ask ourselves at this point is this: the way technology developed since, say, the age of the Greeks and Romans, has it improved human civilization? It will most probably turn us into some kind of 'global tribe'; and it will be left to us to choose if we want to be a tranquil tribe or a warring tribe. If it is the former, then it will pave the way to, in the words of Deepak Chopra, "more collective creativity, collective problem-solving, collective well-being and collective intention as to what we want". Before that, we must accept our 'collective guilt' and its double 'collective punishment', for what all humans have exacted on the planet and other species.

We need a new angle of vision to look at the totality of what living entails. As Jane Goodall puts it, "You cannot get through a single day without having an impact on the world around you. What you do makes a generative difference, and you have to decide what kind of difference you want to make".[355] That difference we can make by how we live, we should realize, is not only to the world we live in, but also to the war within. The practical way is to constantly and consciously try to put someone else on par or above yourself in any reckoning or, to borrow a phrase from William E Henley, "in the fell clutch of circumstance" (*Invictus*, 1888). Concretely, it means putting our sense organs (what in Hinduism are called our *jnanendriyas*) to good use, consciously and deliberately. However much we may try, we cannot entirely dodge existential threats, some of which are now not even on the table, like, for example, as Bill Gates suggests, 'bioterrorism', or what Albert Camus alludes to as those 'that crash down on our heads from a blue sky' (*The Plague*, 1947). The fact is that we cannot avert that which we do not even know about, or envision

---

[355] Goodall, J. 1998. Reason for Hope: A Spiritual Journey.

or apprehend. And you cannot abort human creativity even if it is warped, wicked, or malicious. What the fusion of science and technology has done is to empower and upgrade human innovative capability so much that a single human brain can do what a few decades ago might have needed a 'brigade of brains'. When technologies like man-machine-merger and singularity become operational, there is no knowing what kind of threat it will throw up. The only way is to go to the source: that is, the mind-controlled, corrupted, and compromised human consciousness. If we don't face up to this main malaise, we might soon cross the limits of what Mark Lynas's new book calls the "coping abilities of our civilization" (*Our Final Warning: Six Degrees of Climate Emergency*, 2020). It doesn't mean that we have to go back to our caveman days, or mankind's pre-agricultural times or even pre-industrial times, or give up on modern technology. It does mean that we give up the *war on nature* that we have been waging, and turn our attention to the war within. What we must fully digest is that we are by no means masters of the universe, but we are also not hopelessly helpless in fashioning our future. We can mold it through a virtuous life, which distills into something startlingly simple: try to practice the dictum of Dorothea Brooke, the heroine of George Eliot's *Middlemarch*: "To make life less difficult for everyone you crisscross, collide, and caress every day". Or, to make it more affirmative, in the words of Joseph Campbell,[356] "The ultimate aim of the quest must be neither release nor ecstasy for oneself, but the wisdom and the power to serve others". What we must understand is that 'service is a two-way street'. Serving others, we work on ourselves; and when we work on ourselves, we better serve others.

The key question then is: how can we extract breakaway changes in the current archetype of human life? We cling to what we think we know, as we can no longer imagine a stand-in that wouldn't be even worse. No amount of enhancement of bodily organs or alterations in our sin-soaked life-style or manipulations (of brain) and mergers (with the machine) will

---

[356] Joseph Campbell, author of *The Hero With a Thousand Faces* (1949).

do. A new study has found that the human body has shown an alarming adaptation to technology used in daily life. A recent newspaper headline says it all: 'Mobile users develop horns'.[357] The call of the day is to take honest cognizance of what Carl Jung called, at the individual level, the shadow, and, more particularly, confess and cleanse what the website *LonerWolf* calls 'collective shadow', humanity's sinister side—the sum total of past and present atrocities, cruelties, tragedies, and ghastly horrors perpetrated by humankind and stored at a deep, unconscious, cellular level, all of which we have internalized, in various degrees and ways, at the visceral level. The way to get a handle on them is to get a grip on the three 'M's of *morality, money,* and *mortality.* And without that we cannot ensure that Lincoln's 'better angels of our nature'[358] will prevail over the 'domestic demons' in our consciousness. Money we love; morality we don't mind, and mortality we detest. What we need to do is make money less of a love; morality more central; and mortality not so loathsome. This is the real revolution we should aim to trigger in our life, a 'transformative wave of modification', more anatomic and titanic, more cathartic and metamorphic, than what has occurred or has been attempted in human history.

The simple point is this. We are capable and have the skill and tools necessary to overcome every crisis we face, and to fulfill every aspiration of ours, provided it is righteous and just. What are dragging us down are two: our endogenous enemies and our obsessive 'fandom' for material possessions. These can only be surmounted at our deepest depth, and the way is to see that the forces of evil do not dominate and dictate the dynamics of the war within. Instead, what we must do is to reinforce their strength through how we lead our lives. The American psychologist and philosopher William James said over a century ago that "The

---

[357] Source: Bending Forward Is Affecting Form: Mobile Users Develop Horns. *The Deccan Chronicle*, Hyderabad, India. 22 Jun 2019. p.8.

[358] Abraham Lincoln's first inaugural address, delivered on Monday, 4 March 1861.

greatest revolution of our generation is the discovery that human beings, by changing their intrinsic attitudes, can change the outer aspects of their lives". But nothing has happened since then because we did not sufficiently realize that to mastermind such a metamorphosis warrants waging and winning this War. What we, in the words of Bill Plotkin, "behold [is] the possibility of a radical and foundational shift in human culture—from a suicidal, life-destroying element to a way of life worthy of our unique human potential and of earth's dream for itself".[359] The truth is that from the pristine days there were people and places, there has been a sort of forlorn longing for other, different people, and ideal, perfect places. But the scale and enormity of structural changes needed in today's world is so seismic and cosmic that none of us are constitutionally capable of even imagining, let alone thinking or configuring. What goes as our 'imagination', more than thinking, is what stands in the way of our future. For all its sophistication, our capacity to imagine surrogate states is deeply deficient. Even our fondest imaginings fall far short of complete immersion.

Saint John of the Cross wrote, "If a man wishes to be sure of the road he's traveling on, then he must close his eyes and travel in the dark". When your eyes are closed, only your intuition, not intelligence, can guide you. We are so consumed by our work outside that we are not even aware that the real work is within—in the sanctum sanctorum of the soul, what some describe as 'ensoulment'. The real impediment is that none of us have the tools and the kit needed to do the such work. If we do not even know what the right raw material is, how can the product be right? Nor do we know where we are now, and what we should aim at. When 'soul work' gets done, the elite and powerful will face their own functional obsolescence, and come to realize their faded relevance to the very social structures that once made them feel inevitable. We cannot even

---

[359] Plotkin, B. 2007. Nature and the Human Soul: Cultivating Wholeness and Community in a Fragmented World.

extrapolate what the probable outcome of the technological endgame of making artificially *lifted* humans could be. Soon, such 'lifting' might be a choice, but only in name, and it would come at a crippling cost. The 'cost' is to extricate ourselves from the emotions inseparable from the human condition. While it will entail a serious risk, because attendant technologies like gene-editing carry unknown consequences, not getting it done might leave them socially behind. We may soon have two kinds of persons: lifted, 'god-like' humans; and 'left-behind' humans. The tension between the two could make matters worse. Neither scripture nor science can pull us out of the rabbit hole of our mind. The only way is to summon all our skills and weapons would be to marginalize, not vanquish, the mind in our consciousness. What is encouraging is that we don't need the entire mass of mankind, but a minimum but sufficient critical mass of enlightened citizens, which could trigger, through still unknown processes, a chain reaction and generate unstoppable momentum. But every one of those persona must consciously construct the correct *contextual-change* and trigger the heart-centered *consciousness-change*. To nurture what we may call 'social consciousness'—in which all actions are measured by their effects on the community, and in which the responsibility for these effects is understood as collective—we need such a change at the personal level. We need to be "educated in the heart", to be "able to feel for the sorrows and fears of every fellow human being".[360]

Waging and winning this war is the only way to arrest and reverse what Philip Zimbardo called the *Lucifer Effect*, the tipping point in time when an ordinary, normal person first seamlessly slips from good to evil. It is this war—the way it is waged, how we feed the opposing forces, and its outcome—that will determine the dialectics of *dharma* and *adharma* in the world. And winning this war could not only let us get off, in Bill McKibben's words, the "long escalator down to Hell", but also possibly abort, what Bob Dylan called "the death of the human race; the long

---

[360] Lewis, S. 1935. It Can't Happen Here.

strange trip of the naked ape". Winning this war will, at last, save us from ruminating in desperation and helpless despair.

The time now is to decisively help the forces of good to subdue and surmount the forces of evil in the war within. What offers some help are two things: one, the very power of technology that has brought us to the brink is amenable to be redirected. Two, we don't need universality or unanimity; that is, each and every one of us need not come on board. It is not mandatory that all of us must so behave that it 'feeds' more and better our good inner wolf than its bad sibling. For, just as there is no good man or bad man but only good acts and bad acts, there is no 'good' or 'bad' wolf as such. What we 'do' is what we feed, and therefore for us to feed correctly requires that the behavior of a critical mass among us becomes altruistic, not opportunistic, triggering a process of what is called *autopoiesis*. And that would, like the rising tide that lifts all boats, catapult mankind onto a new trajectory. And then our proclivity to *akrasia* (lack of self-indulgence; the proclivity to act against one's better judgment) will give way to cultivating *enkrateia* (self-mastery, restraint over one's own passions and instincts). Such a visceral shift is necessary as a counter to our braggadocio of having attained mastery over life, to borrow a phrase from Vaclav Smil (*History and Risk*, 2020). About how the world responded to the Covid-19, Smil does not mince his words: "The entire lineup of near-miraculous advances has been exposed as irrelevant, and the notion of *Homo deus* boldly charting the destiny of a godlike species has imploded".

We don't have to be a 'god'—whatever we think we mean by that—or even a supra-intelligent or impregnable superman, to realize our inherent potential. In fact, as the Upanishads say, we already are *divine* in its deepest sense, and all that we have to do is to remove the veils that come in the way. What we need is 'self-abandonment', not self-aggrandizement. We can rectify things right here, just as we are. If we, through our conduct, can bring ourselves to help the forces of dharma or righteousness to prevail over the forces of adharma and wickedness, it could be a huge step towards engineering a human society that the Vedas so eloquently proclaim: *Vasudaiva kutumbakam*; *Om, shanti, shanti, shanti*; *Loka samastas sukhino bhavantu*; *Sarvejana sukhinobhavantu* (The whole earth is a family; Peace, peace, peace; Let everyone everywhere be happy; May all people live happily). A similar sentiment, it is interesting to note, was echoed by Plato when he wrote, "This world is indeed a living being endowed with a soul and intelligence... a single visible living entity containing all other living entities, which by their nature are all related". But the bottom line is that such lofty aspirations will remain just that unless we shift our gaze inwards, energetically intervene in the war within, and 'win' it in the righteous way.

Printed in the United States
by Baker & Taylor Publisher Services